Italian Literature and Thought Series

Selected Writings of
Girolamo Savonarola

Religion and Politics, 1490–1498

Translated and edited by Anne Borelli and Maria Pastore Passaro
Donald Beebe, *Executive Editor*

Introduction by Alison Brown

Foreword by Giuseppe Mazzotta

Yale University Press   New Haven and London

Designed by Sonia Shannon.
Set in Galliard type by Binghamton Valley Composition.
Printed in the United States of America.

Library of Congress Cataloging-in-Publication Data

Savonarola, Girolamo, 1452–1498.
 [Selections. English. 2005]
 Selected writings of Girolamo Savonarola : religion and poli-
tics, 1490–1498 / translated and edited by Anne Borelli and Ma-
ria Pastore Passaro ; Donald Beebe, executive editor.
   p. cm.—(Italian literature and thought series)
 Includes bibliographical references and index.
 ISBN-13: 978-0-300-10326-7
 ISBN-10: 0-300-10326-3 (alk. paper)
  1. Florence (Italy)—Politics and government—1421–1737. 2.
Florence (Italy)—Church history. 3. Catholic Church—Italy—
Florence—History. 4. Savonarola, Girolamo, 1452–1498. I.
Borelli, Anne. II. Pastore Passaro, Maria C. III. Beebe,
Donald. IV. Title. V. Series.

DG737.97.A613 2005
282'.092—dc22

                                         2005050073

A catalogue record for this book is available from the British
Library.

The paper in this book meets the guidelines for permanence and
durability of the Committee on Production Guidelines for Book
Longevity of the Council on Library Resources.

10 9 8 7 6 5 4 3 2 1

To Donald Weinstein

Contents

SILENCING AND EXCOMMUNICATION

MORAL REFORM II

Illustrations

Illustrations follow page 136.

Foreword

The Italian Quattrocentro is replete with extraordinarily creative personalities who brought forth ideas and ways of thinking destined to change and to shape the face of the modern world. At one end of this century one finds, among others, Alberti and Valla. At the other end there stand, among others, two bitter enemies, a Neoplatonic philosopher, Ficino, and a Dominican preacher, Savonarola.

Girolamo Savonarola was well aware of the creative, deeply subversive powers of the imagination and, specifically, of the religious and prophetic imagination. He thought of himself as, and was, a preacher-prophet. Of the many biblical prophets he glossed in his preaching before the Florentines, he identified especially with one, Haggai (Aggeus). Haggai, a relatively minor prophet who stands in the tradition of Ezekiel and Amos, lived and wrote at the time of the brilliant Persian general Darius, a time when the Persians worshipped Zoroaster and, accordingly, practiced a religion based on the interpretation of the stars. By 538 B.C. Cyrus agreed to let Israel return to Palestine. A new consecration of the temple was in order, but Israel's struggle to restore the land that had been defiled and to rebuild the temple was delayed. Some Jews opted to return to Babylon, while those who decided to stay thought rather of their own houses and left the house of God in disarray. Haggai preached against all such delay. He launched his call to holiness by denouncing the alliance between the high priest and the governor and made the political program of rebuilding the emblem of a radical moral reform.

In the history of modern religious consciousness, Savonarola is usually aligned with the sixteenth-century reformers (such as Sozzini, Luther, and Calvin), whose evangelical zeal he is said to prefigure. These reformers are defined by their narrow and intense moral focus: they pursued the retrieval of the pure, spiritual core of the Christian tradition that had been disfigured by the cynical exercise of papal power. In their view, public and private morality had to be made consistent with the unadulterated letter of the Gospel.

More than a moral reformer, Savonarola can be called a moral revolutionary. His vision is broad. Like the reformers who were to follow him, he attacked the dominant paradigms of social life — the unholy conniving of the universal Church with Florence's political despots; the astrological philosophies of the latter-day Zoroastrians; the conceits of hermetic, Neoplatonic syncretism; decadent aesthetic conventions; and private vices. But he saw with great clarity that the spiritual crisis he witnessed in Florence and in the Church would not be solved by the erasure of all bonds between culture and its religious roots or by a return to a simpler form of spirituality. Unlike the reformers, and notwithstanding his own nostalgia for medieval forms of apocalyptic vision and prophecies of doom, he called for a renewal of both culture and religious life, persuaded that the shaping force of the West lies within the horizon of Christian history. He was a revolutionary because his breadth of vision poured over into his call for a new style of art, of thought, and of living. In his mind, the city of Florence had the unique opportunity to become the New Jerusalem. To achieve this vision, he did not flinch from struggling to convince his audience to overcome themselves. Above all, he was a revolutionary because he struggled to overcome himself. His perpetual lamentations adumbrate the phantasms of this inner struggle, the tragic knowledge of a man who lived before his time and, like the true prophets, outside of his own time, and who recognized that his destiny was to lose himself.

Giuseppe Mazzotta
Yale University

Acknowledgments

In preparing the manuscript for this project, I have been sustained by the support, advice, and perseverance of so many people, for which I am deeply grateful. The project began as a natural extension of my dissertation, wherein I sought to reveal relationships between Savonarola's writings and quintessentially Savonarolan images, the illustrations that grace his own publications. I wish to thank Creighton Gilbert for encouraging both my interest in Savonarola and a holistic approach to Quattrocento art. Both Donald Weinstein and Giuseppe Mazzotta enthusiastically endorsed the idea of providing uncut translations of Savonarola's texts into English to fill a huge lacuna in Quattrocento literature available to English-speaking readers. The idea of turning this translation project into a marketable book was Alessandra Comini's. She bolstered my courage to approach Yale University Press about the project. Cynthia Wells, my first contact, presented the project to Jonathan Brent. Throughout the process, I have enjoyed working with Lara Heimert and Keith Condon, both of whom have been remarkably kind, encouraging, and professional. Keith's support, resourcefulness, and gentle nudging were vital in helping us to complete the project. Thanks also to Ann Hawthorne, who meticulously copyedited the text, to Kara Pekar, who created the index, and especially to Margaret Otzel, who shepherded the book through its final revision and proofing. I thank Bob Babcock, Curator of Early Books at the Beinecke Library, Yale University, who introduced me to Valerie Hotchkiss, Director of the Bridwell Library at Southern Methodist University. She took an interest in my research and encouraged me to apply for a Bridwell Library Fellowship. As a consequence, I was invited to curate *A Renaissance Requiem,* an exhibition of incunabula and Renaissance medals at the Bridwell in commemoration of the quinquecentennial of Savonarola's death. The Bridwell has provided encouragement as well as technical and bibliographical support throughout the project. I am very thankful to Eric White, Curator of Special Collections, for his good-natured help in procuring hard-to-find texts and in tracking down recondite quotations. He made the Bridwell Library accessible to me and my colleagues though we were a thousand miles away.

In the compilation of the book itself, I wish to thank Giuseppe Mazzotta for his constant enthusiasm and support over the years as we brought the project to completion. At a critical moment, he introduced me to Maria Pastore Passaro, who made a significant contribution to the book by her translation of the Italian selections. Robin Neas provided an initial translation of the *Dialogue concerning Prophetic Truth,* which made our work with this difficult text easier. Most of all, I wish to thank my good friend Anne Borelli, without whom this book would never have come to be. As the course of my life has taken me outside the realm of academe, Anne continued to labor on the project, adopting it as her own. She has masterfully fashioned and refashioned translations by herself, Maria, Robin, and me into a seamless whole, capturing the simplicity, clarity, and sincerity of Savonarola's voice.

Finally, I wish to thank Alison Brown for writing the introductory essay and bibliography. Her keen insights into Italian Renaissance culture and Savonarola's place within it are a vital part of this book. Her essay frames the sections of the book within a broader context that will certainly be useful to both students and professional scholars.

I hope that this book will be as informative and rewarding for readers as the experience of preparing it has been for me and my colleagues. I hope that it will provide a new way of perceiving an important historical figure who has been lionized and demonized, who looms as large in fiction as he does in history—but who has seldom been taken for the man he was, on his own terms.

Donald Beebe

Introduction

Savonarola remains an enigma, as controversial in our day as he was in his own. He was born in Ferrara in 1452, the grandson of a learned physician who helped him on his way to acquiring a master of arts degree at the University of Ferrara. At the age of twenty-three, however, he rejected the secular world to become a Dominican friar in the Observant monastery in Bologna, where St. Dominic himself had died and was buried. It was there that he acquired the deep learning reflected in his later sermons, as we can now see from the "Borromeo notebook," which he wrote in 1483, a year after he was appointed a teacher in the Observant monastery of San Marco in Florence. There was nothing in it, or in the sermons he gave in Florence at this time, to suggest his later prophetic gift; on the contrary, he drew few listeners ("only some simpletons and a few little women," he recalled in Ruth and Micheas [Micah], Sermon IV, 18 May 1496), and he was faced with dwindling audiences when he left the city after two years. By the time he returned to the monastery of San Marco in 1490, however, he had developed his apocalyptic voice, which came to him (he tells us in one account) just before he left Florence in 1484; and it was honed in the Advent and Lent sermons he delivered in Lombardy and Tuscany in the intervening years. On his return to Florence, he became not only a powerful and terrifying preacher but also, from 1494 to 1498, the most influential figure in Florentine politics, as well as an outspoken critic of the papacy: a combination of roles that led to his being put to death at the stake in June 1498, anathematized and condemned by the Church and the Florentine state alike.[1]

How are we to interpret the extraordinary events of these years? To attempt to understand what happened, we need to investigate not only his political and social milieu but also the religious mentality and eschatology of fifteenth-century Italians, especially as the half-millennium approached. For although Savonarola was in some ways very forward-looking in his organizational techniques and his desire to return to apostolic simplicity, his belief in demonic forces and Antichrist is much less modern, as Donald Weinstein has reminded us.[2] His very success as a leader and reformer in turn drew him into the maelstrom of Florentine confrontational politics that also contributed to his downfall. By 1497, events developed their own dynamic in the aftermath of the increasingly fervent campaign of moral reform

1. For a succinct outline of Savonarola's life, Weinstein, 1994.
2. Weinstein, 1970, pp. 188–189, 228–231.

in the previous year. The Bonfire of Vanities in Lent 1497 was followed by the assault on Savonarola in the pulpit on Ascension Day and his excommunication by the Pope in May. This in turn led to the final drama of the ordeal by fire in April 1498, and the deaths of Savonarola and his companions at the stake the following month.

Historians today are as divided about who should bear the responsibility for what happened as his contemporaries were. Was Savonarola a victim of papal and Florentine politics, or was he so fired by his own success that he was incapable of seeing the havoc he was wreaking by choosing so uncompromising a path to martyrdom? Here his correspondence with the Pope and the chronicles, letters, and political debates of Florentines allow us insight into the position of devout Christians faced with an excommunicated and recalcitrant leader. Even the papacy is finding it difficult to decide whether to sanctify him as a Catholic martyr or to continue to condemn him as a heretic for claiming, as a prophet, to speak directly with God. So this anthology of writings by Savonarola and about him, most of them never before published in translation, is extremely timely. It will enable us to make up our own minds about this controversial figure on the basis of these unique primary sources set in their contemporary context.

The Pastoral Writings

It is appropriate that we are first presented with Savonarola's pastoral writings, for although they are less dramatic than his prophetic sermons, they were what led to the moral transformation that nearly everyone, then and now, agrees was Savonarola's greatest achievement. As Francesco Guicciardini wrote, in the extract translated below, "the work he did in promoting decent behavior was holy and marvellous; nor had there ever been as much goodness and religion in Florence as there was in his time." Savonarola belonged to the Observant, or reformist, branch of the Dominican order, which had been established at the end of the fourteenth century to introduce a return to simplicity and poverty. The movement was led by reformers who worked closely with lay patrons, such as the Este in Ferrara and the Medici in Florence, Cosimo de' Medici being encouraged by Pope Eugenius IV to introduce the new Observant order in San Marco.[3]

So the ground was already laid for Savonarola when he was invited to return to San Marco in 1490. Nor is it surprising that he quickly gathered a band of lay supporters. Florence enjoyed a strong tradition of lay piety expressed in the charitable activities and sermons of ordinary citizens in their confraternities, where they celebrated the Eucharist together as a commem-

3. Rubinstein, 1990, p. 65.

orative love-feast. Even theological debates about sin and grace were held in public, as in 1489, when a debate was held in the cathedral on Adam's sin, to be continued a week later in Lorenzo de' Medici's own home.[4] All this was in addition to the cycles of sermons delivered every year by invited preachers during Advent and Lent. Some preachers were particularly popular, especially the Franciscan San Bernardino of Siena, whose fiery sermons against sodomy and bonfires of vanities in the 1420s anticipated Savonarola's. So too was Bernardino da Feltre, who was expelled from Florence in 1488 for his provocative sermons against the Jews; and also the Augustinian friar, Mariano da Genazzano, a Medici favorite, whose eloquent and learned sermons in the 1480s provided a challenge to Savonarola when he returned to Florence—as one of his friends pointed out in telling him that his "pronunciation and graceless gestures" compared very badly with Fra Mariano's.[5] A manuscript containing an anonymous collection of sermons delivered in Florence between 1467 and 1502 shows how eclectic the Florentine taste was, for it includes a miscellany of sermons preached in different churches by Augustinian, Franciscan, and Dominican friars—and only one by Savonarola (which is the first sermon translated here).[6] So there was already a devout lay audience for topics central to the movement for religious reform.

The two pastoral sermons translated here help to explain how Savonarola differed from his predecessors and competitors among the preachers of his day. When he first began to preach in 1490, as he later reminded his congregation (in Ruth and Micheas, Sermon XVIII), people complained that he did not raise *quaestiones* or moral problems like other preachers, and we can see this is true by comparing his sermons with those of Fra Mariano in the collection referred to above. His Good Friday sermon on 1 April 1496 demonstrates very well his method of preaching. He begins by citing his biblical text for the day, which he quotes in Latin before translating or paraphrasing it in Italian; he then expounds it by comparing the authority of the Old and the New Testaments, explaining Christianity in terms of its humanity (here, Christ's sacrifice upon the Cross) and its naturalism (the natural instinct, shared with plants and birds, being to strive towards self-preservation and perfection). As he explained a few days later, he had initially preached simply, "without philosophy," in order to draw simple people to his sermons, and he began to cite natural philosophy as well as the Scriptures only in response to criticism from the learned elite ("astrologers and philosophers and the wise men of the world"; Amos and Zacharias, Sermon

4. Kraye, 1996, p. 151; on lay piety, Kristeller, 1956; Henderson, 1994.
5. Ridolfi, 1959, p. 34; cf. Weinstein, 1970, p.99. On San Bernardino and Bernardino da Feltre, Origo, 1963, esp. p. 199; Weinstein, 1970, p. 103.
6. Zafarana, 1968, pp. 1058–61 (1 April [1496]).

XLVIII). What made his sermons accessible to the people at large was his use of eloquent images and analogies to make his meaning both clear and relevant. In this Good Friday sermon, he uses the images of the ladder and the Cross to maximum effect—as we can see both from the woodcut of the Cross published shortly afterwards (plate 2) and from the précis of this sermon by the anonymous Florentine. Not only did this Florentine record the seven steps of the ladder with great accuracy—despite claiming to have forgotten many of "the beautiful things" Savonarola said about them—but he also commented that "what particularly pleased the people" was the way Savonarola related the seven steps to the seven mysteries of the Passion. He recorded as well another characteristic of Savonarola's sermons: that whereas other preachers would have tried to move their audience to tears on this sad day, Savonarola said he wanted instead to teach interior devotion.

Interior devotion is also a theme of his All Souls' Day sermon later that year, which uses similar arguments and devices to make its impact. He initially embarks on the theme of naturalism and how difficult it is to get people to think about death when the desire to live is our most natural instinct. His solution to the problem is to offer a set of practical rules to avoid sin and the danger of Hell, which he again expounds by using visual images and analogies: the evocative image of "the spectacles of death" and a detailed description of three pictures to be hung at home as a perpetual aide-mémoire. Printed the following year as a separate treatise, *On the Art of Dying Well,* its three woodcuts (two illustrated here, plates 3–4) successfully imprint on our minds the message of his sermon, evidence in itself of the effectiveness of his novel techniques.[7] These woodcuts were also intended to encourage another common theme of the sermons: the importance of inward reflection instead of the outward outpouring of emotion.

This is the message of his treatise *On Mental Prayer,* printed in Florence in 1495, which also exemplifies another novel feature of Savonarola's moral campaign: the use of the printing press to reinforce the messages of his sermons. Like the treatise *On the Art of Dying Well,* it contains woodcuts to stress the importance of private meditation at home without the trappings of outward ceremonies and cult—as happened in the primitive Church, he said, when Christians were able to empty their minds of worldly matters without the need of songs or organs to raise their minds on high. Music was, of course, another area for reform and simplification where Savonarola again anticipated later reformers, with his preference for plain chant instead of polyphony—although he did not scruple to adapt the secular carnival

7. Printed three times before his death, the treatise is discussed by Weinstein, 1989, and by Polizzotto, 1989.

songs popularized by Lorenzo de' Medici to bond his own supporters.[8] Similarly, he attacked religious art for using images of recognizable Florentines to represent Mary Magdalene, St. John, and the Virgin Mary: "Do you believe the Virgin Mary went dressed as you paint her? . . . You would do well to cancel these figures that are painted so unchastely."[9]

It was in the same vein that he addressed the nuns in the enclosed convent of the Murate and printed a treatise *On Widowhood,* in which he advised widows not to remarry, nor to attend weddings and banquets, nor to chat with men, wander in the streets, or even gaze at the streets from their windows. He had previously attempted to involve women in the work of reform, only to be rebuffed by a woman from a leading Florentine family. But he remained closely involved in women's reforming movements, and even his advice to widows was consistent with his desire to encourage inner spirituality free from external distractions. When the Medici were restored after 1512, the convents he had reformed insisted on retaining a certain independence and responsibility for themselves as Savonarola's legacy to them.[10]

The common themes running through the whole of Savonarola's pastoral ministry are the desire to return to apostolic simplicity and to base his teaching on the Scriptures. Both are exemplified in his treatise *On the Simplicity of the Christian Life,* which one of his followers, Girolamo Benivieni, translated for the printed edition of 1496. Another humanist admirer of Savonarola also praised him for his "simplicity of heart . . . bodily simplicity, too, and simplicity of cult," describing Savonarola's brilliance in expounding the Scriptures "to us" as a norm to be absolutely obeyed, "like an evangelical missionary."[11] Similarly, the Florentine merchant chronicler Bartolomeo Cerretani recorded in his *Storia fiorentina* that Savonarola introduced "an almost new way of pronouncing the Word of God, that is, like the Apostles, without dividing the sermon, or posing questions, without singing or rhetorical tropes, his sole aim being to explain something of the Old Testament and introduce the simplicity of the primitive Church."[12]

So it was as a reformer that Savonarola won the support of many Florentines, for "until now," Girolamo Benivieni's brother Domenico wrote in his 1496 *Tractato,* "people never knew what the true Christian way of life was . . . believing that good living consisted in ceremonies and external

8. See Macey, 1992; also Aggeus, Sermon VII, below.
9. Gilbert, 1980, pp. 157–158; Hall, 1990, pp. 499–500.
10. Polizzotto, 1993, 1996 (esp. p. 236 on Le Murate), 1997; Kent, 1983. On *Vita viduale,* which ran to four editions between 1490 and 1496, Eisenbichler, 1996.
11. Nesi, 1973, pp. 163, 165.
12. Cerretani, 1994, p. 192.

works, which were praised by the clergy and friars because they brought them personal honor and profit."[13] The implicit criticism of the religious in this passage suggests one source of future hostility to Savonarola: the old-established clergy in Florence whom he was to nickname "the lukewarms," or *tiepidi,* those who spoke fine words but refused to reform, like the former Mediceans, the Greys or *Bigi,* who also stood midway between Savonarola's angry opponents (the *arrabbiati*) at one extreme and the puritan Whites or *Bianchi* (whom their opponents nicknamed the Snivellers or *Piagnoni*) at the other.[14] Although he suggested abolishing the party labels of "White" and "Grey" in his sermon of 28 December 1494, he and his own supporters helped to encourage this factionalism, to which they themselves fell victim.

The Prophecies

Savonarola was transformed from a pastoral reformer into the scourge of Florence and the papacy by his role as a prophet—although in fact there was no initial contrast between these roles, since his earliest prophecies were made in the context of pastoral reform. Reform of Florence's clergy and its ruling elite, not the forthcoming scourge of Italy, was the theme of his very first prophecy in Florence. It was delivered in February 1491 as part of his cycle of sermons on the Apocalypse of St. John. The importance of these sermons can be seen in his claim (made at the end of the cycle) that in them he had preached "new things in a new way," *nova dicere et novo modo,* which he regarded as a sign of their divine origin; and also in the care with which he dated them in October 1492 as beginning "two years and three months ago, that is, 27 months, that is, 810 days."[15] What they contained was an assault on the greed and self-interest of the leading men in Florence, not only the religious but also lawyers, judges, brokers, bankers, and merchants, as well as members of the great families who competed for ecclesiastical benefices and were able to "buy anything with money," an attack he summarized in a later note in the margin of the manuscript: "I said that the devil uses the great to oppress the poor so they can't do good, etc."[16] This is the context for his first prophecy on the second Sunday in Lent 1491, in what he later called his "terrifying" (*spaventosa,* or in Latin *terrifica*) sermon that he preached after a sleepless night. In it, he predicted a time when men

---

13. Benivieni, 1496, fol. a3r–v (with the woodcut shown here as plate 2).
14. Brown, 2000b, pp. 22–26; Zancarini, 1997, pp. 49–51. On the "lukewarm," Aggeus, Sermon VII.
15. Sermon 49 (5 April 1491), Savonarola, 2001, p. 297; and *"In domino confido"* (21 October 1492), Savonarola, 1992, p. 83, discussed by Verde, 1998, p. 136.
16. Sermon 5 (20 February 1491, repeated a year later), Savonarola, 2001, pp. 29–35, 312, n. 12.

would risk their lives for Christ, would not amass riches or build great palaces or become clients of the powerful but would carry Christ in their hearts (a sermon, according to a later marginal note, "in which there are many prophecies and other things"). As Armando Verde points out, the overall message of these sermons was about Christ's compassion, however, not his anger.[17]

So we must be careful not to confuse the prophecy in this early cycle of sermons with either Savonarola's earlier visions or the later visions described in the important "Renovation Sermon" of 13 January 1495, translated here, and in the *Compendium of Revelations* printed later that year in Florence. According to the 13 January sermon, his visions began in the years between 1475 and 1480 and were first preached in Brescia in 1489. As Giulio Cattin argues, however, these early sermons are strongly influenced by scholasticism despite their attempts at a new simplicity and lightness of touch; and even those preached after his "illumination" in the church of San Giorgio in Florence in 1484 are not visionary but are instead careful meditations on the theme of why the Church needed to be scourged.[18] Encouraged by the sermons of itinerant preachers, as well as by the new invention of the printing press, there was at the time a widely diffused belief in millenarianism and portents.[19] As the half-millennium approached, fears of the end of the world preceded by the rule of Antichrist were accompanied by portents of "the second Charlemagne," who would return to Italy on his way to recover the Holy Land, from the Turks. Other widely believed portents included the striking of the cupola of the Duomo in Florence by a thunderbolt three days before Lorenzo de' Medici died on 8 April 1492, which caused its marble lantern to crash onto the north side of the cathedral. Because it fell towards the Medici palace, the chemist Luca Landucci (like many others) interpreted it as a portent of Lorenzo's death three days later, and even the skeptical Machiavelli and Guicciardini cited this as evidence that serious events, in ancient and modern times, are always foretold by "divination or revelation or by prodigies or by other heavenly signs."[20] At the same time, there was growing interest among Renaissance scholars in the prophecies of ancient magi rediscovered in Hermetic writings and oracles. So Savonarola's predictions, like his pastoral work, found fertile ground in Florence in which to develop.

What is difficult for us to pinpoint is the moment when Savonarola

17. Sermon 12 (27 February 1491), ibid., pp. 75–83; cf. Savonarola, 1974, pp. 9–10, 135–136; Verde, 1998, pp. 143–147.
18. Cattin, 1953, pp. 155–161.
19. Niccoli, 1990, esp. pp. 3–29; also pp. 33–34; Hatfield, 1995, pp. 106–114.
20. Machiavelli, 1983 (I, 56), p. 249; Guicciardini, 1970, p. 70.

began to have visions of specific future events. He had begun to preach publicly but "very circumspectly" about the forthcoming scourges and tribulations before Lorenzo de' Medici's death in April 1492. Since Lorenzo had made himself unpopular for driving out Savonarola's rabble-rousing predecessor, Bernardino da Feltre, he did nothing to stop the sermons. Nevertheless, as Savonarola told a fellow Dominican in 1491, he had always to be careful, preaching the renovation of the Church and future tribulations but not "absolutely" and always with a basis in Scripture, "so no one can reproach me."[21] So without either accepting the visions at face value or rejecting them as later inventions, we can see how their message became transformed under the pressure of events—the French invasion and the political revolution in Florence—that made it easy, with hindsight, to interpret them as fulfillments of his predictions of the scourge to come.

The sermon of 13 January 1495 is important for the claim Savonarola made in it that his prophecies were based on what God said to him and not simply on his interpretation of the Bible ("believe me, Florence, it is not I, but God, who says these things"). It is also important for containing Savonarola's first public account of his mission, including his two earliest "mental images," or visions. The first of these (later ascribed to 20 April 1492 and printed as the treatise *Triumph of the Cross* in 1497) describes two crosses: a black cross above Rome, on which rained down swords, knives, and lances; and a golden cross above Jerusalem. The second vision (later ascribed to 22–23 December 1492) describes the hand of God poised to strike the wicked, "Gladius Domini super terram cito et velociter," with angels offering men red crosses and white mantles, both visions influencing the illustrations reproduced here (plates 2, 8).

These prophecies are described in greater detail in his *Compendium of Revelations,* written in response to the Pope's request in July 1495 (in the letter translated below) that he explain himself.[22] In the *Compendium* Savonarola claims to have predicted the deaths of both Lorenzo de' Medici and Pope Innocent VIII in April and July 1492, but only to friends, and also the crossing of the Alps into Italy by someone like Cyrus.[23] Although Charles VIII had announced his intention to claim his rights to Naples in 1491, and had supported his announcement by vigorous propaganda to influence public opinion, it was only two years later that the invasion began to be discussed seriously (together with the idea of using it to foment a revolution in Flor-

---

21. Guicciardini, 1970, p. 103; Weinstein, 1970, pp. 102–103.
22. In Italian in August and in Latin in October (Ridolfi, 1959, p. 135), Savonarola, 1974, pp. 12–14, 22–23, and 138–140, 148–149. English translation by McGinn, 1979, pp. 192–275; discussed and quoted at length by Weinstein, 1970, pp. 67–78.
23. Savonarola, 1974, pp. 14–15, 140–141.

ence), and only in the late summer of 1494, after considerable opposition within France, that it was finally agreed on.[24] When Savonarola preached on Genesis in Lent 1492 and Lent 1494, he failed to give Florence the special role referred to in later sermons, in the *Compendium*, and in his *Dialogue concerning Prophetic Truth*, that Florence was "especially decreed to receive the seed of this divine word in order to propagate it throughout the world."

By the time Savonarola had reached the Flood in his Genesis sermons, in the month in which Charles entered Italy, the appropriateness of God's message finally sank in, making the eminent humanist Pico della Mirandola's hair stand up on end (Savonarola tells us in the *Compendium*).[25] The sacking of Florence's fortresses and the revolution followed swiftly. From then on, Savonarola's predictions corresponded closely to the course of events. The controversy aroused by his prophecies led to the events described in his 1495 correspondence with the Pope, translated below. But far from silencing him, the Pope succeeded only in bringing the controversy into the public arena by provoking Savonarola's Open *Letter to a Friend* and the so-called pamphlet war of 1496–97.[26] Savonarola's long *Dialogue concerning Prophetic Truth* was written to confute the charges made against him in this war of words, but it would perhaps have been better if it had remained "terrifying" and enigmatic than for Savonarola to have attempted to rationalize with scholastic arguments what was not susceptible to scientific proof.[27] Faced with the hostility of the papacy and his eloquent critics, however, Savonarola had little option but to answer the charges that his dialogue, the *Compendium*, and the Open Letters summarize so well.

Politics

Savonarola's political influence in Florence was foremost among these charges, which accused him of getting involved, as a cleric, "in the administration of the city."[28] The truth of the charge is indisputable. Even before the Medici regime fell on 9 November, Savonarola was elected one of five ambassadors to Charles VIII in Pisa to renegotiate the terms of submission that Piero de' Medici had agreed to with the king without authorization. He interceded with the king again in Florence, and although the Florentines had to agree to pay Charles a large indemnity of 120,000 florins and make concessions to the Medici, it seemed to them miraculous that a settlement

24. Peyronnet, 1995, pp. 49–53; Mallett, 1995; Brown, 2000a, pp. 16–22.
25. Savonarola, 1974, pp. 11, 137.
26. See Ridolfi, 1959, pp. 132–143; Polizzotto, 1994, pp. 66–67, and, on his critics, pp. 64–69; Weinstein, 1970, pp. 227–239.
27. As Toussaint suggests, 1996, p. 171.
28. Cf. Savonarola, 1974, p. 65.

had been reached five days after the intercession of "this holy man and prophet," and that Charles had left the city only two days later, on 23 November, without sacking it and with very little bloodshed. It was just a week later, in his seventh sermon on Aggeus (Haggai), translated here, that Savonarola celebrated Florence's release from the potentially serious danger posed by the large number of French troops billeted within the city: "O Florence, if things had ended badly, as they could have done, many, very likely . . . would today be in Hell."

This sermon provides a bridge from his earlier pastoral and prophetic sermons to the politically engaged sermons that proposed the program of legislative reforms largely achieved in 1494 and 1495. The program consisted, first, in the creation on 23 December 1494 of a Great Council, modeled on that of Venice. In Florence, however, the members were to be not a closed noble caste but some 3,500 former officeholders (qualified by holding one of the three "major" elective offices over four generations). This council passed the reform program that Savonarola summarized in the cathedral on the Feast of St. Victor on 28 July 1495.[29] It included the amnesty law of 19 March 1495 and the law abolishing *parlamenti* of 13 August 1495; both measures were intended to strengthen the rule of law against the threat of the sudden plebiscites and the tyrannous "vote of Six Beans," which could sentence people to death, without appeal, by only six of the eight votes of the Signoria, or the Eight of Ward. Then there were laws against sodomy, gaming, and taverns; the abolition of arbitrary taxation in favor of assessment by neighbors; the establishment of a charitable *Monte di Pietà;* the building of a great hall in which the new Great Council could meet; and provisions for the time of plague and for the publication of laws a day before they were voted on.[30] Although he was criticized for creating "a government of madmen," these laws provide convincing evidence of Savonarola's influence on the reform of the state. As a result, the old Medicean oligarchy was transformed into a new, much broader system of government, in which — Bartolomeo Cerretani recorded — "for the first time, nearly the whole of Florence participated."[31]

The coherence of this program suggested to his critics that Savonarola was politically ambitious, not content with the simple life of a friar but eager to "meddle in affairs of state." For this reason, it is important to look care-

---

29. The law of 23 December is edited by Cadoni, 1994, pp. 33–60; Savonarola, 1969, II, pp. 168–176 (*Prediche sopra i Salmi,* sermon XXVI, 28 July 1495).
30. Cadoni, 1994, pp. 108–118, 185–195. On this program, Polizzotto, 1994, pp. 28–36.
31. Cerretani, 1993, p. 270. On the charge and the chancellor's defense against it, Open *Letter to a Friend;* Scala, 1997, p. 400, cf. 407–408.

fully at the political sermons and the treatise translated here to see how fully integrated they are with his pastoral writings and with his writings on moral reform. The first sermon, for instance, adopts the pattern of his earlier pastoral sermons in its use of naturalistic, Thomist arguments and striking images to make his point, followed by specific advice on how to achieve salvation. So he begins by explaining that whereas animals are guided by unerring instinct, and saints and the elect are unerringly guided by God's special light, man's uniqueness lies in having free will and a soul as well as a body; hence he stands "as if between two magnets," pulled both upwards and downwards and needing God's special light to achieve certainty. How to acquire this special light provides the context for introducing his reform program. In this sermon he talks about repentence and the need to live uprightly, whereas in his more famous sermon on Aggeus XIII on 12 December he goes on to propose "what the natural government of the Florentine people should be"—recapitulated in his 1498 *Treatise on the Government of Florence,* which is equally indebted to Aristotelian-Thomist arguments.[32] It was only after this, on 16 December, that he began to quote Haggai as relevant to his theme of rebuilding, concluding on 28 December by emphasizing the need to establish a hierarchy of order within this greatly enlarged and socially mixed government. So it is misleading to regard either the prophet Haggai or political ambition as the main inspiration of the program, since its purpose was entirely consistent with the aims of his pastoral ministry, to teach people how to achieve salvation.

During these years, Savonarola also maintained his reputation as a successful prophet and defender of the city. He was invited into the government palace to discuss reform with the Signoria at the end of 1494. He was sent on another successful embassy to the king of France in June 1495 in order to deter Charles from passing through Florence on his return from Naples to France. And in October 1496 he was ordered by the government to deliver a public sermon in order to protect the city from being attacked at Livorno by the imperial fleet, his prediction of divine help being once more miraculously fulfilled by the destruction of the fleet in an unexpected storm. Given this apparently unbroken success, why did he fail?

The most obvious reason, apart from the continuing failure of his pro-French policy to recover Pisa for the Florentines, was the Pope's hostility to his claim to be a prophet and to his repeated onslaught on the Church, which led to his preaching being frequently prohibited and to his eventual excommunication in May 1497. But there were also other reasons relating to his political role in Florence. Although he was invited to Florence by Lorenzo

32. Savonarola, 1974, p. 27; Rubinstein, 2000; Weinstein, 1970, pp. 289–316.

de' Medici and soon got taken up by Lorenzo's circle of friends, his open and repeated criticism of the wealth and unbridled ambition of the ruling elite cannot have failed to hit its target, especially when his 1491 Lent and Advent sermons were followed by the equally hard-hitting 1492 Lent sermons in San Lorenzo.[33] Lorenzo may not have been mentioned by name as an extravagant palace builder, as Filippo Strozzi was, but he must have been implicated in the charge of "buying villas and shops from the poor at a low price, joining one field to another," and certainly in the charge concerning the dowries and wealth of contemporary marriages, which Savonarola boldly made in a sermon in San Lorenzo on the morning of the very day that Lorenzo was buried there. In another sermon he imagined the magnates protesting that he should not " 'say these things in the pulpit, because you make us despised by the people.' " And he much later recalled that "at the time of Lorenzo de' Medici" he had been cautioned about his preaching by five leading citizens, who he assumed came at Lorenzo's behest.[34] So although his onslaught was essential to his reform campaign and was not in itself politically motivated, it nevertheless drew him irrevocably into the field of politics, making constitutional reform a priority after the fall of the Medici.

Constitutional reform in turn drew Savonarola further into the political arena. He made his proposals for reform ten days after the Medici constitution had been revised by the oligarchs in their own favor. Despite being firmly associated with the popular party, Savonarola found himself opposed to later attempts to radicalize the government by choosing it by lot instead of by nomination, so detaching himself from the very people who had been his early supporters.[35] Moreover, by pardoning the Mediceans in his amnesty law, he had ensured the continuance of factionalism in the city, getting drawn into the party system himself by the need to join with other groups in order to gain a majority in the vast new Great Council. So gerrymandering became part of the now frequent and contentious process of electing officeholders, "and what's worse, I hear there are some who say, 'He belongs to the friar's party, let's vote for him.' "[36] And as a party leader, he found himself offering increasingly tempting rewards to his followers—more wealth and power, the recovery of Pisa, lower income tax—making him vulnerable to the charge that instead of criticizing the old propitiatory view of religion, he was now

---

33. Polizzotto, 1989, 2000; Verde, 1992.
34. Verde, 1992, pp. 516, 519–20; Savonarola, 1956, II, pp. 326–327 (*Prediche sopra l'Esodo,* sermon XXII, 18 March 1498).
35. Prodi, 1997, pp. 47–48; Brown, 2003, pp. 304–306.
36. Prodi, 1997, pp. 45–46; Brown, 2000b, pp. 24–25.

pandering to "the credulous multitude."[37] In the long run, these develop-
ments helped to compromise Savonarola's initial message of reform and to
reveal the ambiguities in his situation. When he was unwilling to allow Medicean conspirators the right to appeal to the Great Council in August 1497,
he was accused of even greater hypocrisy, making it "plain to all," Machiavelli
famously wrote in his *Discourses on Livy* (I, 45), "that at heart [Savonarola]
was ambitious and a party-man," which "ruined his reputation and brought
on him much reproach."

The final paradox of Savonarola's political position concerns the question
of his leadership. From the fall of the Medici in 1494 until his *Treatise on the
Government of Florence* in 1498, he had consistently preached against allowing
a single head *(capo)* to recapture power. Faced with the need to fill the vacuum left by the Medici, however, he first proposed Christ as the Florentines'
king and leader, a year later extending this idea to include the people through
the Great Council. "Who is our Lord?" he asked in October 1495; "Christ
is. Who holds the place of Christ? Not the Signoria, but the people are the
Lord, and therefore I say to you, keep your eye on the Lord, that is, on the
Council." But by behaving like Moses in claiming to enjoy undisputed authority as God's mouthpiece and by appearing to want "to be lord," as he
put it in the *Compendium,* he ended up being accused of the very vices of
irreverence and hypocrisy that he had condemned.[38] These ambiguities help
to explain the increasing weakness of his position in Florence, despite the
success of his fervent moral crusade against corruption.

Moral Reform

Palm Sunday, 27 March 1496, in many ways marks the high point of Savonarola's fortunes. He had remained silent since the papal ban on his preaching in July 1495, when the Pope had also tried to reattach San Marco to the
Lombard Congregation (attempting a year later, with equal lack of success,
to make it join a new Tuscan-Roman congregation).[39] So his return to the
pulpit in Lent 1496, at the request of the government, was celebrated with
unusual fervor. What impressed contemporaries was the transformation of
the Carnival rites that preceded Lent, as well as the spectacular procession
that ended it. Traditionally, Carnival was celebrated by boys hurling stones
at passersby and barricading streets to prevent them from entering without

---

37. *Epistola responsiva,* ed. Garfagnini, 1991, pp. 106–107; and on propitiatory religion,
    Brown, 2004, pp. 26–29.
38. Brown, 1988, pp. 57–65, citing Altoviti, 1991, pp. 123, 125; cf. Savonarola, 1962, I,
    p. 27 (*Prediche sopra Ruth e Michea,* sermon I, 8 May 1496); Savonarola, 1974,
    pp. 65, 190.
39. Ridolfi, 1959, pp. 132–143, 178–180.

paying a toll. Now, however, the boys collected alms and placed crucifixes on the street corners where the barricades had been. On the last day of Carnival they processed in large numbers through the city to collect alms and gifts, and on the following day and throughout Lent, they attended Savonarola's sermons in the cathedral with great devotion. This transformation reduced their elders to tears, who saw it as another miracle; but nowadays it perhaps interests us more for what it tells us about the organizational techniques that Savonarola displayed in using youth groups to spread his message. Preadolescent children were seen at the time both as the scourges of their day and as holy innocents, and we find Savonarola (like others before him) organizing them to tame them as a potentially disruptive force and also to use their purity as the means through which to mediate reform.[40] Savonarola's awareness of the dramatic effect of mass processions of these children and of their apparel is demonstrated by his last Lenten sermon, on Palm Sunday, translated here, in which he wanted both boys and girls to be dressed in white for the procession with red crosses in their hands and olive garlands on their heads. The impact of this procession — which also served as a successful fundraising event for the newly established *Monte di Pietà*[41] — is reflected in the chronicles of Landucci and Piero Parenti, who also commented on its sheer size: "five thousand boys, and also a great number of girls," according to Landucci; "six to seven thousand children," according to Parenti. Music played its part, too. Girolamo Benivieni's poem of celebration and other lauds were sung in the Piazza della Signoria during the celebrations, and afterwards the friars of San Marco danced and sang in the piazza in front of their monastery. "Long live Christ who is our King!" was the cry that went up throughout the city.

A year later, the famous "Bonfire of Vanities," on 7 February 1497, was intended to repeat the purifying ceremony with the same success. Contemporaries regarded the exceptional size of the bonfire and its destruction of so many treasured possessions as dramatic evidence of what could be done "through the agency of children," the culmination of Savonarola's moral campaign through his youth vigilantes. Yet there were already signs of unease, even among Savonarola's supporters, that the zeal of the vigilantes was not "eliminating", but simply "recycling", the ritualistic aspects of this pagan-Christian festival.[42] For although the current head of government, Francesco Valori, was a strong supporter of Savonarola, his partisanship stimulated

---

40. Bertelli, 1980–81; Plaisance, 1993, 1997 (esp. p. 125); Niccoli, 1997; Terreaux-Scotto, 1997; also Trexler, 1980, pp. 474–482; Polizzotto, 2004, pp. 110–123.
41. A charitable pawnshop intended to replace usurious moneylending by Jews, Menning, 1993, esp. pp. 1–63; cf. Plaisance, 1997, pp. 125–126.
42. Ciappelli, 1997, p. 139.

factionalism, and disorder broke out again two months later. On Ascension Day, 4 May 1497, a group of young aristocrats hostile to Savonarola, the so-called Compagnacci, caused a riot during Savonarola's sermon in the cathedral, having previously planned to put explosives in the pulpit (which were replaced by nails and ordure on the day).[43] The government had already banned all preaching in public after Ascension Day, so four days later Savonarola had to resort to an open letter, as in 1495, to keep up the spirits of his followers. Only five days later, on 13 May 1497, Alexander VI issued a bull of excommunication against him. This marks the final period of Savonarola's life.

Excommunication and the Last Year

The papal bull of excommunication was promulgated in Florence on 18 June, transforming the controversy about Savonarola from a local issue to one of wide ecclesiastical and political concern.[44] No longer able to preach or to say Mass, Savonarola again reacted by writing open letters in his own defense. Then he devoted himself to writing devotional works that circulated widely through the printing press and exercised a powerful posthumous influence on the religious reforming movement. The events of this last year are described eloquently in the documents translated here and need little additional comment. Savonarola's fate hung not only on the Pope and his situation vis-à-vis the French in Italy, but also on the flux of Florentine politics as friendly and hostile priorates succeeded each other every two months. The division of opinion in Florence was so equally balanced that two quite new coalition magistracies of "peacemakers" were appointed to deal with the crisis in April and July. The consultative meetings of citizens held to discuss Savonarola's fate in July (as again in March–April 1498) were equally divided in their views, as we can see from the unparalleled evidence of their debates in these crucial months, which pondered whether Savonarola's authority as a prophet overrode that of the Pope as Christ's vicar on earth (or, as they put it, whether God's power was greater than Christ's), and whether the threatened interdict would damage Florence's economic interests.[45] They provide an interesting counterpoint to the epistolary debate described here between the Pope and Savonarola, which led to the turbulent events of 1498.

The Pope warned the Florentine ambassadors in Rome on 25 February 1498 that Florence would be interdicted if Savonarola continued to preach

43. Violi, 1986, pp. 73–74. On the Compagnacci, Rocke, 1996, pp. 220–222.
44. Ridolfi, 1959, pp. 197–205.
45. Ed. Fachard, 2002, pp. 493–500; 1993, pp. 41–71; discussed by Brown, 2000b, pp. 29–34.

and summoned him again to Rome (his response is translated below).[46] On the same day as this audience, Savonarola made himself a hostage to fortune by declaring in his Carnival Sunday sermon that if he was deceiving the people, he might be swallowed into Hell by a fire from Heaven. Since he failed to be swallowed up when he issued the challenge two days later, the chronicler Parenti saw it as a clever device to endorse the truth of his teaching, as well as a source of disillusionment among those who had hoped for a miracle that never materialized. Disillusionment was in fact the ultimate outcome, for although none of his opponents responded at the time to his challenge to put themselves to the test, the Franciscan fra Francesco da Puglia did later challenge Savonarola's substitute preacher, fra Domenico da Pescia, to a trial by fire. Savonarola professed to be willing to undergo the ordeal himself, as did his religious and lay followers, several thousand of whom, he claimed, cried out in response to his sermon in San Marco, "Here am I, here am I, I will go into this fire for your glory, O Lord."[47] But the opinion of the citizens whom the government consulted about the ordeal was more skeptical, as we can see from their debates. In arguing (on Christ's authority) that to seek for a sign was a mark of depravity, the lawyer Guidantonio Vespucci put his finger on the most dangerous aspect of Savonarola's initial proposal to challenge God on 25 February, the archaic notion that truth could be proved by a sign.[48]

The events that ensued are well known. Plans for the ordeal went ahead despite widely conflicting views about its legitimacy, until on 6 April the looked-for "sign" was provided by a sudden downpour that doused the flames of the bonfire. Even believers had been scandalized by the Dominicans' plan to take the consecrated Host, "the most sacred Body of Christ," into the flames, "something horrendous and execrable even to talk about," one Florentine wrote; and after the event was aborted, everyone felt frustrated and disillusioned.[49] The following day, Palm Sunday, San Marco was attacked by an angry mob, and Francesco Valori and his wife were murdered. Savonarola was declared a rebel, and he, fra Domenico, and a third friar were imprisoned. After interrogation with torture, they were condemned by the state, as well as by the papal commissioners sent from Rome, for being schismatics and heretics and for preaching

---

46. Florence, Archivio di Stato, Signori, Dieci, Otto, Legazioni e Commissarie, Missive e Responsive, MS 30, fol. 16v ; Ridolfi, 1959, pp. 221–230.
47. Ridolfi, 1936, p. 238; on these events in general, Weinstein, 1994, pp. 13–14.
48. Fachard, 1993, p. 65, cf. Brown, 2000b, pp. 32–34. On ordeal, first abolished in 1231, Bartlett, 1986 (and on Savonarola, p. 22, n. 32).
49. Florence, Archivio di Stato, Acquisti e Doni, MS 142, ins. 7, fol. 14 (9 April 1498); cf. Cerretani, 1994, p. 245.

"new things." They were handed over to the secular authorities to be hanged and burnt on 23 May 1498.[50]

The manifest contradictions in Savonarola's life are reflected in the comments of contemporaries translated here, which range from the faith of supporters like Landucci, Simone Filipepi, and Lorenzo Violi, to the criticism of the neoplatonist Marsilio Ficino and the balanced assessment of Francesco Guicciardini. Another Florentine, Tommaso Ginori, deleted a whole page he had written in his journal describing Savonarola's trial and death, for the reason (as he explained overleaf in huge letters) that because many lies had been spoken during his trial, he didn't know what to think—except that Savonarola was a man "of great learning and from what one could see in San Marco of good and perfect life . . . and I think a great error was committed in depriving him and other friars of their lives."[51] What stands out in the assemblage of texts presented in this volume is the contrast between the didacticism and gentle pietism of the earlier pastoral sermons and treatises and the demagogy and violence of the later sermons and writings, which resorted to invocations of hellfire and the threat of a "great multitude of demons" reserved by God "in this caliginous air of ours" to test our faith. In addition to Ficino's criticism of Savonarola's "violence" and Machiavelli's description of Savonarola tearing up the Bible and repeatedly stabbing at it (to illustrate Moses' attack on the Egyptian in Exodus), he was also criticized by the humanist Marcello Adriani, who countered Savonarola's attacks on pagan philosophy with his own measured defense of a curative god, very different from Savonarola's vengeful Old Testament God, who, like a pawnbroker, needed propitiating with gifts.[52]

After the trauma of his legal process with torture, Savonarola wrote two last *Prison Meditations on Psalms 51 and 31*.[53] Liberated from the scholastic and prophetic language of his sermons, his "Exposition of Psalm 51" takes the form of a simple humanist dialogue between Hope and Sadness that movingly conveys the alternating shifts between these two emotional states. It provides us with a valuable link between the simple piety of the early reformer and the trapped and angry victim of his often self-inflicted wounds. The *Meditations* became, with Thomas à Kempis' *Imitation of Christ,* one of the most popular books on inner piety linking him with reformers north and south of the Alps. It can be read as a fitting memorial to his conflicted life and legacy.

---

50. Weinstein, 1970, pp. 285–288.
51. Ginori, 1910, p. 104.
52. Machiavelli, 1961, p. 88 (letter to Riccardo Becchi, 9 March 1498). On Adriani, Brown, 2004, pp. 27–29.
53. Savonarola, 1994.

Bibliography

Abulafia, D., ed. 1995. *The French Descent into Renaissance Italy, 1494–95: Antecedents and Effects.* Aldershot.

Altoviti, Francesco. 1991. *Defensione de' magistrati e delle leggi di Firenze contra alle invettive di Fra Girolamo Savonarola* (Florence: Francesco di Dino, c. 1498). In Garfagnini, pp. 121–130.

Bartlett, R. 1986. *Trial by Fire and Water.* Oxford.

Benivieni, Domenico. 1496. *Tractato in defensione et probatione de la doctrina et prophetie predicate da frate Hieronymo da Ferrara nella città di Firenze.* Florence (F. Bonaccorsi).

Bertelli, S. 1980–81. "Embrioni di partiti alle soglie dell' età moderna." In *Per Federico Chabod (1901–1960).* Annali della Facoltà di Scienze Politiche dell' Università di Perugia, pp. 17–35.

Brown, A. 1988. "Savonarola, Machiavelli and Moses: A Changing Model." In *Florence and Italy: Renaissance Studies in Honour of Nicolai Rubinstein,* ed. P. Denley and C. Elam, pp. 57–72. London.

———. 1997. "Partiti, correnti, o coalizioni: Un contributo al dibattito." In Fontes, Fournel, and Plaisance, pp. 59–79.

———. 2000a. "The Revolution of 1494 and Its Aftermath." In *Italy in Crisis, 1494,* ed. J. Everson and D. Zancani, pp. 13–40. Oxford.

———. 2000b. "Ideology and Faction in Savonarolan Florence." In Fletcher and Shaw, pp. 22–41.

———. 2003. "Uffici di onore e utile: la crisi del repubblicanesimo a Firenze." *Archivio storico italiano* 161, pp. 285–321.

———. 2004. "Intellectual and religious currents in the post-Savonarola years." In *La figura de Jerónimo Savonarola y su influencia en España y Europa,* ed. D. Weinstein, J. Benevent, and I. Rodríguez, pp. 23–50. Florence.

Cadoni, G., ed. 1994. *Provvisioni concernenti l'ordinamento della repubblica fiorentina (1494–1497).* Vol. I. Rome.

Cattin, G. 1953. *Il primo Savonarola: Poesie e prediche autografe dal codice Borromeo.* Florence.

Cerretani, Bartolomeo. 1993. *Ricordi.* Ed. G. Berti. Florence.

———. 1994. *Storia fiorentina.* Ed. G. Berti. Florence.

Ciappelli, G. 1997. "I bruciamenti delle vanità e la transizione verso un nuovo ordine carnevalesco." In Fontes, Fournel, and Plaisance, pp. 133–147.

Eisenbichler, K. 1996. "Il trattato di Girolamo Savonarola sulla vita viduale." In Garfagnini, pp. 267–272.

Epistola responsiva a frate Ieronimo da Ferrara. 1991 (Florence, L. Morgiani, 1496). In Garfagnini, pp. 102–120.

Fachard, D. ed. 1993. *Consulte e pratiche della Repubblica fiorentina, 1498–1505.* Geneva.

——— ed. 2002. *Consulte e pratiche della Repubblica fiorentina, 1495–1497.* Geneva.

Fletcher, S., and C. Shaw, eds. 2000. *The World of Savonarola: Italian Elites and Perceptions of Crisis.* Aldershot.

Fontes, A., J.-L. Fournel, and M. Plaisance, eds. 1997. *Savonarole: Enjeux, débats, questions,* Paris.

Garfagnini, G. C., ed. 1991. "L'*Epistola responsiva* e la *Defensione* dell' Altoviti." *Rinascimento*, 2d ser., 31, pp. 93–130.

———— ed. 1996. *Studi savonaroliani. Verso il V centenario.* Florence.

———— ed. 1997. *Savonarola e la politica.* Florence.

———— ed. 1998. *Savonarola: Democrazia, tirannide, profezia.* Florence.

Gilbert, C. 1980. *Italian Art, 1400–1500: Sources and Documents.* Englewood Cliffs, N.J.

Ginori, Tommaso. 1910. "Ricordanze." *Quellen und Forschungen zur Geschichte Savonarolas.* Ed. J. Schnitzer. Munich, I, pp. 94–104.

Guicciardini, Francesco. 1970. *The History of Florence.* Ed. and trans. M. Domandi. New York.

Hall, M. B. 1990. "Savonarola's Preaching and the Patronage of Art." In Verdon and Henderson, pp. 493–522.

Hatfield, R. 1995. "Botticelli's *Mystic Nativity,* Savonarola and the Millennium." *Journal of the Warburg and Courtauld Institutes* 58, pp. 89–114.

Henderson, J. 1994. *Piety and Charity in Late Medieval Florence.* Oxford.

Kent, F. W. 1983. "A Proposal by Savonarola for the Self-Reform of Florentine Women (March 1496)." *Memorie Domenicane,* n.s., 14, pp. 335–341.

Kraye, J. 1996. "Lorenzo and the Philosophers." In *Lorenzo the Magnificent: Culture and Politics,* ed. M. Mallett and N. Mann, pp. 151–166. London.

Kristeller, P. O. 1956. "Lay Religious Traditions and Florentine Platonism." In *Studies in Renaissance Thought and Letters,* pp. 99–122. Rome.

Machiavelli, Niccolò. 1961. *The Letters of Machiavelli.* Ed. A. Gilbert. Chicago.

————. 1983. *The Discourses.* Ed. B. Crick. London.

Macey, P. 1992. *Bonfire Songs: Savonarola's Musical Legacy.* Oxford.

Mallett, M. 1995. "Personalities and Pressures: Italian Involvement in the French Invasion of 1494." In Abulafia, pp. 151–163.

McGinn, B., ed. and trans. 1979. *Apocalyptic Spirituality.* New York.

Menning, C. B. 1993. *Charity and State in Late Renaissance Italy: The Monte di Pietà of Florence.* Ithaca.

Nesi, Giovanni. 1973. *Oraculum de novo secolo* (Florence, Lorenzo Morgiani, 1497). In Vasoli, pp. 161–179.

Niccoli, O. 1990. *Prophecy and People in Renaissance Italy.* Princeton.

————. 1997. "I 'Fanciulli' del Savonarola: Usi religiosi e politici dell' infanzia nell' Italia del Rinascimento." In Fontes, Fournel, and Plaisance, pp. 105–120.

Origo, I. 1963. *The World of San Bernardino.* London.

Peyronnet, G. 1995. "The Distant Origins of the Italian Wars: Political Relations between France and Italy in the Fourteenth and Fifteenth Centuries." In Abulafia, pp. 29–53.

Plaisance, M. 1993. "Florence: Le Carnaval à l'époque de Savonarole." In *Les fêtes urbaines en Italie à l'époque de la Renaissance,* ed. F. Decroisette and M. Plaisance, pp. 9–29. Paris.

————. 1997. "1496: Savonarole metteur en scène de la procession des rameaux." In Fontes, Fournel, and Plaisance, pp. 121–131.

Polizzotto, L. 1989. "*Dell'arte del ben morire:* The Piagnone Way of Death 1494–1545." *I Tatti Studies* 3, pp. 27–87.

———. 1993. "When Saints Fall Out: Women and the Savonarolan Reform in Early Sixteenth-Century Florence." *Renaissance Quarterly* 46, pp. 486–525.

———. 1994. *The Elect Nation: The Savonarolan Movement in Florence, 1494–1545.* Oxford.

———. 1996. "Savonarola, savonaroliani e la riforma della donna." In Garfagnini, pp. 229–244.

———. 1997. "Savonarola e la riorganizzazzione della società." In Garfagnini, pp. 149–162.

———. 2000. "Savonarola and the Florentine Oligarchy." In Fletcher and Shaw, pp. 55–64.

———. 2004. *Children of promise. The confraternity of the purification and the socialization of youths in Florence, 1427–1785.* Oxford.

Prodi, P. 1997. "Gli affanni della democrazia: La predicazione del Savonarola durante l'esperienza del governo popolare." In Garfagnini, pp. 45–46.

Ridolfi, R. 1936. "Due documenti Savonaroliani sopra la prova del fuoco." *La Bibliofilia* 38, pp. 234–242.

———. 1959. *The Life of Savonarola.* Trans. C. Grayson. London.

Rocke, M. 1996. *Forbidden Friendships: Homosexuality and Male Culture in Renaissance Florence.* Oxford.

Rubinstein, N. 1990. "Lay Patronage and Observant Reform in Fifteenth-Century Florence." In Verdon and Henderson, pp. 63–82.

———. 2000. "Savonarola on the government of Florence." In Fletcher and Shaw, pp. 42–54.

Savonarola, Girolamo. 1956. *Prediche sopra l'Esodo.* Ed. P. G. Ricci. 2 vols., 1955, 1956. Rome.

———. 1962. *Prediche sopra Ruth e Michea.* Ed. V. Romano. 2 vols. Rome.

———. 1969. *Prediche sopra i Salmi.* Ed. V. Romano. 2 vols., 1969, 1974. Rome.

———. 1972. *Prediche sopra Amos e Zaccaria.* Ed. P. Ghiglieri. 3 vols., 1971, 1972. Rome.

———. 1974. *Compendio di rivelazioni e Dialogus de veritate prophetica.* Ed. A. Crucitti. Rome.

———. 1992. *Scritti vari.* Ed. A. Verde. Rome.

———. 1994. *Prison Meditations on the Psalms 51 and 31.* Ed. and trans. J. P. Donnelly. Milwaukee.

———. 1998. *Sermones in primam divi Ioannis sermones.* Ed. A. Verde. Florence.

———. 2001. *Il Quaresimale del 1491.* Ed. A. Verde and E. Giaconi. Florence.

Scala, Bartolomeo. 1997. *Apologia contra vituperatores civitatis Florentiae* (Florence, A. Miscomini, 1496). In *Humanistic and Political Writings,* ed. A. Brown, pp. 394–411. Tempe, Ariz.

Terreaux-Scotto, C. 1997. "La place des enfants dans la réforme Savonarolienne de la cité." In Fontes, Fournel, and Plaisance, pp. 81–103.

Toussaint, S. 1996. "Profetare alla fine del Quattrocento." In Garfagnini, pp. 167–181.

Trexler, R. C. 1980. *Public Life in Renaissance Florence.* New York.

Vasoli, C., ed. 1973. "Giovanni Nesi tra Donato Acciaiuoli e Girolamo Savonarola: Testi editi et inediti." *Memorie Domenicane,* n.s., 4, pp. 103–179.

Verde, A. 1992. "Fra Girolamo Savonarola e Lorenzo de' Medici: Il quaresimale in S. Lorenzo del 1492." *Archivio storico italiano* 150, pp. 493–605.

———. 1998. "Girolamo Savonarola: Ideologo e profeta. Il quaresimale del 1491." In Garfagnini, pp. 127–147.

Verdon, T., and J. Henderson, eds. 1990. *Christianity and the Renaissance: Image and Religious Imagination in the Quattrocento*. Syracuse, N. Y.

Violi, Lorenzo. 1986. *Le Giornate*. Ed. G. C. Garfagnini. Florence.

Weinstein, D. 1970. *Savonarola and Florence: Prophecy and Patriotism in the Renaissance*. Princeton.

———. 1989. *"The Art of Dying Well* and Popular Piety in the Preaching and Thought of Girolamo Savonarola." In *Life and Death in Fifteenth-Century Florence,* ed. M. Tetel, R. G. Witt, and R. Goffin, pp. 88–104. Durham, N.C.

———. 1994. "Girolamo Savonarola." In *Girolamo Savonarola: Piety, Prophecy, and Politics in Renaissance Florence,* ed. D. Weinstein and V. R. Hotchkiss, pp. 1–16. Dallas (Bridwell Library).

Zafarana, Z. 1968. "Per la storia religiosa di Firenze nel Quattrocento: Una raccolta privata di prediche." *Studi medievali,* 3d ser., 9, pp. 1017–1113.

Zancarini, J.-Cl. 1997. "La question de l'ennemi dans les sermons et écrits de Savonarole." In Fontes, Fournel, and Plaisance, pp. 45–57.

Alison Brown

Text Sources

Alexander VI, Pope. *Le lettere di Girolamo Savonarola*. Ed. Roberto Ridolfi. Florence: Olschki, 1933. Appendix III, pp. 229–235.

Benivieni, Girolamo. *Commento di Hierony[mo] B[enivieni] a pius canzone et sonetti dello amore et della belleza divina*. Florence: S. Antonio Tubini, Lorenzo di Francesco Venetiano and Andrea Ghyr, 8 September 1500. Pp. cxii^v–cxiiii^v, cxvi^v–cxvii (leaves ooii^v and oovi^v). Bridwell Library Special Collections 06109.

———. "Commento." In *Canzona d'un Piagnone pel bruciamento delle vanità nel Carnevale del 1498 [sic]*. Ed. Isidoro del Lungo. Florence: Grazzini, 1864. Pp. xvii–xxv.

(Pseudo-)Burlamacchi, Fra Pacifico. *La vita del Beato Ieronimo Savonarola*. Ed. Prince Piero Ginori Conti [and Roberto Ridolfi]. Florence: Olschki, 1937. Pp. 118–136.

Ficino, Marsilio. *Supplementum Ficinianum: Marsilii Ficini florentini philosophi Platonici opuscula inedita et dispersa*. Ed. Paul Oskar Kristeller. Florence: Aedes Leonis S., 1937. Pp. 76–79

Filipepi, Simone. *Estratto della cronaca*. In *Scelta di prediche e scritti di Fra Girolamo Savonarola*. Ed. Pasquale Villari and Ernesto Casanova. Florence, 1898. Reprinted in Herbert P. Horne, *Botticelli, Painter of Florence*. Princeton: Princeton University Press, 1980. Pp. 362–363. See also Creighton Gilbert's English translation in his anthology, *Italian Art, 1400–1500: Sources and Documents*. Evanston: Northwestern University Press, 1980. Pp. 218–219.

Guicciardini, Francesco. *History of Florence*. Ed. and trans. Mario Domandi. New York: Harper and Row, 1970. Pp. 145–148.

Landucci, Luca. *A Florentine Diary from 1450 to 1516*. Trans. Alice de Rosen Jervie. London: J. M. Dent, 1927. Pp. 101–104, 130–131, 142–143.

Nardi, Iacopo. *Istorie della città di Firenze di Iacopo Nardi*. Vol. I. Ed. Agenore Gelli. Florence: Le Monnier, 1858. Pp. 90–94, 114–117.

Parenti, Piero. *Diary*. In *Savonarola nach den Aufzeichnungen des Florentiners Piero Parenti*. Vol. IV of *Quellen und Forschungen zur Geschichte Savonarolas*. Ed. Joseph Schnitzer. Leipzig: Verlag von Duncker und Humblot, 1910. Pp. 159–161, 230–232.

———. *Storia fiorentina*. Vol. I. Ed. Andrea Matucci. Florence: Olschki, 1994. Pp. 326–328.

Savonarola, Girolamo, O. P. *Compendio di rivelazione . . . e Dialogus de veritate prophetica*. Ed. Angela Crucitti. Edizione Nazionale delle Opere di Girolamo Savonarola. Rome: Belardetti, 1974. Pp. 247–376.

———. *Lettere e scritti apologetici*. Ed. Roberto Ridolfi, Vincenzo Romano, and Armando Verdi. Edizione Nazionale delle Opere di Girolamo Savonarola.

Rome: Belardetti, 1984. Pp. 71–90, 149–151, 161–162, 204–205, 226–227, 239–264, 271–282, 404.

———. *Prediche sopra Aggeo con il trattato circa il reggimento e governo della città di Firenze*. Ed. Luigi Firpo. Edizione Nazionale delle Opere di Girolamo Savonarola. Rome: Belardetti, 1965. Pp. 105–122, 208–228, 409–428, 435–487.

———. *Prediche sopra Amos e Zacaria*. Ed. Paolo Ghiglieri. Edizione Nazionale delle Opere di Girolamo Savonarola. Rome: Belardetti, 1971. Pp. 144–158, 239–285.

———. *Prediche sopra i Salmi*. Vol. I. Ed. Vincenzo Romano. Edizione Nazionale delle Opere di Girolamo Savonarola. Rome: Belardetti, 1969. Pp. 37–62.

———. *Prediche sopra l' Esodo*. Vol. I. Ed. Pier Giorgio Ricci. Edizione Nazionale delle Opere di Girolamo Savonarola. Rome: Belardetti, 1956. Pp. 68–98.

———. *Prediche sopra Ruth e Michea*. Ed. Vincenzo Romano. Edizione Nazionale delle Opere di Girolamo Savonarola. Rome: Belardetti, 1962. Pp. 362–397.

Somenzi, Paolo. Letters to Lodovico Sforza, Duke of Milan. *La storia di Girolamo Savonarola*. Ed. Pasquale Villari. Florence: Le Monnier, 1910. Document XXVI, vol. I, pp. cxi–cxii; and Document XII, vol. II, pp. li–liii.

Violi, Lorenzo. *Le giornate*. Ed. Gian Carlo Garfagnini. Istituto Nazionale di Studi sul Rinascimento: Studi e Testi XIII. Florence: Olschki, 1986. Pp. 78–79.

Biblical Abbreviations and Equivalencies

Abbreviations of biblical book titles follow the Vulgate. Proper names in the text follow the Douai spelling. Equivalencies with spellings from the King James Version are given below where differences are distinct enough to require mention.

Abbreviation	*Vulgate*	*King James*
Abac.	Habacuc	Habakkuk
	Aggeus	Haggai
Apoc.	Apocalypse	Revelations
	Baltasar	Belshazzar
	Bersabee	Beer-sheba
	Chanaan	Canaan
Col.	Colossians	Colossians
Eccles.	Ecclesiastes	Ecclesiastes
	Eliseus	Elisha
	Ezechias	Hezekiah
Ezech.	Ezechiel	Ezekiel
	Gedeon	Gideon
Ier.	Jeremias	Jeremiah
Iob	Job	Job
Ioh.	John	John
Ion.	Jonas	Jonah
Ios.	Josue	Joshua
Luc.	Luke	Luke
Marc.	Mark	Mark
	Micheas	Micah
	Nabuchodonosor	Nebuchadnezzar
	Noe	Noah
	Osee	Hosea
I Reg.	I Kings	I Samuel
II Reg.	II Kings	II Samuel
IV Reg.	IV Kings	II Kings
	Sedecias	Zedekiah
Sir./Eccles[us].	Sirach/Ecclesiasticus	[No equivalent]
Zach.	Zacharias	Zechariah

Pastoral Ministry

Amos and Zacharias, Sermon XLIV

Good Friday

1 April 1496

Venite ad me omnes qui laboratis et onerati estis et ego reficiam vos.[1] —
Matt. 11:28[2]

Dearly beloved in Christ Jesus, so great has been the love of God Omnipotent toward rational creatures that, seeing that man had been alienated from Him by the sin of his first ancestor such that he did not know his intended end, He sent His only-begotten Son to take human flesh and suffer on the wood of the Cross to make satisfaction for this sin. From this Incarnation and Passion there have resulted so many advantages and so many favors for the world that human tongue could not recount them.

First, since man on his own did not know either his own end or the truth, God deigned to come down in His own person in order to show them to him, whereof the Savior says: *"In hoc natus sum et ad hoc veni in mundum, ut testimonium perhibeam veritatis"*[3] [Ioh. 18:37]. The intended end of the rational creature is to see God *facie ad faciem*[4] [I Cor. 13:12]. This would have appeared impossible for human nature—that the intellect of man might be joined to God, given that God is infinite and our intellect finite

---

1. "Come to Me, all you who labor and are burdened, and I will refresh you."
2. Latin citations from the Bible are named and numbered according to the Vulgate. In selections translated from Italian, Latin quotations are given in the body of the text with a literal translation (not always in full agreement with Savonarola's own Italian translations) in footnotes. Comments are added where Savonarola differs from the authoritative modern edition of the Vulgate; in some instances, his quotations may be true to his own copy of the Scriptures. Nonbiblical Latin quotations are also translated in footnotes, except where they consist of a single word or short phrase of no interpretational significance (such as *ergo* or *tamen*), in which case they are translated in the text and italicized. In selections originally in Latin (*A Dialogue concerning Prophetic Truth*, the papal correspondence, Ficino's *Apologia*), quotations are translated along with the rest of the text. The reason for this difference in treatment is that in Savonarola's oral delivery of a sermon in Italian, a quotation in Latin would have interrupted the flow of his oratory; retaining the Latin achieves something of the same effect. In the Latin treatises and letters, there would be no such highlighting.
3. "For this I was born and came into the world, so that I might bear witness to the truth."
4. "Face to face."

(and *finiti ad infinitum nulla est proportio*)[5] — but, although this union seemed impossible, God wanted to join human nature to His divinity, which union of divinity and humanity is far greater than that between man's intellect and God's essence,[6] in order to show that if this greater union could be achieved, we ought to believe all the more easily that man would be conjoined with God in seeing Him *facie ad faciem*.

Another advantage derives from this Incarnation: since man has some creatures superior to him, perhaps it would have seemed to him that some one of those creatures nobler than he was God. Thus, man gains this advantage from the Incarnation and Passion of Christ: that he understands his worth and does not turn to a creature as his intended end, but only to Christ. And because man ought to be certain of his end, God could not have made man more or better assured of his end than by coming to speak in His own person and proving it by His own words and miracles. And because it does not suffice simply to know one's end, but is also necessary to know the means conducing to that end, He wanted to teach us this means by Himself with both His words and His life. And because the means is justice, which consists in this: *declinare a malo et facere bonum*[7] [I Pet. 3:11], our Savior took on flesh and agreed to suffer to free us from evil. And so that we might know that we need to divorce ourselves from sin, He also agreed to do works of justice in His own life to give an example to you, man, in His own person. For, if you had had to follow the example of another man, you could have said, "He is a man and can err," but because it was God, you cannot err by following in His footsteps. And because one's end must be vehemently loved, and so, also, the means conducing to that end, God wanted to stir our hearts to love Him; this could not be done in any better way than by becoming man and making Himself like us, so that we would have interchange and friendship with Him. And because, following Him, we would do it with great love, He agreed to suffer and die for us, nor could He have drawn us to Him by a better means than this.

The other particular advantages which follow from His Incarnation and death are endless and cannot be recounted, but we know that many other advantages hinge upon the mystery of this present day. Thus, from the wood of the Cross, our beloved Savior today cries out and says: *"Venite ad me omnes qui laboratis et onerati estis et ego reficiam vos."* By reflecting on these words, we wish to console your minds this morning.

---

5. "There is no proportion between the finite and the infinite."
6. I.e., divinity joined to an individual human nature (the dual natures of Christ) would seem to present a greater difficulty than humanity encompassed within divinity (the soul's union with God).
7. "To turn from evil and do good."

When the patriarch Jacob had received the blessing from his father, Isaac, Isaac said to his son Jacob: "Do not take a wife from the daughters of Chanaan, but go to Mesopotamia and take one from the women there" [Gen. 28:1 ff]. *Et egressus Iacob ex Bersabee*[8] [Gen. 28:11]; he came to a certain place called Haran, and, wanting to rest here *post occasum solis,* he put some stones under his head and slept, and he saw *in somnis*[9] a ladder that had its foot on the earth and its summit in heaven [Gen. 28:12], and from atop the ladder the Lord said: *"Ego sum Deus Abraam;* the earth on which you sleep *dabo tibi et semini tuo"*[10] [Gen. 28:13]. This is the place where the temple was built, where Abraham attempted to sacrifice Isaac, and where Christ was crucified. Jacob took some of those stones, some say one, others three that then became one. We want to lead you this morning to Paradise up this ladder. At the top of this ladder is the Lord, Who says: *"Venite ad me omnes qui laboratis et onerati estis et ego reficiam vos."* This ladder has seven steps.

The philosophers say that every movement under the heavens depends entirely on the movement of the heavens, such that if the movement of the heavens were to cease, every other motion of the world under the heavens would cease; thus they say that the movement of the heavens is the life of all natural things, and, *therefore,* if that were to cease, all things composed of elements would dissolve into those elements. If, then, the heavens were not moved, nothing would be generated down here, and there would be no motion. It is obvious that this is true, for nothing in nature is in vain: *Deus et natura nihil agunt frustra.*[11] If the heavens were able to do these things here below without being moved themselves, their movement would be pointless, especially given that movement leads to the perfection of the things moved, and so, it must be that the movement of the heavens causes all these other things.

If the heavens are moved, then, they must of necessity be moved by another mover; therefore, the heavens are the instrument of another agent,[12] *quia omne quod movetur ab altero movetur.*[13] Since the heavens cannot operate except through motion, this is a sign that they are an instrument, as are the

---

8. "And Jacob went out from Bersabee."

9. "After the sun had gone down . . . in a dream."

10. "I am the god of Abraham . . . I will give to you and your seed."

11. "God and nature do nothing in vain."

12. Aristotle, *Metaphysics* XII (Λ).vii.2 (1072a, ll. 24–25). Citations from Aristotle follow the numbering used in the Loeb Classical Library editions.

13. "Since everything which is moved is moved by another." Thus the text, but it would make more sense if the first *"movetur"* were instead *"movet,"* the line then meaning: "since that which moves is moved by another"; ibid., viii.4 (1073a, ll. 26–27). Aristotle is quoted by Thomas Aquinas, *Summa theologica,* part 1.1, quest. 2, art. 3.

saw, the hammer, and the file, which cannot operate on their own if they are not moved by some principal agent; in the same way, the heavens are an instrument which operates because it has been moved by another. But because the things of nature are orderly and nature has an admirable order (especially the heavens), and because nature always proceeds to its end by predetermined means, it necessarily follows that he whose instrument the heavens are has intelligence such that he may know how to make them turn and never err, as we see that he never errs; thus, the philosophers say that this is the work of an unerring intelligence. For this reason, some say that this is the soul of the heavens (*l'anima del cielo*) and, thus, that the heavens are animated. Nonetheless, if this were true, it would still be necessary to postulate another mover, because the soul, in its turn, needs to be moved; wherefore, it cannot itself be the prime mover, because one must find a prime mover who is completely immovable, and this is God.

This intelligence, then, the angel which moves the heavens, is first moved by God as its object of love and desire, so that it desires to be assimilated to Him. In the same way, every other effect of nature desires to be converted and assimilated to its cause. Although this operation of nature is extrinsic, nonetheless, God moves this angel as its beloved and desired and as the beginning and cause of everything, since He brings forth and sends out everything toward its own being and its own perfection. And because the perfection of every creature is to be assimilated to its cause, and the beginning and cause of everything is God, everything desires to draw near to God and to be converted to Him, and this is a turning back. God moves everything as its object of love and desire, not only as the beginning, but also as the end of everything, to which it desires to be assimilated. Accordingly, Dionysius says: *Ad se omnia convertit Deus*.[14] God, then, moves everything as the One Whom it loves and desires, and He moves the angels, who, by intrinsic operation, desire to be assimilated to Him as to the ultimate end of everything.

Now, why have you said this, friar? Because I set the Crucifix[15] in the middle of the world, and I want to show you that This is the intended end of man, Which moves everyone as the thing he loves and desires; It cries out and exclaims: *"Venite ad me omnes qui laboratis et onerati estis et ego reficiam vos."* So, God says to all creatures: *"Venite ad me omnes qui laboratis et onerati estis et ego reficiam vos;* be like Me, come, for I shall give you your consolation and your felicity." I set the Crucifix in the middle of the world.

The philosophers say *quod homo est minor mundus:* "man is a lesser

14. "God turns everything back towards Himself."
15. The Italian, *il/el Crucifisso,* can mean either "the One Crucified" or "the Crucifix" or both at the same time.

world," because he contains within himself and partakes of everything—angels, animals, plants—and man generates another man, through whom all these other things are created. But because man has free will and can do good or evil as he wishes, some, following evil, are disordered and do not live according to reason. From the order of the heavens we know God, Who is most wise; likewise, from the order of men who live according to reason we know that they are men, but of those others who live evilly, we say and know that they are beasts. You can thus see which are those who are moved by God. I say that all men who live uprightly are moved by this Crucifix as the thing they love and desire, for if you look around and read carefully all the histories in accordance with moral philosophy, you will not find—nor can one even imagine—any life more ordered than that of the Christian, a life such as Christian saints have not only described, but also as they have lived it. And if you were to say, "In the philosophical life, one can also find those who have lived in a most orderly manner," you would be able to list so few of them that all of them could stand in this pulpit. You would cite Socrates and Plato and a few others, who, *however,* have committed some errors in their lives, such as worshipping idols and certain other sins. If you were to continue in this fashion of yours, you will find either none or only a few who are perfect. But all those who have followed this Crucified One as the thing they loved and desired—those who lived before Him as well as those who have lived since then—were all perfect, beginning with Abel, the first just man, up to the time of Christ, and these also were Christians, in that they were intent on nothing other than Christ and on the Messias Who was to come. Read the whole Scripture; you will see that all of them were well ordered in their lives and were made so by none other than this Crucifix which moved them as a thing loved and desired. All desired and intensely loved this Messias and this Christ, Who, although He had not yet taken on human flesh, was awaited by them with the greatest desire. Similarly, all those after Christ who have lived uprightly and in an orderly way have been moved and drawn by this Crucifix, *tamquam ab amato et desiderato.*[16] But I want to say a word about this Crucifix to the Jews and to the pagans.

Jew, come forward. Either this is the Messias or He is not: if you affirm that He is, then convert; if you say that He is not, I ask you what it means that all the prophecies are verified in Him and that all fit Him, not by distorting them, but easily. Go, see the Doctors [of the Church], who show that the whole of the life of Christ and what He has done is described and prophesied in the Old Testament. And if you were to say, "You extract from them what you want to interpret them as being about this Christ of yours," tell me, why is it that no other person can be found in whom these things

16. "As if by a thing loved and desired."

are verified? Pick any patriarch you wish or any other man in whom these scriptures are verified and to whom the conditions specified in the Old Testament are applicable. Excepting Christ, you will find no one. Why, then, since God has said that when a man is born to whom these conditions are applicable, we should believe in Him as in God and that He will be the Messias and His Son, why, then, if this is not the Messias, has God allowed this man to be born and all those conditions to be verified in Him? Either one must say that God did not know that this man would fulfill these conditions, or that, if He knew, He could not prevent it, or that He did not want to. That He did not know, this cannot be said, because such a statement cannot apply to Him, since God knows everything. That He could not, neither can this be said, since God can do anything. If you say that He did not want to prevent it, then He has deceived us because, having told us that we are to believe in the One Who fulfills these conditions as we believe in Him, if this one is not the Messias, and God has allowed these conditions to be verified in Him, then God has deceived us. This is not a fitting thing to say about God, because God is good and deceives no one. You must, then, O Jew, acknowledge by necessity that He is the Messias.

Now I turn to the pagans. Pagan, I ask you: if these matters concerning Christ were predicted so far in advance and have been fulfilled in this man, this then is a sign that they have been predicted not by a man but by God. The astrologer could not predict them because he cannot see particulars; he wants to see a person's natal day and then give his opinion. But of Christ there were predictions hundreds of years before He was born. Go, see that the astrologers said nothing of it beforehand; afterward, yes, because future contingencies cannot be seen except by God, Who is eternal. And so, pagan, acknowledge that this Scripture comes from God, and if it is from God, then it is true, and if it is true, it says that this Christ is the true Messias. This, then, is the true salvation of human nature, which God has sent and which He had prophesied not only by the prophets but also by sibyls and pagans, and the Apostles, the martyrs, and innumerable people followed after Him, all drawn to living uprightly by Him much more than by the philosophers.

Behold, then, the Crucified One in the middle of the world; He has restored human nature, which had fallen into ruin through man's sin. All those who have lived uprightly, whether before Christ or after, all have understood this, moved by Him as their object of love and desire. Still today He moves the good but not the wicked. And we see all those who live uprightly love this Crucified One, and the others who do not love Him live evilly. Tell me then: why is this so? Because He is the Prime Cause. And if you were to say that this flesh of this Crucified One or this wood of the Cross are the things which draw men, I answer that this is impossible on its own; there must be another principal agent which moves this instrument, just as the heavens are moved by another cause. Therefore, I say that this flesh stands here in the middle as do the heavens between men and God, Who moves men *tamquam amatum et desideratum*.[17] This instrument may be either good or evil, you will say. If it is evil, we would see that by this instrument men are drawn to live uprightly, but then the effect would be worthier than its cause, which is unfitting. If it is good, He [Christ] has said that He is God and has convinced the whole world. To this, then, it is necessary to add that He is both God and man, and that this divinity has drawn men to itself as the thing loved and desired. And so, this Crucifix stands in the middle of the world and says: *"Venite ad me omnes qui laboratis et onerati estis et ego reficiam vos;* come to Me and live uprightly, and I will give you consolation."

Out of reverence for so great a solemnity, I shall tell you what I have seen on this feast. The unfaithfulness of many causes the deprivation and withdrawal of many consolations. And yet, on this very account, I am glad to tell it. *Levavi oculos meos et vidi*[18] [Dan. 8:3; 10:5]. I saw the whole world before my eyes, bit by bit, on a very great plain all full of many men and women of every condition in the world (I do not want to tell you particulars about such and such because it is not permitted). In the middle of the plain, there was a little mount all full of roses and lilies, and on top of the mount a Crucifix was pouring forth red blood which radiated all the way round the world, around and around, and it splashed into the air here and there with the most splendid rays. It also poured onto the ground most abundantly, and it seemed to me that it formed a river which divided the world into two parts. And the Crucified One was crying out: *"Venite ad me omnes qui laboratis et onerati estis et ego reficiam vos."*[19]

I stood and watched: on the left side of the river there was Rome with all the Christians; on the right side, there was Jerusalem and all the pagans. The blood was spreading out on the right side and appearing on the foreheads of each of those Moors and pagans, and it seemed to me that it made on the foreheads of all of them a red cross more splendid than a ruby.[20] And as they felt themselves marked with the sign, they would run to that river and throw away their clothes and enter into it and drink of that blood and become inebriated, and then they would come forth gentle and sweet, beau-

17. "As the beloved and desired."
18. "I raised my eyes and saw."
19. See "Adoration of the Cross," plate 2.
20. In Ezech. 9:4–6, God sends an angel to mark in ink with a *tau* (Greek T, symbolic of the Cross) the foreheads of those who had not fallen into idolatry. This is perhaps conflated with the lamb's blood used to mark the lintels of the Israelites to protect them from the Angel of Death (Ex. 12:7).

tiful as angels. Likewise, on the left side, the blood was spreading out, and I saw that it made a mark on the forehead of every Christian of whatever condition—I saw Rome, in particular—and a red cross would appear on their foreheads because of the rays of that blood coming from the Crucified. And I saw that some would put on a cap to cover the cross; others would put up a hand; others a mask (there were different masks: some were lions, others wolves, others foxes, some others different animals). The preachers were standing there, and it seemed to me that they cried out and said, "Do you not hear what He says? *'Venite ad me omnes qui laboratis et onerati estis et ego reficiam vos.'"* But they did not want to hear or remove the masks or uncover the crosses. The angels came from heaven and wanted to take off their masks, and they did not allow it, but they ran toward the clothes which the infidels had left and were grabbing them and putting them on.

I keep watching: what is this? Lo and behold! lances, swords, bombs, and pestilence were coming. Meanwhile they were told, "Come to the Crucified!" But many did not want to come; they ran to the weapons and the rocks. Yet some of those on the left, who had the crosses on their foreheads, ran to that river and drank of the blood of the Crucified and emerged from it in the likeness of angels, and I saw that many of these were from Florence, my city, and were Florentine citizens. And when the sword had arrived, all those who ran to the arms and to the rocks ended up badly, all dead, and afterward in Hell, and few people remained. And it was said to me, "Tell my people that there is no other remedy than the Crucified; have recourse to Him Who says: *'Venite ad me omnes qui laboratis et onerati estis et ego reficiam vos.'"*

I do not want to expound this figure for you any further because the conclusion is clear. As for the particulars, what that red cross, the clothes, the sword, those masks, and the other particular things signify, examine them on your own; I leave this exposition to you. It is enough for you to know that this figure demonstrates that you should fall in love with Christ as one enamored and come to drink His blood, and that there is no other remedy for escaping from these tribulations than the Crucified. Thus says the Lord God.

You do not believe, eh? You do not believe me. "Well, sure, a vision." What do you say about the one Jacob had *in somnis* [Gen. 28]? This one has not been *in somnis,* but while waking. What do you say about this one of Jacob? And yet it is part of the Canon [of the Scriptures]. It is true that, though he had it in his sleep, he nonetheless had the light within him, for when the prophets receive a vision *in somnis,* they have the light of prophecy within them, which assures them and allows them to discern whether it is a dream or not and teaches them to know if it is or is not a prophecy. So had Jacob, whose name is interpreted "the uprooter" [Gen. 27:36] and signifies one who has uprooted vices and sins and left them behind in order to return to living a good life. To him the Lord says, "Do not take a wife from the house of Chanaan" [Gen. 28:1] — Chanaan is interpreted as *change* — that is, "do not take things that are mutable; material goods, honors, and philosophy are mutable things of the world; do not collect these things, because they will deceive you. But there is one I shall give you, and it is eternal wisdom, of which Holy Scripture is composed." Therefore, Jacob came out of Bersabee, which is interpreted as *puteus iuramenti*[21] [Gen. 21:32], which is the Holy Scripture. Man dwells in Bersabee; depart from it and begin to contemplate and go into Haran, that is, on high, and through the medium of creatures begin to contemplate the highest things, such as the Trinity, the goodness of God, and other elevated things.

But, although divinity cannot be known by man in this life, nonetheless, Dionysius says that when man is engaged in such contemplation, he comes to a certain place so exalted that he does not know how to express what he sees,[22] but he well knows that he contemplates God, and, like Jacob, he would like to sleep and rest in this place and in this contemplation. However, because our intellect is not powerful enough to contemplate without symbols and to rise so high, Jacob took three stones or else one stone, which are symbols, that is, man needs them to contemplate God, Who is three Persons and one nature, when he has come to a certain place of contemplation which he cannot express; however, the three stones can also mean the soul of Christ, His body, and His divinity, which are in one Person. And he begins to contemplate and to sleep in order to contemplate.

Suddenly he saw the ladder, which signifies the Cross of Christ, which is a ladder leading to Paradise. And the angels, ascending and descending the Cross of Christ in order to aid anyone wanting to climb up to Paradise, descend to help the one who climbs. This ladder ascends by seven steps; one must climb up these seven steps, for the Lord is above and says: *"Venite ad me omnes qui laboratis et onerati estis, et ego reficiam vos,"* for there is no other way to climb and ascend to Paradise. And the Lord says: *"Ego sum Deus Abraam et Deus Isaac* [Gen. 28:13]; follow their lives and their footsteps, for I want to lead you by means of this ladder. The earth on which you sleep, *that is,* contemplate, I shall give to you and to your seed, if you first follow this ladder in the tribulations, and afterward you will have consolation."

Now, let us begin to climb up this ladder; let us go, for, indeed, the Passion of Christ teaches us to go step by step.

Come, come, put your foot on the first step, which is called *fides* [faith]. What faith? Faith in the goodness of God and of His love toward humanity.

21. "Well of the oath."
22. Pseudo-Dionysius the Areopagite, *Mystical Theology,* chap. 3.

If you suffer tribulations, there must be in you a firm faith that God loves humanity with the greatest love. This is a great comfort for the one who begins to climb. Anyone who loves a thing vehemently, especially if he loves it as the ultimate end, quickly makes this assessment within himself: if he does not have it, even if he has everything else there is, he is not happy, but miserable; similarly, if he has that and nothing else, he considers himself happy. For the sake of argument, take a fervent lover: he has this view of the situation in his mind that, if he does not have the woman he loves, he seems to have nothing; if he has her, it seems to him that he has everything. Take one who has set his aim on riches: if he does not have riches, it appears to him he has nothing and he is unhappy, but if he has riches, it seems he has everything and is supremely happy.

Fides est substantia sperandarum rerum, argumentum non apparentium[23] [Heb. 11:1]; faith is a beginning and a light which makes you see and places before your eyes [man's] intended end of eternal life, a light which makes you have such certainty of that eternal life and such appreciation of it that, without it, nothing seems to go well, and with it, you consider yourself happy. Faith, then, reveals this to you. What is more, living faith assures you that God is so good toward souls, that not only has He given this end to man, but He also wanted to give it through the blood of His Son and through the death of Christ because He wanted to magnify human nature and give it an excellence even greater than He gave to the angels. *Sic Deus dilexit mundum ut Filium unigenitum daret, ut omnes qui credunt in eum non pereant sed habeant vitam aeternam* [Ioh. 3:16]. *Si Filio proprio non pepercit, [. . .] quomodo non etiam cum illo omnia nobis donabit?*[24] [Rom. 8:32] If, then, His love is so great, believe and have faith that He will not send you any tribulation or anguish but for the sake of your well-being and your medicine, for so great is His love that you ought not to doubt that if He takes away your possessions, He does all for your good, to illuminate you, to purify you, and to incite you toward these spiritual matters, and thus, they will be meant for your healing and not for death. Moreover, faith, by revealing these things, warms the heart of men to divine love such that it [the heart] cannot help but love God, considering how much it is loved by Him. And so, they have the greatest joy in this love. Thus, through this faith, man becomes stronger in his tribulations.

Set your foot up here and listen to what the Lord says: *"Venite ad me omnes qui laboratis etc."* Leave the love of earthly things; confirm yourself in

23. "Faith is the substance of things to be hoped for, evidence of things not seen."
24. "God so loved the world that He gave His only-begotten Son so that all who believe in Him might not perish, but have eternal life./If He did not spare His own Son . . . will He not also give us all things else along with Him?"

this faith, for it will free you from all tribulation because it reveals the end, which is so great that, beside it, you account every other happiness as nothing. So, even if you were to lose everything, you would not care; you would think that God wants no ill for you, but does all for your good, and that He is your Lord, your Physician, and that He acts in this way because He loves you, and then you would think that in any case you must die, and love will bear the burden of it.

God, wishing to show this love for humanity, deigned to come to be incarnated, to take up flesh, and to enlighten us and to perform miracles, and ultimately, He came for the sake of humanity. And *further,* as His Passion drew near, He summoned His disciples: *Cum venisset in mundum et dilexisset suos, [. . .] in finem dilexit eos*[25] [Ioh. 13:1], that is, He did not abandon them at the end. Although He departed, He showed them a sign of great devotion, as if to say, "See, man, how much care I have for you and how much love I bear you!" He arose from the supper and laid aside His vestments; He did not call the angels, nor the servants; rather, with His holy hands He girded Himself and set about washing the feet of His disciples [Ioh. 13:4 ff.]. See how much love! The Creator kneels before the creature: the Creator humbles himself to the creature and shows His devotion—He wanted to show His love and He stopped at nothing to show us His love—He began to wash the feet of His disciples with such great humanity![26] Come here, proud man, you do not want to humble yourself; come, you will see your Lord before Judas, before the traitor. And He began to wash his feet, as if saying, "O Judas, you will betray Me, and I call you to penitence; I would like to show mercy even to you."

So, man, take this example of the Savior, Who has shown you humility, which is the foundation of all the virtues. Be humble in this way likewise, and come to this first step. Reaffirm, men, the faith in your hearts that God loves humanity, and have this great confidence in Him, Who will not allow anything bad to happen to you, except for the sake of your salvation. And even if you suffer tribulations, say, "I know that God is good and that He will not abandon me, and, therefore, what He sends me is for the sake of my salvation, for His love is so great that He has become incarnate and washed the feet of His disciples. Because God has shown so much love to me, let any tribulation whatsoever come, since, if God has sent it, and since

---

25. "When He had come into the world, He had loved His own; He loved them even to the end." The first clause, added by Savonarola, echoes Ioh. 12:46: *Ego lux in mundum veni.* The brackets indicate an omission: *qui erant in mundo.*
26. Thus the text, the Italian *humanità* having the sense of "humane" or "benevolent" or "gracious." Divinity here exhibits truer humanity than do humans.

He is as good as He is, I know that all is for my salvation." Come, then, all, and climb up this first step.

Set your foot on the second step, which is called *necessitas:* it means that in this world it is necessary to suffer in one way or another. If you are good, you have to go *per multas tribulationes [. . .] ad regnum Dei*[27] [Act. 14:21]. On the other hand, if you are wicked, you will still have to suffer, since we see that in this world both the good and the bad have tribulations. Since you must suffer, then, it is better to suffer for Christ than for the world. It is necessary, I say, to suffer in one way or the other, because there are many contraries in us which make us suffer, inborn in us after the sin of our first ancestor, when the Lord in his anger said: *"Maledicta terra in opere tuo"*[28] [Gen. 3:17], *that is,* in your humanity, your intellect, your flesh, because they *continually* make you suffer tribulations. There are many reasons for this. First, because of our contrarieties; second, because of the necessity [compelling] men, for they are not self-sufficient; third, because the end of man is supernatural. First, you see that the heavens are incorruptible because they have no contrarieties; actually, they do have some contrarieties, not of quality, but of motion, for the movements of the heavens are in some way oppositional. The elements have an extrinsic, not inherent, contrariety, that is, one element is contrary to another; things compounded of elements have contrariety within themselves because they are composed of contraries, and they have the extrinsic contrariety of other bodies as well.

You will not find anything which is composed of elements that has greater contrariety than man, because he is composed of four contrary elements. Man has both intrinsic and extrinsic contrarieties: intrinsic in a number of ways, that is, by reason of the contrariety in the qualities of the elements, the contrariety of flesh and spirit, and the contrary reasons in the intellect, and other similar contraries, but the major contrariety is the one between flesh and spirit; the flesh is opposed to the spirit and the spirit to the flesh. There is also an opposition between opinions and intellects, whereby different minds have different opinions. *Item,* there are infinite tribulations among men, and this is because man is not self-sufficient like the other animals, which are provided by nature itself with clothing, shelter, food, and weapons with which to defend themselves, but it is not so for man. *Item,* the other creatures are directed to their end by the law of nature, but man has many contrarieties which impede him. On account of this, discord arises among men and more conflicts among them than among all the other animals. And because man is unable to regulate himself by the law of nature alone, you see that every day they make more laws. *Item,* man is

27. "Through many tribulations . . . to the kingdom of God."
28. "The earth shall be cursed in your work."

not self-sufficient, because his intellect is confused and is not clearly set on any one thing. And because his end is supernatural, he must get to it by another way than that of nature; besides which, when man is *in a pure state of nature,* he is not at rest. Therefore, it is necessary that man have many tribulations; if he were to have no other but death—and to think that man has to die and not know when he will die—it seems that this would create anguish, for man will do anything so as not to die. It is necessary to die, but you do not know when; if you had no other tribulation but this, it would not seem small. It follows that human nature is more miserable than any other animal, if he has no other end than what one sees. If this is so, we must all have some tribulation.

It is better, then, to suffer with Christ and enter upon this way of the ladder rather than the way of the world, for those who choose tribulations for the sake of the world get no relief and are like the damned, who are deprived of every consolation, and so they suffer great tribulations. They do so, first, because they are deprived of grace and glory: *item,* they desire things which cannot be carried out; *item,* external tribulations; *item,* the men of the world are without grace and have no consolation above in that they are turned toward the things of the world, from which they draw no consolation, for the more you own, the more you are anxious. But those who are in the grace of Christ, grace enlightens, draws, and leads. And so you see, all those who love Christ are glad and joyful in their tribulations, while those others, among all their pleasures, do not have such joy, and even if they do, it lasts but a short time. But those who serve Christ are always glad, whether in tribulation or not.

As our Savior was walking along, *egressus est trans torrentem Cedron*[29] [Ioh. 18:1]; He passed over tribulation with His disciples. Cedron was a channel that passed through the middle of the valley of Josaphat. *Egressus Iesus trans torrentem Cedron* (*id est, cedrorum,* because here there were many cedars); this torrent signifies the tribulations of the world; the cedars are the saints of Christ, odoriferous and lifted on high like the cedar, who have been in the tribulations of this world. Suppose He were to say, *"Venite ad me omnes,"* and they had said, "For what?" To suffer in this world.

Set down your foot and consider that each one has to cross this torrent and bear this cross. Either you wish to carry it with Christ or with Simon of Cyrene. Christ bore it willingly; Simon was forced [Matt. 27:32; Marc. 15:21; Luc. 23:26]. Everyone must bear it. Bear it willingly, I tell you, for this is the way the world works, especially in these times; I say none can escape it. Whoever survives the sword will not survive the plague; whoever survives the plague will not survive the sword, or death, or famine, or tribulations.

29. "He went across the stream Cedron."

All men have to suffer in some way; one will lose his property, another his life, still another, children or brother or husband. What do you want to do? I want to follow Christ. Set your foot here and say, "Necessity compels me; therefore, so must it be. Let us follow Christ. Let us make a virtue of necessity."

So, you see, all His disciples, all who followed Him, were glad and joyful; they went gladly to trial, for the Lord had considered them worthy to follow Christ, and they said:

> *Nisi quia Dominus erat in nobis, dicat nunc Israel,*
> *nisi quia Dominus erat in nobis, cum exsurgerent homines in nos,*
> *forte vivos deglutissent nos.*
> *Cum irasceretur furor eorum in nos,*
> *forsitan aqua absorbuisset nos.*
> *Torrentem pertransivit anima nostra;*
> *forsitan pertransisset anima nostra aquam intolerabilem.*
> *Benedictus Dominus qui non dedit nos in captionem dentibus eorum.*
> *Anima nostra sicut passer erepta est de laqueo venantium:*
> *laqueus contritus est et nos liberati sumus.*
> *Adiutorium nostrum in nomine Domini*
> *qui fecit coelum et terram.*[30] [Ps. 123]

The wicked, who have not followed Christ, cry out amidst their tribulations, desperate and anxious: *Lassati sumus in via iniquitatis nostrae.*[31] Follow Christ, then, and say, "I believe that God desires my welfare so much that He will not allow any tribulations to befall me, except insofar as it is necessary for my salvation, and I am glad, since it is necessary to suffer in some way, the good as well as the bad, to suffer rather for the love of my Lord, Who has suffered on my account, than to suffer for the world." Come, then, set your

---

30. "If the Lord had not been with us, let Israel now say,
    if the Lord had not been with us when men rose up against us,
    they might perchance have eaten us alive.
    When their fury raged against us,
    the waters might have engulfed us.
    Our soul has passed through the torrent;
    our soul might perchance have passed through intolerable waters.
    Blessed be the Lord, Who has not handed us over as captives into their teeth.
    Our spirit, like the sparrow, has been snatched from the hunters' snare:
    the snare has been destroyed, and we have been freed.
    Our help is in the name of the Lord
    Who made heaven and earth."
31. "We have languished in the way of our iniquity."

foot on this second step; let us go with Christ into the garden, and let us cross this torrent, since it is necessary to suffer anyway.

Venite ad me omnes qui laboratis et onerati estis, et ego reficiam vos. Since it is necessary to suffer somehow, let us climb to the third step, called *conformitas,* which means that you conform your will with God's; make every effort to do this and say, "I want to conform myself wholly to God, and to praise whatever things He does, and to say that whatever comes is well done." One must be steadfast in this because all the passions men have proceed from the root of love. Love is the prime passion, or even the first act of the appetite, and the first act leads us always to all the other acts which follow; thus, love always leads us to all the passions and is their root. For example, if you have a desire for something, you could not have [such a desire] unless you love [the thing]; if you have delight, it is only because of what you love. If you hate something, you do so only because it is contrary to what you love, and in the same way, if you have sorrow, it is because you have lost what you love. If you have hope, it is hope of having what you love or else to overcome what is contrary to what you love; if you feel despair, it is either because you cannot have the thing you love or because you cannot flee its contrary. Similarly, if you are bold, it is boldness to acquire what you love; if you fear, you fear not to have what you love. If you have anger, that anger is desire for revenge in order to remove what is contrary to what you love, and so, all passions proceed from love. Love is the unitive virtue of lovers; therefore, a lover would want to stay always with the beloved, and both lovers together would desire to become one single thing and stay together always. And the more things are natural to us, the more they are loved. Nothing is more natural than being; therefore, being is loved in the highest degree. Yet, a creature loves its own being in God more than in itself, for a being is much more perfect in God than in itself, and, loving itself, it would like to assimilate to its cause as much as possible because in God it is more perfect and because God is infinite. Thus, the love of God and love of oneself go together, and although they may seem to be contrary, nevertheless, they are not when you love yourself in God.

Note, however, that our will is to be considered in two ways: one way is with respect to nature; the other is with respect to reason. Of course, there is no one who does not love being and who would not grieve at not being, and who does not love his own flesh, and who would not feel passion when he suffers tribulations, and who would not feel pain, since he is flesh and bone. This is true. Nonetheless, a well-ordered reason ought to be always united with God and must feel so much love toward God that the will is conformed in everything to the will of God so that what God wills, you also will. And although the natural love of your fleshliness[32] may object so that

32. *La sensualità;* the English cognate "sensuality" carries too heavy a burden of neg-

you feel some tribulation within, let your reason hold steady and be confirmed in the will of God, and say, "I know that He is truly God; if my property or any other thing is taken away from me, I am content at once with what God wants, and I conform myself to His will." Fleshliness resents it, but reason must say, "Since it is pleasing to God that things do not happen otherwise, I am happy." And given that the flesh finds it repugnant, reason must remain strong and say, "Nothing can happen without God's will; there can be neither plague, nor war, nor martyrdom, nor other tribulation without the will of God, and if this is so, although I may feel injury, nevertheless, since God Himself wills it so, I myself will it. If the plague should come, may I be steadfast in God's will; it could not come if God had not sent it. Since He has sent it, though I should suffer, nonetheless, I am glad; I want to be wholly conformed to God." This will free you from many tribulations and temptations because when you remain fixed in God, tribulations can strike their hardest, for the man who has this support does not fall down. But when a man is not conformed to the will of God, *as soon as* tribulations come, he takes a fall, and, made desperate, he loses his possessions, as well as both this world and the next. Now, pay attention to the reason why I have said this. *Venite ad me omnes qui laboratis et onerati estis et ego reficiam vos.* Come, I say, and learn to conform yourselves to the will of God. See all the things Christ has done: He has done them all for us.

These women would like to weep with the Virgin. But do not think that she cried the way they say. She suffered the greatest sorrow. The Virgin was illuminated within more than any other creature (except for the soul of Christ). Do you suppose that she did not know the whole Passion of Christ step by step, and that our Savior did not speak to her about it when they were together? She would ask about everything in Paradise, and about His Passion, and about things that are to come all the way up to the Antichrist. At the last, Mary held within her most sacred breast almost all the secrets of Christ. The Virgin was so conditioned that fleshliness could not move her against reason, if she did not will it; if fleshliness had wanted to move her against her will, it would not have been able to, and she would have felt no sorrow, because the Virgin was restored to the original righteousness of Adam, in that, through the Incarnation of Christ, the tinder of the fleshly part was stifled in her. Not that she never had a spark of fleshly feeling; St. Thomas says that she had it, but it was always held in check, and at the Incarnation of Christ it was extinguished, whence it follows that she never sinned. I shall leave aside the question of her conception, whether or not

---

ative connotation. This term, and the related *la parte sensitiva* below (rendered variously as "fleshly/natural feelings" or "fleshly/natural part"), refer to the nonspiritual part of every human being, the senses and all that responds to them.

she was conceived with original sin, and I will leave it to be determined in the court of Paradise. The glorious Virgin, then, fixed her soul and will and reason in God, and she was so firmly attached to the will of God that she could not be moved in any way. She did not want her Son not to suffer; rather, she wanted it and was grateful for it because she was wholly conformed to the divine will. Nonetheless, because she knew that it was reasonable to feel pain, she let her natural feelings run their course and said, "I, too, want to suffer along with my Son, because if the Innocent One has to suffer, so will I suffer." And she experienced such a sorrow that her suffering exceeded the suffering of all the martyrs because she let it go full force, and because she had a tender imagination, she let it run free, although reason never failed her. In her rational faculties, she was glad and joyful on account of the great salvation that was to follow; in her fleshly part, however, she was sad and mournful such that, if you had seen her outward form, she would have seemed to you partly sad and partly joyful, such that, without and within, she had both mirth and sadness. And Christ also was in the same position in that, with respect to reason, He was glad and joyful; His natural part mourned because He had given it free rein, and it represented the Passion to Him beforehand in its entirety.

And so, when Christ and the Virgin were together, they looked at each other, and each saw the heart of the other; each saw the other both joyful and sad. Thus looking at each other the Son would say, "Well, Mother, what do you want to do? It must be so." And she would reply, "I am content, and yet I feel sad." Their natural feelings grieved and said, "Let us suffer together," but reason would remain steadfast. And do not imagine that she would go through the streets wailing, her hair down, or in any way indecent, because she could command her natural feelings not to grieve. She would follow her Son, yet with mildness and great modesty, shedding few tears. On the outside, she was not all sad, but joyful and sad, such that men would marvel that she did not behave as other women usually do. Nor is it true that she was comforted by Mary Magdalene; rather, she comforted the Magdalene. She had no need to be consoled by the other women, she who would encourage them in the faith and say, "Be steadfast, let Him suffer, for this is what has been prophesied. Do not doubt, for my son is the Son of God, and He has come for this; He must suffer to redeem the human race." She comforted the other women and had no need of comfort herself except from her Son. She stood next to the Cross both joyful and sad, utterly astonished at the mystery and the great goodness of God, and although she grieved in her fleshly part, even so, she was partly joyful and comforted the others. Well, let us see what our Lord does in such a situation.[33] Behold, the example

33. This sentence seems out of place, as though Savonarola had finished with his

you have in the Virgin. Because of the great conformity she had to the will of God, she stood resolute in this tribulation, both joyful and sad. In the same way you, who have conformed your will to God's, will in your tribulations be both joyful and sad. The fleshly part will be troubled; the rational will be joyful.

Christ crossed the torrent while He was in the garden. Because the Savior's Passion was great, He wanted to grieve in His natural part, primarily out of charity, since He bore great love for the Eternal Father, and yet He grieved over human wickedness: that the Eternal Father had abandoned men on account of their sins and that souls would go to perdition. He had a vivid and most exquisite imagination, and so He felt sadness all the more, and although His intellectual part was joyful and happy, even so, in His natural part His strong imagination represented to Him internally the whole of His sufferings. And it set before His eyes, first, all the vituperations by which the honor of God was offended; second, He saw particularly the insults of the Hebrew people, of His relatives and disciples, who were about to sin: Judas would betray Him, Peter would deny Him, and all the others would flee, and then the tears and sadness of Mary, and beyond that He was to be insulted by all conditions of men: princes, priests, Jews, Gentiles, the great, tyrants, servants, women, maids, the faithlessness of Jews and Gentiles. Then His imagination presented to Him His body and His most precious life, which He loved very much, and also His chastity: He grieved that He was to be crucified naked in the sight of so many people, insulted between two thieves. Regarding the Passion of His body, He suffered first in His eyes, because He had to see evil men insulting Him; next, in His taste, because of the vinegar mixed with gall; then, in His nerves, His head, His hands, and in His feet—so exquisitely sensitive. And He let the sadness of His natural feelings run free in order to give an example to men that if their fleshly part feels pain, they should always be steadfast in Christ. In His senses He felt sadness, for He was to see His Mother and all those other Maries, mourning and weeping at the foot of the cross.

Therefore, Christ went apart from His disciples and said: *"Tristis est anima mea usque ad mortem"*[34] [Matt. 26:38; Marc. 14:34]. And so, as His natural part represented this Passion to Him to give an example to us that in our tribulations we ought to turn to God, He in His grief turned to the Father and prayed: *"Pater, si possibile est, etc."*[35] [Matt. 26:39] Fleshliness says

---

analysis of the Virgin's role in the Passion, but then thought to add a summation of his points. It would be more appropriate at the beginning of the next paragraph.

34. "My soul is sorrowful unto death."
35. "Father, if it is possible, etc."

that it does not want to suffer, but reason steps in and considers that the honor of the Father must take first place. Thus, He said: *"Si non potest fieri [. . .], fiat voluntas tua"*[36] [Matt. 26:42]. Take example, when you are in trouble, to have recourse to prayer and say, "Lord, if it is possible, I do not want to die of this plague; I would have You free me from this tribulation. I beg you, if it is possible; otherwise, let Your will be done." Once again He returned to His disciples and said, "Do not sleep. *Vigilate et orate, etc.*[37] [Matt. 26:41; Marc. 14:38] I do not sleep. Peter, even you sleep. My natural feelings will not allow Me to sleep." A second time He represents His Passion to Himself and is greatly disturbed, but once more He prays: *"Pater, si possibile est;* Father, behold Your beloved Son. My natural part grieves, but reason remains steadfast. It is necessary that I drink this cup for the salvation of souls." And so He says, *"Si non potest fieri, fiat voluntas tua."* Again He returned to His disciples, and thereby shows that one who is troubled must often turn to prayer and say, "If it is possible, my Lord; otherwise, Your will be done." A third time He returned and prayed in the same way. Nonetheless, His natural feelings forcefully represent His Passion to Him; so great was the agony in His breast that He sweated blood, which poured down to the ground. Alas, Lord, O my Jesus, how great then must Your Passion have been *in reality,* when only imagining it was so painful that You sweated blood which poured down to the ground! Oh, how great, then, was your Passion!

Immediately the angels came down from heaven [Luc. 22; 43]. Do not think that He had need of them as if they were superior to Him. They came as servants and friends; not to give comfort, not even to His fleshly part, since His reason was capable of comforting Him, but they came as does a friend who goes to another friend when he is in trouble. "Lord, what do you want to do? Well You know that You want to bear this pain for the salvation of souls." He did this to show you that when you suffer tribulations, you ought to pray, and although your fleshly part may resist and make you sweat blood, stand firm, nonetheless, for Christ will send His angels to comfort you.

Then Christ embraced His Passion: "Now, Father, since nothing else can be done, I conform Myself to Your will." What do you suppose were His thoughts while He was in the garden, after accepting His Passion? He was thinking, "O Jesus, O Son of God, where will You be in a little while? Betrayed by Your disciple Judas, seized by the crowd, beaten and scourged, then put on the wood of the Cross, crowned with thorns which pass through to the brain. O My head, you will be all beaten and broken. O My hands,

---

36. "If it is not possible to do this [. . .] let Your will be done." Savonarola substitutes *fieri*, imported from Marc. 14:35, for a longer explanatory clause.
37. "Watch and pray, etc."

you will be pierced, and so, will you, feet. Son of God, You have to be abused for the sake of human sinners."

Oh, how ungrateful we are not to acknowledge so great a favor, when, just by imagining it, He sweated blood, and, even so, He did not hesitate to go to His Passion! You do not consider this great favor. *Venite ad me omnes qui laboratis et onerati estis et ego reficiam vos.* Come, consider His sorrows, and that Christ suffered so cruel a Passion voluntarily. Conform your will to His, and, you, too, bear your tribulations willingly. This is the third step. Let us go to the fourth.

Living faith, necessity, conformity: conform your will to God's, since it is necessary to suffer tribulations, and you will not feel them as such. Once your will is conformed to God's, you will climb the fourth step, which is called *promptitudo*. What is one to do, since, in one way or another, one has to bear this cross? Be conformed to God and be ready to go, and you will be made ready by keeping continually in mind that this present time is short and these tribulations are leading you to eternity. So, be ready to suffer and say, "And what of it? Is it more than life? I must at any rate take this step. If it is to be short, I want to be ready and suffer for the love of Christ, for I shall go to that destination where nothing is ever lacking."

Thus Paul says: *Id enim quod in praesenti est momentaneum et leve tribulationis nostrae supra modum in sublimitate aeternum gloriae pondus operatur in nobis, non contemplantibus nobis quae videntur, sed quae non videntur; quae enim videntur temporalia sunt, quae autem non videntur aeterna*[38] [II Cor. 4:17–18]. He says, "Let us be ready and prepared to die for the love of Christ, and feel no tribulation on this account, but joy." He says, "Let us be ready," as if to say, "This tribulation is small compared with that of Hell, which is the greatest there is, to be without God's grace and His glory." This present tribulation is transitory and very small. It is present, as if He said, "It occurs down in this place where time is; if it is in time, it will have an end—at some point it will be over. It is momentary and so brief and light in comparison to eternity that it is but a puff of air. What will it matter, then, if there is war or plague? It is momentary. For whom? For one who has the grace of God; he can support it because he is strong. One who does not have the grace of God cannot bear it because he has no strength. The infirm cannot bear it. Thus, tribulations will seem heavy to those who do not have grace and light compared with those who do. Tribulations are the best preparation for an eternal glory beyond all measure. And note that the Apostle

---

38. "For these present tribulations, which are momentary and light, work beyond measure in us an eternal weight of glory on high, since we do not contemplate things which are seen, but those which are unseen, for things which are seen are temporal; however, those which are not seen are eternal."

makes happiness respond to tribulation in this way: where it says "tribulation," he responds "glory," and where it says *id, that is,* "little," he responds "weight," that is, a great and precious and weighty thing; where it says "present," that is, in these places down here of present time, he responds "on high"; where it says "momentary," he responds "eternal." So this is what he says: for this little tribulation which we have *at present,* but for a moment, there will be worked in us a great weight of eternal glory in the highest heaven.

This, then, is a strong mental image for me: that time is short, and tribulations are light compared with that glory which is prepared for you. So, set your foot up higher, and not only conform yourself to God, but be ready for tribulation. You see [how it is with] spiritual things—the more spiritual they are, the stronger they are; whence, the celestial powers, on account of their spirituality, are incorruptible and impassive. Likewise, one who is spiritual lives his life with vigor; no tribulation can break him. For spiritual things have more efficacy than corporeal ones.

Now, our Savior did this because He wanted to give us this example: that when He had shown the conformity of His will to the Divine Will, He came to rouse His disciples and said to them, "Let us go to the Passion, which will pass like a puff of wind, and we will go to eternal life, where I will no longer suffer." So, He gives you example. Therefore, embrace your tribulations readily, as did Christ, Who readily went to the Cross. Let us now see in what manner He went there.

See, our Savior, as an example for us, goes to meet Judas; do not suppose that He went there much troubled, afflicted, or weary, nor that He went laughing; rather, He went with a certain gravity and cheerfulness, as was His custom. He did not change after conforming His will to God's. He goes forward. Oh! so many are the Judases who betray Christ and do not believe in the Catholic faith, and, even so, take Communion! *[Iudas] osculatus est eum*[39] [Matt. 26:49; Marc. 14:45]. Do not trust every kiss and every embrace, because there are many Judases. Hear what the villain says: *"Ave, Rabbi"*[40] [Matt. 26:49]; he wants Him destroyed, and he says: *"Ave,"* and he says: *"Rabbi,"* and he calls Him "Teacher." Now, tell me this: is this what your Teacher has taught you, to become a murderer? Ah! you traitor, Judas, has He taught you in such a way that you would come to the sacrament without faith, contrition, or sorrow for your sins, with the intention of returning once again to your vanities? Even so, with mildness He calls him "friend": *"Amice, ad quid venisti?"*[41] [Matt. 26:50] Then He turned to the

39. "Judas kissed Him."
40. "Hail, Teacher."
41. "Friend, what have you come for?"

scribes and Pharisees and said: *"Quem quaeritis?"*[42] [Ioh. 18:4] As if to say, "It appears that you do not know Me, yet Judas has given you the sign." Judas gave such a sign because it was said that James looked much like Jesus. And you, Judas, did not want them to go wrong. Then he says: *"Ducite eum caute"*[43] [Marc. 14:44]. It was not enough to betray Him and give the sign; you also wanted Him led away cautiously by night. Why by night? Because if it had been in daylight, the people would perhaps have made a rumpus.

Jesus said to the crowd: *"Quem quaeritis?" Et illi: "Iesum Nazarenum"*[44] [Ioh. 18:4–5]. O fools, are you looking for the One Who has performed so many miracles? Do you not fear Him? This is He Who has raised the dead and given sight to the blind. He can kill you in a moment and annihilate you and, likewise, make you live, and you try to kill Him! See what blindness! They ought to have been afraid because they ought to have considered and said, "If He has raised the dead and enlightened the blind, He could destroy us with a single word." But one who is blind and obstinate must go along the path of error. God turned then and said to the crowd: *"Ego sum"*[45] [Ioh. 18:6]; "I am Jesus." O blind ones, if He wanted to kill you all, He could do it. Christ wanted to convert them. O blind ones, you will see if you can withstand a single word from Him. So, He said: *"Ego sum,"* and they all fell to the ground, not face down, but on their backs [Ioh. 18:6]. They did not fall like the saints and good people, who fell on their faces, but backward like the damned.[46] The Lord says once more, "Here I am. I give you permission to seize Me." What do you, Judas, and you, Pharisees, say at this point? *Et iterum dixit: "Quem quaeritis?"*[47] [Ioh. 18:7], as if He said, "If I had not given you the power, you could do nothing. Do you not know that I am God? Are you so blind?"—They did not consider this because of their sins and infidelity.—"But know this: if I wanted, I could have twelve legions of angels from My Father to defend Me [Matt. 26:53]. But I do not want it. I am glad that you seize Me. I die willingly for man's salvation." With a single word He could have done anything. *Et illi iterum: "Iesum Nazarenum." Et Iesus: "Ego sum"*[48] [Ioh. 18:7]. "Take Me, then, for I give you the power to do it. I am ready. I am that Host, Victim, and Sacrament, Who must be sacrificed for man's salvation. I am ready." Accord-

---

42. "Whom do you seek?" The wording in passages from John is abbreviated throughout by Savonarola.
43. "Lead Him away warily."
44. " 'Whom do you seek?' And they: 'Jesus of Nazareth.' "
45. "I am He."
46. An iconographic convention. To fall on one's face shows proper respect for a superior.
47. "And He said again, 'Whom do you seek?' "
48. "And they repeated, 'Jesus of Nazareth.' And Jesus, 'I am He.' "

ingly, He restrained the force of His divinity and gave the Jews power over His humanity, but not over His Apostles.

See, then, how great is His readiness as He willingly points Himself out. Now what do you suppose these rabid dogs[49]—especially the Pharisees— were going to do? Because they were rabid, they gnashed their teeth and quivered with rage. Even so, Christ went willingly and readily to the cross. You come too, my son, come after Christ, come readily to tribulation. Go the way of the Savior, and if you lose your possessions, have no fear, even if you lose your life for the love of Christ. Go readily to tribulation, and climb up this fourth step as your Lord did, for He calls you and says: *"Venite ad me omnes qui laboratis et onerati estis, et ego reficiam vos."*

The fifth step is called *humilis confidentia* [humble confidence or trust]. I have said to you that you are to be ready and prepared to sustain anything for love of the Savior, but because a certain prideful confidence could arise from this readiness, in order that you might proceed with humility you must climb to another step, called *humilis confidentia*. Note that all the excellencies attributed to creatures, [all those things] which are good and perfect, are also attributed to God; in fact, all the excellencies of any cause whatsoever are attributable to the First Cause, given that it is the cause of every other cause. The builder is a cause in making a thing only, but not in preserving it, because, even after the builder's death, the edifice is preserved, and so, the First Cause is the cause which preserves everything. The sun, though it gives light and preserves, nonetheless, because its being comes from God, its every operation proceeds from God, for every creature has its being from God and not from itself. This is why, in the definition of a creature, one does not include being, but, in the definition of God, one does, because He is being. If God withdrew His hand from them, all creatures and their being would cease to exist. For this reason, Job used to say: *"Si Deus destruxerit, nullus est qui aedificet; si incluserit hominem, nullus est qui aperiat ei, etc."*[50] [Iob 12:14] To be enclosed by God refers to one who has closed his mind against acting uprightly and will not open it; if man, in some difficulty, falls away from the faith, that is, if you go off on your own and God leaves you, no one can open to you. If God, I say, does not give you the light of faith, no one else can enlighten you. Therefore, he who considers himself to be something, since he is really nothing, deceives himself.

Everyone must acknowledge that his every operation comes from God, and so, he must not exalt himself, but remain humble and know that every-

---

49. Savonarola calls the Pharisees *cani arrabbiati,* implicitly linking them to his enemies, the Arrabbiati.
50. "If God has demolished [it], there is no one who might build [it] up; if he has shut a man up, there is no one who might open for him, etc."

thing depends on the will of God, *apud quem est fortitudo*[51] [Iob 12:16]. We see that in all natural things every effect exerts itself to remain grounded in its cause so that it may be led to perfection. Considering that all their strength and their every operation depend on the First Cause, they strain with every effort to ready themselves for it and to draw it to themselves, like a plant, which exerts itself, through the strength it receives from the sky, to draw moisture from the earth and submits itself to its cause, however it can, in order to be better able to preserve itself. Look at the birds, which migrate to places where they know they will be better able to preserve their lives — see the swallow, it goes to a warm place, and the fish remain always in the water the better to preserve themselves. Thus, it is necessary that all your trust be fixed in God and that you understand that all your strength, your every operation and grace, depend on God. If He removes His hand, you are sold up. So, you must not place your confidence in yourself, because to suffer these tribulations and rely on your own strength would be as if a plant, relying on its own strength, were to say, "I want to leave the earth behind and bear fruit," but then you would see the plant dry up, and this would happen to you if you were to rely on your own strength.

All your trust, then, must be in God so that it may not dry up. You must be humble and not rely on yourself for anything, for even the most perfect and saintly would fail when tribulations come, if they were not aided by God. Therefore, do not rely on yourself, but be humble and say, "I could in no way stand firm, if God were not with me." In this way, let your trust be humble and in God. Just as causes produce effects when they are prepared to receive their influence, so will the First Cause do to you when you are prepared, and it will give you the strength to be able to keep yourself cheerful in your tribulations. See here Peter, who deceived himself when the Savior said to His disciples that Satan had taken up the sieve in order to sift them as the wheat is sifted, and by afflicting them with tribulation to draw some of them away; He said this for Peter's sake *ut non deficeret in fide*[52] [Luc. 22: 32; slightly altered], in order to demonstrate that faith comes from God. But Peter said, "No, Lord, I do not doubt at all. I am prepared to die, if need be," because he trusted in himself and had not properly understood the words of Christ, that is: *"Oravi pro te, Petre, ne deficeret fides tua"*[53] [Luc. 22: 32]. And so, Christ said to him: *"Antequam gallus bis cantet, ter me negabis"*[54] [Marc. 14:30]. And so it was.

My children, those who do not have the grace of God cannot withstand

51. "With Whom there is strength."
52. "So that he might not be lacking in faith."
53. "I have prayed for you, Peter, so that your faith might not be lacking."
54. "Before the cock crows twice, you will deny Me three times."

tribulation; likewise, those who have it, but trust in themselves, fail. However, those who have grace and trust in God alone will be strong. See here Peter: because he relied on himself, he denied several times, and when pointed out by a maidservant, swearing, he denied the Savior. At this, the cock crows, and Christ, remembering his love and that Peter had sinned out of frailty, turned His eyes toward him, and Peter came to his senses and went out, wept bitterly, and repented. Likewise, you, even if you have failed in your tribulation, do as Peter did: weep for your sin, do penance, and return to the fifth step, trusting wholly in God, Who calls us: *"Venite ad me omnes qui laboratis et onerati estis, et ego reficiam vos."*

The sixth step is called *mansuetudo*. Mildness is the contrary of wrath. This step tells you to be meek and to consider that our Savior, in all His tribulations and sufferings, was meek in order to show you that you must be on guard against anger, so that you may always be in a state of purification and can better understand the truth. Anger darkens the intellect, blinds you in a way, and drags you to the ground so as not to allow you to see the truth. Look at natural things: the more a thing is dragged down and immersed in materiality, the more imperfect it is, but the more it is abstracted from matter, the more perfect it is and the more knowledge it has. Look at men: because they are more elevated above matter and have an intellect and are steadier, they have more knowledge than other animals, and man, the more he is elevated above the corporeal things of this world, the more he is capable of truth. Because God is pure act, He is absolutely separated from every materiality and from every passion; therefore, He is truth itself.

Now then, climb this step of mildness and leave behind anger and the passions. Come up on this ladder. I do not care to drive you to a great outpouring of tears this morning. I want to pull you up to Christ on these steps; these are very useful. And if you will keep in your mind and memory these steps of Christ's Passion, you will be so set afire and stirred up by His love, that when you suffer tribulations, you will also feel joy, joy, I say, along with sadness, as I have told you He had, and you will fear nothing. See what I have shown you: the more you are elevated in Christ, the more you will have knowledge of truth. The more the intellect is prepared, the more you will see, and the more it is prepared, the more it is alien to the passions; the more you are alienated from the passions, the closer you are to Christ. If you want to draw close to Christ, flee evil imaginings. But because man cannot understand without imaginings, which are the lenses through which we see, if you position these lenses in the seat of wrath, you will be blinded and unable to see the truth. *Quia qualis quisquis est, talia et sibi videntur.*[55] Therefore, when you are in trouble, take care not to get angry with either

55. "For such as a man is, so will things seem to him."

God or men; rather, remain calm and peaceable, and say, "God cannot err, and if He sends me these tribulations, He does so because He loves me and for the sake of my salvation. He at least loves my soul, and so, this tribulation can only be for the sake of my salvation," and thus, you appeal to reason. If men persecute you, you ought to consider that it comes from their ignorance and that they are blind and do not have the light. Have compassion for them, and in this way you will begin climbing this step of mildness.

The Savior, in order to summon us to this sixth step, came into this world, where He received many insults, but He bore them all mildly, and so, on this day, when He was asked about His teaching in the house of Annas, He mildly answered: *"Ego palam locutus sum mundo: ego semper docui in synagoga et in templo quo omnes Iudaei conveniunt, etc.*[56] [Ioh. 18:20] If you had wanted to give due consideration to My teaching, which I have preached in the synagogues and in the churches, you would not say this, but because you put no faith in it, ask those who have heard it." Then a proud servant, because it seemed to him that He had not answered appropriately, slapped Him [Ioh. 18:22]. This servant was like one of those flatterers who, as I have told you, always crowd around these lords and grandees; they do not mind doing evil to please their lords. Flee these flatterers, and take example, you men, from your Savior, Who remained so mild. If someone had given you a blow on the cheek, you would have knifed him. If you, women, had been slapped by your maid, you would have eaten her alive. The Savior gives you an example to answer and to bear abuse meekly. Now, do you not see that man has slapped God, and that the sinner has struck the supremely Just One? And He, the meek One, suffers it, although He could have annihilated him, if He had wanted to, in an instant. But He answered mildly, saying: *"Si male locutus sum, testimonium perhibe de malo"*[57] [Ioh. 18:23]. See what mildness this is. This is an example to us.

The second insult took place in the house of Caiaphas, where He was asked many things and was accused by false witnesses. But truth cannot be confounded. Caiaphas said: *"Dic si filius Dei es"*[58] [Matt. 26:63]; "tell me if You are the Son of God." Jesus answered: *"Ego sum, etc."*[59] [Marc. 14:62] Caiaphas tore his garments and said: *"Blasphemavit"*[60] [Matt. 26:65], as if Christ had blasphemed. It was customary to do this, if one heard blasphemy,

56. "I have spoken in public; I have always taught in the synagogues and the temple, where all the Jews gather, etc."
57. "If I have spoken evil, point out the evil."
58. "Say if You are the Son of God." The wording is slightly altered. Note that this exchange occurs in Mark also, but that the Latin words quoted by Savonarola will more exactly fit one or the other version. See also Luc. 22:70.
59. "I am, etc."
60. "He has blasphemed!"

out of horror at the sin. The Lord bore everything mildly. So you have no excuse not to want to pardon, because example has been given to you. These Jews insult our Lord with spitting and blows and say to Him insultingly: *"Prophetiza, si tu es Christus"*[61] [Matt. 26:67–68; cf. Marc. 14:65]. And He bears it mildly. Now consider a moment: who would not have lost the faith, seeing Christ held in such opprobrium? Consider that everyone down to the lowest said, "We have been deceived; look, He cannot help Himself."

The third insult took place in Pilate's house, when he sent Christ to Herod, who was curious to see Him and to watch Him perform some miracles. But our Savior did not answer him and did not want to perform any miracles [Luc. 23:7–9], because Herod was not worthy and because if He had performed a miracle, Herod might, perhaps, have spared Him, but He wanted to die. So Herod, like a madman, disparaged Him and, like a madman, sent Him back to Pilate [Luc. 23:11], who wanted to satisfy the people more than justice; he tied Him to a column,[62] some say on the ground, others, standing up; it could be either way. O Lord, none has compassion to see God exhausted before men, while men beat and strike their God, Who never moved, but stands meek as a lamb.

Another insult is that He was robed in purple, with a reed put in His hand, as if He were a madman, and they said mockingly: *"Ave, rex Iudaeorum,"* and they placed a crown of thorns on His head, and they beat with reeds on the crown [Matt. 27:28–30; Marc. 15:17–19; Ioh. 19:2–3] in such a way that those thorns thrust through flesh and bone, and the whole head shed blood; nonetheless, like a lamb He stood completely docile. Behold your Lord, O man, Who has given you an example to be meek in tribulations. But this was not enough, for Pilate showed Him to the people, saying: *"Ecce homo"*[63] [Ioh. 19:5]; "look at this innocent man, and have compassion for Him; look at Him, scourged and crowned with thorns, dripping blood; I say, have compassion for Him." Nonetheless, the Jewish dogs are unmoved, but cry out: *"Crucifige! Crucifige!"*[64] [Ioh. 19:6; also Luc. 23:21; Marc. 15:13–14; Matt. 27:23]

Another insult is that Barabbas, the murderer, was preferred to Him

---

61. "Prophesy, if You are the Christ."
62. Pilate had Jesus scourged (Marc. 15:15; Ioh. 19:1), but no column is mentioned in the Gospels; however, iconographic convention depicted Christ tied to one. The second Sorrowful Mystery of the Rosary, a form of prayer particularly associated with the Dominicans, focuses on the "Scourging at the Pillar." By 1481 the Dominican-sponsored lay confraternity at Florence had adopted the practice of saying fifteen mysteries of the Rosary; Michael Walsh, *Dictionary of Catholic Devotions* (San Francisco: Harper, 1993), s.v. "rosary," p. 221.
63. "Behold the man!"
64. "Crucify Him! Crucify Him!" Matthew has *Crucifigatur!*

[Matt. 27:21; Marc. 15:11; Luc. 23:18; Ioh. 18:40], and He bore it all with sweetness and mildness. Then He was condemned to die. Alas, meek Lamb! Here is the cross on His shoulders, and He was carrying it, but He cannot because He is faint. The Lord could well have been strong, but He wanted to allow His natural feelings full rein. O creature, look at your Creator, how, in such great affliction, He remains completely meek and summons everyone, "Come, come to this sixth step. Learn to be meek. Come and carry this cross with Me. Come and drink this chalice. *Venite ad me omnes qui laboratis et onerati estis, et ego reficiam vos.*"

Trust that God loves you; set your foot on this first step. The second is necessity, for you must suffer one way or the other. So come to the third, which is *conformitas;* be conformed to the will of God. And come to the fourth, which is *promptitudo.* In order not to be proud, come to the fifth, which is *humilis confidentia;* trust in God and not in yourself. Climb higher then; when you have tribulation, try hard not to become angry, and come to the sixth step, which is called *mansuetudo;* be meek and suffer meekly. The seventh and last step is *perseverantia;* you will persevere *usque ad finem,*[65] for if you are to persevere till the end, you must not doubt that you will find your end and a crown prepared for you in life eternal. Look at all natural things: every cause that moves, moves for some end, and it never ceases, if it is not impeded, such that it continues its work up to its ultimate end. Look at the plant: if it is not impeded, the sky will never cease giving it its influence such that it will bring forth fruit. The vine will never cease till it makes wine. If God, then, conducts everything to its own end and perfection, all the more will He lead you, if you live uprightly, for He loves man more and cares more for him than for any other creature, since He died for him. God will never cease sending His influence to lead you to your end; persevere, for He will give you your crown, if you are not impeded by your free will.

However, Florence, although I have told you that it seemed to me that in that vision few Christians would be saved, nonetheless, it seemed to me that Florence had a large share of the saved. Do, then, what I have told you; entrust yourselves to God, live in charity, do away with all hatred. My children, love the spiritual good, love the common welfare of the city, for somehow you will have all that has been promised you. Have no doubt: God has not begun this undertaking in order to stop midway, but to go through to the finish. In this way, you will persevere in living uprightly, and do not doubt, for you will have everything. Perseverance, I say, is necessary.

The Savior, wanting to show this, willed to persevere *usque in finem* [Matt. 10:22]. Thus He has given this example to men, that it is a vain thing

---

65. "Up to the end." Matt. 10:22: *qui autem perseveraverit in finem hic salvus erit.*

to go on to the midpoint and then turn back, for all your effort is lost. See Christ, Who remains constant and strong amidst so much insult and villainy. They said to Him: *"Descende de cruce"*[66] [Matt. 27:40; cf. Marc. 15:30, 32, context given below], and He remains strong till the end in order to have that glory and to lead us to that beatitude. He offers the sacrifice for us like a priest. *Tu es sacerdos in aeternum* — our Lord was a priest eternally — *secundum ordinem Melchisedech*[67] [Ps. 109:4], who sacrificed bread and wine, as Christ did His body and blood. And when our Lord, the immaculate Lamb, had come to the place of His Passion, because He was a priest and had to offer this sacrifice, He said: *Ecce, venio*[68] [Ps. 39:8; quoted in Heb. 10:9]. Do not suppose that He would have acted or spoken in this way under constraint, for He was not forced at all, but believe that He did it willingly.

Et oravit ad Patrem[69] [cf. Matt. 26:42], "O My Father, You have answered the prayers of the patriarchs and prophets. See, I am ready; see, I offer Myself willingly. I am here to go up on this wood and be offered as a holocaust and victim *in odorem suavitatis*[70] [Eph. 5:2]. And so, I pray You, Father, accept this sacrifice to free those fathers. I commend to you the Hebrew people, the sinners, the Gentile peoples, and the whole world, all souls present and future, and My city of Florence." As He offered this sacrifice, they put Him on the cross. They took that holy hand and began to strike it with a hammer and to pierce it and pass through it with nails[71] and to fasten it to the wood; then they took the other hand, and with the same cruelty they fixed it to the wood. Likewise, they pierced the holy feet with nails such that blood poured forth abundantly from every part, and the whole body was stretched on the Cross.

O my Lord, O sweet Jesus, in what a way do I see you stretched out for love of us! Angels, how can you look at this spectacle? O heavens, hold still for the Passion of our Lord! Sun, do not give any more of your light! Earth, tremble! [Matt. 27:45, 51; Marc. 15:33; Luc. 23:44–45] Stones, break apart! Mountains, split open! And you, what did you do, holy Mary, when you beheld this spectacle? Think how her heart was bursting. O man, behold

66. "Come down from that cross."
67. "You are a priest forever, according to the order of Melchisedech."
68. "Behold, I come."
69. "And He prayed to the Father"; adapted from Matthew's *et oravit dicens, Pater mi* . . .
70. "In an odor of sweetness."
71. The nails are never mentioned specifically in the Passion accounts. Their use is verified by doubting Thomas' insistence on touching their imprints for verification of the Resurrection: *Nisi videro in manibus eius figuram clavorum et mittam digitum meum in locum clavorum* . . . (Ioh. 20:25; "Unless I see the mark of the nails in His hands and put my finger in the place of the nails . . .").

your Lord nailed and dying for you on this wood. Acknowledge this favor, leave your wicked life, return to Him Who waits for you with arms wide open, call for mercy from Him, for He wants to grant it to you.

[Transcriber's comment: "Note that here he cried out, 'Mercy!' and the sermon was finished. Note also that this sermon was taken down by many writers."]

Ruth and Micheas, Sermon XXVIII

The Art of Dying Well

All Souls' Day

Delivered 2 November 1496

In omnibus operibus tuis memorare novissima tua, et in aeternum non pec-cabis.[1] — Sir. (Eccles[us].) 7:40

Dearly beloved in Christ Jesus, it is not difficult to prove to man that he has to die, because, without need of any other argument, daily experience demonstrates this to us. But it is very difficult to induce man to meditate on death and to try to engage him so that he is always thinking about death. And the reason is this: that every inclination[2] follows some sort of knowledge, but not always its own particular knowledge, because natural inclinations follow the extrinsic knowledge with which nature governs them; just so, the natural inclination of a rock, which inclines it to go toward the center, follows a knowledge not its own, because it has no other knowledge than that from which it derives that inclination. It is the same with all other natural things, but about such knowledge as this and such inclinations as this we will say nothing now, because it is not to our purpose; however, the animal or rational [obedient to reason] inclination follows sensible [derived from the senses] or intellectual knowledge, which is intrinsic to the animal or man.

It sometimes happens, then, that the cognitive power represents to the appetite some thing under a semblance of such great delectation that the appetite follows it with great vehemence; and at other times the appetite is so strongly attracted that the cognitive power makes it stay fixed on that thing so that, *in a way,* it does not know how to turn aside from it. For example, a man beholds a woman, and when he begins to think about her, appetite draws him so forcefully that, *in a way,* it makes him immovable from that matter, for all his thoughts and all his mental concentration are then ordered toward that end. It so happens also that when one is enamored

---

1. "In everything you do, remember your last hour, and you will never sin."
2. The word used is *lo appetito*, which, depending on context, may have the sense either of "inclination" or "appetite." In English parlance, a rock, for example, has no "appetite," though it can be said to have a "tendency" or "inclination"; in speaking about man and animals, however, "appetite," which conveys a sensory nuance, seems more appropriate.

of God, through the knowledge which one has of Him, that love wholly constrains him so that he is drawn entirely into God; all his mental concentration is ordered toward Him, and his every thought is engaged in pleasing only his Creator. To the point, then: I say that although the rational, animal appetite follows its own particular knowledge, nonetheless, because great violence has been done it, it holds firmly to that first consideration which was the cause of its love, and this afterward draws back to itself other knowledge and considerations and renders the man effectually unable to think of anything other than what he loves. Now then, because the desire and appetite for existence is the most natural thing, and existence is more beloved by man than any other thing, so appetite for existence draws man so forcefully that it makes him remain fixed on this thought to such an extent that all his mental concentration and virtually all of his actions are ordered toward this will to be, and he does everything to sustain it. Likewise, just as the enamored never thinks of trying to separate himself from his love and, if he should try to think of it, would experience great difficulty, so it is difficult for man to separate himself from thoughts of and care for life and to think about death. As the logicians say: *Sicut se habet oppositum in opposito, ita se habet propositum in proposito;*[3] therefore, just as man vehemently loves life, with equal vehemence he hates death and flees, as much as he can, everything which might be contrary to this existence and this life. And so, he flees meditation about death as a thing contrary and wholly unpleasant to him, for the very thought of it is odious to him. Thus, it is a most difficult thing to make man turn aside and to make him think about death and to lift him up from his very natural concern for life and from his desire for existence, which is very delightful to him, while the thought of death is so very hateful to him. Therefore, the more easily a man yields to these concerns about life, the more difficult it is to lead him to think of death, because, as I have said, *sicut se habet oppositum in opposito, ita se habet propositum in proposito.* This difficulty is caused by the senses, to delight in which we are overmuch given, and the knowledge of the senses does not induce a man to think, except about present and delightful things. It is also caused by solicitude and anxiety about human affairs, in which men are much occupied, so that they cannot think about death as well.

This morning, then, since I want to speak of the art of dying well and, as I said yesterday morning, to give you a bit to chew on, we do not want to tire ourselves in proving that man has to die, because this would be superfluous, and you would say, "Father, you are wasting time; we know that we have to die," and so, I want to leave that aside and try to persuade

3. "Just as opposites are held in opposition, so like purposes are held alike." The pun is impossible to render in English.

you that man should seek to have this concern always fixed in his mind, that he has to die, and I will show that the man who thinks about death extracts great fruit therefrom and that, certainly, if a man held to this thought continuously, he would be blessed. All the saintly men of the past have had this thoughtfulness about death, which made them live in this world with great rectitude, so much so that they are now in the beatitude of Paradise. So, the thought of death is a thing very useful to man, because, in the Christian religion, the beginning and the middle are of no use apart from the end. Therefore, it is necessary to think always about making a good end, and this is to think always about death. And so, the sage in Ecclesiasticus states the theme we have proposed: *In omnibus operibus tuis memorare novissima tua, et in aeternum non peccabis,* that is, "in all your works, O man, remember your last days," *that is,* your end. Remember, man, that you have to die and, having this remembrance always fixed [in your mind], *in aeternum non peccabis, that is,* "you will not commit any sin." Now, dearly beloved, we will speak about death and give everyone a prescription for dying well. First, I will speak of those who are healthy, who ought to think that at any hour they may grow sick and die. Then we will speak about those who have already begun to sicken, how they ought to think of death. Third, we will speak about those who are gravely ill and are confined to bed, virtually *in extremis,* what they *also* ought to do. God give us grace to speak of this death in such a way that it will be strongly impressed in your brains so that you might bring forth fruit from this preaching.

If I had told you, [my] people, that I want to prove to you through reason, authority, and example that man has to die, you would say that this was foolishness. Similarly, it seems foolishness to me that man, although he knows he has to die, does not want to think about death, but rather, all his concern seems to be thinking about how to stay here and build beautiful palaces and amass possessions and so to become rich. On such as this, it seems, man would expend all his thought, but about death and the next life, it seems he thinks not at all, as though the hereafter were of no account. Oh, what foolishness is this, to think only of the here and now! You seem unaware that you have to die one way or the other and leave everything here, I say, whether you would or not, and you know not the time nor the manner, when and how you have to die. Solomon says in the Proverbs, in the thirtieth chapter, that some animals are wiser than man: *Quattuor, inquit, sunt minima terrae, et ipsa sunt sapientiora sapientibus: Formica, populus infirmus, quae praeparat in messe cibum suum; lepusculus, plebs invalida, qui collocat in petra cubile suum; regem locusta non habet, et egreditur universa per turmas suas; stellio nititur manibus et moratur in aedibus regum*[4] [Prov. 30:24–28];

4. "There are four things which are the least on earth, and these same are wiser than

"four animals are wiser than the wise: first the ants, a weak population, who gather [the fruits of] summer for the winter; the second is the hare, which makes its nest in rock, so that it might be more secure; the third is the locusts, that is, crickets, who have no king but always go leaping here and there in ordered rank upon rank; the fourth is the lizard [*lo stellio*], *that is,* the gecko, which walks on its hands and lives always in the house of the king." These four creatures, says Solomon, are wiser than the wise.

Anyone who seeks to be wise orders all his affairs toward an end, *quia sapientis est ordinare.*[5] But note that there are many [kinds of] ends. Some are particular: for example, the end of the builder is the form of the house, and so he orders every aspect of his building to that end. Similarly, the end of a captain of the army is victory, and he orders the whole of the army toward that end, and so it is with the ends of other particular matters. But the philosophers say that men who order all their affairs to ends such as these are seeking wisdom *secundum quid, et non simpliciter,*[6] that is, they are called wise with respect to that pursuit [in which they are engaged] and not wise absolutely. Anyone who seeks to be absolutely wise considers the ultimate end of man and of human life and orders all his affairs and his life toward it. The ultimate end of man is God, and anyone who ponders well upon this end is truly wise. But these sages of worldly wisdom, who do not consider well this ultimate end, cannot truly be called wise. Rather, one would find more wisdom than theirs, first, among the ants, which, as Solomon says, are a weak population. For me, the ant signifies good little women, who are of the weak and fragile sex, but are devout and have ordered the whole of their lives toward God, and they go about always accumulating merits before God through their good works so that they might rejoice in the next life. These women, then, signified by the ants, are wiser than wise merchants who go scouring all the earth and all the sea in order to collect possessions which they know they have to lose anyway, that is, [they will have] to leave them here. But the simple woman, who has all her attention directed toward God, gathers a treasure here in order to take possession of it in Paradise, where she will never lose it. The hare is also wiser than the wise. The hare to me figures certain good men of utter simplicity, given wholly to God, who think continually of death; they make their bed on rock, that is, they have entrusted their end and their peace to Christ: *Petra*

---

the wise: the ants, a weak people, which prepare food for themselves at the harvest; the hares, a powerless class, which lodges its nest in rock; the locusts have no king, but all go about in squadrons; the stellion moves about on its hands, but dwells in the apartments of kings."

5. "For it belongs to wisdom to put things in order."
6. "For some purpose and not simply for itself."

autem erat Christus[7] [I Cor. 10:4]. They are always thinking that they have to die, and so they remain fixed on Christ, Who can save them after death. These little hares are wiser than princes and great masters and prelates who have not placed their nest on rock, but wear themselves out in preserving their position, which they have to lose in any event. The locust, that is, the cricket, is also wiser than these wise men. Crickets signify for me certain good peasants, who get on well together; these are like the crickets, who have no king; similarly, these peasants have no one to rule over them or to teach them; they do not have so much in the way of preaching or laws or learning as we do, but they have arranged their life once and for all and ordered it toward God; they observe God's commandments simply, without learning, and they go leaping about in an orderly way and elevating themselves above earth as much as they can; they are united in charity, thinking always about death. These are wiser than the wise theologians, philosophers, legists, orators, and poets, who spend their time in thinking up arguments and subtleties and sophistries, but do not think of God nor of death. The lizard, *that is,* the gecko, is also, as Solomon says, wiser than the wise; this creature, he says, walks on its hands and dwells in the king's house. This lizard signifies certain serious men who have no particular genius, but have good works; they do not know how to speculate, but they know how to do good, and so, he says they walk on their hands, as if to say, "He does not fly; he walks on his feet, and yet he ascends on high"; thus, they engage in such good work that many times they mount up to the heights of contemplation; hence, they are of a certain simple goodness, which is of avail where the wisdom of these wise men avails not. Such as these, I say, dwell in the house of the king, *that is,* through their simplicity they dwell with the saints, who are all kings and are in the presence of the first King, *that is,* with God. Note well, then, you who want to live uprightly: learn to be wise like the ant, the hare, the cricket, and the gecko; think about death and about what will come after death. And if you will learn from them, you will live uprightly and be wiser than these sages. But let me rest a bit, and I will show you that true wisdom consists in thinking about death.

St. Jerome says that in the circle of Plato, this adage was in vogue: *Vera philosophia est meditatio mortis,*[8] that is, "true philosophy is thinking about death." "Philosophy" means love of wisdom. True wisdom, then, is thinking about death, and anyone who seeks to be truly wise is always thinking that he has to die and that the end of human life is not here. And so, he disposes all his affairs in such a way that, whenever death should come, he is prepared to die well, in order to go to that ultimate end to which he has been ordered

7. "And the rock was Christ."
8. "True philosophy consists in meditation on death."

by God. This statement of Plato's then, that is, that true philosophy and true wisdom consists in thinking about death, was well said. But we Christians understand it better than did he. Let's go a bit further. Sometimes you are in doubt about the faith. If you were to think and meditate frequently within yourself about death, you would have no doubts about the faith; rather, you would be confirmed in it. Take this, then, as rule number one: think sometimes of death within yourself and say, "I must die in any event"; consider your flesh and your hands also sometimes and say, "These hands and this flesh must become dust and ashes; soon they will stink wretchedly; everyone has to die—that great master, that youth, the rich, the handsome, the strong. One minute they were alive, the next they are dead; they are all stink and ashes. I also will perhaps die soon; in a single breath everything to do with this life will have passed away." Then think more closely about and enter a bit more deeply into the profundity of this consideration of death and say, "What is to come after our death? Where does man go after he dies? He is seen no longer. What shall we say has become of him? Man is surely the most noble creature on earth. What is the end of man?" "The contemplation of God," the philosophers have said; so consider this and say, "Is the contemplation of God the end of man? The end of every thing is the place where it rests content and at peace. We see that in this world man is not at peace; on the contrary, he is always distressed by numerous passions. It seems, then, that the end of man is not here." Aristotle thought so and went to a great deal of trouble to prove this point, although he did not understand that the contemplation of God was the end of man, whether in this life or afterward. But you, Christian, if you want to arrive at this conclusion, you will say thus: "God governs the world and makes provision for it and for every least little thing; He also has a more special providence for man than for any other thing in the world because man is the most noble creature; if this is so, God, being just, must repay the good with good. But we see that in this world the good are always in distress and undergoing tribulation; therefore, the end of man is not here," and so you will profess that God, just and wise provider that He is, has prepared another life after this. To whom, then, will this peace be given in the hereafter? Certainly, you will say, "To the good." *Indeed, it is true* that there is no better person in the world than the Christian because the Christian life is the best life one can possibly imagine. You will say, then, that the true Christian, who lives our faith, will possess that beatific life hereafter, which God has prepared for all His beloved; considering this, you will reaffirm that the faith is true, for, if our faith were not true, it would follow from this that no other faith could be true, and that man is the most unhappy creature living; however, since the faith is true, you will have to think about Hell and Paradise, and consider that, if you should go to Hell, you must stay there not a hundred years, nor a thousand, nor a hundred thousand, nor a hundred million, but for ever and ever to infinity.

The philosopher was not sure of this, that there is a Hell and that evil men must go there, and yet he said: *Terribilissimum autem mors, terminus enim est, et post mortem nescit homo utrum bene vel male habeat;*[9] "death," he says, "is the most terrifying thing in nature, because it is the end of life, which is so well loved, but it is even worse, if one adds to this that after death, no one knows what happens to man, whether it be good or evil." But we, through the light of faith, know and are certain of this, that if man dies without the grace of God, he will go immediately to Hell. You could die today and not know if you are in God's grace or not, *quia nemo scit utrum amore an odio dignus sit*[10] [Eccles. 9:1]; therefore, O man, think of death, and arrange your life in good order, and learn to remain always in God's grace so that you may not fail on this point. O man, the devil is playing a game of chess with you, and is looking for a way to get at you and checkmate you on this point, so be prepared, mull it over well, for if you win on that point, you have won everything, but if you lose there, you are left with nothing. So then, keep your eye on this checkmate, think about death constantly, for if you are found ill prepared on this point, you have lost everything you have ever done in this life. See how much attention you should give to this concern. Now let me rest.

Oh, what great madness it is, not to think about death and say, "If I do not win on this point, I have accomplished nothing, I have lost everything." O merchant, if you had to receive a sentence which in one fell blow would bring about the loss of everything you own, you would have no peace day or night; you would turn the whole world upside down to make provision for this. And so, man, think about death, and whither goes your soul, which is worth more than all the world.

Now, I recall that another time, when I was preaching to you on a similar topic, I told you that, if you wanted to be well prepared for death, you should have three illustrations depicted for you. The first was that you should have depicted an illustration [showing] Paradise above and Hell below and keep it in your room in a place where it would often be before your eyes, but not that you should make a habit of looking at it, for then it would no longer move you. And I told you that you should be always thinking about it and should say, "I may die today," and look well on this image, for death is always before you, ready to remove you from this life, as if it were to say to you, "You have to die in any event, and you cannot escape from

9. "But death is the most terrifying, for it is the end, and after death, no one knows whether he will receive good or ill."
10. "For no one knows whether he is worthy of love or hate."

my hands; consider where you want to go—to Paradise above, or down to Hell?" All saintly men and women have engaged in this meditation on death, and in whatever work they do, all their thoughts turn continually here to death. So, have this picture painted, which will be very useful to you in making you consider that you must die. Now listen to another remedy and rule which I want to give you before we go on to the second picture.

In omnibus operibus tuis memorare novissima tua, et in aeternum non peccabis; "remember always that you have to die, and you will not sin." Every sin committed by man stems either from ignorance or from thoughtlessness, because it is not a sin if it is not of the will, and the will does not err unless the intellect errs. The intellect errs either through ignorance or through thoughtlessness. Error in the will, then, comes about because the intellect has deceived it, either because it does not know or because it does not consider what it does. You will say that, surely, there are some sins committed either through malice or through frailty, which do not proceed from ignorance or from thoughtlessness. I would answer you that although it is true that some sins are committed through malice or through frailty, nevertheless, understand that all of them can be traced back to ignorance or thoughtlessness, because malice and frailty cause a man either not to understand what he does or not to think about it. For example, women swear by the faith even things that are not true. St. Thomas says, in his *Secunda secundae,* that such an oath is a mortal sin, when she knows that what she swears is a lie.[11] "Oh," the woman will say, "I did not know it!" So, you see, this sin was committed in ignorance. But anyone who commits fornication, since he knows that it is a sin, sins not through ignorance, but through thoughtlessness, for his pleasure causes him to give no consideration to it while in the act. If he had considered with fixed attention that it was evil, he would not have committed the sin, for, as St. Dionysius says: *Nemo respiciens ad malum operatur,*[12] that is, "no one who gives careful consideration to evil can carry it out." Therefore, if, when some temptation to sin comes to you, you keep your thoughts firmly fixed on the fact that it is a sin, and that what you would do is against the commandment of God, you will certainly not sin. The same thing would happen if you were to think continually of death; you would abstain by and large from sin because there are two things which lead one to perform any good deed, love and fear, and these two spurs are the teachers of all the arts.

Consider the woman who learns to tend children: all of a sudden she has it, instructed by nothing other than love. The swallow learns to build its nest and tend its young moved solely by love for its little ones. Love,

---

11. *Summa theologica,* part 2.2, quest. 98, arts. 1, 3; also quest. 89, art. 2.
12. "No one reflecting on evil engages in it."

then, is the master which teaches you how to do anything. And so, if you loved eternal life, you would exert yourself to spend your life acquiring it and would not sin. The second thing is fear. Consider the hare: when it is followed by a dog, it flees and in its flight makes certain twists in order to disrupt the pursuit of its enemy, which cannot catch up with it. It is taught to do this by nothing other than its fear and terror of the dog. Similarly, if you were to think of Hell as your enemy, you would not sin as you do, but would devise every means to escape it, and, when the temptation to do evil came to you, you would say, "Do I want, for the sake of a trifle of pleasure, for a trifle of honor, for a trifle of worldly goods, which things are all transitory, to lose Paradise, where there is perpetual consolation, and go to Hell, where there is continual suffering?" Anyone who considers death steadily in this way will also consider Paradise and Hell, and the love and fear of God will enter your heart, and these will make you do good and flee evil.

This then is the reason for that saying of the wise: *In omnibus operibus tuis memorare novissima tua, et in aeternum non peccabis*. On the other hand, ignoring thoughts of death causes you to commit many sins. Meditation on death prevents man from sinning through ignorance or thoughtlessness because, as we have said, it generates fear and love within the heart, which are the teachers of everything. Therefore, man, when he loves and fears God, quickly learns the path he is to follow, so that he might not sin through ignorance. It also makes man meditate continually upon the other life, for the sake of which he takes care not to sin. And so, my son, when temptation comes to you, think right then and say, "If I were just now on the point of death, would I not want to have done all the good the saints have done? Yes, indeed, and, therefore, I do not want to commit this sin, but rather to think that I must die, and that, if I do good, I will go to Paradise, where the saints have gone, but if I do evil, I will go to Hell, where all the wicked are punished." Do this, my son; think about death, and you will drive away every temptation. Now let us rest a bit, and then I will show you, step by step, the way in which you must enter into this meditation on death, so that you might flee every sin.

Do you want to learn this true wisdom, my son, which the worldly wise do not want? Ask God often to enlighten you, and pray that He might infuse your intellect with His light, so that you might hold steadfastly to this consideration of the next life. Note, now, that I have told you that sin comes from ignorance or from thoughtlessness. One who does not fall into ignorance or thoughtlessness, then, cannot sin; this is the property of Divine Intellect alone, which, through its very nature, never falls into ignorance or thoughtlessness, because God is infinite and boundless wisdom, and the closer an intellect approaches to God and the more it is assimilated to God, the more perfect it becomes, and it falls into fewer errors because the closer an effect approaches to its cause, the more perfect it becomes. Since God is the Prime Cause of everything, the closer one approaches to God, the better and more perfect he becomes. Therefore, the blessed and the angels cannot sin any more through either ignorance or thoughtlessness, because they are so close to God and are strengthened in His grace through the light of glory, and they are very like to God. The soul of Christ, *also,* before He suffered on the Cross, could not sin through either ignorance or thoughtlessness because it was united with the Divine Essence, which it saw always. The Virgin, likewise, could not sin, not because she had already seen the Divine Essence in this life, as did the soul of Christ, nor as the blessed do now in their heavenly homeland, but through the great abundance of the Holy Spirit with which she was filled, and so she was strengthened in such a way that she could not sin. But the Apostles could indeed sin venially because they did not have such a plenitude of grace and of the Holy Spirit, and so they were not strengthened as was the Virgin. See how St. Paul rebuked St. Peter, since, while he lived and ate with Gentiles, he ate *even* foods prohibited to the Jews, *but* with the Jews, he pretended to remain Judaized. And so, St. Paul said to him: *"Tu iudeus cum sis, et gentiliter vivis, quare cogis gentiles iudaizare?"*[13] [Gal. 2:14] and then he adds: *Reprehendi eum, quia reprehensibilis erat*[14] [Gal. 2:11], that is, "I rebuke Peter because he has merited to be rebuked." Thus, the Apostles, although they had a great abundance of the grace of the Holy Spirit, could *nonetheless* err and sin venially through thoughtlessness, and those inferior to the Apostles all the more so. Think, now, how it must be for one who is without the light of God's grace and is left *in a purely natural state.* Consider how you think his condition would be and whether he could live without sin. I tell you that, in order to be on guard against sin, one must have the grace of God, and one cannot be on guard against it without that and without the light of faith, and so, it is necessary for anyone who wants to live uprightly and to be on guard against sin to ask first of all for light from God. Take this as your first rule then: that you pray every day and ask for light from God, that He may enlighten your will, and that through this light you might keep firmly fixed in your mind a consideration of death and of the next life, that is, of Paradise and of Hell, because I tell you that without this light you cannot live uprightly. And it would be very much to our purpose if you would say that psalm: *Usquequo, Domine, oblivisceris mei?*[15] [Ps. 12:1] That is, fly to the Lord and

---

13. "Since you yourself are a Jew, and yet you live like a Gentile, why do you think of Judaizing the Gentiles?"

14. "I rebuked him because he was deserving of rebuke." The introductory clause, *Reprehendi eum,* is Savonarola's alteration of the Vulgate's *In faciem ei restiti.*

15. "How long, O Lord, will You remain oblivious of me?"

say to Him, "O Lord, how long will you remain unmindful of me?" because God is said to be unmindful of us when He does not give us His light. So then, say this psalm and conclude at last with David: *Illumina oculos meos, ne unquam obdormiam in morte; ne quando dicat inimicus meus: Praevalui adversus eum*[16] [Ps. 12:4–5]; "O Lord, give me light so that I might not sin." Yes, it will be very useful to you to say this psalm often and to pray to God to give you light, because this is a gift which God gives to His beloved; ask it of Him, that with this light He might keep your intellect firmly fixed in its meditation on death. This is the first rule and the first remedy that I want to give you; let us move on now to the second.

The second remedy is to try to abstain from sin; make for yourself a pair of spectacles which are called the spectacles of death, which I told you about another time, but we will repeat a few things about them this morning. These philosophers say: *Oportet intelligentem phantasmata speculari,*[17] that is, "a man who wants to understand a thing must form images in his imagination," and such images are the spectacles of the intellect. Anyone who reads with glasses has before him the open book, and the glasses between his eyes and the book, and the light, through whose power the things seen, or rather, the similitude of the letters, come to the spectacles and by means of the spectacles to the eyes. This is like the understanding of our intellect. First, the intellect which understands, which is called the "possible [passive or receiving] intellect" by the philosophers,[18] is like the eyes; the intellect required as their "agent" is like the light; sensible things are like the letters of the book; the mental images, which are between the sensible things and the possible intellect, are like the spectacles. So, then, if you had red spectacles, the whole book would appear red to you; if they were green, the book would seem green, and the same for the other colors. In this way, our intellects are often deceived by the imagination, and moved in amazing ways, because the intellect has to make its observations through images. For example, you have here some glasses, and you want to read; with your eyes, you give your attention to the letters and not to the glasses, yet you must be careful about your glasses if you want to see the letters and understand them. If you have good glasses, your intellect will always see well, *and the contrary,* if you have bad ones. Put on a pair of yellow glasses, and you will see everything yellow; if you have red glasses, you will see everything red. The yellow glasses are images of envy, or, if you prefer, of avarice; the red, of anger, because the images are formed by the passions within the soul, in

16. "Enlighten my eyes so that I may never fall asleep in death, lest my enemy one day say, 'I have prevailed against him.' "
17. "Anyone who would understand must speculate using images."
18. Aristotle, *De anima* iii.4.

conformity with that passion, for *qualis unusquisque est, talia et sibi videntur,*[19] that is, "whatever sort of disposition a person has, things will appear to him to be of the same sort." The red glasses, then, signify anger and revenge. Take, for example, one who is angry, full of rage and hate: his spectacles, or mental images, will be like that rage and hate, and it will seem to him a good thing to take revenge because he sees everything full of rage and of hate; but remove that rage and hate, and he will immediately say, "I do not want revenge anymore," because the bad eyeglasses have been removed. Note, then, that the imagination, when firmly fixed, moves man forcefully wherever it will, and if the imagination is full of goodness, it will draw man to goodness; if it is full of evil, it will draw him to evil, because the imagination moves man *even* against reason. For example, if you walk across a beam set up high, and it comes into your imagination that you might fall, straightaway you fall; if lustful thoughts come into your imagination, all of a sudden you are afire with evil. So, then, if you want to do good and flee from sin, make for yourself a forceful image of death. These are the spectacles I am talking about: make death be impressed upon your imagination at all times, and in whatever you do, be mindful of death; in the morning when you arise, first make the sign of the Cross, then put on your spectacles of death; that is, you should say, *"Memento homo quia cinis es et in cinerem reverteris,"*[20] "remember, man, that you are dust and ashes, and to ashes you must return." Then, turn to the Lord and say, "O Lord, I have offended You and I have committed so many sins; pardon me, [for] I may perhaps be close to death; give me the grace not to offend You anymore." Put on these spectacles of death, my child, and you will see that they will be of the greatest use to you in life. You who must go to the Council, when you are there, take care to counsel justly; put on your spectacles of death and say, "I must tell the truth because I have to die and will have to give a reason then for what I have done and suffer punishment for whatever unjust counsel I have given." You who strive to amass possessions and to become rich and contrive evil contracts, be mindful of death; put on these spectacles and say, "I will be held accountable for this in Hell, and all the riches in the world will not buy my way out of there." You who go after ambition and honors, remember that you have to die; put on the spectacles of death and consider that all the honors in the world, if you go to Hell, will not get you out of there. Ladies, if the fancy takes you to preen yourselves and to strive for a fine display, put on these spectacles of death, and you will not want to go

19. "Such as an individual is, so will things seem to him."
20. "Remember, man, that you are ashes, and unto ashes you will return." This admonition, based on Gen. 3:19, is used at the imposition of ashes on Ash Wednesday.

with your finery to eternal damnation. Children, when you are tempted to sin, put on these spectacles of death; remember that you have to die, and give yourself wholly to the service of Christ with purity of heart and of body. Priests and religious, when you suffer any temptation, put on these spectacles of death, and you will find them very useful to you against every temptation. This is the second remedy and the second rule which I am giving you this morning: that you keep these spectacles of death on always, that is, this continual thought in your mind that you could die at any time. These spectacles, my child, make you see the brevity of this life and how much solicitude you should have to be constantly prepared for death. So, make these glasses for yourself through which—because you will always be in a state of preparation, considering that you could die at any moment—your life will be well ordered, and you will avoid many sins. Now, stay and listen, for I am going to give you another rule so that you might sustain this thought of death all the better.

You have understood this rule about the spectacles of death, but because the spectacles frequently fall off, you need to put on a cap or some sort of hook to attach them so they will not fall off. The hook with which you have to fasten these glasses is some sensible object which will make you remember death because the imagination comes from sensory perception, which is moved by sensible objects. Thus, philosophers say: *Phantasia est motus factus a sensu.*[21] And so, because it is necessary to form a firm habit of wanting to think always about death, if you form such a habit within you, this thought will keep you steady. All holy men and women have had this habit and custom of thinking about death, and in all their affairs they were ever mindful of this. When holy men feel a touch of pride, they recur to these spectacles of death and say, "I am dust and ashes; I have to die," and then they do not want to encourage themselves to think about affairs of this world. Likewise, when they are persecuted and find themselves in tribulation, they recur to the spectacles of death and say, "We have to die; soon these tribulations will pass, and we will enter into Paradise," and in this way, they never let the spectacles of death fall off. In order to instill this habit in yourself, so that your spectacles will not fall off, you must reinforce them with some sensible object. So, take this as your rule: go frequently to see the dead buried; go often to the graveyard; look often on those near death; make it your practice, if you know that one of your relatives or a friend or some other person is dying, to stay by them to see them die, and then go to see them buried, and consider well that this thing is a man, and consider what a transitory thing man is, and it will be very effective in guarding you from sin. But if you are much prone to [spiritual] frailty, you should have death depicted in your

21. "The imagination is a movement made by the sense."

house and *also* carry around in your hand a small relic of bone and look upon it often. And when you feel yourself tempted by ambition, recur to death and say, "Fool that I am, where are the many lords and many great men who devoted themselves to ambition and to seeking honors and dignities? All are dead, all are dust and ashes, all are stinking corruption!" And so, leave ambition alone; attend to living uprightly; restore any ill-gotten gains. In this way, you will be withdrawing from the temptations of avarice and of the flesh and of other iniquities. And if you do this, you will surely begin to want to think about dying well, and you will ask for counsel from someone who is expert in such matters, and he will say to you straightaway, "Since you do not know when you have to die, do not put off doing penance any longer, but go to confession immediately and say, 'I want to confess today and not tomorrow, because tomorrow I could die.'" Take example from that holy man whose thoughts said to him, "You could do it just as well tomorrow; tomorrow you will begin," and he responded, "Let us do it today, not tomorrow, for tomorrow we may perhaps be no longer among the living." *Item,* make your will, organize your affairs, and arrange everything as if you had to die tomorrow so that, whenever the Lord wants you, you can say, *"Ecce me, Domine,"*[22] "Here I am, Lord," I am prepared to die.

My son, be like the courier who arrives at the inn and, without removing his spurs or anything, eats a mouthful, and though it seems to him he has been a thousand years ahorse, he says, "Up, up quickly, let's get going!" In the same way, you should keep in mind that you are not going to remain here, but must pass on and go elsewhere, and that any hour could be your [last]. If war, or pestilence, or famine comes, have no fear, but say, "I have to die in any event." And if your imagination tells you that it is a hard thing to die by the sword, or by pestilence, or by famine, answer, "I have to suffer the pain of death once, whatever sort of death it may be." Indeed, to die from a pain in the side or any other illness is to suffer the pain of death; through this pain we must pass one time. Note that it is written in the Scriptures: *Pretiosa in conspectu Domini mors sanctorum eius*[23] [Ps. 115:15], and in another place: *Mors peccatorum pessima,*[24] "the death of the saints is precious, but that of sinners is the worst." Have no fear, then, about your manner of death, but, rather, of what follows after the death of the wicked. Consider that the saints have been sawed in half, shot with arrows, stoned; [they have] died in any number of ways after undergoing the worst tortures. Many a sinner has died in his bed and gone to the house of the devil, but the saints have gone to Paradise. So be prepared to die, and do not fear the

22. Perhaps echoing Samuel, I Reg. 3.
23. "Precious in the eyes of the Lord is the death of His holy ones."
24. "The death of sinners is the worst."

manner of death, because, as St. Augustine says: *Mala mors putanda non est, quam bona vita praecesserit; non enim facit malam mortem nisi quod sequitur mortem;*[25] "do not consider that death evil which has been preceded by a good life, for the only thing that makes a death evil is what follows after it," that is, the tortures of Hell. Therefore, if war comes, have no fear, but say, "Let death come as it may, for I am prepared; that death which is preceded by a good life is not evil." This consideration is good medicine against the tribulation of war. But, if you want a good remedy against the pestilence, make yourself familiar with some saint or with your [guardian] angel, and pray to them every day, for I promise you that if you make yourself familiar with some saint or your angel, even if you are abandoned by men at the time of the pestilence, you will not be abandoned by these, but they will come to you, *even* visibly if necessary, to watch over you and provide for you. *Item,* in time of famine, you who are poverty-stricken, who do not have enough to live on, do what I tell you: first, help yourself in whatever way you can—go to confession, go to Communion, and live uprightly; if you possess any superfluities, sell them, and buy what you need to live, and do as much for yourself as you can; then, when you have been reduced to utter poverty, do not be ashamed to go to your friend, to your neighbor, to your relatives, and say, "I have need of some things; help me," because if you do not want to do it, this would be an act of pride, and you would be unworthy of God's assistance. But if you do this and you are straitened by extreme necessity, do what I say, have recourse to God and say to Him, "My Lord, you have said: *Primum quaerite regnum Dei et iustitiam eius, et haec omnia adiicientur vobis*"[26] [Matt. 6:33]. I have acted with my utmost diligence, I have no other remedy, I have no more to live on; help me, Lord." If you do this, have no doubt, have faith that God will aid you and provide for you in every way; I say in every way because He has said so, and He cannot deny Himself. These are the remedies I wanted to give you this morning to teach you to die well, all of which pertain to you who are healthy, but who ought to consider that at any moment you could sicken and die, because this thinking of death is a rule very useful in the spiritual life. Now then, this suffices for the first picture in the book which I have told you to have illustrated. Let us come now to the second.

The second illustration, which I have already told you about another time, is this: that you have depicted a man beginning to grow ill, with death

25. "A death which has been preceded by a good life must not be thought bad, for nothing makes a death bad except what follows death"; *De civitate Dei,* bk. I, chap. II.

26. "Seek first the kingdom of God and His righteousness, and all these things will be added unto you."

standing at the door and knocking to gain entrance. You know that the devil is very attentive at the point of death, as indeed it is written: *Insidiatur calcaneo eius*[27] [Gen. 3:15]. So, when the devil sees that you are infirm, he does not know if you have to die from this illness or not, but in order not to be surprised, he says right away, "This may be it," and he prepares all the traps he knows of and can contrive in order to catch you unawares at this point, and he tries every art he can to make you damn yourself inadvertently, as he damned himself in Paradise.

The devil, when he was created in Paradise and saw how beautiful he was, began to fall in love with himself and said, "It would be a wonderful thing if I did not have to acknowledge favors from anyone, but possessed this excellence through my own natural power; I would pay no further heed to the vision of God," and he acted like certain fools who say, "I have no great desire for Paradise; I would take care of myself if God would let me stay in this world forever." In this way, the devil, through disregard for what he ought to have thought about very carefully, deceived even himself. Similarly, thoughtlessness made the lady Eve sin, when she neglected to think carefully about what had been said to her. She did not sin through ignorance, because she had been created with natural wisdom. But the devil got at her because of her thoughtlessness and began to say to her, "Why did God command you not to eat from this tree?" as if he had said, "It certainly seems an indignity that you, who are so noble a creature and above all the other corporeal creatures, cannot eat from any tree you please." Thus, he tempted her with pride, not gluttony. And so, little by little, he led her to entertain this thought, so that it seemed an indignity to her not to be able to eat from it, and bit by bit, she entered into pride. As soon as it had taken possession of her, it weakened the flesh, and she fell into sin through thoughtlessness and ate the apple which had been forbidden her by God.

The devil, then, who knows that one falls into error and sin through thoughtlessness, when he sees a man growing ill, says within himself, "Since we, who had great knowledge, sinned in Paradise through thoughtlessness, and since Adam and Eve, who possessed much wisdom and original justice, also fell into sin through thoughtlessness, man, who is much more thoughtless, will fall all the more easily." So, the first thing the devil does when he sees that you are sick, he tries to catch you unawares through thoughtlessness, and he tries his best to think of every device he knows of to turn you away from thinking about death. He begins to put everything but death before your imagination; he calls up images of your house, of your shop, of your farm, of the state, and says, "When this bit of fever has gone away, I will do this thing and that." My son, be wise, and have recourse then to the

27. "He lies in ambush at His heel."

Crucifix; be thinking that you could die of this illness. The first penitential psalm will be much to the purpose then: *Domine, ne in furore tuo arguas me*[28] [Ps. 6:1], so that the Lord may not allow you to be overcome by the temptations of the devil.

When the devil sees that he cannot overcome you through thoughtlessness, he will try to overcome you through your confidence of recovery, and he will put it into your head that you are only a little sick. My son, do yourself a favor and do not say, "I am only a little sick," but think that you could die of that "little" sickness, because many times a little sickness becomes great, and the pain of death does not always come all at one stroke, but begins feebly and then grows. The devil, when he sees that you are trying to think about death, incites others to distract you from this thought, and he puts it into the heads of your wife and your relatives, as well as your doctor, to tell you that you will recover soon, and that you should not give yourself up to thinking [about death], and that you should not suppose that you are going to die from this [disease]. Hold steady then, and do not allow yourself to be persuaded, but think that, if you should be on the point of death, no doctor can cure you, and keep this always in mind, that these are all enticements of the devil to distract you from thoughts of death.

When the devil sees, too, that you are steadfast in thinking about death and that you put no trust in your recovery, but are instead making plans to be confessed, he begins to make you put off your confession and says, "You are not ready to be confessed today; you haven't examined your conscience very well; you will confess tomorrow." If you hold firm in your resolve to confess yourself today, the devil goes about inciting your farm workers and your shop manager and innumerable tasks and impediments to interrupt your confession. But be mindful of death, my son; let the other matters go, and say, "This is the most important matter I have to attend to; my soul is at stake here," and do not let yourself be interrupted, but make your confession. When the devil sees that you have confessed, he exerts himself to distract you from your devotions and begins to incite your wife, and your children, and your relatives to bother you about your possessions: this one wants you to leave him one thing, and that one [wants] something else, and someone, in order to keep you in a good mood, tells a story, and somebody else tells another; all these are enticements of the devil to distract you from your confessional devotions and to keep you utterly confused. Therefore, my son, keep this in mind: that, when you feel yourself growing sick, you should choose some good man or woman who is spiritually inclined to take care of your health, whether it be a priest or a layman, a religious brother or a nun, who will stay with you at all times and remind you continually that you

28. "Lord, in Your fury do not condemn me."

have to die, and that you should confess yourself and set yourself straight with God, because sometimes it happens that your relatives, or *even* your own children, out of fear that you might leave your possessions to another or revoke your will, when your confessor comes, they say, "He is asleep, and now is not a good time to disturb him." So, you can see how much trouble the devil takes on this point. Think constantly about death, and when you feel yourself growing sick, consider that this may be your final moment. This is the second picture; let us go on now to the third.

If you will do as I say, it may be that you will not only escape from Hell, but even perchance from the pains of Purgatory, where there are very grievous punishments, and to anyone who is there, every hour seems a thousand before he can leave those torments behind. Indeed, everyone ought to pray every day for the dead, because they are waiting for our prayers, since they cannot merit anything more for themselves, if they are not aided through the prayers of the Church. Oh, if only you could know how harsh the pains of Purgatory are, you would much sooner choose to have all the wars, famines, and plagues of this life come down on you than to remain in those torments of Purgatory. Now then, let us go to the last picture, and then we will make an end of it.

The final illustration, which I have told you about, is that you have depicted a sick person in bed; he has arrived at the last moment to do penances, at which point few [penitents] are saved. It is indeed possible that a man reduced to that state may be saved, but you should know that it is very difficult for him. But in order that we might describe this state to you in detail, let us begin here.

God sets our free will astir and has given man a term up till death to reform and turn to Him, during which time He aids him and lends him a hand. But when this term has passed, God no longer shares his burden and no longer aids him. And so, when a man is dead in mortal sin, he remains obstinate in that sin and can no longer turn back, because he is destitute of divine assistance, without which he cannot be unburdened; therefore, by his own efforts he can no longer be unburdened of his sin. And so, when men have been brought down to that final point without having repented or confessed themselves, it is difficult for them to turn back, since they are already so close to the time of that [perpetual] obstinacy which follows after death. For this reason, men must not let themselves be reduced to this extremity, because rarely, rarely, I say, are they converted from it. Consider well, then, my son, what a dangerous thing it is to be reduced to this extremity without first having done penance. Why, then, do you hesitate to act now while you are well? I tell you, my son, do penance now, and do not let yourself be reduced to that point, for those who want to do evil while they live and reform at [the point of] death, many times God does not convert them then. This is perfectly just because they have been called so many times to turn to God and have had no desire to turn to Him; therefore, it is reasonable that they should not be converted then at the last moment either. Whence it is written: *Vocavi, et renuistis; extendi manum meam, et non fuit qui aspiceret; despexistis omne consilium meum, et increpationes meas neglexistis: ego quoque in interitu vestro ridebo, et subsannabo cum vobis, id quod timebatis, advenerit*[29] [Prov. 1:24–26]. The Lord God says: "You do not want to turn to Me, and although I have called out to you many a time, you have made mock of Me; I will laugh, too, at your predicament in the hour of death." For this reason, the man who has delayed up to the end and has remained unreceptive to God's invitation also merits to have God retract His grace at that moment, and so, it is difficult to be saved at that point.

Another reason is that the pain of death is most intense, and the soul suffers grievously at its separation from the body, and since the soul is a single entity, it is wholly absorbed in that pain and little able to think then about its sins and to have recourse to God. Another reason is that man, feeling himself weighed down by the pain of death, has so great a desire to escape that he thinks of little else. Another is that even if a man should think [of repentance] at the point of death, *in most cases* he does so through fear of Hell; this is not satisfactory, if he is not converted by love, as St. Augustine says. Another reason is that his wife and relatives gather round him and persuade him that he is not dying, and they tell everyone, "Don't upset him; tell him he'll recover; the sick don't need to be discouraged." And in this way they fill him up with airy nonsense instead of being mindful of his true needs. If anyone comes to say a word to him, [the visitor] calls out and asks, "Don't you recognize me?" And he squeezes his hand and says, "He recognizes me," and they do not know what else to say, nor do they give the least attention to what would be healthful for the soul. Thus, in such extremity it is difficult to be saved. Another [reason] is that at that moment the devil sets despair before him and shows him that he has committed so many sins that it seems utterly beyond reason that God would want to save him, and so he says to him, "Your tongue has always been prompt to speak ill; your eyes have always been delighted to view disgraceful things, your ears to hear muttering and wickedness; your taste has always sought after exquisite sensations; your sense of smell likewise." And thus the devil carries on about all his iniquities in every one of his senses and every part of his soul. And then he expounds on those words which our Savior, Jesus Christ,

---

29. "I called, and you shook your head 'no'; I held out My hand, and there was no one who would regard it; you have spurned all My counsel and ignored My rebukes. I also shall laugh—at your destruction! and mock when what you fear comes to pass."

said about the Last Judgment: *"Erunt signa in sole, et luna et stellis, et in terris pressura gentium prae confusione sonitus maris et fluctuum, arescentibus hominibus prae timore et expectatione, quae supervenient universo orbi"*[30] [Luc. 21:25–26]; " 'Signs of damnation will appear in the sun,' *that is,* in the intellect which has never thought of any but earthly matters; and 'in the moon,' that is, in the will which has loved the creature more than the Creator; and *'in the stars,'* that is, in the exterior and interior senses wrapped up in physical sensations; and 'on earth,' that is in the worldly heart; 'distress of nations,' that is, of a multitude of thoughts which run through the mind of the sick and torment him at that point along with the aches of his sickness"; and so the man is lost through fear and expectation of divine judgment. On the other hand, in order to prevent his finding rest anywhere, the devil begins to tempt him even about his faith and says, "If I can't have you one way, I will have you another," and he puts it into his head that the faith is not true and says, "Why do you believe in the faith? Dead body, dead soul." Yes, indeed, for all these reasons and many others, it is a difficult thing for one reduced to that point to be saved. But what is wanted, in order to overcome these temptations of the devil, is that there be someone there to say the Creed continually, as our brothers do when one of the brothers is dying; all are summoned by a brother who goes beating on a board throughout the household, and when they hear that signal, they immediately rise up and begin to say, *"I believe in God, the Father,"* and as they walk to the cell of the sick, they continue saying the Creed. Indeed, it is a serious matter to be reduced to that point without having prepared the way beforehand. "Well, now, Father, when someone has been reduced to that point, what should he do then?" Listen, and I will tell you in a moment.

My son, do not let yourself be reduced to that point. I tell you, O soul, if you let yourself be reduced to that point, I fear that it will be necessary to weep over you, as Jesus wept for the city of Jerusalem [Luc. 19:41], saying: *"Si cognovisses et tu, scilicet fleres"*[31] [Luc. 19:42], that is, "if you knew what evil and punishment will come upon you, you, yes, you also would weep." *"Et quidem in hac die quae ad pacem tibi est"*[32] [Luc. 19:42], that is, "and

30. "There will be signs in the sun, and the moon, and the stars, and on earth distress of nations, caused by the confusing thunder of the sea and the waves; men will shrivel with fear and expectation of what will happen to the whole world."

31. "If you knew, you also would weep." *Scilicet fleres* is added by Savonarola, along with several other alterations to the clauses of this verse, which in the Vulgate reads: *Quia si cognovisses et tu et quidem in hac die tua quae ad pacem tibi; nunc autem abscondita sunt ab oculis tuis.*

32. "Certainly on this day which is peaceful to you." The obscurities of the Vulgate are not elucidated by Savonarola's emendations. There is no *est* in the Vulgate, and *quae* is the neuter plural subject of *abscondita sunt,* referring back to *tua,* the

indeed you will weep on that day when it seems to you there should be peace." *"Nunc autem abscondita sunt ab oculis tuis"*[33] [Luc. 19:42], that is, "you do not weep now, for your ills are hidden from your eyes." *"Quia venient dies in te, et circumdabunt te inimici tui vallo, et circundabunt te, et coangusta-bunt te undique, et ad terram prosternent te, et filios tuos qui in te sunt, et non relinquent in te lapidem super lapidem, eo quod non cognoveris tempus visitationis tuae"*[34] [Luc. 19:43–44], that is, "the days are coming against you when your enemies will surround you," that is, the devils will hedge you round and lead you to Hell, and they will draw you down into great torments and anguish, and they will hurl you down through the earth into the depths of Hell with all your works. "And they will leave not one stone in you upon another," *that is,* your good works will avail you nothing. *Eo quod non cog-noveris tempus visitationis tuae,* that is, "for you have not recognized the time of your visitation"; you would not listen when you were summoned by the Lord.

O soul, do not let yourself be reduced to that point, but still, if you are so reduced, do not despair, take hold of these remedies. First, have recourse to the Crucified; consider the goodness of Him Who wanted to be crucified and to die to save you. Have great confidence in Him, that, if you have recourse to Him with a contrite heart, He will help you, even if you have committed thousands of sins. Consider how benevolently He pardoned the thief, and do not despair, but have faith that He will pardon you also, if you have recourse to Him in all humility, for He has poured out His blood for you. Second, repent for your sins with all your heart and resolve not to return to them, and if it is pleasing to Him that you recover, resolve to try always to do better and not to offend your Lord anymore. Third, summon a good confessor and make a full confession as carefully as possible, and receive Communion. Fourth, make sure that someone will always be there with you praying. And you, if you happen to be with a sick person as he is dying, do not make a great clamor, but all pray for him, for prayer will be of more avail to him then than anything else, and he will need the prayers of others because he will not be able to say many for himself.

And in order to give hope to anyone reduced to this extremity and to show how much the prayers of others avail him, listen to what St. Gregory

object of *cognovisses,* rather than a feminine singular, referring back to *die;* hence: "Would that you also had known, even [now] in this [present] day [i. e., in advance], those things which pertain to your peace . . ."

33. "But now they are hidden from your eyes."

34. "For the days are coming upon you when your enemies will encircle you with a ditch; they will encircle you and cut you off in every direction. They will throw you to the ground, and your sons within you, and they will leave in you not one stone upon another, for you have not recognized the time of your visitation."

writes in his *Dialogues*. He says that there was a brother of one of his monks, [a man] named Theodore, who was very restless, but felt himself bound to the monastery through his sympathy and love for his brother monk. Although the other monks admonished him many a time, he did not want to accept correction; rather, he became angry and outraged and made mock of the monks, and he said that he would never become a brother. There was a plague [raging] at that time, and so God sent it upon him, and when he became gravely oppressed with that malady as though he would die, the brothers gathered around him, and all, on their knees, prayed fervently to God for him. All of a sudden, he began to scream, "Go away! Go away, all of you!" And when the brothers asked why he wanted them to leave and what was the cause of his screaming, he replied, "Do you not see the serpent there which has nearly devoured my whole body? Only one part remains which the serpent cannot devour because of your prayers, and this is a more grievous torment to me than if he had devoured me whole." Then the brothers realized that a demon possessed him, and they said to him, "Make the sign of the Cross," but he replied, "I can't, because this serpent holds my arms in a bind." At this, all the brothers threw themselves on their knees and took up their prayers again even more fervently, begging God to free him. In a moment he began to say, "Thanks be to God, thanks be to God, I have been freed through your prayers; I now want to become a brother." Afterward he lived uprightly and, in short, died so.[35]

After this, St. Gregory cannot help but add another example of a man named Crisaurus [Chrysaorius], who was rich and had as many vices as he had possessions. Proud, avaricious, lecherous, he never in his life paid attention to any but worldly matters. Finally, as he lay sick in bed and reduced to the last extremity, a multitude of demons appeared to him who indicated that they wanted to separate his soul from his body. He grew pale and began to tremble and sweat and cried out to his son, Maximus, screaming, "Maximus, help me, protect me!" At that cry, Maximus ran to him, together with everyone in the house, and when he reached [his father's] bed and asked what he wanted, [the father] turned his face so as not to see the demons, but they appeared still before him, so he turned the other way, and when they appeared on that side, he turned away again. After tossing again and again in this way, he finally began to scream over and over the following, "*Inducias vel usque mane, inducias vel usque mane*[36] — O Lord, give me time till tomorrow." But in the end, he could not get it, and so he died in this way.[37]

35. Bk. IV, chap. 40.
36. "Truce till the morning, truce till the morning."
37. Bk. IV, chap. 40.

St. Gregory puts forth these two exempla, one after the other, which he says are for our example, in order to show us that we should not let ourselves be reduced to this extremity, so that we might not end up like the second man; however, if we are so reduced, we must hope in God, as did the first. So, then, no one should delay doing penance till the last moment of his life, but one should always be prepared, confessing frequently and going to Communion; one should be purified and well disposed, as if he expected death at any moment. For the man who is always in such a state of preparation and who continually thinks that he has to die will refrain from most sins. Indeed, as the wise man says: *In omnibus operibus tuis memorare novissima tua, et in aeternum non peccabis,* that is, "if you want to live uprightly, be mindful in everything you do of death, and you will not sin"; such meditation on death will be very useful to you and yield great fruit. Thus, dearly beloved, let everyone attend to living well if he wants to die well, and always have in mind that last extremity of his death, so that, acting thus, we might have grace in this life and, in the next, the glory of our Savior, Jesus Christ, Who was crucified and died for us, *Cui est honor, gloria et imperium per infinita saecula saeculorum. Amen.*[38]

---

38. "To Whom be honor, glory, and power for endless ages upon ages. Amen."

Prophecy

Psalms, Sermon III

Renovation Sermon

Octave of the Epiphany

Delivered 13 January 1494[5]
  Ecce gladius Domini super terram cito et velociter.[1]

Our intention this morning is to repeat all that we have said and preached in Florence over these past years about the renewal of the Church, which will happen *all at once* and soon. We will go through this repetition so that those who have not heard [these things] in the past may understand and know that [this] renewal must certainly occur and soon. And may those who have heard it before and believe be confirmed this morning [in their belief]; may those who have not believed or do not believe be converted; and may those who will not believe, ever obstinate as they are, at least be left blankly confounded by the reasons we shall adduce.

In every creature, its creation is limited, both its being and its power; eternity has no limit or end, *quia aeternitas est interminabilis vitae perpetua possessio.*[2] Time is not all joined together, while eternity is, because time is partly past, partly present, and partly future. But God, Who can do anything, is eternal and embraces all time because everything is present to Him; what has been and what is and what will be are always present to Him, and He sees and understands everything in the present. And just as we have said God can do everything and understands everything, so a creature, the more it rises above materiality, the more it is able to do and the more it understands; for this reason, man is more capable and understands more than any other animal. So, then, the angel, elevated above the material even more than man, understands and knows more than man and is capable of more. Therefore, angels know the order of the whole universe, but future things, which are contingent, which can be or not be, and which depend upon man's free will, neither angel nor any other creature knows them, for God has reserved to Himself alone this knowledge of the future and communicates it to whomever He pleases, however much and whenever He likes. Indeed, it is true that angels know those future things which come about through a necessary cause, just as the astrologer does who predicts a future eclipse by the necessary motion of the heavens. Angels also see and assess things

1. "Behold, the sword of the Lord [will be] over the earth soon and swiftly."
2. "Because eternity is the perpetual possession of unending life."

through causes *quae contingit ut in pluribus,*[3] such as, for example, that the olive tree will bear olives, that wheat will make wheat, for this almost always happens *et contingit ut in pluribus,* though at times, the opposite happens *et contingat ut in paucioribus.*[4] On account of this, it can obviously be concluded that divination and that branch of astrology which seems to divine *de futuris contingentibus*[5] are utterly false, for future things and those things which depend upon free will, which can be or not be, only God and any creature to whom God wants to reveal them know, as we have said. Therefore, I say that astrology, since it tries to divine the future, is the cause of much superstition and heresy.

Why such astrology is altogether false I can prove to you as follows: either philosophy is true or it is false; if it is true, astrology is false, for philosophy says that *de futuris contingentibus non est determinata veritas;*[6] if philosophy is false, then astrology is also false, because philosophy demonstrates those things which the astrologer presupposes *tanquam principia.*[7] If, then, philosophy is false, and it demonstrates the first principles of astrology, then they will be false; if the principles of the astrologer are false, then whatever follows from them will also be false.

In the second place, I [will] prove it to you: either our faith is true or it is false. If it is true, then astrology is false, for the canons of the faith reprove it; if the faith is false, then astrology is also false because the faith of Christ—which began *a principio mundi,*[8] because then they believed that Christ would come, while we believe that He has come—according to the astrologer, comes from the inclination of a fixed star which inclines men to this faith, but this faith is false. Therefore, astrology is false, because these stars, which incline [men] to falseness and on which astrology is founded, are a false thing; therefore, astrology is false.

Item, if the faith of Christ is false, in which there is more goodness, justice, and morality than in any other faith, then every other faith is false; therefore, it follows that astrology is false, since it inclines [men] to believe

---

3. "Which happen most of the time." The *quae* refers back to a singular *causa.* Statements on the angels' knowledge of futurity derive from Thomas Aquinas, *Summa theologica,* part 1.1, quest. 57, art. 3. The analogy of the astrologer comes from quest. 86, art. 4 and quest. 95, art. 1.
4. "And it may happen very rarely."
5. "Future contingencies." Savonarola's following *reductio ad absurdum* of astrology, though he does distinguish between the astronomical and divinatory aspects, is peculiarly apposite for the season of Epiphany.
6. "The truth concerning future contingencies has not been determined"; *Summa,* part 2.2, quest. 171, art. 3.
7. "As first principles."
8. "From the beginning of the world."

this falseness. You must conclude, then, from what has been said above, that divination and suchlike astrology is false, and that future things which depend on free will are uncertain to every creature, but they are certain to God and to those to whom He reveals them.

Moreover, first principles are more certain than their conclusions, which are inferred from them by our intellects, but for God there is no such intervention because He does not know causes through their effects; to Him conclusions are known from their principles and effects from their causes without reasoning it out. Angels also partake of this light, for they understand without reasoning it out. The prophets also had some of this light from God, and so David has said in the psalm: *In omnem terram exivit sonus eorum*[9] [Ps. 18:5], meaning the Apostles, who would come many, many years after David; and *nonetheless,* he, with that light, already saw their works as accomplished fact. Through this light, also, the holy prophets understand from external signs what they mean intrinsically, as Daniel did when, at the time of King Baltasar, that hand wrote those signs on the wall, that is, *Mane, Thecel, Phares;* he understood the sense and intrinsic significance of those signs and extrinsic letters [Dan. 5:25–26]. Therefore, this light is a participation in eternity, which God communicates to whomever He wants.

"Come now, brother, what do you mean by this? Where did you get these things which you have predicted here for four years?" I do not need to tell you this, because the mind is not disposed to understand it. I have shared it with some of my friends, one or at most two. But I want to tell you that you must believe, for I am not mad, and I do not exert myself for no reason. In the past, I, too, would laugh at such things, but God allowed this [to happen] to me so that I would feel compassion for you when you disbelieved like this. But, truly, you ought to believe, because you have already seen a great many of the things I have preached here verified, and I tell you that the rest will also be verified, and not one iota will be lacking; I am more certain of this than you are that two and two make four, more certain than I am that I touch the wood of this pulpit, because this light is more certain than the sense of touch. But I want you to know that this light still does not justify me; Balaam, who prophesied, was nonetheless a sinner and wrongdoer even though he had this light of prophecy [Num. 22:32–33]. I say to you, Florence, that this light has been given me for your sake, not mine, for this light does not make a man pleasing to God. I also want you to know that I began to see these things more than fifteen, maybe twenty years ago, but I began to speak of them only in the last ten years; first in Brescia, when I preached there, I said some things; later God allowed me

9. "The sound of them has gone out through all the earth." The Vulgate has *universam terram.*

to come to Florence, which is the navel of Italy, so that you might give notice of them to all the other cities of Italy.

But you, Florence, have heard with your ears not me, but God. Other [cities] of Italy have heard only from what others have said, so you will have no excuse, Florence, if you are not converted; believe me, Florence, it is not I, but God, Who says these things. This is understandable because you have seen this nation, which was headed down an evil path, turn back to penitence; do not suppose that such an effect could be brought about by a poor little friar if God had not worked in him. Believe, then, Florence, and be converted; do not think that your scourge has passed away, for I see the sword turning back.

The stone, by its nature, is drawn downward and knows not why; the swallow makes its nest on the ground and knows not why, for they do so by natural instinct, and they do not know the reason why they act in this way. But man is guided by free will. Similar to this are those who, in their simplicity, have foretold many things without knowing why. Some others have foretold many things not from simplicity, but knowing the cause and the reason why. And so, in whichever of these two ways you want to say that a thing can be predicted, I have predicted this: that all Italy will be turned upside down, and Rome, and afterward the Church, must be renewed. But you do not believe; however, you should believe, because God has told you so, rather than I.

Let us now begin with the reasons I have been citing for many years gone by, which demonstrate and prove the [coming] renewal of the Church. Some reasons are probable, and, so, they can be contradicted. Others are demonstrable and, so, cannot be contradicted because they are founded upon Holy Scripture. Those which I will tell you are all demonstrable, all founded on Holy Scripture.

The first is *propter pollutionem praelatorum.*[10] When you see a good head, you say that the body is well; when the head is bad, woe to the body. So, when God allows ambition, lechery, and other vices to be [found] in the head of government, believe that God's scourge is near. I [will] prove it to you: go, read IV Kings about Sedecias' end, where it says: *Dominus irascebatur contra Jerusalem*[11] [IV Reg. 24:20]. *Item,* in I Kings, where it says that God allowed David [*sic;* Saul?] to sin in order to punish the people. One reads the same about Manasses [IV Reg. 24:3]. So, when you see God permitting the heads of the Church to overflow with wickedness and simony, say that the scourge of the people draws near. I do not say that it *is* [now] in the heads of the Church; I say *when* you see it.

10. "On account of the uncleanness of prelates."
11. "The Lord was enraged against Jerusalem."

The second is *propter absumptionem*[12] of the good and the just. Whenever God takes away the holy and the good, say that the scourge is near. This can be proved: when God wanted to send the Flood, He removed Noe and his family [Gen. 6]. *Item,* He rescued Lot from Sodom when He wanted to burn it [Gen. 19]. Consider how many men can be found nowadays whom you can call just and good, and so, say that the scourge is near and that the wrath and the sword of God has moved.

The third is *propter exclusionem iustorum.*[13] When you see that a lord or leader of government does not want the good and the just near him, but banishes them because he does not want the truth to be told, say that God's scourge is near.

The fourth is *propter desiderium iustorum.*[14] When you see that all men of good life desire and call for the scourge, believe that it has to come soon. Look today and see if everyone cries out for the scourge; believe me, Florence, your punishment would already have come if it were not for the prayers and devotions of the good; believe me that today you would be a wasteland.[15]

The fifth is *propter obstinationem peccatorum.*[16] When sinners are obstinate and do not want to be converted to God and neither value nor appreciate those who call them to the good way, but always go from bad to worse and are obstinate in their vices, say that God is angry. This reason and the two preceding can be proved by what God did to Jerusalem, when He sent so many prophets and holy men to try to convert that people, but they remained obstinate and hunted down the prophets and stoned them, while all the good seemed to be crying out for the scourge. Likewise, many miracles were sent to Pharaoh, but He remained obstinate [Ex. 7–10]. And so, Florence, expect the scourge, since you know how long you have been told to be converted, and yet you have remained obstinate. And you, Rome, Rome! You, too, have been told, and yet you remain in your obstinacy, and so expect the wrath of God.

The sixth is *propter multitudinem peccatorum.*[17] Because of David's pride the plague was sent [II Reg. 24]. Consider whether Rome is full of pride, lust, avarice, and simony! Consider whether her sins are continually multiplied, and say, therefore, that the scourge is near, and the renewal of the Church is near.

12. "On account of the removal."
13. "On account of the exclusion of the just."
14. "On account of the desire of the just."
15. The word used is *giardino,* "garden," but the sense is obviously negative.
16. "On account of the obstinacy of sinners."
17. "On account of a multitude of sinners" (*sic*).

The seventh is *propter exclusionem virtutum primarum, scilicet charitatis et fidei*.[18] In the time of the early Church, no one lived without complete faith and complete charity. Consider how much of these are in the world today. You, Florence, want to look after your ambition instead, and everyone promotes himself. Believe that you have no remedy but penance, for the scourge of God is near.

The eighth is *propter negationem credendorum*.[19] Consider that today it seems that no one believes and has faith any more, and everyone, in effect, says, "So what?" When you see this, say that the scourge is near.

The ninth is *propter perditum cultum divinum*.[20] Go, see what is done in God's churches and with what devotion people attend. Today divine worship has run to ruin! You will say, "Oh, there are so many religious and so many priests, more than there have ever been before! Would that we had fewer!" O clergy, clergy, *propter te orta est haec tempestas!*[21] [approximates Ion. 1:12] You are the cause of all this wickedness! And yet, everyone thinks himself blessed if he has a priest in the house. But I tell you that the time will come, and soon, when they will say, "Blessed is that house without a tonsure in it!"

The tenth is *propter universalem opinionem*.[22] See, everyone seems to be preaching and waiting for the scourge and tribulations, and everyone seems to feel it would be just that punishment for such great iniquity should come. The abbot Joachim [da Fiore][23] and many others preach and announce that this scourge has to come at this time. These are the reasons why I have preached to you about the renewal of the Church. Now let us talk about symbols which demonstrate it.

In order to discuss the figures of Holy Scripture, it has to be borne in mind that Scripture has two senses: first, a literal one, which is what the one who composed and wrote the letter understands by it; the second is a mystical sense, which is conveyed in three modes: allegorical, tropological, and anagogical.

We will take the allegorical sense. Understand that in order for any writing to have an allegorical sense, three things are necessary: first, that it have a literal sense; second, that it be historical and not fictional—therefore, poems do not have an allegorical sense; third, that it be Holy Scripture; fur-

18. "On account of disregard for the primary virtues, that is, charity and faith."
19. "On account of the denial of belief."
20. "On account of the decay of divine worship."
21. "Because of you this storm has arisen!"
22. "On account of universal opinion."
23. 1132?–1202; Cistercian mystic, whose prophecies were condemned in 1256 by Pope Alexander IV, largely because of their appropriation by the radical Franciscan Spirituals.

thermore, allegorically speaking, the Old Testament signified and figured the New.

Item, there was a cherub on the Ark of the Law, and he faced another cherub [Ex. 25:19; 37:8–9]: they figured the Old and New Testaments.

Item, rota erat in rota[24] [Ezech. 1:16; 10:10]: the two wheels signify the same thing.

In another place it says: *Et factum est verbum Domini et vidi.*[25] This message begins from *"et"* (for it is customary with the prophets, in whom the Spirit of God begins first to speak within them, and later they utter the words and join the words within to those without), and continues to say: *et vidi virum cum funiculo venire et mensurare Hierusalem, et postea tacuit*[26] [Zach. 2:1–2]; the prophet saw someone, and this figures Christ, Who came to measure Jerusalem—*that is,* the Church and how great the charity of the Church was—and He measured it with a cord, *that is,* with the wisdom of God, which measures everything. And after He measured the breadth, he remained silent, that is, from the breadth He also knew the length, which must be proportioned to the breadth. And so, He knew how great was the Church's charity, which must be broad and long, because it is broadened and extended to one's neighbor, and even to one's enemy. But when I expounded this prophecy to you, I told you that the Church has two walls: one is the prelates of the Church, the other, the secular princes, who also have to support the Church. But when God comes to measure the Church, He will find neither of these walls, because one has fallen on top of the other in such a way that both are ruined, and all the squared stones of these walls have been broken and are no longer square, that is, they do not have the breadth of charity, and they have become round stones, converted to their own welfare and gathered within themselves. With these stones they have

---

24. "A wheel was within a wheel." The Vulgate has *quasi sit rota in medio rotae* ("as if there were a wheel in the middle of a wheel").

25. "And the word of the Lord was done and I saw." This conflates two prophetic locutions: *et factum est verbum Domini ad me dicens* ("and the word of the Lord was directed to me, saying") and *et levavi oculos meos et vidi* ("and I lifted my eyes and saw").

26. "And I saw a man with a cord come and measure Jerusalem, and afterward, he was silent." This significantly differs from the Vulgate: *et levavi oculos meos et vidi et ecce vir et in manu eius funiculus mensorum/et dixi quo tu vadis et dixit ad me ut metiar Hierusalem et videam quanta sit latitudo eius et quanta longitudo eius/et ecce angelus qui loquebatur in me egrediebatur* (Zacch. 2:1–3; "And I lifted my eyes and saw, and behold! a man and in his hand a cord for measuring; and I said, 'Where are you going?' and he said to me, 'To measure Jerusalem, and I shall see what may be her latitude and what her longitude.' And behold! the angel who was speaking within me went forth").

bombarded the city, that is, with their bad example they have corrupted and ruined the city and its citizens. The scourge, however, is near, as it was and came to be in Jerusalem.

The second figure I explained to you was the one in which no one in Jerusalem was allowed to possess weapons for any reason, and no blacksmith could make any weapons; even goads for pricking oxen had to be blunted[27] [I Reg. 13:19–22]. The smith, who is always at the fire, signified the fire of charity, which must always stay and burn within us. The hammer, which pounds, is constant prayer, which must always pound away at God: *"Pulsate et aperietur vobis"*[28] [Matt. 7:7; Luc. 11:9]. The blunted goad was philosophy, which does not prick as forcefully as does knowledge of Holy Scripture. But King Nabuchodonosor came and cruelly scourged that people, which had no weaponry[29] [IV Reg. 24:14, 16], that is, charity. The same will soon happen to the Church, in which there remains today no single speck of charity.

The third figure I explained to you was that of the Apocalypse, in which he said he saw four horses, one white, the second red, the third black, and the fourth pale [Apoc. 6:1–8]. And I told you that the white signified the time of the Apostles; the red signified the time of the martyrs, which was the second stage of the Church; the black signified the time of the heretics, which was the third stage of the Church; the pale signified the time of the lukewarm, which is today. Therefore, I told you that the renewal of the Church had to be undertaken, and soon. Otherwise, God will give His vineyard, that is, Rome and the Church, to others to cultivate, because in Rome there remains no charity at all, but only the devil. And this suffices for the figures. Now I will explain the parables which signify the Church's renewal.

The first parable is this. A citizen has a farm, on which two pieces of land touch each other, one full of rocks and thorns and weeds and everything unproductive, and this field the citizen does not plow or cultivate. The other field he plows and cultivates every year and prepares it with all solicitude, for it seems to be good land for producing crops; nonetheless, that citizen has never extracted any harvest from it. Tell me: what do you think that citizen will do with these two fields? Certainly, if he is prudent, he will take all those rocks and thorns which are in the first field and throw them all in this field. He will begin to plough and cultivate this other land. The citizen is Christ, Who has become a citizen, that is, a man like you, and has a stony and thorny field, that is, the land of the infidels, full of hardness, like rocks,

---

27. Conditions imposed by the Philistines.
28. "Knock and it shall be opened to you."
29. Another conflation; Nabuchodonosor scourges the people before taking away their smiths, but this is a separate incident from the one above.

and of heresy, like thorns; He also has the land of the Christians, which He has cultivated till now, and *yet,* it yields no harvest. However, He will convert the infidels and sow His law in that land, and this, which He has cultivated so much, He will abandon, and it will be left full of heresy. At last, the renewal of the Church will come about, and many who are here at this preaching will see it.

The second parable: a fig tree was planted, which, in the first year, produced many figs without any leaves; the second year, it again produced many figs and some leaves, but very few; the third year, it produced as many figs as leaves; the fourth year, it produced more leaves than figs; the fifth year, it produced very few figs and very many leaves. As time went on, it came to produce nothing but leaves in such abundance that it not only produced no fruit, but with its excessive foliage it overwhelmed the other plants, which were unable to grow. What do you think the gardener should do to that fig tree? Indeed, he will cut it down and give it to the fire. This fig tree is the tree of the Church, which, although at its beginning it produced much fruit and no leaves, has today come to the point that it produces no fruit at all, but only leaves, that is, ceremonies, pomp, and superfluities, with which they overshadow the other plants of the earth; that is, with their bad example, the prelates of the Church make other men fall into many sins. The gardener will come, that is, Christ, and cut down this fruitless fig tree; then the Church will be renewed.[30]

The third parable: a king had one only-begotten son. He found a poor woman, ragged and covered with mud; the king, moved to compassion, took her and led her into his house and raised her up to be his legitimate spouse. With her he had two daughters, whom he gave as wives to his only-begotten son. The king's lady, having lived in this way for some time, became amorous and began to commit many evils with her courtiers and servants. The king learned of this; he seized her and threw her out and sent her back into poverty and mud, as she was at first. After awhile, one of his daughters began to sin in the same way as the mother had done and much worse; the king, angered by this, sent her away and drove her off from him and his son and ordered that no bread be given to her. The other daughter, taking no warning from the sin and punishment of her mother and sister, began to sin likewise and to behave much worse and much more wickedly than they. Tell me, you who are wise, what does she deserve? Surely, she deserves much more punishment than her mother and sister.[31]

Now I want to explicate this parable for you. The king is God, Who

---

30. Compare with Christ's parable of the fig tree (Luc. 13:6–9). See also Matt. 21:19; Marc. 11:13–14.
31. Cf. Ezech. 23.

took that poor woman for His spouse, that is, the Synagogue of the Jews as His Church. She sinned, and you know how God drove her away from Him and sent her back into the mud where she first was; that is, He sent her into the slavery, misery, and blindness [she had known] before. The two daughters are the Eastern Church of the Greeks and the Roman Church, given as spouses by God to His only-begotten Son, Christ Jesus crucified. In this [Church] we have to serve under the faith of His Son, Christ Jesus. The Eastern Church sinned in her heresy, and so God has driven her off from Himself and His Son, Jesus Christ, and has commanded that no bread be given to her, so that no preacher or anyone else goes there any more to give her the food of the soul, spiritual food, nor to enlighten her. The other one is the Roman Church, full of simony and wickedness, who has sinned much more than [either] the first or the second. What do you think she deserves? Do you not suppose that God wants to punish her? Surely, you believe it is so, and even more harshly than her mother and sister, for they would rightly complain to God, saying, "When we have sinned, You have made us bear the penalty, but this other one, who has sinned more than we, why don't You punish her?" Therefore, be assured that the Church will be renewed, and soon.

Having told you these parables, we shall speak of the renewal of the Church insofar as we have seen, known, and predicted it. And so that you may better understand, you should know that there are two [kinds] of knowledge. The first is when we know by some external sign what that sign means intrinsically. The second [type of] knowledge comes through mental images.[32]

With regard to the first: when Pope Innocent died, something happened on account of which you used to amuse yourselves about things I had done, since I had said that the Church had to be renewed, and you believed, because of that sign, that I was in great error and that what I had predicted could not come to be. But I, because of that external sign, saw that, *yes, indeed,* the renewal of the Church had to be carried out, and I based this on what you used to say, which was against me.

With regard to the second, which is that of mental images, I saw, through the power of the imagination, a black cross above Babylonian Rome, on which was written: *Ira Domini,*[33] and upon it there rained swords, knives, lances, and every [other sort of] weapon, a storm of hail and stones, and long, awesome streaks of lightning in dark and murky skies. And I saw another cross, of gold, which stretched from heaven to earth above Jerusa-

32. The term used is *per imaginazione,* though one may conclude that they are not idle imaginings, but sent with a purpose, i.e., visions.
33. "The wrath of the Lord."

lem, on which was written: *Misericordia Dei*,[34] and here the skies were calm, limpid, and clear as could be; wherefore, on account of this vision, I tell you that the Church of God must be renewed, and soon, for God is angry, and afterward the infidels have to be converted, and this will be soon.[35]

Another image: I saw a sword over Italy, and it quivered, and I saw angels coming who had a red cross in one hand and many white stoles in the other. These angels gave this cross to be kissed to everyone who wanted it and also handed them the white stoles.[36] There were some who took these stoles; others did not want them; still others not only did not want them, but also encouraged others not to take them and acted in such a way that many, because of their persuasion, did not take them. After this, when these angels had left, more angels returned with chalices in their hands, filled to the brim with good sweet wine, but with very bitter dregs at the bottom. These angels offered the chalice to everyone, and those who had willingly taken the stoles willingly drank the wine, which was sweet at the top, and enjoyed its taste. To the others they gave the very bitter dregs, because they did not have the stoles, and they did not want it and would twist and turn, but they had to drink it. All of a sudden, I saw that sword which quivered above Italy turn its point downward and, with the greatest tempest and scourge, go among them and scourge them all. But those who had taken the white stoles felt the scourge less and drank the sweet wine from the chalice. The others were forced to drink the most bitter dregs, and in [the midst of] that scourge, they begged those who had the stoles and said, "Give me a bit of your stole, so that I won't have to drink these bitter dregs," but they were answered, "There is no longer time for this." This is why I tell you that the renewal will happen, and soon.

I will explicate it for you. The sword which quivered—I must say this to you, Florence—is that of the king of France, which is appearing all over Italy. The angels with the red cross, the white stoles, and the chalice are the preachers who announce this scourge to you; they give you the red cross to kiss—that is, martyrdom—so that you might bear up under this scourge which has to come during the renewal of the Church. The stole signifies the purification of her [the Church's] conscience, cleansing her of every vice, so that she may be white with purity. The chalice, full to the top with good

34. "The mercy of God."
35. This vision (datable to Good Friday 1492) and the following are all repeated in slightly altered form and in a different order in Savonarola's *Compendium of Revelations,* readily available in Bernard McGinn, ed. and trans., *Apocalyptic Spirituality* (New York: Paulist, 1979), pp. 192–275; see esp. pp. 206–207. For the Latin text of the *Compendium,* see *Girolamo Savonarola: Compendio di rivelazioni e Dialogus de veritate prophetica,* ed. Angela Crucitti (Rome: A. Berlardetti, 1974).
36. White robes are given to the martyred just in Apoc. 6:11.

wine, signifies the passion of which everyone ought to drink; those who have taken the stoles and cleansed their consciences will drink the sweet wine, that is, they will feel only a little of this scourge, which is signified by the sweet wine at the top of the chalice, that is, they will be the first to be scourged, but it will be sweet because they will bear it patiently, and if they die, they will go to eternal life. Those others drink the very bitter dregs under duress because it will seem bitter to them, as it surely is. This sword has not yet turned its point downward, even though it has appeared throughout all Italy, because God still awaits your repentance. Be converted, Florence, for there is no other remedy for us but penitence. Clothe yourselves with the white stole while you have time; do not wait any longer, for later there will be no room for penitence.

Now I shall speak about this renewal with respect to the intellectual part, and this is in two modes. First, I have spoken about this renewal with formal words and with informal words. The formal words I spoke, understand that I did not draw them from Scripture, nor did I find them in any [other] place, nor have I composed them out of my own fancy, nor did I get them from a man come down from heaven, but from God. I cannot say it any clearer: understand me, Florence, God says these words. Now then, I say that I have spoken them, Florence; understand me well; the words are these:

> *"Gaudete et exultate, iusti, veruntamen parate corda vestra ad temptationem lectione, meditatione et oratione et liberamini a morte secunda. Vos, servi nequam, qui in sordibus estis, sordescite adhuc: ventres vestri impleantur vino, lumbi vestri dissolvantur luxuria, et manus vestrae sanguine pauperum polluantur; haec enim est pars vestra. Sed scitote quia corpora vestra et animae vestrae in manu mea sunt, et post breve tempus corpora vestra flagellis conterentur, animas autem vestras igni perpetuo tradam."*[37]

The other formal words were these:

> *Audite, omnes habitatores terrae, haec dicit Dominus: "Ego Dominus loquor in zelo sancto meo, ecce dies venient et gladium meum eva-*

---

37. "Rejoice and exult, you just, yet prepare your hearts against temptation with reading, meditation, and prayer, and you will be freed from the second death. You, you vile slaves, who dwell in filth, wallow as you will: let your bellies be full of wine, your loins loose in lechery, and your hands stained with the blood of the poor, for this is your portion. But know that your bodies and your souls are in My hand, and after a short time, your bodies will be scourged to a pulp, and your souls I will hand over to the everlasting fire." The divine messages recorded in this sermon are also found in the *Compendium;* for the foregoing, see McGinn, *Apocalyptic Spirituality,* pp. 197–198.

ginabo super vos. Convertimini ergo ad me antequam compleatur furor meus. Tunc enim angustia superveniente requiretis pacem et non invenietis.[38]

Concerning the words which are not formal, remember when I said, three years ago now, that a wind will come, as in that figure from Elias [III Reg. 19:11], and that this wind would shake the mountains. This wind has come, and this has been the report which has spread throughout Italy for a year; it was told concerning this king of France, and this report has flown all over like the wind and has shaken the mountains, that is, the princes of Italy, and it has kept them vacillating this past year between believing and not believing that this king would come. And, behold, he has come, [although] you were saying, "He will not come; he has no horses; it is winter," and I would laugh at you, for I knew how things had to turn out. See now, he has come, and God has made summer from winter, as I said then. Remember that I also said to you that God would go beyond the mountains, and that He would seize him by the bridle and lead him over here, in spite of and against the opinion of everyone, and behold, he has come. Remember also that I said to you that great fortresses and walls would be of no avail; see whether all has been verified. Tell me, Florence: where are your fortresses and strongholds? And of what avail are they to you? Remember, also, that I told you that your wisdom and prudence would be of no avail and that you would get everything back to front; you would not know what to do or what to take hold of, like a drunk out of his senses. Now he has come, and it has been verified, and *even so,* you never wanted to believe me, and still you do not believe. I say to you, obstinate as you are: you will not believe the rest either, for God will not give you the grace to believe, because your obstinacy does not deserve it. Remember that at times during the past three or four years, when I preached to you, I used so much breath and fervor and vehemence in speaking that it was doubted whether a vein in my chest would not rupture. You did not know, my child, why it could not be otherwise.

Remember the Sunday of Lazarus three years ago,[39] when the arrow fell on the dome,[40] what I told you that morning, that I had not been to sleep that night, and that I had wanted that night to take up the Gospel about

38. "Listen, all you inhabitants of the earth, the Lord says these things: 'I, the Lord, speak in My zeal; behold, the days are coming, and My sword will wave over you. Therefore, be converted to Me before My fury reaches full strength. For when distress overcomes you, you will search for peace and not find it.'" Ibid., pp. 198–200.

39. Second Sunday of Lent, 1492.

40. Of the cathedral Santa Reparata/Santa Maria del Fiore.

Lazarus in order to preach from it, but it had not been possible to get a hold on it in my imagination. Know, then, that this saying came out of my mouth at that time: *Ecce gladius Domini super terram cito et velociter.* So I preached to you that morning and told you that God's wrath was stirred up and that the sword was ready and near at hand, and so I tell you again; you simply must believe.

Remember also that it was three years ago that I began reading Genesis, but I did not then know the reason why. I did everything to rework the old topic a bit, but when I came to the Flood, it was impossible to go any further, so abundant was the material; afterward, it was appropriate to preach about something else. Then, last Lent, I began again where I had left off, at the Flood, and I began to gloss the Ark, which I thought I would finish, but suddenly there was so much material that I could not possibly finish that Lent. When later I resumed it, before I had a chance to finish it, I could not, because I had to go on your behalf to the king of France. Two sermons, as you will recall, remained to finish it and close, and no sooner were they finished than the flood came, and everything was upside down here that day because of the French. I infer from this that this was a divine work and mystery and no ordinary thing, nor an arrangement conceived by me, and to a certainty, you simply must believe, Florence, and try not to be so hardened in your unbelief.

Remember also that I told you that in the past I had been a father to you and God had been a mother, because I had reproached you bitingly and bitterly and cried out loudly that you must be converted, as a father does when he diligently reproaches his children, and that now I wanted to be the mother and God wanted to be the father. So, just as a mother, when she sees her child erring, threatens and shouts and says she will inform the father when he comes and have him punished, and later, when the father has come, she does not report him but says, "If you ever again lapse into this error, I shall have your father punish you," so, although I reproach you now, I do not reproach you with that vehemence and harshness I used in the past, because I see that the father, that is, God, has come to punish you. Yet I say to you and beg you in a low and humble voice: my children, do penance, do penance.

Remember also, Florence, that I told you that I have given you an apple, as the mother does when she gives an apple to her child, when he cries, to quiet him, and then, when he still cries and she cannot quiet him, she takes the apple away from him and gives it to another child. So I say to you, Florence: God has given you an apple, that is, He has chosen you as His own; if you will not do penance and be converted to God, He will take the apple away from you and will give it to another; truly, it will be so, as surely as I am up here. And so, Florence, do these four things I told you, and I promise you that you will be richer than ever, more glorious than ever, more powerful than ever. But no one believes that the angels take part in men's lives today and hold converse with them, nor that God speaks to any man. And I say to you *quod similitudo est causa amoris*,[41] that is, "similitude is the cause of friendship." So, the closer one draws near to God and the angels through faith and charity, the more he becomes a friend of God and His angels, and they speak to him and hold converse with him.

I am not saying by this, nor have I ever told you, that God speaks to me; I say neither yes nor no; you are so far from the faith that you do not believe; you would sooner believe in some devil who spoke with men and foretold future things. You are devoid of sense and outside [the bounds] of the faith. Tell me, if you believe that Christ became incarnate through the Virgin and that He was crucified, which is more difficult to believe than [what I say], you should also believe this, which is easier, that is, that Christ speaks to men. *Moreover,* if you are a Christian, you must believe that the Church has to be renewed. Daniel says that the Antichrist has to come and has to persecute the Christians in Jerusalem[42]; it follows that there must be Christians there; therefore, those who are there must be baptized. But to effect this, there is a need for other men than those the Church has today. *Therefore,* the Church has to be renewed so that men may become good and go there to convert the infidels to Christianity. Go and read the Fathers on that passage in the Gospel of Matthew where He [Christ] says: *"Evangelium hoc praedicabitur in toto mundo et tunc erit consummatio"*[43] [Matt. 24:14]. Believe me, Florence! You simply must believe me because, from all that I have told you, you have not seen a single iota lacking up to now, and in the future as well, you will see nothing fail.

I predicted, quite a few years ago, the death of Lorenzo de' Medici and the death of Pope Innocent. *Item,* [I predicted] the turn of events here now in Florence concerning this recent change of government. *Item,* I said that

41. "That likeness is the cause of love." Aquinas, *Summa,* part 1.2, quest. 27, art. 3. Savonarola uses *amicizia* ("friendship") rather than *amore* ("love").
42. In *A Dialogue concerning Prophetic Truth,* bk. VI (below), Savonarola says: "It is also written in Daniel concerning this: *Introibit in terram gloriam* (without a doubt Jerusalem) *et multi corruent. Hae autem solae salvabuntur de manu eius: Edom et Moab et principes filiorum Ammon"* (Dan. 11:41; "He shall enter into the glorious land, and many shall fall. These only, however, shall be saved from his hand: Edom and Moab and the princes of the sons of Ammon").
43. "This Gospel will be preached through all the world, and then will come the consummation." The Vulgate has: *Et praedicabitur hoc evangelium regni in universo orbe in testimonium omnibus gentibus et tunc veniet consummatio.*

on the day when the king of France should arrive in Pisa, there would be a renovation in the government here. I did not say these things up here *publicly,* but I said them to some who are here at this sermon—I have witnesses here in Florence.

I know that this morning I am crazy *et quod omnia haec insipientia dico*[44] [II Cor. 11:21], but I want you to know that this light does not make me just; rather, if I am humble and have charity, I will be made just. And this light has not been given to me for my own sake, nor on account of my merit, but for you, Florence. And so, Florence, this morning I have told you these things so openly, having been inspired by God to say them to you in this way, so that you might know the whole and have no excuse later when the scourge comes and cannot then say, "I did not know." I could not say it more clearly, and I am aware that I shall be considered crazy this morning, for many have come here to point at me. If you say that I am crazy, I will have patience. I have spoken to you in this way because God wanted me to speak to you so. Since I began on this Apocalypse, we have had many contradictions. You understand some of them, God [only] some, and His angels some.

It is necessary to fight *contra duplicem sapientiam,*[45] that is, against those who have both the Old and New Testaments; *contra duplicem scientiam,*[46] that is, against philosophy and against astrology and the "science" of the Holy Scriptures; and *contra duplicem malitiam,*[47] that is, against the evil done today by the lukewarm, who know that they do evil and want to do it. This was not so at the time of Christ, for then there was only the Old Testament, and although they erred, they thought they were acting properly. Thus, I tell you that if Christ were to return here today, He would once again be crucified. I say, I have revealed next to nothing, because if I were to reveal everything, I would be here at least a week.[48] Believe me, several times already I have been in mortal danger.

I have declared to you: *Gladius Domini super terram cito et velociter.* Believe me that God's dagger will strike, and soon. And do not make a jest of this *cito;*[49] do not say that it is one of these Apocalyptic *citos,* which take hundreds of years to occur. Believe me, it will be soon. Believing does you no harm; rather, it helps you in that it makes you turn to penitence and

44. "And that everything I say is foolishness." The Vulgate has simply *in insipientia dico.*
45. "Against duplicitous wisdom."
46. "Against duplicitous knowledge."
47. "Against duplicitous malice."
48. "Almanco sei dì."
49. "Soon."

makes you walk in the way of God. Not believing could harm you and does you no good, so believe that the time is near. One cannot say exactly when, for God does not allow it, in order that His chosen ones may be always in fear and in faith and in charity, and keep always in the way of God. This is why I have not told you of a set time, so that you might always do penance and make yourselves pleasing to God, because if, for example, I were to say to men, "The tribulation will come within ten years," everyone would say, "I can still wait a bit to be converted." It would be tantamount to giving license to evildoing in the meantime, which would be detrimental. Therefore, God does not want a fixed time to be preached. So, I say this: now is the time for penance. Do not make a jest of this *cito,* for I tell you: if you do not do what I have told you, woe to Florence, woe to the people, woe to the great and the small!

Finally, I will conclude: I have been crazy this morning, this is what you will say, and I knew you would say it before I came up here. God willed it so, yet I say—and take this as my conclusion—that God has prepared a great dinner for all Italy, but all the dishes are bitter. I have given only the salad, which was a bit of bitter lettuce. Understand me well, Florence: all the other dishes are yet to come, and they are all bitter and plentiful, for it is a grand dinner. Thus, I conclude, and keep it in mind that Italy is now on the verge of her tribulations.

O Italy, and princes of Italy, and prelates of the Church, the wrath of God is upon you, and you have no remedy but to be converted! *et a sanctuario meo incipiam*[50] [Ezech. 9:6]. O Italy, O Florence, *propter peccata tua venient tibi adversa! Oh, nobiles, oh, potentes, oh, plebei, manus Domini est supra vos, et non resistet potentia, sapientia, vel fuga!*[51] And it will come about not because you do not know how things have been ordered. O princes of Italy, flee the land of the North; do penance while the sword is not yet out of its sheath, and while it is not yet bloodied, flee from Rome! O Florence, flee from Florence, that is, flee from sin through penitence and flee from the wicked!

50. "And I will come forth from My sanctuary." The verb in the Vulgate is the imperative plural, *incipite,* because this is God's instruction to the "men" He sends to destroy all who do not have a *tau* (Greek T, symbolic of the Cross) on their foreheads. Cf. Savonarola's vision described in his Good Friday sermon above.
51. "On account of your sins adversity will come upon you! O nobles, O princes, O commoners, the hand of the Lord is upon you, and power cannot resist it, nor wisdom, nor flight!" From the *Compendium;* see McGinn, *Apocalyptic Spirituality,* p. 202.

This is the conclusion. I have said all these things for reasons both divine and human, with moderation and tempering my tongue. I have begged you; I cannot command you, for I am not your lord, but your father. Do it, Florence; I pray to God for you, that He may enlighten you, *Cui est gloria et imperium per infinita saecula saeculorum. Amen.*[52]

52. "To Whom is glory and power forever and ever. Amen."

A Dialogue concerning Prophetic Truth

by Brother Girolamo Savonarola of Ferrara of the Order of Preachers

1496–97

The Argument

Meeting with Girolamo while he is walking in solitude meditating within himself on matters divine, the Seven Gifts of the Holy Spirit are introduced under mystical names, as if they were certain unknown foreigners who have set out abroad seeking disputation. There is much discussion with each of them about prophetic truth, concerning those things which have been foretold through him [Savonarola] to the whole Church and especially to the people of Florence in this present year, the one thousand four hundred ninety-seventh from the birth of Christ. Finally, when truth has been established and the disputation completed, they reveal themselves.

Book One
Speakers: Vrias,[1] Girolamo, Eliphaz, Rechma, Iechimham, Thoralmed, Abbacuc, Saphtham

VRI. May the Lord, Who made heaven and earth, bless you.

GIR. And may the Lord bless you. But whereto are you journeying through this solitude?

VRI. Indeed, we were told a short while ago that Girolamo, a friar from the Order of Preachers whom we wish to meet, had retired here, and you have opportunely happened upon our way. Perchance you might point him out to us, for that habit shows you to be of the same profession.

GIR. And what purpose leads you to this man?

VRI. A good one, I assure you. When he has learned it, he will rejoice exceedingly.

GIR. What a marvel indeed that among so many persecutions, by which

---

1. In Latin orthography, *v* and *u* are interchangeable. In order to emphasize the anagram spelled out by the names of these seven sages, Savonarola renders the initial letter of the first sage's name, though a vowel, with a *v*.

this innocent man is now agitated, good news should suddenly present itself!

VRI. Hence we may hope for good, for to be Christian is to do good and to suffer evils.

GIR. I begin to entertain good hope from this conversation even now at the outset. But who are you? And say whence you have come, if I may ask.

VRI. We are from the East, having traveled here out of foreign places, and our lineage is most ancient, as our ancestral names, coming from the primeval language, prove: first among these, I am called Vrias; the next is named Eliphaz; third, Rechma; fourth, Iechimham; fifth, Thoralmed; sixth, Abbacuc; seventh, Saphtham; and we understand every kind of language. But come, quickly point the man out to us so that we may all the sooner confer together as we wish, for then our identity, whence is our coming, and our purpose will be more readily made apparent.

GIR. Behold, you both see and address the man.

VRI. Hah, *you* are that Girolamo, about whom so much is going around?

GIR. However poor and weak you see me, I am he. And would that so many lies were not fabricated about me!

VRI. We have come for this purpose: so that, when we have inspected the matter in person, we might thoroughly dispel this poisonous vapor, for a double fame flies about, and contradictory rumors concerning you are spread among the people.

GIR. Fame is light and empty, and the rumor of the people is as a reed [cf. Matt. 11:7 and Luc. 7:24].

VRI. However, one ought to attend to the matter of a good name.

GIR. Indeed, I agree, but truth is to be preferred to glory and to all precious things.

VRI. Many men who are wise (in that they know as much as I) accuse you equally of rashness and of falsehood.

GIR. "The wisdom of the flesh," as the Apostle says, "is the enemy of God, for it has not been submitted to the law of God, nor can it be" [Rom. 8:7].

ELI. But I have often heard from wise and inspired men that you are damned.

GIR. Surely the Holy Spirit is not contrary to Himself?

ELI. Therefore you assert that your teaching is from the Holy Spirit?

GIR. Why not?

ELI. If one agrees to this, it follows that wisdom opposed to you is base and diabolical.

GIR. I must confess it is so.

REC. You alone are wise? And with you wisdom will pass away?

GIR. Perish the thought. For God does not abandon His people.

REC. But few agree with you.

GIR. Is it not written: " 'Many are called; few, however, are chosen' "? [Matt. 20:16 and 22:14] Have not the wise always been few?

REC. Therefore you profess that you are one of the wise.

GIR. Friends, I believe that which the prophet said at his own death: "All men are liars" [Ps. 115:11]. Truly, in these things which I prophesy I am not mistaken, and by God's grace I am that which I am.

IEC. I implore you, my Girolamo, admit to me frankly, do not conceal anything from me (for I understand perfectly arts of this sort): are you not deceiving people?

GIR. Ah, what could be more disgraceful and more worthy of severe punishment?

IEC. But it could hardly seem a disgrace to anyone to make people good by means of these deceptions, which harm nothing.

GIR. You are wrong, brother, for every lie is evil in that it is the opposite of truth. For if every truth is good, one is compelled to agree that every lie is evil. Moreover, evil must not be done, so that good might come about.

IEC. But perhaps no one would disapprove of committing small evils in order that we might attain the greatest good.

GIR. On the contrary, anyone who is wise will think this ought to be condemned. But I beseech you, does it seem to you a light offense or one worthy of indulgence to make a lie of the person of Christ in the presence of everyone, and to repeat that same lie by confirming it countless times? Would you say that it is a good thing or a minor fault to make pretensions about the Person of the First Truth, to spread falsehoods, and to make God a liar?

THO. Although you acknowledge that evil deceives people, nevertheless, certain people say that you do it deliberately and cunningly so that what you want most you might obtain by this means.

GIR. If this were so, I can certainly hope for nothing from Christ. What, indeed, is left to me to hope for from mortals, me, to whom nearly the whole world is hostile? Does anyone clever or shrewd or with an appetite for worldly glory and wealth follow in my footsteps and walk with me?

THO. On the contrary, they go along by the opposite way.

GIR. If, therefore, I were busied solely with the hope of this world, and if, for the sake of obtaining what I desire, I were to deceive people, and by deceiving them I were to stir up against myself the wealthy and the powerful and nearly the whole world besides, truly I would not be cunning, but mindless and insane, nor indeed would I be deceiving, but I myself would be utterly deceived.

THO. And many people are saying *that*.

GIR. Men, believe me, I neither deceive nor am deceived.

ABB. Are you not a man? Or is every man not able to be deceived?

GIR. I say, I am a man; but "is able" and "is" differ from each other more than a little.

ABB. What if perhaps you *are* deceived?

GIR. I am certain that I am not deceived.

ABB. Whence arises your certainty?

GIR. From the fact that God does not lie, for He is not able to deny Himself.

SAP. God has spoken to you?

GIR. What if God *has* spoken to me? It is not impossible nor difficult nor unbecoming to God to address sinners, seeing that He was crucified for them.

SAP. But, I beseech you, speak more clearly (for I am somewhat ignorant): how has it been made certain to you?

GIR. Although it may be true that Scripture says on this score: "No one knows but him who receives" [Apoc. 2:17], nevertheless, if you will patiently and piously listen each in turn, you will fully understand, God willing, that I neither deceive anyone at all nor am I deceived.

SAP. Certainly I greatly desire to hear it. For although I am very ignorant of letters, nevertheless, practical experience has not taught me nothing, and age itself has made me more cautious.

GIR. Unless perhaps it displeases the others, I shall by all means comply.

VRI. Indeed, we will all most willingly attend to your conversation, and respond one at a time, as our rank requires.

GIR. Let me, too, set this down as a gain today, considering that I may depart from you better instructed.

VRI. See, this place welcomes us. Let us sit down together by this fountain, in the green grass under this leafy plane tree, so that we may confer with you more quietly and more pleasantly concerning divine illumination.

GIR. Since it pleases you, let us now be seated. You I consider entirely worthy of admiration, for indeed I sense that your hearts burn inwardly with incredible longing; furthermore, the number seven, which you make up, and which in the Scriptures is highly commended, promises something good at the outset.

VRI. I ask about these messages which have been sent to you, and that you also explain to us in greater detail how you are not deceived.

Book Two
Speakers: Girolamo and Vrias

[Vrias is concerned with how Girolamo can be sure of the truth of his prophetic gift? Girolamo's reply follows an Aristotelian analysis of how the form, or essential character of a thing, is led by nature to its proper end. Each sensory organ perceives accurately objects appropriate to its peculiar capability. The eye, for example, formed for sight, accurately perceives colors. But this peculiar power may be limited, as is sight by darkness; thus

> [v]ision has not been given the power by nature to see in dark-
> ness but in light, by whose action the environment is made
> transparent and the appearance of the object conveyed to the
> eye through it; the light informs the eye, and thus informed, it
> sees.

Proceeding with light for his example, Girolamo then distinguishes among "peculiar objects," qualities such as color, perceived by one sense alone and, so, accurately; "common objects," qualities such as size, shape, and motion, perceptible to more than one sense or by several senses conjoined and, so, less certainly; and "accidental objects," qualities which may be inferred by a sense or senses not peculiarly formed to perceive them (as vision may infer taste from appearance), perception of which is most prone to error. About the objects peculiar to it, a sense cannot be mistaken, if they are presented within an appropriate range (distance, for example, may affect the eye's perception of color).

Just as certain objects or qualities are perceptible to individual senses, so are there objects perceptible to the intellect, as, for example, philosophical first principles and mathematics. The intellect's accuracy of perception, as with the senses', also varies; the more remote an object is from reason, the more likely the intellect is to err. Natural things, Girolamo says, are like "common" objects to the intellect, while supernatural matters are "accidental" objects. Intellect operates on the

human level by the light of reason; for matters supernatural, it requires
a divine light for guidance, the light of faith. The operation of the intellect under the light of faith, or revelation, can be understood by
analogy to the operation of sight in natural sunlight. All of scriptural
revelation is to be given equal credence by the Christian believer, but
not all is equally understandable. Just as distance affects clarity of visual
perception, so some objects of faith are closer and clearer to our understanding than others. The oneness of the Godhead is indisputably clear
and easily grasped; the union of a human nature to the divine Word is
no less to be believed, but difficult to understand. Faith perception,
like visual perception, is certain of objects peculiar to it at due distance.

From this springboard, Girolamo explains the power of his prophetic vision as a fourth level of enlightenment beyond the corporeal,
the intellectual, and the credal, but similar in its operation. As with
these other means of perception, prophecy has its peculiar, common,
and accidental objects. The one endowed with this gift is as certain of
its first principles as the sighted are that white is not black. To ask a
prophet to demonstrate the truth of his prophecies is equivalent to asking for proof that a lily is white. Though a prophet could err initially
in interpreting the common or accidental objects presented to his view
(as with Jonas [Ion. 3:4] and Nathan [II Reg. 7:1–17]), God would
swiftly step in to correct such misperceptions, lest His people be subverted in their faith. True prophecies can be tested against natural reason, Scripture, and Christian doctrine, and, Girolamo asserts, his
prophecies meet these tests. The faithful are not required actively to affirm them, but neither can they obstinately oppose them, for to do so
would be to stand opposed to the accepted tenets of faith, with which
they are in agreement.]

Book Three
Speakers: Eliphaz and Girolamo

[Not fully satisfied with the foregoing discussion, Eliphaz agrees that a
true prophet could not be deceived in his gift, but that others, feeling

equally sure within themselves that they also perceive by this light, are, nonetheless, deceived by the devil. How can Girolamo be certain that he is not of the latter sort? Girolamo replies that pride is key. False prophets are not ignorant of their errors; rather, because of pride they choose to ignore their own doubts and therefore affirm to be true things which they ought to question. Blinded by pride, they continue in error till they can no longer distinguish truth from falsehood, like dreamers who think that they are awake. Eliphaz counters pointedly, "Perhaps you also snore and lie in darkness while you believe yourself nonetheless awake and in the light." To answer this challenge, Girolamo says, unaided reason is insufficient; experience must be the touchstone. As a man assures himself that he is awake by grasping solid objects, so the true prophet feels the solid reality of what he sees as surely as if he held it in his hands. Nonetheless, his assurance can be, and should be, tested against "the natural light of reason and the supernatural light of faith," not because he doubts but in order to confirm for others that his gift is real and true.

> [T]he revelations of the prophets can nonetheless be proved to originate from God by inerrant signs and manifest results, to which, however, a prophet does not cling as to a foundation, since only by the light of prophecy might he be made certain, but his spirit is happier and livelier when he finds that truth accords with truth.

Eliphaz accepts this explanation and desires Girolamo to set forth these probative reasons. Girolamo cites first his overriding devotion to truth, rather than sectarianism: "Socrates is dear to me, but dearer still is truth."[2] This thirst for the truth has led him to lay out proofs of Christianity drawn from natural reason, fully convincing even without the supernatural gift of faith (in his *Concerning the Truth of Faith in the Triumph of the Lord's Cross*) and, further, drawing on philosophy, to

---

2. *Amicus Socrates, magis amica veritas.* The saying, more usually *Amicus Plato, sed magis amica veritas,* is attributed to Aristotle.

outline the virtues leading to beatitude, most purely distilled in Christian simplicity (in his *On the Simplicity of the Christian Life*). Putting this accumulated knowledge into practice, he has modeled his own life in accord with the Christian ideal. Eliphaz affirms that Girolamo's manner of life *was* a model of holiness—until he began prophesying without restraint, but that this outspokenness has set many former admirers against him. Indeed, Girolamo scathingly replies, had I kept to basket-weaving in my cell, no one would find fault with me, but because I have proclaimed a difficult message in public, I have discomfited those set in the enjoyment of their evil ways.

Girolamo explains that his greatest assurance of the validity of his prophetic gift rests in the "rectitude of (his) soul toward God"; that the uprightness of his life and his continual prayers for enlightenment would not go unanswered by God, the First Cause and Perfecter of all His creation. Beyond these rational proofs and good works, Girolamo finds his ultimate assurance in his own openness to God's correction and willingness to hand on the task to another, should that be God's will, for the glory he seeks is God's, not his own.]

Book Four
Speakers: Rechma and Girolamo

[The third sage, Rechma, to clarify the foregoing discussion, summarizes using Girolamo's own simile: just as, when a natural agent impresses form on receptive matter, it is God Who not only perfects the action of the agent but also predisposes the matter to receive it, so with divine illumination, God shapes the disposition of the one receiving it by rectitude of life. Girolamo's sincerity in his devotion toward God is a strong argument for the truth of his claims. Still, Rechma is not entirely convinced that Girolamo's own consciousness of his rectitude cements his argument, for the Pharisee in Christ's parable of religious pride was likewise sure of his high standing before God [Luc. 18: 9–14].

Girolamo acknowledges that what serves as proof for himself does not suffice for others, but external proof can be adduced from the effects of his prophetic gift. Recurring to his analogies with natural light, he extracts from Rechma the conclusion that a greater light does not dim a lesser, but expands it, for

> light is not extinguished by light, but rather is strengthened,
> just as one sort of knowledge is not contrary to another nor
> does it occlude it, but rather reveals it; truth rejoices in truth
> and like delights in like.

Demons, though they retain a natural light, pervert even the limited truth they know to an evil end; likewise, those who consort with them are disturbed and confounded in mind. On the contrary, those who commune with God and His angels grow daily more enlightened, as Girolamo feels himself to be; disclaiming spiritual pride, but "boasting in the Lord," he avers that his zeal for the First Truth and for leading others to Him burns ever brighter. Furthermore, the prophetic light he has received has augmented his intellectual capacity for lesser lights in both natural and moral philosophy, as well as economics and politics.

His own faith, too, has become less a matter of belief than of actual knowledge and palpable experience of things divine. With this, his understanding of Scripture has deepened to such a degree that he cannot by any means record the fullness of its revelation. Yet this expansion of spiritual and intellectual power has always been accompanied by humility and a keen sense of his own frailty. The purpose of his prophesying is not to overwhelm his audience with tantalizing curiosities, but to supply only the needful. Nor does he abuse his prophetic powers as a shortcut to knowledge otherwise available, whether from standard exegesis or the wisdom of other men, for to do so would be to test God.

Finally, he has not sought celebrity for himself by an exaggerated and crowd-pleasing asceticism or flashy wonder-working, but rather has conformed himself to the moderate discipline of his order. As Rechma pronounces himself satisfied with these proofs, Girolamo concludes with a plea not to misconstrue what he has said of his gifts as self-praise.]

Book Five
Speakers: Iechimham and Girolamo

IEC. From these matters which you have pursued in the foregoing disputation, I have concluded that all the certitude of these things which
you have prophesied depends on the light which you attest that you
have received, along with the reasons put forth—that you are
strengthened both by the rectitude of your mind before God and by
the increase of natural as well as of heavenly light and of spiritual
life, especially with regard to the subjugation of pride and vainglory,
which the ray of that light and your spirit strive to extirpate utterly.
This, if I am not mistaken, is a recapitulation of the whole essence.

GIR. You understand the matter correctly and have summarized everything clearly.

IEC. In truth these things pertain to you alone; however, we, who in no
way see either that light, nor the increase of your illumination or
[spiritual] life or humility, and nothing of these things which dwell
within the innermost depths of your heart, cannot be assured by
these reasons. You must make known to us the *first* principles, from
which your reasons are deduced; *these* principles [the ones already
stated], however, are known to God alone and to you.

GIR. You asked me, when I told you that I have certitude of these things,
whence I have it. I responded to your questioning; I made no attempt to prove the truth to you from those prophecies which have
been preached by me, but I revealed to you by what reasons, bound
within me, I could in no way be doubtful. Therefore, such reasons,
as I said a little earlier, are not efficacious except among those who
have faith in me.

IEC. It is true that one who believes the inward signs which have been
offered to you for your own sake is strongly assured, for it is advantageous if the students are not in doubt regarding the first principles
of knowledge—the learner, the Philosopher says, must believe. But
the one who faithfully receives your assertions about yourself will
easily grasp the rest of what you have said, even without reasons;
now, how will you prove them to those who do not believe you at
first blush or who consider the truth of your words suspect and uncertain?

GIR. Reasons are scarcely lacking to me for refuting others and for driving out from their minds all suspicion of error and of deception with which they think me bound.

IEC. That, indeed, I desire and demand from you, and I hope that these our friends, likewise, will listen no less willingly and attentively.

GIR. And I am ready to oblige you in all things according to my ability.

IEC. Go on then, speak.

GIR. Although a cause carries out the disposition of matter, it does not otherwise introduce form; do you think that the natural agent is able to negate the form of the disposed matter, so that it [the matter] may not introduce the form?

IEC. Not in the least. For it acts not by purpose but by nature.

GIR. From where does it obtain this nature?

IEC. From the first cause, which is God.

GIR. Does the first cause act through its own will or through nature?

IEC. Through will.

GIR. Would God then be able *not* to give form to prepared matter?

IEC. Indeed, He would be able, but He is not accustomed to do it.

GIR. Why?

IEC. His infinite wisdom brought order to this universe, to overturn which would seem repugnant to His wisdom.

GIR. Does He never act against this order?

IEC. Sometimes He acts above or beyond it, when He works miracles, but against it, I cannot easily imagine.

GIR. On the contrary, He seems to have acted against the order of nature when, at the command of Josue fighting the battle, the sun stood immovable [Ios. 10:12–13]; and when, at the time Ezechias was ill, an interval of several hours ran backward [IV Reg. 20:8–11]; and at the death of our Savior, an eclipse came to pass when the moon, standing then at the farthest distance from the sun, instantaneously traversed the immense span of the sky and was seen to be conjoined to it outside its accustomed course and then, suddenly sliding back, was deflected to its proper place [Matt. 27:45; Mar. 15:33; Luc. 23:44–45];[3] likewise, when the three children escaped unharmed from the fiery furnace, combustible matter had been disposed and an agent prepared, and, nevertheless, He did not introduce the form [Dan. 3:19–94].

IEC. If we are talking about the sun or about the sky, it would be better to say that God acts against the will of the moving intelligence

---

3. The full details are not given in the Gospels, but see the discussion in Aquinas, *Summa,* part 3, quest. 44, art. 2, reply to objection 2.

rather than against nature, for the sky is not moved in the same way as heavy things are borne downward and light things upward, but rather by the will of a moving intelligence. Nevertheless, I say that those miracles performed in the sky were not against but beyond the will of the angelic mover; moreover, concerning the three youths in the fire, He similarly worked not against, but beyond nature, because, granted that nature were inclined to and disposed for combustion, nevertheless, it would be more inclined to obey God its Creator than its own proper form; therefore, He acted beyond rather than against the condition of its particular nature. But, so that I may cut off all caviling, if anyone should wish to contend that God sometimes works against the order imposed in the universe, I would say that He sometimes acts against some particular order on account of some particular greater good, or rather for the sake of universal good.

GIR. You have not answered absurdly. But again I ask of you whether in spiritual matters God might do anything contrary to the order imposed in them.

IEC. It is not proper to fight against spiritual good, but against sin. If, therefore, you interpret it in this way, it is certain that God does not act against the order of spiritual good.

GIR. I do not interpret it in this way, but since some things can be done against the given order without sin, supposing that, if someone were, with God's assistance, disposed by final disposition to receive grace, and God did not want to confer it upon one thus prepared, especially since He acts in accordance with His will, not by necessity of nature, I ask you whether this is in fact possible for God Himself.

IEC. If we are speaking of absolute power, certainly it is possible, for He is not compelled nor bound to give grace to anyone. But He will never do it with His ordinary power.

GIR. For what reason?

IEC. Because the difference between natural things and rational creatures is great; natural things have a certain particular good on account of their intended end, from which they are sometimes cut off for the sake of the good of man, for whom they have been ordained, or for the sake of universal good. But since all natural things were made for man and man for beatitude, because it is a universal good chiefly redounding to the glory of God, no greater good is to be discovered for the sake of which our most excellent Begetter would desire that one so disposed should be made destitute of so great a gift as His grace. And so, there is no suitable reason why grace would not be conferred upon one who is perfectly disposed to receive it, especially since that same disposition is made by God and is ordained, through His ineffable wisdom, toward that aforesaid grace just as toward an end; therefore, it would be contrary to the order of divine wisdom not to grant this grace to one so disposed, because it is not appropriate for God.

GIR. Does God not daily allow men to be involved in sin, and, nevertheless, He converts that evil to the glory of His own justice?

IEC. The rationale for those who sin willingly is different from those who dispose themselves for grace through abstaining from sins as much as they are able, for those He prunes away for the glory of His justice, but in the case of the others what glory would there be for God if He were to dismiss those trying with all their strength to live righteously and to serve Him alone, and if He were to render unperfected those whom He especially assists and prepares to receive grace?

GIR. You have answered correctly, as I see it. Therefore, it must be said that God will fully endow such men with grace.

IEC. Without a doubt, although He is constrained by no necessity, He will do it.

GIR. Therefore, just as natural things, having been well disposed, prepare themselves for their own forms and men washing away their sins with tears prepare themselves for grace, so those who live uprightly and already partake of divine grace prepare themselves for absorbing and understanding divine illuminations. And so, concerning those things which pertain to salvation, which do you think will be more illuminated by God: the good or the evil?

IEC. The good, of course, on account (as I have said) of their right disposition.

GIR. By what inferences are good Christians to be distinguished?

IEC. It is written: " 'By their works you will know them' "⁴ [Matt. 7:16].

GIR. Those, therefore, who observe the commandments of God or who, having abandoned the world, turn to religion [i.e., join a religious order] so that, by more freely devoting themselves to the spirit and contemplation, they might serve God in that place in peace and in charity, without complaint, would you call them good or evil?

IEC. I would, indeed, hardly dare to call them evil, and so I will declare them good.

GIR. Let us come then to the matter proposed, so that I may prove that my [prophecies] are not from the devil nor from human industry or sagacity, but from God. For, so that we may begin from matters

4. Substituting *operibus* for *fructibus*.

closer and more connected to me, see, we should count the nearly two hundred fifty brothers now in fellowship and in this congregation of ours serving God by rejecting every worldly solicitude, of whom some who were endowed with ample means and nobility and others who were learned and wise in worldly matters and occupied with [acquiring] honors, when they heard my preaching and exhortations, very eagerly flew to holy poverty and humility, and, persevering with me in my tribulations, they dread no threats of persecution nor any of its darts, but rejoicing in these tribulations and singing praise to God, they are unanimously prepared to die for the sake of this truth.

IEC. Among the prudent this might claim the most faith, and it has been repeated very often by many, and when they hear obloquy of you, they marvel, saying, "How can so many learned men, prudent and good, among whom some are expert in Greek and Latin, some in Hebrew, and who are also extraordinarily erudite in philosophy, theology, and the Sacred Scriptures, in canon and civil law, and in whatever branch of knowledge you please, *not* examine this error carefully, even though they are incessantly occupied with it? If, however, they do examine it carefully, how can they, who are called brothers, foremost in nobility, favor, and authority, sustain and tolerate in their own community for so long this same stranger and alien, now made contumacious (if so it might go on) to God and men—?"

GIR. But add this further: how is it that so many men and men of such a character not only desire and beseech, but also compel me, a foreigner, to preside over them? For they could more easily shake off this yoke from their necks, especially in this tempest, than rouse someone from sleep [Matt. 8:23–27; Mar. 4:36–40; Luc. 8:22–25]. And so, does it seem to you that these men are seeking worldly consolations or pleasures when in so many and such great persecutions they happily and unanimously accept this yoke and fiercely and most steadfastly resist those who seek to loose it?

IEC. Perhaps they tolerate all these things because, under this regimen of yours, they live more freely than they would do under other prelates.

GIR. Perhaps this response of yours might solve the argument if these persecutions had been inflicted on us before they came to the cloister. But very many, yes, almost all of them, received the habit [i.e., friar's robes] in the midst of these tribulations, and even more did so after excommunication was brought to bear against us, and although they were free, of their own accord they submitted to this

free servitude, because "where the Spirit is, there is freedom"⁵ [II
Cor. 3:17]. Moreover, it is well known that we have revoked the
loose reins of religion for the rule of our predecessors, desiring to
preserve every day the stricter way of life and to subject ourselves
more and more to obedience to Christ.

IEC. What if the lower ranks consent through fear, while the few leaders
among you, by an amicable agreement, divide the duties and the
emoluments of ruling?

GIR. Believe me, brother, if among us there were any blemish of ambition
or avarice, it could not lie so hidden but that from some secret place
at some time an undertone of murmuring would arise and would
whisper into the attentive ears of spies, since among the proud and
avaricious there are always conflicts and quarrels. Moreover, concerning the lower ranks, fear is an untrustworthy guardian for the long
haul, because from it they might very easily release themselves by
means of favor obtained from the superiors [of the order], by whom
they would be graciously and very gladly received on an opportune
occasion; might they not either express this to them through letters
or at least hint at it to their relatives? But, see, among so many attacks of those who rage against us, they all persist so unanimously in
this truth that quite often they fervidly cry out in a single body and
attest that for the sake of defending it they would eagerly undergo
every extremity.

IEC. To be sure, I do not know what more I might object to this assertion of yours, but proceed further in the direction your reasoning
was tending.

GIR. Since, therefore, they walk righteously before God, and, on account
of this, they have despised the world and have been and daily are
better disposed for divine illuminations, do you think them deceived? Why would God allow His own to be so deceived? Why
would He not disclose the truth to them? And who are more fit for
laying hold of this truth of salvation than they? If, therefore, to
think this is sacrilege, let us concede that this which I prophesy is
truth, and, moreover, let no one presume either that I am deceived
or that I deceive others. But I would add one thing more, if it
please you.

IEC. Yes, please do.

GIR. I want you to know that all these things which you see accomplished through us in our congregation as well as in the city—indeed, exceedingly arduous and incredible [as they are] if they are

5. In the Vulgate: *Spiritus Domini.*

considered among so many difficulties and adversities—have been effected and sustained by us not by arms nor force nor any means other than faith, patience, and prayer. For this reason, those who have heard are my witnesses in what manner I have been accustomed to say to them often that if we persevere in these things by living uprightly, we will always follow through to victory and suffer and accomplish mighty things; they know also how many prayers we have in the past poured out before God and how many we are pouring out, while on account of these matters we are almost constantly offering supplications to heaven. Do you think, then, that God, Who has promised to listen to our prayers, Who indeed makes us pray, as the Apostle says, "with inexpressible groanings"[6] [Rom. 8: 6], will not listen to so many prayers of His servants? Or would He not already have made this deception (if it were a deception) public? For where [in this] is the goodness of God? Where His zeal? Where the multitude of His heartfelt affections and His mercies? Where is our kind and sweet Lord Jesus Christ, Who poured out His own blood for us? For what do we seek by praying assiduously and doing good, if not the truth, so that God may be glorified and our souls saved?

IEC. This reasoning seems most valid. But it has perturbed many that God in recent days has struck you with a wasting plague; they are saying that if you had in truth been servants of God, by no means would He have punished you with this contagion.

GIR. But those people do not in the least discern what things are of God as long as they distinguish the servants of God from the adherents to the world through those things which are seen to be common to the good and the evil, for the favorable and unfavorable things of the world are common to both, or, rather, unfavorable things more often strike the good than the evil. Therefore, each side should be examined, not by means of those things which happen commonly and indifferently, which can be called truly neither good nor bad, but by means of those things which are particular to each individual, namely, a good life or a bad.

IEC. You said that right.

GIR. And so, God has tested His elect, nor yet has this blow fallen upon them unforeseen, for already five or six years ago I warned them to prepare themselves because death, standing at the door, ready to ravage cities, villages, and towns with sword, pestilence, and widespread famine, was also about to carry off many from among us,

---

6. In Romans, it is the Spirit Who prays *pro nobis* with inexpressible groanings.

whom, however, we consider not as dead, but as resting in blessed repose, nor does it matter by what kind of death they departed to their fatherland, because, as Augustine says: "A death which has been preceded by a good life must not be thought bad, for nothing makes a death bad except what follows death."[7] I beseech those who are saying these things to consider what the Scripture threatens against the guilty, namely: "If the just man receives [recompense] on earth, where shall the impious and the sinner appear? And if this is done in the green wood, what shall be done in the dry? For it is time," Peter says, "that judgment must begin in the house of God."[8] For in this very city God has taken away many good people of both sexes so that what I have often prophesied may be fulfilled, namely, that many good people are still about to perish in these calamities, who, though now unconcerned about the reward for labors and afflictions, will view this renewal of the Church on earth from Heaven and will encourage it. If, therefore, the judgment begins first with these, what do you think the future one will be on those who do not believe and live evilly?

IEC. Assuredly, I think that there will be judgment without mercy for them, and, when you have proclaimed these things publicly, certainly people ought, in my opinion, to be more confirmed in truth.

GIR. You understand well. But our Lord Jesus Christ says: "Every plant which My Father has not planted will be uprooted. Leave them alone: they are blind and leaders of the blind, but if a blind man should lead a blind man, both will fall into the pit" [Matt. 15:13–14]. But let us return to the point from which the conversation has slipped away.

IEC. I think that nothing can now be added to these arguments, because I am already strongly impelled to believe.

GIR. There is also this: that since it is written, "By their fruits you will know them" [Matt. 7:16], the fruits of my teaching and preaching are already manifest, for, after I began to preach, as is very well known, many were deeply affected, of whom some, relinquishing

---

7. *De civitate Dei,* bk. I, chap. 11.

8. A strange conflation of several passages: Prov. 11:31: *Si iustus in terra recipit quanto magis impius et peccator?* ("If the just man receives [recompense] on earth, how much more shall the impious and the sinner?"); 1 Pet. 4:18: *Et si iustus vix salvatur, impius et peccator ubi parebit?* ("If the just man will scarcely be saved, where shall the impious and the sinner appear?"); Luc. 23:31: *Quia si in viridi ligno haec faciunt, in arido quid fiet?* ("For if they do these things in the green wood, what shall be done in the dry?"); and 1 Pet. 4:17: *Quoniam tempus ut incipiat iudicium de domo Dei* ("For the time is come that judgment must begin at the house of God").

the shipwreck of this world, fled to the port of religion [i.e., joined a religious order]; others, indeed remaining in the world, embraced the simplicity of Christ and changed their lives for the better. By their example, this grace has been diffused throughout the country-side and many cities, and in both sexes of whatever age, condition, or rank has produced manifold fruit. But why am I dwelling on so public a matter? For there is no one who does not know these things.

IEC. So I understand, for everywhere there is nothing else in everyone's mouth, nothing else is discussed, nor are attackers wanting, and, on the other side, those who very fiercely defend it, so that there is scarcely any home, any cottage in which there is not some conflict concerning such matters, as our Savior says: "Do not think that I have come to bring peace into the world. I have come to bring not peace, but the sword, for I have come to set a man against his own father, and a daughter against her mother, and a daughter-in-law against her mother-in-law, and a man's enemies are those in his own household" [Matt. 10:34–36].

GIR. If, then, this tree has borne and daily bears good fruit, why should it be called bad? "Either make," says the Lord, "the tree good and its fruit good or the tree bad and its fruit bad, since by the fruit the tree is known" [Matt. 12:33]. Can the effect be better and more per-fect than its cause?

IEC. Doubtless, if this teaching makes people good and induces them to live uprightly and blessedly, I do not see how it may be called bad.

GIR. We see from experience that by this teaching people are directed to a right way of life, and all who live righteously become lovers and de-fenders of it, and the more they advance in living uprightly, so much the more fiercely do they uphold it and guard it; however, those who live evilly regard me with hatred as their accuser and conscience and the one censuring their open crimes, and they attack me.

IEC. Nevertheless, I have heard certain people of an approved way of life and religious [i.e., persons in vows] also very aggressively attack it.

GIR. In the first place, this is sure and certain: that those who are openly evil are likewise opposed to this teaching, as is crystal clear from our persecutors, for almost all of them are held to be infamous in the common estimation, and their perverse works are known to the whole world, and it is agreed in this city as well as elsewhere that it is mainly those who chase after vices who detest this teaching. How then ought they to be judged good who make common cause with the worst people with zeal equal to theirs?

IEC. They say that they join with them only on the part of truth, not in the depravity of morals.

GIR. This response can indeed persuade little girls; for us it is truly frivolous and inane.

IEC. In what regard?

GIR. Furthermore, we see that those who are recognized as not dissimulatingly but truly good (whose number is hardly small) follow and defend this truth all the way to death; however, those who are manifestly evil attack it vehemently. And so, given a choice between them, which do you think ought rather to be followed?

IEC. Wherever and however I might discover the truth, I would follow it alone. For just as it makes no difference whether pure gold is extracted from mud or from Parian marble, so also the truth may be elicited however you please, because by whatever means it may have been drawn forth, it is from God.

GIR. But now attend more carefully to my words. Whatsoever I have preached and taught, it is the Gospel and the doctrine of the Church, to which I have always testified and do testify I have subjected myself; moreover, whatever seems superadded by me is some prophecy of things to come, which is contrary to no doctrine, nor can it be reproved. Therefore, the good wholeheartedly drink in this evangelical teaching and very steadfastly believe in the things prophesied for the future; however, the evil, although they do not dare to do so with words, contradict this evangelical discipline with their deeds; moreover, they inveigh against my prophecies without moderation, both in word and in deed, because it is permitted with impunity. And so, to which of these would you rather attach yourself?

IEC. As I truly confess, I would rather join myself to the good, because when something cannot be proved or refuted by any reason, one ought to yield to the judgment and authority of the man of proven quality, for, as I said before, it must be believed that the good are more genuinely and certainly illuminated by God than the evil. Therefore, since so many good people so steadfastly maintain these things, certainly this must support their opinion.

GIR. And this also: that to grow so insolently and blindly inflamed, with detractions and maledictions against those who assert and obey this teaching, as they do, is in no way characteristic of a good man, but of an evil man—not to say of the worst sort of person—since nothing against faith, against good morals, and against natural reason can be elicited from this [teaching]. From which it is clear that such persons, whether religious or whoever else, under a guise of goodness, are from the number of those no doubt lukewarm people, whom I often refute and with whom I am in constant conflict, as I prophesied many years ago, who indeed are the worst of them all. For how might one be good who with pertinacious malignity impugns a teaching so fructifying in the Church of God, as is seen daily, and joins himself to the bad and the worst?

I E C . Indeed, their iniquity is inexcusable.

G I R . These are Pharisees (believe me!), who have taken counsel with the Herodians to catch me out in what I say. For if they were sincere cultivators of justice, they could not delight in the friendship of those among whom truth is odious; such persons, nearly all magnates, ecclesiastical as well as secular, are conspicuous in this uproar, whose favor and goodwill those whom just a while ago you were calling good hunt after with all diligence and skill, for if they were to publicize the truth, which engenders hatred, they would not in any case be esteemed by those [whose favor they seek].

I E C . But many people say that they deprecate neither the evangelical teaching nor the prophecies of the things to come, but your involvement in the administration of the city, since it is written: "No one serving God involves himself in secular affairs"⁹ [II Tim. 2:4].

G I R . In this, likewise, they all too clearly reveal their chicanery and their wickedness, since they rest upon a false foundation, and this is well known: that day and night, devoting myself to the divine office, to readings, prayers, exhortations, and the writing of books, and to the instruction of my brothers, which matters demand my whole attention, I exercise no solicitude or concern for such command, and that my way of life differs from nothing more than from secular occupations, [in that] for me contemplation alone of the Sacred Scripture and the precious purchase of the Dominical¹⁰ pearl [Matt. 13:45–46] are among the supreme delights. How, then, is he good who wrongly detracts from another's reputation? since it is a good man's nature not only to speak sparingly and restrainedly about anyone's disgrace, even though it might be true and known for certain, so that he may not offend in his talk, but also not lightly to suspect something bad about his neighbor. How much more, then, will he beware of false or dubious detraction!

I E C . How can you say that you are not implicated in the administration of the city, when you have effectually preached many things pertaining to its government?

G I R . I have already cleared away this objection a thousand times before, for just as it is inhuman and impious to neglect a very great and

---

9. Inserting *Deo* for the implied *eum* referring back to *Christi Iesu* in the preceding verse.

10. No doubt a pun, the Lord's pearl being hidden in the Dominican cloister.

common good when you have the power to assist in any way, so it is also especially displeasing to God, Who commends charity above all things. And so, it was proper to propose to this wavering and endangered people, when they had just claimed liberty for themselves, useful and necessary solutions for settling matters and restraining hatred, dissension, tumults, and the impending massacre of many people along with the overturn of the entire city. Since so much good has come to pass from this work, which is not my own but divine, those who do not labor under the supreme vice of an ungrateful spirit readily acknowledge what indeed all good people publicly confess and give the highest credit to the most clement God. And unless certain ungrateful and seditious persons should confound everything—whom (as I have often forewarned), if they do not come to their senses, divine vengeance will obliterate any moment now—this city would gain even greater advantages.

IEC. To tell the truth, your reasoning proves most acceptable to me, for those whom I said a little while ago seemed good, if you know them inwardly and privily, you will find seething with pride and envy, and they, just as you have often declared, display an exterior of simulated religiosity.

GIR. Judge, then, how effective our argument is here, since the good pursue this teaching even to the consequence of death, while the evil persecute it,[11] [an effect] which is peculiar and particular to Christ's doctrine. For just as the influence of sun and air causes trees planted in earth to sprout, but dries them out when they have been uprooted, so the doctrine of Christ illuminates the well-disposed and, ripening them with an enlivening heat, brings forth good fruits, but shrivels and scorches the ill-disposed, so that they may bear no fruit at all; rather, they become more sterile and go from bad to worse; not otherwise is the teaching I have introduced, because it is Christ's.

IEC. No one can now deny that through the exposition of this teaching the good indeed have been made better, the evil, truly worse.

GIR. But let us further consider that no teaching in our times seems to have had weightier and longer-lasting adversaries and to have been torn apart by so many people, while against it (as I have often prophesied long before now) the double edge of power and malice is brandished; nevertheless, it has never succumbed amid so many insulting darts, but rather has been increased, because the more truth is assailed, the more it gathers strength, while falsehood is worn down and exhausted.

---

11. *Boni sequuntur . . . mali autem persequuntur.*

IEC. These are no insignificant nor obscure points you have added.

GIR. Believe me, the half of this plot has not been found out, which if it were known would inspire even more astonishment. For [my teaching] has contended against the shrewdness and cunning of seducers not for a few months only but has endured unconquered in the line of battle for seven whole years now completed; indeed, made more robust [in this conflict], it makes faith in my truth and reasoning more certain.

IEC. I hear, however, that many have defected from it.

GIR. And many defected from Christ. But it is of little concern, because others have risen up in their place.

IEC. Do you think that all who say that they believe do in fact think accordingly?

GIR. Not at all.

IEC. Then how can you distinguish those who speak the truth from hypocrites?

GIR. They are tested in tribulation. For in tranquil times hypocrites and lightweights and the unstable make a show of adhering to us and believing absolutely, but in time of trouble they withdraw. But truly the good "bless the Lord at all times, His praises ever in their mouths"[12] [Ps. 33:1]. Therefore, those who turned away from us were not marching faithfully, but as John the Evangelist says: "They went out from us, but they were not of us" [I Ioh. 2:19].

IEC. How, then, has this teaching increased, as you say, in tribulation?

GIR. First, the truth has been brought out more clearly into the light, while, like purest gold tested by quarrystone and by fire [cf. I Pet. 1: 7], it is neither discolored nor diminished, but has emerged brighter and stronger. Second, as the outcome of the matter has shown, it has been further roused up and strengthened in the hearts of the faithful, who, undertaking its defense like lions, have been more ignited with zeal than before. Third, because the present tribulations will increase its confirmation even more among the foreign nations, to whom report has lately reached, as well as future generations. For what moves our hearts more efficaciously to support of the Christian faith than the insuperable and wonderful patience and constancy of the martyrs in every kind of temptation and persecution?

IEC. This is certainly worthy of admiration, that, in the midst of so many adversities, neither you nor they have defected, since you, as I understand, have remained immovable in the assertion of these things, and they have inviolably persevered with you, although the matter

12. Third person plurals are substituted for David's first person singular.

would seem, in the opinion of outsiders, less to succeed than to be diminished.

GIR. At this point, then, you can understand that, unless these [teachings] were mine from God, having weighed the persecutions and perils in which I was daily engaged and am still engaged, I would have thought that I ought to look after my own interests more carefully, nor was easy access to escape wanting.

IEC. How?

GIR. Do you not know how easily I could have pleased certain magnates, if I were seeking temporal advantages? For do you not suppose that, just as with threats and persecutions, I have been tempted likewise with promises and bribes by those who try to get theirs? They leave nothing untried, who walk among great [events] and marvels beyond them.

IEC. But I pray you: if what you prophesied *had* been deficient in truth, how would you have escaped the perpetual stigma of a hypocrite and pseudo-prophet?

GIR. I would cautiously have avoided these things lest I should have fallen into snares.

IEC. How?

GIR. First, I would have committed nothing to writing, so that there would always be a means for changing and exchanging words, and I could in any case say, "I did not speak thus, nor have you fully understood." Then I would have confirmed these things none too often nor in too clear a style, but I would have spoken enigmatic and ambiguous words suitable for opportune interpretation — something which certain persons prophesying, though very imprudently, on their own account [i.e., not from God] nevertheless have watched out for, for when they perceived that their own predictions were not coming to pass, but rather tended to the contrary, turning to glosses and coverings for their shame, they excused themselves with whatever subterfuges they could.

IEC. I know whom you mean, but would that they had not put a bold face on it, so that their vanity might cause them shame and so that they might not rashly dare to slander other innocents and condemn them!

GIR. Let us pass over these things and pursue the matters with which we began.

IEC. Do you have other arguments?

GIR. This also is of significance to the matter: experience has attested how inept I would naturally have proved long since in this office of preaching, for when I had exercised this office for ten years by the command of my superiors, I was considered, not only in my own judgment but in that of all my listeners, so very unsuitable that, for example, I possessed absolutely no grace either of voice or of delivery nor a manner of gesture to please the minds of my listeners, whom I knew rather to be weighed down by boredom. But now, in fact, I do not even use the superinduced artifice of the rhetoricians or any cosmetic, but very simple and familiar words, for God is my witness that I do not plan ahead what words I may offer or what gestures or manner I may employ, but, intent only upon meaning, I am simply carried along to whatever place its urging and fervor of spirit move me. Nevertheless, a throng of people since that time even to this day has been recruited to my sermons, so that larger and more attentive crowds are seen nowhere else. And although a public orator of two or three years, by his very familiarity, as you know, usually grows to some degree weak and stale in the minds of his listeners, nevertheless, although these people have heard me for seven whole years, often repeating the same things in the manner of Sacred Scripture, they listen avidly (which is amazing!) as if I were fresh and offering new things and are pained when I desist.

IEC. Perhaps the crowd acts this way out of expectation or curiosity to hear future things from you.

GIR. On the contrary, sometimes through the whole interval of Advent and of Lent I have deliberately abstained from prophesying new things, warning my listeners that they should not expect anything extraordinary from me during that time; nevertheless, they gathered in no fewer numbers and with no less fervor.

IEC. Indeed, I have understood not only from you, but from others also who have known you, how obviously unpolished and hardly pleasing an orator you once were, as you say, while few could patiently bear with you even with difficulty; and this, since you seem changed by this new gift poured out from above, very powerfully argues that this teaching is not yours.

GIR. And so, this confirms that it is from God, not from man, for the more divine matters come to one's knowledge, because they still exceed it so much, the more they are desired, and the more they are tasted, the more they delight, in accordance with this [saying]: "Those who eat of me will still hunger, and those who drink of me will still thirst" [Sir. 24:29]. But human affairs, on account of their imperfection, make one foolish and grow worthless the more they become known and are possessed at will.

IEC. Your conversation pleases me marvelously. But lest I take up more time than is fair, with thanks for your politeness I will give place to those who remain.

GIR. Rather, it is more advantageous to complete the conversation we have begun.

IEC. Are there still other things remaining?

GIR. Indeed, a few.

IEC. Proceed. Because of their courtesy, our companions will, I know, willingly grant this short delay.

GIR. The identity of effect likewise shows that this teaching is from God, since, in the good as in the bad, it produces no other fruits than Sacred Scripture, for that which was first preached by the Apostles, then by other saints, formed in the hearts of men charity, joy, peace, patience, et cetera, which the Apostle recounts [Gal. 5:22–23], so that there was among all in the early Church one soul and one heart in God [Act. 4:32], but among the reprobate on account of their demerits it exacerbated their blindness of mind and hardness of heart. One will observe nothing different in the offspring of my teaching, for those who faithfully obey it live uprightly and, united in spirit, enjoy to the full incomparable joy and peace in the house of the Lord; on the contrary, our adversaries, because of their pride and envy and other sins, for which they do not want to be censured, become like the scribes and Pharisees and the rest of the persecutors of the saints, and, wasting away with spite, they are disturbed with perpetual unrest and pestiferous discord among themselves, in accordance with the Gospel: "And there was schism among them" [Ioh. 9: 16].

IEC. This needs no proof, since it cannot be kept secret by any evasion.

GIR. But, what makes it all worthwhile, our results so accord with Sacred Scripture that they, as though directed by the same Spirit, if they were well considered, would suffice for explanation of it, and as if those earlier teachings of the Old Testament as well as of the New were dictated and written down on purpose as a sort of sign. For even these women, as soon as I recite the Gospel or other readings from the Sacred Canon and before I can elucidate them, sense beforehand what from among those things which are immediately apparent will give counsel to us by its elucidation, and indeed they know that the ancient lessons of the Scriptures were composed and collected for these our times.

IEC. From the report of many I have heard this, not without admiration.

GIR. There are countless witnesses at hand as to how exposition of either Testament, whether by reading or by preaching, readily suits us for application to present affairs and how very similar to the acts of the prophets or of the Apostles and martyrs and other saints [the present situation] appears. For this reason, those who have listened dumbfounded are now so confirmed in their faith in this teaching that they cannot persuade themselves that it is from somewhere other than from God, for surely they do not gather grapes from thornbushes or figs from the vine? Naturally, neither of those trees will degenerate from its own proper and usual seed, but the same form will always produce the same effects. So also, the same light and the same teaching will draw forth works exactly alike. Since, therefore, these things which are just now happening and this teaching of ours completely agree with those earlier things, acts as well as writings, no one should doubt but that the same Holy Spirit works such things in us.

IEC. Some contend that the sense of the Scriptures is torn and twisted by you.

GIR. These are undoubtedly those who have not heard me. Let them hear first, and only then confer judgment. Or let them at least read my writings, where they will find no violent or oblique interpretation, nothing against faith or good morals or the teaching of the saints, and finally nothing against natural reason, but rather everything equable and sincere. For if, as they say, I twist the Scriptures, this could not be hidden in so crowded a throng of people or in a not so small assembly of very learned men, nor could deviant teaching, alien to the intention of the Holy Spirit, produce the fruits spoken of before and be thoroughly confirmed by the sayings and the remnants of the prophets and the Apostles.

IEC. You assuredly say what is true.

GIR. And finally, I will add this: since this teaching of ours has persisted for many years and does persist even to this day unshaken in the midst of so many and such great struggles, and since it has so many proofs of truth (especially in the good lives of men), and since now, diffused throughout the whole world, it has laid such foundations that it scarcely seems about to fall, if it were false, nothing more pernicious could be contrived against the Christian faith. For if God had allowed so many good men to be deceived, by the same argument all authority of the earlier Fathers would have been easily invalidated. Accordingly, it is not to be credited that God, Who was crucified for us, would have wished that such a great error as this would be should go unpunished for so long a time under such an effective covering of truth, for hereupon anyone could be rightfully afraid lest the whole faith be abolished, which is so rare in these times that it subsists in few people and with difficulty. But in truth it must rather be believed that God wished me to announce these future things, as you understand, and prove them by the sort of reasons such as I have given already, and also, as I hope, that He will daily confirm them with greater and stronger arguments, so that the faith, which is now nearly extinct, may revive. For when these prophecies have come to pass, men will understand that all things are governed by divine Providence and that future contingencies cannot be foreknown unless God, by Whose command these things are done, reveals them. For this reason He has made these things to be foretold so that it might be made known that He Himself has by no means forsaken His Church.

IEC. I am indeed completely persuaded, since you have labored so mightily to assert the faith, as your book, *On the Triumph of the Cross,* shows. And so, it is proper that there should be an abundance of disputation no less useful than agreeable for these men also. Indeed, as a challenge to every one of them, I gladly await [each] encounter in this contest.

Book Six
Speakers: Thoralmed and Girolamo

THO. So far you have explained well enough that you are certain about these things which you have prophesied not only by means of supernatural light, but also by reason and by very evident signs. I truly desire to know further whether you have also drawn understanding of them out of the Sacred Scriptures, to which I have given attention.

GIR. Whatever I know of future events has indeed shone upon me, dearest brothers, by means of that light about which we have spoken. But besides that, many things present themselves to me as if described in the Scriptures.

THO. What are those things? Go on, out with them.

GIR. The renewal of the Church and the future tribulation in the last days. Those specific things such as I have brought to attention with regard to the city of Florence and to individual persons are, of course, stated nowhere in the Sacred Scriptures, but they can, nevertheless, be thoroughly evaluated, if we carefully advert to certain signs.

THO. Indeed, all these affairs of the future are agreeable to us, but since you have assiduously preached this most important renewal, let us first have discussion regarding that.

GIR. As you wish.

THO. Then, so that we may agree in this matter, first I desire to know what you mean by this term "renewal."

GIR. Let me resolve a few things. I understand that this renewal of spirit and of the Christian life will be poured out throughout the whole world through the grace of the Holy Spirit, just as was done in the time of the Apostles.

THO. From what Scriptures do you presage such a renewal of the Church?

GIR. From many in both the Old Testament and the New.

THO. I ask you to choose one important passage, in which the proof is particularly forceful, lest, if many things were discussed, we might seem to have neglected consideration of time or of our fellows.

GIR. You have decided prudently.

THO. But now speak.

GIR. This writing concerning the Apostles is of importance: "The sound of them has gone out into every land and their words unto the ends of the earth" [Rom. 10:18]. And the Lord says in the Gospel: "This Gospel of the Kingdom will be preached throughout the whole world, as a witness to all the peoples; and then will come the consummation" [Matt. 24:14].

THO. These things have already been fulfilled through the Apostles and their successors.

GIR. If the Holy Spirit announced true things through the prophets and Christ [also announced them], either they have already come to pass in their entirety, or they will come to pass down to the last detail.

THO. I accept what you say, but these things, as I have said, have already been completed.

GIR. But I ask you rather to direct your attention to what Augustine thinks about this.

THO. I am listening.

GIR. For that exceptional teacher says:

Some suppose that this which is said, "The Gospel of the Kingdom will be preached throughout the whole world" [Matt. 24:14],
was accomplished through the Apostles, but this has not been
proved by means of sure evidence to be so, for there are in Africa
innumerable barbarian peoples, among whom the Gospel has not
yet been preached, as has been readily ascertained from those
brought thence in captivity. Nevertheless, it cannot by any means
be rightly said that the promise of God does not pertain to them,
for He has promised not only the Romans, but all peoples by His
oath to Abraham's seed. And so, among those peoples where the
Church is not yet present, she will have to be so in the future, not

so that all who are there may believe, for how will that saying be fulfilled—"You will be hated by all peoples on account of My name" [Marc. 13:13]—unless they are among all peoples and there are those who hate? Therefore, that preaching has not been completed by the apostles, since there are still peoples among whom it has not yet begun to be fulfilled. Moreover, that which the Apostle said, "the sound of them has gone out into every land" [Rom. 10:18], although he spoke in the past tense, nevertheless foretold what was to be, not what had already been done and completed, just as the same Prophet whom he used as a witness also said that the Gospel would fructify and grow throughout the whole world so that he might thereby indicate up to what point it would continue to grow. If, therefore, it is unknown when the end will be, to be sure, it will not be before [this].[13]

> And so it is clear from this that Augustine would affirm that the Scriptures of the Old and New Testaments have not yet been fulfilled, but that he would say that they certainly will be fulfilled before the end of the world.

THO. Nothing could be stated more clearly.

GIR. In the same way Origen wrote before Augustine: "When all peoples have heard the preaching of the Gospel, then will be the end of the world," and this is what follows: " 'And then will come the consummation' [Matt. 24:14]: for many, not only among the barbarians, but also among our own peoples, have not yet heard the word of Christianity."[14]

THO. From these words indeed it is obviously to be concluded that the Church will be renewed before the end of the world.

GIR. But, from the witness of the Scriptures, is not the Antichrist himself, who rages ferociously against the saints, still to come?

THO. So, I say, I understand it, although some people think that he has already come.

GIR. Whom do they assert that he is?

THO. Mohammed.

GIR. They are deceived, just as in the time of the Apostles some judged Nero to be the Antichrist, but the Scriptures concerning the Anti-

---

13. *Ep. CXCIX, to Hesychius, De fine saeculi,* chaps. 46–51, abridged, and with the opening altered.

14. *Commentary on Matthew,* PG XIII, col. 1650, 39D, though the two passages are presented in reverse order.

christ do not agree with them. For the Apostle writes to the Thes-
salonians: "Unless dissension has come first and the man of sin has
been revealed, the son of perdition, who opposes and is raised up
over all which is called God or which is worshipped, so that he
may sit in the temple of God presenting himself as if he were God";
and a little after he adds: "And then that iniquitous one will be revealed, whom the Lord Jesus will slay with the breath of His
mouth and destroy by the light of His coming, and whose coming
is, in accordance with the work of Satan in all its signs and lying
prodigies and every seduction of iniquity, to those who are lost, because they did not receive the love of truth so that they might be
saved"[15] [II Thes. 2:3–4, 8–10]. Which words, indeed, cannot apply
to Mohammed, for he did not make himself God, nor was he outstanding (as he himself testifies) in performing miracles, nor was he
slain with the breath of the mouth of Christ. Moreover, many other
Scriptures, which I omit for the sake of brevity, repudiate that
opinion.

THO. Besides, these things suffice.

GIR. Who could believe that the Antichrist, for the sake of avoiding
whose seduction there are so many great writings, has already come
and is hidden from all Christians? For his coming will not be con-
cealed, nor is it reasonable that the universal Church of the faithful,
which thinks that he is yet to come, is being deceived.

THO. Indeed, I hold this to be so.

GIR. If, therefore, we rightly believe that the Antichrist is yet to come,
Christians ought to bear witness that as a result of his coming there
will be most grievous massacres, since it is written: "Then there will
be great tribulation, such as there has never been from the beginning of the world until now nor will be, and if those days had not
been cut short, no flesh would be saved, but on account of the
elect those days will be shortened" [Matt. 24:21–22].

THO. No one can deny this.

GIR. In what part of the world do you suppose that these persecutions
from the Antichrist will chiefly be?

THO. In the Land of Promise, especially in Jerusalem, for thus we are
warned from the writings of the Canon and the saints.

GIR. You understand correctly, for thus it is also written in Daniel concerning this: "He will enter into the glorious land"—without a
doubt Jerusalem—"and many will fall to the ground. Moreover,

---

15. With *dissensio* for *discessio* ("division") and the alteration of *omni virtute et signis*
to *omnibus signis*.

only these will be saved from his hand: Edom and Moab and the princes of the sons of Ammon" [Dan. 11:41]; where blessed Jerome says: "The Antichrist will leave unharmed Idumaeans and Moabites and the sons of Ammon, that is, Arabia, because the saints will flee there to the desert."[16] What is necessary, if we agree on this, is that Christians be in those parts and, indeed, such Christians as are able either to stand against the Antichrist or to endure steadfastly those most abominable afflictions.

THO. It must be confessed that this is so.

GIR. Therefore, it follows that, with regard to the sense of the Scripture, the Church must first be extended into those parts and that, as we have said, the Gospel of the Kingdom must be preached throughout the whole world.

THO. I think it cannot be otherwise understood. But I want to know from you: how will God do these things or by what means will God convert the infidel to Himself?

GIR. If it can be conjectured from the past, I think that He will do these things through His ministers, [i.e.] preachers, sowing the seeds of the divine Word, for so God has been accustomed to do.

THO. But where, oh where, in this day and age are such patrons and heralds to be found, who would be suited to regenerating in Christ so great a multitude and good enough to pasture and govern it by word and example?

GIR. The priests and preachers of our time, with very few exceptions, seem fit more for destroying the Christian life than for building it up or preserving it.

THO. Let us not, I beg, embark upon so deep a sea, for it is shameful to call to mind their behavior, much less to speak of it, but only answer this: how, if the preachers are lacking, can the infidel be converted?

GIR. God in His own good time will provide new ones, just as He once chose the Princes of His Church from fishermen, for God is able to raise up sons of Abraham from these stones [Matt. 3:9; Luc. 3:8].

THO. How will he raise them up?

GIR. He will flood them with a heavenly light, for so He taught the Apostles through the outpouring of the Holy Spirit, as it is written: "By the Word of the Lord the heavens were made firm and by the breath of his mouth all their power" [Ps. 32:6].

THO. From what kind of people do you think that they will be taken up?

GIR. From the Christians. For from the faithful root of the Jews He se-

16. *In Danielem prophetam*, bk. III (IV: *De Antichristo in Danielem*), xi: 41b.

lected the Apostles for the regeneration of the Gentiles, for God makes all things wisely and disposes them agreeably; for that reason, since the Christians would be more apt for this task, He will elect preachers from among the flock of them.

THO. What you say is acceptable.

GIR. It is fitting, then, that by their persuasion and effort the Church may begin to be reformed and the effulgence of truth and grace be poured out first upon the Christian people, then widely among the infidel, and in this way it is necessary, according to the Scriptures, that the Church be thoroughly renewed.

THO. So, many reasons persuade and lead [one] to this conclusion. But I ask again whether you think that, just as among the Hebrew people only a few fully believed and [yet] a multitude of [other] races were converted to the faith, it will be so among the Christian people?

GIR. From these things which are now happening it is easy to understand: for just as the wickedness of the priests and Pharisees once subverted the Jews, the depravity of our priests and religious now will bring about the same thing, for, in the judgment of the saints, the worst of men such as these are incurable. These, therefore, agitated inwardly by infernal fury, will persecute those who assert divine truth and will condemn them as seducers and heretics, attempting to abrogate from them every ounce of faith among the people, as it was also done then. Accordingly, the followers of Mohammed will be more easily converted than the Christians.

THO. Let us not look afar for examples; we already see today that good men are being attacked by these people, but when they obtain both spiritual and earthly power, whereby the hearts of the righteous, dreading the stroke of either sword, are not a little stirred, I do not know how it will be that the Church can emerge by virtue and grace.

GIR. For God nothing is impossible.

THO. Regarding His power, there is no doubt, but we are searching for a means conformed to His wisdom.

GIR. In natural matters does not God preserve the order of things? Thus He always produces grapes from the vine, olives from the olive tree, although He could do otherwise.

THO. What then?

GIR. So in spiritual matters He maintains the order established from the beginning in accordance with His wisdom.

THO. But what order has been observed in them from the beginning?

GIR. In the Old Testament as well as the New, He has always renewed His Church when it has collapsed under the lash; the same thing now must be hoped for.

THO. Indeed, I believe that the Church cannot be relieved in any way unless by those men raised up from her midst. But when will these things happen?

GIR. Soon and swiftly.[17]

THO. Naturally it is this about which doubt emerges, for it seems to be clear from the Divine Scriptures that the Church will be renewed and that it will be persecuted by scourges, but what pertains to the instant of present time cannot perhaps be gathered and clearly discerned from them.

GIR. Although I asseverate this by the illumination of that same light by which I have been made more certain of other matters, nevertheless, we can in addition elicit from the Scriptures probable enough reasons.

THO. This indeed is the very thing which I long to hear.

GIR. I suppose you would agree that it is fitting that every large group of people be subject to one head, and that this government of the group which is entrusted to one person is best for it.[18] Therefore, since the government of the Church is superior to the rest, all Christian assemblies are brought under one head, just like the members of the whole body; thus, all parishes are under the authority of their priests, and cities are under their bishops, and all of these, finally, are under the pope. And so, because the principal power is assigned to this same head, it is inevitable that the good and the bad of the group depend upon it. Therefore, whenever God is angered and prepares to punish the people's crimes, He takes away the good leaders and in their places permits the evil to rule, just as in Job: "On account of the sins of the people He will make a lying prince to rule"[19] [Iob 34:30]; likewise in Osee: "I will give you a king in My anger and I will take him away in My indignation" [Osee 13:11]; and Solomon says: "Woe to you, land whose king is a child and whose princes squander the morning" [Eccles. 10:16].

THO. Of course, this shows that God is angry with the people; nevertheless, it cannot necessarily be concluded from what was said earlier that the people will be punished right away.

GIR. Yes, but if the aforesaid authorities do not perhaps suffice for proving the matter, this will, at any rate, become clearer from compari-

17. *Cito et velociter:* the watchwords of Savonarola.
18. See Savonarola's *Treatise on the Rule and Government of the City of Florence,* First Treatise, chap. 2, below.
19. Reordered and with *principem hypocritam* for *hominem hypocritam.*

son of the divine punishment of the Hebrew people to the situation in this endtime: for there was in the past a presage of an imminent and proximate scourge when good leaders, namely good princes and priests, were done away with in various places within a short time, and the evil substituted for them; here, in the fourth book of Kings, although King Sedecias, the last to rule at that time, had been established in Jerusalem, thus it is written about him: "He did evil before the Lord, like all that which Joachim had done, for the Lord grew angry against Jerusalem [. . .], until He cast them forth from before His face" [IV Reg. 24:19–20]. The fifty-second chapter of Jeremias also testifies to the same [Ier. 52:2–3], for when good protectors are lacking, who, positioned in an intermediary place between God and the people, offer an acceptable sacrifice to God for all, indeed no one remains who might withstand the anger of God. What, then, is to be expected except for it to be poured out? For this reason it is written in Ezechiel 22: "And I sought from them a man who would set up a hedge and stand opposite Me on behalf of the land, so that I might not destroy it, and I did not find one; and I poured out My indignation upon them and consumed them in the fire of My anger" [Ezech. 22:30–31]. Moreover, God's anger is all the more aroused the more openly and impudently He is sinned against, especially by those who are held in honor because of reverence for Holy Orders and who do harm to many by their deadly example, sitting in the cathedra not of doctrine but of pestilence, in which vice is extolled and venerated in place of virtue. What, moreover, should I say of our time, since the matter is so out in the open that there is no need of spies or informers? Let no one be incensed against me, who accuses no one; rather, they should complain against themselves, who want to seem the sort such as it is not possible either to speak or think of.

THO. We are well agreed at this point, for what is the use of dissembling when more crimes are heaped up before the eyes of all than can be told? For we blush to tell those things which they boast in front of everyone of doing. And so this plague has grown so strong, that this [prophecy] of Micheas is fulfilled today: "The holy man has passed away from the earth, and there is no just man among mankind," and it is added: "Whoever is the best among them is as a thorn, and whoever is upright is as a prickle from a hedge" [Micheas 7:2, 4]. Whoever does not perpetrate sins of flaming passion and robberies or certain manifest crimes is considered holy among them, since they are always and everywhere troubled with pride and ambition, and, panting after positions of high rank with the utmost anxiety, they stop at nothing for their sake, but they become dangerously wound up in all the reins of government; these I consider more wicked than the others to the same degree that a demon, inflamed and swollen with the sole crime of pride and envy, is worse than men.

GIR. If you would also hear of another sign, it would be easier to persuade you that a scourge is drawing near.

THO. Say it, whatever it is; I will listen attentively.

GIR. Every day we see the good and the just, not only priests, but also people of lower position, giving up entirely, and the depraved replacing them. Look around, I ask you, at the habits and morals of either sex, clerics as much as religious and the laity as well, and earnestly ask where you may find a lamp worthy to be placed upon a lampstand or a city set upon a mountain [Matt. 5:14–15; Marc. 4:21; Luc. 11:33]; what sign, then, could be more certainly indicative of an imminent scourge? For when God wanted to engulf the earth in a flood, He closed Noe in the ark [Gen. 7:1 ff.], and at the burning of Sodom He removed Lot from among them [Gen. 19:15–25], and so also before the Romans' siege and devastation of Jerusalem, He called forth His disciples and scattered them abroad throughout the other regions of the world; for this reason it is written in Isaias: "The just man passes away and there is no one who reflects upon it in his heart, and men of mercy are withdrawn, because there is no one who understands, for the just man has been drawn away from the face of malice" [Is. 57:1].

THO. Truly, we can lament today with the Psalmist, saying: "Save me, Lord, for the holy man has gone away, for truths disappear from the sons of men" [Ps. 11:2]. And so, as the good depart and the evil increase, malice doubtless grows stronger, and so the anger of God hastens nearer.

GIR. And this also is added to the mass of evidence, that if honest and upright men are to be found (granted, they are quite rare), not only can they not be heard, but they cannot even be tolerated; rather, they are mocked, driven out, and afflicted with persecutions, which is the final token of ruin, as the Gospel parable very beautifully declares, when the faithless vinedressers, who were supposed to hand over the harvest, killed the master's servants who had been sent to them and afterward the master's son; therefore, it justly concludes: "He will destroy the evil with evil and lease his vineyard to other gardeners," and turning to the priests, the Lord said: "Therefore, I say to you that the Kingdom of God will be taken away from you and given to a people who will produce its fruits" [Matt. 21:33–41, 43].

THO. We also see daily that those especially who enlarge their fringes and love to be first when reclining at table [Matt. 23:5–6] not only commit crimes publicly, but also are incorrigible and of such great depravity that they try to demolish good, which, like an impediment to their eyes, they are unable to endure, and, therefore, they will not allow others to live well.

GIR. If, therefore, every order of men is cast so far down into the depths of sin that no toehold for correction shows itself, why does God's no longer beneficial patience delay further? For though summoned by persistent warnings and threats and scourges, they not only stop up their ears but fall into worse sins; does this not portend a sickness next-door to death and grace utterly withdrawn and the heavy hand of the Lord? The Lord Himself says this in the sixth book of Isaias: "Go and say to this people: 'Hear, hearers, and do not understand; see what is to be seen, and do not recognize it. Make blind the heart of this people and dull its ears and shut its eyes so that it may not by chance see with its eyes and hear with its ears and understand with its heart and be converted so that I might heal it.' And I said: 'How long, Lord?' And He said: 'Until the cities are left desolate without an inhabitant and the homes without a single man'" [Is. 6:9–11].

THO. I seem to see it now, for hope does not show itself anymore, so that the Christian people may be torn asunder by inveterate depravity.

GIR. Consider furthermore that, although some good people remain (granted, they are quite rare), whose not-to-be-abandoned seed God, ever assisting His Church, will save according to this [passage]: "Behold I am with you always, even to the end of the world" [Matt. 28:20], nevertheless, they are not able to apply themselves to beseeching God to avert this scourge, but rather, at the Spirit's dictation, they long eagerly for it to be hastened, and as I have gathered from many people, who have learned likewise from others, all seem to agree in their desire for this event.

THO. I also have heard the same thing in various places, and, to reveal the desire of my own conscience, a similar ardor dwells in me, for it is better that bodies be punished than that souls be swallowed into Hell all at once and in endless numbers, since worldly peace and tranquility are the Church's ruination, in that in tribulations she always advances, for virtue is made perfect in weakness.

GIR. And so, does this not seem to you a divine inspiration? Since according to what the Apostle says: "We do not know as we ought what we should pray for, but the Spirit Himself asks for us with inexpressible groans. But the One Who scrutinizes hearts knows what the Spirit desires, because He makes petitions for the saints in accordance with God" (Rom. 8:26–27). Since, therefore, God inculcates this desire in His saints, He shows that He will surely hear them in favor of a quick vengeance for crimes.

THO. That is an important argument.

GIR. This, furthermore, argues a faith already nearly extinct, as it is written in the seventh chapter of Jeremias: "This is a people who heard not the voice of the Lord their God nor accepted instruction; faith has perished and been removed from their mouths. Cut your hair and throw it out, and take up lamentation toward heaven, because the Lord has rejected and abandoned the generation of His anger" [Ier. 7:28–29].

THO. Nor have they made clear by their works that they have at least an unformed faith, since they rush forth into every crime, detained by neither shame nor fear.

GIR. Moreover, because of the fact that all charity is utterly lacking, this has no doubt been done here and not elsewhere, seeing that their whole faith is deformed, which can be considered a sign of the end-time according to the word of the Savior concerning the end of the world: "And because iniquity has abounded,[20] the charity of many will grow cold" [Matt. 24:12].

THO. Surely their rivalries, divisions, hatreds very plainly confirm this, for the whole Church, cut to pieces, enfolds few in whom there is one spirit and one heart, since all look out for what is their own.

GIR. And so, we gather from the words of the Redeemer that the Christian establishment will not be far from destruction when He says: "Every kingdom divided against itself will be laid waste, and house will fall upon house" [Luc. 11:17]. Truly, if you add besides how much the divine and true worship has been obliterated or how much many priests today burn with thoughtless and abominable contrivances of luxury and gluttony and also with execrable avarice and the simoniac heresy as well as pride and an overabundance of offenses, you will not doubt but that the day of the Lord's wrath and vengeance is at hand. But you will marvel at His slowness, you will be astounded at the patience of His so grievously offended Majesty; and if once, when zeal for His house consumed Him, He

---

20. *Abundabit* (future) in the Vulgate.

seized cords and expelled from the Temple the buyers and sellers of those things which even so pertained to the sacrifice [Ioh. 2:14–17; also Matt. 21:12–13; Mar. 11:15–17; Luc. 19:45–46], who doubts but that at any moment now He may rush with an iron rod not only upon those simoniacs, but also upon those entangled in every kind of lust, so that, together with the foulest swarms of His servants, both men and women, they may be expelled from the Church?

THO. Indeed, I shudder just hearing these things, nor can anything truer be said; nevertheless, you will not deny that some good clerics and religious remain, repaying the worship owed to God.

GIR. I believe that they are very few. But what of moment could one or two, counted on a finger, bring to bear against such a great number of sinners? Assuredly, at this very moment, many, imitating the scribes and the Pharisees, with their prolix prayers are devouring the homes of widows, and they are "like whited sepulchers, which do indeed appear beautiful from the outside, but inside they are full of the bones of the dead and every filth"21 [Matt. 23:27]; should not lukewarm people of this sort be held to account, so much worse to others the more secretly and destructively they do harm, while, of course, they are disguised in sheep's clothing? [Matt. 7:15] These are the ones, I say, "who penetrate homes and lead the silly women captive, burdened with sins [. . .], always learning and never arriving at the knowledge of truth" [II Tim. 3:6–7].

THO. Now, truly, it is scarcely to be wondered at if they, with rabid fury and ferocious snapping, attack you especially, who strive to drag off their disguise. But, indeed, I myself have often found by experience that such lukewarm people are the cause and the flashpoint of many evils, while under the cloak of virtue they ruin wretched souls, for they are proud, envious, murmurers and detractors. What they, moreover, admit in secret, modesty does not allow me to reveal. But what need is there of numbers? For when no fear of God dwells in the heart, the magnitude of a crime is not considered, only how this false façade can conceal it.

GIR. But again consider carefully with how many great sins the Church of God boils over or how long this most evil behavior of men has endured, for from this you will judge that the scourge is now approaching. For what is missing from this heap of crimes? Do they not sin more grievously than those who perished in the inundation of the Flood on account of their fornication? Do they not exceed

21. Altered from second to third person.

the unbridled lust of the Sodomites and the perfidy of the Jews also and the Greeks, who have all now vanished, utterly destroyed? Perhaps you may say that they are not idolaters and that they have not crucified Christ (as did the Jews), but, I ask, what more execrable worship could be given to idols than the assiduous pursuit of simony and of avarice, which is slavery to idols? Because if they did not crucify Christ, it was not the will that was lacking, but the opportunity, for if at this moment He were to go to Rome in mortal guise and, just as once against the Jews, so also now against the chief priests and the evil clerics and the lukewarm religious He were to inveigh by publicly condemning vice, I ask you, what do you think? What would they plot against Him?

THO. They would devise not just one, but a thousand crosses.

GIR. Therefore, God pays attention not to the deed itself, whose execution powerlessness generally impedes, but to the will to do.

THO. Concerning yourself, Girolamo, if you were to fall under their control, what do you think they would decide [to do with you]?

GIR. Make your own guess.

THO. But indeed it would be sacrilege to conceal further the evident disgraces of the clergy, nor can we now; furthermore, the priests themselves surpass the filth of all the impious, past as well as present, in both magnitude and number, and, therefore, they are the more grievously delinquent because they, set in a position of eminence, give a ruinous example not only to the Christian people, but also to the whole world. Accordingly, the other princes subvert and confound everything; thus justice has utterly perished, while they assert that evil is good and good is evil.

GIR. And so, if divine justice exacted the merited punishment so many times from the Jews, if it completely overturned many kingdoms and empires for this reason, if with the Eastern Church it destroyed the Greeks, if it has also laid waste the Roman Church many times through the Goths, the Lombards, the Vandals, and other barbarian nations, will it now spare these utterly wicked people? Or is God not the same? His power not impartial? His examination of merits and demerits not the same? Does not the same Church flourish under His special care?

THO. There is no one sound in mental judgment who, in a case so manifestly meriting divine revenge, can now have any doubt regarding this impending scourge, for everyone now believes that it is not far off, and many also desire it.

GIR. For this very reason your faith surely ought to be made secure, for, in the well-known proverb, "The voice of the people is the voice of

God."[22] As if we ourselves have not seen the beginning of great
evils! For, after the speedy course of the king of France through Italy, has everything not been disturbed by a certain commotion? Nation has risen up against nation and people against people; hence
pestilence and famine have leapt in upon us. What else should we
consider these things but the beginning of sorrows? What more is
required? Or do you demand signs and portents from heaven? You
will learn that not even these things have been wanting, if the many
signs and prodigies performed in various places at this time were to
be considered, but the dumbstruck mind understands nothing of
these things. For the sinner, as Solomon says, "when he has fallen
to the depths of sin, is defiant" [Prov. 18:3].

THO. All these things, as you say, are well known; nevertheless, no one,
even if he thinks about them, comes to his senses; no one goes
back from the path which leads to the precipice; no one even
shows any indication of penitence. It is a shame, I say, and a crime
now to turn aside from evil; good is an object of ridicule and reproach.

GIR. Does it not seem to you, then, that during this time of the rod of
fury and the outstretched arm the Church will be snatched away?

THO. I am now persuaded enough and more than enough of such a
thing. But you have prophesied many other things about the affliction of the city of Florence and about her felicity besides, which
cannot be proved through the Scriptures.

GIR. I would not say that these things are plainly signified in the Scriptures, but if these things which have most recently been done in
this place were to be considered, one will find much of account and
probability.

THO. Explain this to us.

GIR. First, since many of the things I have already predicted in my
prophecies have come to pass, they make faith in future [predic-
tions] also not doubtful. Furthermore, since this city itself has been
especially decreed to receive the seed of this divine word in order to
propagate it throughout the world, I do not doubt that it is loved
by God more especially than other [cities], for which evident signs
of love correspond to it; the tremendous light of faith and of evangelical doctrine, of course, which shines even in women and chil- ·
dren; delight in and zeal for the simple and true Christian life also

22. The "well-known proverb" is cited by Alcuin in a letter to Charlemagne, *Ep. 127;*
Alcuin, however, advises against giving ear to the "voice of the people," since
"the uproar of the rabble is next-door to madness."

flourishes in many; likewise, although no other city has more fully embraced religion and penitence for sins, nevertheless, no other is to be found which has patiently endured harsher calamities in these times or has sustained more attacks from its enemies, from which it has been rescued not by human strength or industry, but by divine miracle only, when many of the nobility aspired to tyranny and tried to subject this city to themselves while it was involved in intestine and external dangers nearly to the point of extermination. On their heads, for the most part (as I have often forewarned), the undermined wall has collapsed. From these events we detect that the city is protected by the privilege of divine love, because God, repeatedly trying the good through patience in adversity, yet in no way allowing them to be overwhelmed, makes them stronger and better, but, because this is the reward for such work, in this same city good and righteous men suffer many persecutions from the dissolute and the impious (for often the unfruitful weed is mixed in with the crops [Matt. 13:24–30, 37–43]), and they bear them not only patiently but even joyfully. The good, therefore, religious as well as secular, steadfastly attend to my prophecies and look purposefully ahead. Will God permit them, then, to be deceived who constantly ask this from Him not for their own sake, but for the sake of His honor and for the salvation of souls? Moreover, the impious and profane citizens attempting to demolish the holy things and the fatherland, will they—I ask you—be granted their wishes? Will the good and upright in heart be in the end defrauded of their desire?

THO. May it not be so.

GIR. There are many other particulars also, which are not without their own reasons. But lest my speaking exceed the limit of agreeable time, this, as the chief point, must suffice: that since many earlier things have come to pass and I have not been deceived so far, from a like argument, the rest will also follow. But all the reasons explained above agree with this point and, together with the outcomes of these events, show that this teaching is from God.

THO. I think we have left nothing undiscussed, and I offer you the greatest thanks, my Girolamo.

GIR. But let us rather give thanks to God, Who has given us the best of everything.

Book Seven
Speakers: Abbacuc and Girolamo

ABB. Not without great pleasure have I heard these things which you have pursued so far among yourselves in energetic disputation. But lest we leave any point untouched, it causes me some amazement that many people bitterly inveigh against you and your teaching in writing as well as in preaching.

GIR. We contemn their invective as easily as we confute it, and hence our [teachings] are made stronger, since the knowledge of truth is the solution of objections.[23]

ABB. And yet I have heard that the objections of your adversaries against you have often not been solvable for those who take up your side.

GIR. If they were wise in the truth itself, they would solve everything very easily, for even women and children accustomed to my preaching refute the objections against me of the wise men of this age in the same way that one might tear a slender thread or a spider's web.

ABB. I think it would be difficult for the inexperienced and the simple to stand against the learned and the clever.

GIR. It is easy to defend the truth, especially that which is from God and which is believed and understood through the illumination of faith and grace together with rectitude of life, first, because God, Who is the First Truth, aids and protects truth; then, because truth is stronger than falsehood; finally, because the intellect by its very nature is inclined toward truth, all truths further support it; add that, once darkness has been scattered, grace and faith illuminate it; besides, rectitude of life deservedly claims such authority for itself; indeed, even while a truth proposed to the minds of listeners is being disputed, it will readily sink in. Furthermore, its adversaries are usually hated by others on account of their blameworthiness of life; therefore, less trust is commonly accorded to them; even in a prepared speech they exert themselves not without a certain perturbation of spirit, and with a covering of words they lay bare the mark of their own confusion. Finally, the more truth is attacked, the more clearly it shines forth; falsehood, on the contrary, is besmirched; therefore, for those who live uprightly, defense of truth is easy.

ABB. I fully approve what you say, and I now perceive that, wherever the defense of these affairs of yours is weakly upheld by anyone, it ought to be imputed not to the difficulty of the truth itself, but to their own ignorance.

23. Aristotle, *Metaphysics* III(; ds).i.2 (995a, ll. 28–32).

GIR. But I should like you to acknowledge this as a last resort: I have not placed this among the principal points against my adversaries, even though they certainly, however expert and subtle they may be, are very easily overcome by those who hear me and live uprightly.

ABB. But surely if the matter is as you say, it is not a trivial but a very powerful indication of truth.

GIR. The matter is now carried on so publicly, that there can be no doubt about it, and, in fact, in this city one can see daily disputes and conflicts because of this, in which so many confused, ridiculous, and false things are put forward by my adversaries, that many are forced to blush in shame at their own complicity.

ABB. It is amazing that among so many objections some true ones do not stand out.

GIR. Rather, the great inconsistency in their words and the dissonance among them convicts them of falsehood, since some call me good but simple and captive to mental delusion, and others call me cunning and a seducer, and there are as many opinions about me as there are heads [to form them]. But those in agreement with me conduct themselves otherwise, for, unanimous and like-minded, they asseverate and maintain the same thing together.

ABB. It is scarcely credible that, although you are being attacked with so many accusations, you, though contradicted, are convicted of none, and that those others maligning you, especially religious, are constantly lying.

GIR. There is an ancient proverb: "Whoever has once been evil is always presumed to be evil." Accordingly, my detractors have been repeatedly found to be frivolous and evil; for countless times, by fabricating many lies, they have incited a tumult among the people, but again and again, confounded by emerging truth, they have melted away; they, however, deterred by no shame, have prepared yet again to fabricate new lies, but the truth has always overcome them nonetheless. And so, who would think that trust should rightly be granted to such people?

ABB. Rumor has it that letters and books, erudite, indeed, but defamatory, have been written against you.

GIR. I have not heard from anyone, I say, that it was done by a learned man; indeed, I have seen writings worthy of contempt by certain people who are "learned" only to themselves; for this reason, my truth is more strongly confirmed.

ABB. How?

GIR. For very knowledgeable men in whom is the spirit of God would not be able to pass over in silence false teaching preached to the people, nor to put up with it, for what has been quoted from the mouth of one, namely, "zeal for Your house consumes me" [Ps. 68: 10; Ioh. 2:17], pertains equally to all. And so, if I were to seduce people by false preaching, all would rise up against me, not secretly, indeed, but openly, and my errors, accordingly produced in public and confuted, they would eliminate from the Church by sanctions and by everlasting proscriptions, which has not been done nor can it rightly be done. If, however, they are not moved by the breath of God but, clinging to this world, are swollen up with windy[24] knowledge, since doubtless they are eager for princes and great men to applaud them and strive mightily to show off their own teachings, they surely, both for the sake of the adulation of certain powerful people, who hate me for no particular reason and persecute me, and so that they might seem to be led by zeal for God, would already have burnt the midnight oil to compose volumes of rebuttals against me, if only they could find anything of truth and of substance against me. But we see this has not yet been done, because truth defends me and the good and the just agree with me; indeed, they are likewise fighting for the sake of this same truth. Others, crafty and sly, spew out in snarling words what they do not dare commit to paper, lest what has been written, which does not, like words, pass away, betray the insipience and malignity of the author, for they see that they will bring back no praise, but much shame from what they have written, should they publish it.

ABB. Nevertheless, many skillfully produced [works], as I have heard, are being circulated against you.

GIR. Certain people, deceived by the arrogance of learning, who are pleasing themselves in their own estimation more than anyone else, have dared to write against me, however with name withheld, which is a sign of their too-little trust in their own conscience, for since they were not ignorant that they were attacking truth, they did not wish to show themselves in the light, for whoever acts evilly hates the light; naturally, no one labors to hammer out an extraordinary work under a secret or strange title, and so it has turned out none too happily for them. But among those who have written under their own names, the works used against me have divulged their

---

24. *Sin autem spiritu Dei non aguntur sed ventosa tument scientia* . . . A subtle wordplay is at work here: *spiritu Dei,* the "breath of God," is, of course, the "Spirit of God," Who blows into or inspires the holy; *ventosa,* in contrast, is simply empty wind.

own ignorance and temerity, so that it would not be proper to trouble ourselves to refute them.

ABB. But a certain Samuel, a man who (so it is said) is not ignorant, seems to have entered the field in open combat with a book published against your revelations.[25]

GIR. If you have perused his book carefully, you will easily understand that this person did not study to seem learned so much as refined; however, he has achieved neither, for he has proceeded so absurdly that he deserves to be laughed at rather than confuted, and yet, Giovanni Francesco Pico, Count of Mirandola,[26] ornamenting his illustrious race with piety and learning, following in the footsteps of his uncle Giovanni Pico,[27] who in genius and learning excelled above even the most famous men of his age as much as the cypress does the pliant viburnum, has written brilliantly against him.[28] In confutation of the others, the venerable priest Domenico Benivieni has advanced his pen,[29] assuredly a most religious man and second

25. Samuele Cassinens de Cassinis, *Invectiva in prophetiam fratris Hieronymi* (Milan, 1497); presumably the same Samuele de Cassinis, a Franciscan, who, ten years later, issued a series of pamphlets arguing against the persecution of witches. See Carlo Ginzburg, *The Night Battles: Witchcraft and Agrarian Cults in the Sixteenth and Seventeenth Centuries* (New York: Penguin, 1985), p. 194, n. 10. Though this identification was independently noted, it is also made by Lorenzo Polizzotto, *The Elect Nation: The Savonarolan Movement in Florence, 1494–1545* (Oxford: Clarendon Press, 1994), p. 79, n. 86.

26. Giovanfrancesco (1469–?) was one of Savonarola's most illustrious and loyal adherents, devoting his writing talents to the Piagnone cause throughout his life. His was one of the first biographies of Savonarola. His career—and those of all the following contributors to Savonarola's defense in the ongoing pamphlet wars—is detailed in Donald Weinstein, *Savonarola and Florence: Prophecy and Patriotism in the Renaissance* (Princeton: Princeton University Press, 1970), pp. 220–226 and passim; Polizzotto, *Elect Nation*, pp. 81, 89–91, 98–99, 146–149, 162–167, 324–328, and passim; see also Alison Brown, "Ideology and Faction in Savonarolan Florence," in *The World of Savonarola: Italian Elites and Perceptions of Crisis*, ed. Stella Fletcher and Christine Shaw (Aldershot: Ashgate, 2000), pp. 22–41, esp. 34–39.

27. Count of Mirandola (1463–1494); he was an outstanding philosopher, most renowned for his nine hundred *Conclusions* (1486), in which he sought to reconcile all the major philosophies and religions known to him, and for the introduction to this work, now known as the "Oration on the Dignity of Man." A great favorite among the Laurentian circle, he persuaded Lorenzo to recall Savonarola to Florence. Though he disagreed with Ficino on the subject of astrology, he found his own esoteric outlet in the Jewish Kabbalah.

28. *Defensio Hieronymi Savonarolae adversus Samuelem Cassinensem* (Florence, 1497).

29. *Trattato . . . in defensione e probazione della dottrina e profezie predicate da frate Ieron-*

to none in erudition in philosophy and sacred theology. Many others besides, inflamed with zeal for this truth, reproach the garrulity and petulance of the slanderers; among the former that most learned man from far-off Ragusa in Illyria,[30] Giorgio Benigno [Salviati], of the Minorite profession [i.e., a Franciscan], who is numbered among the foremost philosophers and theologians of our age, has been stirred by report alone and by my publications to write a dialogue in confirmation of my teaching because of his zeal for truth.[31]

ABB. Are there, perhaps, any others?

GIR. I could enumerate for you many more theologians and natural philosophers and men of letters, such as Giovanni Nesi, a refined writer (as his little book proves),[32] whom I deliberately pass over, lest I seem now to enter into the custom of flattery in returning favors and to entice others into my favor by equal emulation; therefore, let it be enough to have cited from among the many, one religious of no mean reputation, one priest of extraordinary life and teaching, and one secular but a very rare nobleman with respect to doctrine and morals, so that you might have in these three ranks of Christians those whom you can compare with his own kind and with anyone whomsoever.

ABB. What if perhaps some very learned men (whom we do not know) have sharpened the pen against you? For many of them have very gravely taxed you from their pulpits with various abuses.

---

imo da Ferrara (Florence, 1496); *Epistola responsiva a certe obiezioni e calunnie contro a frate Ieronimo da Ferrara* (Florence, 1496). Domenico (1460–?), canon of San Lorenzo, friend of Ficino and Pico, was the brother of Girolamo Benivieni, author of the Piagnone laude included in this volume. See Polizzotto, *Elect Nation,* pp. 68–75, 85–86, 108–117, and passim.

30. Dubrovnik, in present-day Croatia.

31. *Propheticae solutiones* (Florence, 1497). Benigno had been exiled from Florence to his native land (present-day Croatia) because of his close association with the Medici (Polizzotto, *Elect Nation,* p. 80). He is paired by Guicciardini with Ficino and Pico della Mirandola as a leading light of philosophy in Laurentian Florence (Francesco Guicciardini, *History of Florence,* ed. and trans. Mario Domandi [New York: Harper, 1970], p. 72; referenced by Polizzotto, ibid.). He later defended, and exonerated, Savonarola's writings from charges of heresy before the Fifth Lateran Council (1516). In Polizzotto see also pp. 80–81, 204–205, 249, 302, and passim.

32. *Oraculum de novo saeculo* (Florence, 1497). Nesi (1456–?) was an associate of Ficino who sought to reconcile Ficinian Neoplatonism with a Savonarolan-inspired mysticism. See Weinstein, *Savonarola,* pp. 192–205 and passim; and Polizzotto, *Elect Nation,* pp. 86–87, 102–108, and passim.

GIR. Those who commit to the winds harsh but quickly perishable words against me have published no writings to be examined as I have done, for these learned men dread to entrust to paper what they despair of being able to sustain; and they, unless they are insane, will not dare to oppose themselves to what we have said.

ABB. Why?

GIR. I have preached two things chiefly, if you consider them correctly, which are: the Christian faith and life and every proof for the Holy Roman Church, along with the future renewal of the Church. Will those who are truly wise publicly protest against Catholic doctrine?

ABB. Not at all, for they will fear either God or the fire.

GIR. Will they contend that prophecies of things to come are false?

ABB. Perhaps they will attempt this.

GIR. Do not believe it.

ABB. Why?

GIR. If they were learned, they would know that these things cannot be proved nor disproved by natural reasoning; therefore, if they take upon themselves this business of attacking, first they show themselves to be ignorant and inexperienced, then they fall into that error which they condemn, since they, confuting prophecies, would indicate that they themselves are prophets.

ABB. In what way?

GIR. Does a prophet not foretell the future resulting from some contingency?

ABB. Absolutely.

GIR. Is the verdict not the same regarding either of the two contradictories in future contingencies, which is that neither of them, in the opinion of the philosophers, is conclusively true?

ABB. Yes, I agree.

GIR. Therefore, if I prophesy the future renewal of the Church and the scourges [to come], but another asseverates the opposite, do we not both set ourselves up as prophets?

ABB. Certainly, both do.

GIR. You see, whoever contradicts a prophet's predictions makes himself a prophet.

ABB. However, they would in no way assert that they are prophets if they presume neither to deny nor to affirm the uncertain outcome of future events, but it is because you boast that these things are divinely revealed that they mock you so much.

GIR. Certainly, if they deny that they are prophets, they prove that they are at least audacious and impious.

ABB. What are you saying, please?

GIR. This: if, as I have repeatedly mentioned, I have put forth nothing impossible, nothing foreign to God, nothing jarring against faith and reason, nothing inconsistent with morals and the circumstances of the times, then either they are making themselves scrutinizers of hearts and of the Divine Majesty, audaciously and insolently passing judgment regarding another's secrets, since they deny that these things have been revealed by God (which is possible), or, in their contempt for my revelation, they believe that the oracles of the ancient prophets are empty, professing one thing with their mouths, another in their hearts, while they deride [the idea] that these things are in any way possible, things which were watched for among the prophets and promised to their posterity through them.

ABB. Doubtless, one must admit this. But when nothing else remains of which they may accuse you, they say that you have predicted that certain things will come about at a certain time, which will become invalid from that time.

GIR. I have prophesied nothing verbally with regard to the future that I have not committed almost entirely to writing; therefore, this must be established not from the fictions of my adversaries, but from the exemplars themselves, in which no one will be able to discover anything false.

ABB. But they will say that you have written one thing, but publicly announced something else.

GIR. There are innumerable witnesses who remember very well that they have heard [spoken] exactly the same sort of things as have been written; and since they are very prudent and honest men, if they had even once detected that I was lying or duplicitous, at that point I would have utterly slipped from their hearts, and I would have been publicly pilloried for the lie ever after. But my writings, published everywhere, have passed through fire and water, believe me, and those who have heard me as well as those who have not, men most learned and well trained, both here and at Rome and elsewhere, have very diligently pondered them; on top of that, so many very powerful adversaries are setting snares for my steps, that if even the least little error had been established, they would have imputed it to me as the greatest.

ABB. But when they fulminated a sentence of excommunication against you, did they act so very impudently in order to allege absolutely no cause?

GIR. Indeed, they allege many causes, but they are manifestly false.

ABB. If this calumny and injury are so public, why does the Pope not notice it?

GIR. The bishops and cardinals, exiled in a way within the inner courts, although they have an abundance of every other thing, are destitute of that sole truth which is more precious than any treasure; affluent in the rest, in this they are indeed beggars.

ABB. What is the cause of so great a lack?

GIR. Do you not know that they have been surrounded on all sides by yes-men and flatterers, by whom the entranceway to truth is closed off? And if at any time [truth] should finally barely penetrate to a cardinal, it is immediately butchered like an enemy and dismembered, or it is secretly strangled with a noose or poison.

ABB. This, then, is a wretched class of men, for what is more wretched than to be without truth?

GIR. Yes, if they do not take great care and are not especially supported by divine assistance, both for this reason and many others which it would be too prolix to recount, they are the most wretched class.

ABB. Nonetheless, they seem happy.

GIR. To those who gaze bleary-eyed or with rose-colored spectacles, but it does not appear so to the purified.

ABB. Let us return to the matter at hand.

GIR. Accordingly, I have said that it would not be difficult to suggest falsehoods to the Pope.

ABB. But "the judgment of a pastor, just or unjust, ought to be feared."[33]

GIR. This is a very familiar and frequent[ly cited] authority, although many others of no less approbation say that an unjust excommunication does not need to be feared;[34] nevertheless, no one readily calls those [authorities] to mind. In my opinion this one, because it is willingly heard, is often trotted out in order to flatter prelates; however, it is necessary to bring up those contrary ones to restrain them. But I have already answered these and other objections very often; besides, many good and learned men have made it clear in

33. *Pastoris sententia, iusta vel iniusta, timenda est;* Gregory the Great, *Homilia XXVI in Evang.,* quoted by Aquinas in his *Summa,* suppl., quest. 21, art. 4. More accurately: *Sed utrum juste an injuste obliget pastor, pastoris tamen sententia gregi timenda ęst (PL* 76, col. 1201; i.e., "But whether the pastor binds [one] justly or unjustly, the judgment of a pastor ought to be feared by his flock"). The "common dictum," as given by Jean Gerson, whom Savonarola quotes at length in his Open *Letter against the Recently Imposed Sentence of Excommunication,* is *Sententia praelati, vel iudicis, etiam iniusta, timenda est* ("The judgment of a prelate or judge, even if unjust, is to be feared"); see at page 304, note 18, below. See also Exodus, Sermon III, at page 317, note 4, below.

34. See Savonarola's letter against his excommunication, below, in which he relies most heavily on the opinions of Jean Gerson.

their writings that this excommunication is null, and, since these [works] are extant, it is not necessary to repeat them.

ABB. I ask you, are you touched sometimes by some prick of conscience?

GIR. Certainly not.

ABB. Do you sometimes doubt whether this [sentence of excommunication] ought to be obeyed?

GIR. The one who has been deemed worthy to reveal the future to me has also taught me that this should be neither obeyed nor feared.

ABB. This, as it happens, is unknown to others; therefore, for the sake of avoiding scandal, it would seem safer to obey it.

GIR. I ask you, surely you are not unaware that for many years now past I have predicted that such sentences would be imposed against me and that I would have to struggle against a duplicitous power?

ABB. So it has been reported both in your writings and in the talk of the whole populace.

GIR. Do you think that the Holy Spirit, Who advised me of these things in advance and trained me for such a struggle, would want His words to be received in this sense, so that I would evidently be fighting impiously against the just punishment of the spiritual sword?

ABB. By no means. For God is just; He cannot deny Himself.

GIR. Therefore, if God Himself, alone prescient of future contingencies and their Governor, wanted them to be foretold in this way and permitted it to be done, as the outcome of affairs very plainly demonstrates every day down to the smallest detail, no one ought to marvel or be disturbed if I neither obey nor dread this sentence, which I have shown not obscurely through my letters to be invalid.

ABB. Nevertheless, many men of exacting conscience, and your friends, even after hearing and reading your reasons, do not agree.

GIR. Friend, believe me that the time approaches and is yet to come, in which God will make manifest what is hidden in hearts and in darkness [I Cor. 4:5].

ABB. I do not understand these words sufficiently.

GIR. Some people used to pretend to believe me; some, in fact, were led by their opinions formed from conjectures about the things which were happening rather than by faith; but others, walking righteously before God and doubtless illuminated by His effulgence, did believe and persevere in the faith up to this day. And so, tribulation has laid open the hearts of all these, which in tranquil and propitious times were unknown.

ABB. How was this done?

GIR. Those who were feigning belief, of course, when they supposed that

I had been crushed by ill treatment, heaping obloquy upon me, defected at once to my adversaries; those who were actually driven by opinion, not by effective arguments, wavered with unsteady purpose; but these whose faith derives from on high, who, as the Apostle says, "according to [His] purpose have been called [to be] holy" [Rom. 8:28], remain steady and do not deviate from the truth even for a moment. And so, if adverse times had not agitated us, the unexplored hearts of many would have remained hidden.

ABB. Then those who fear this sentence do not truly believe.

GIR. Who doubts this?

ABB. The sort of people who would follow a safer path think that it must be obeyed, for what harm could or can its observance do?

GIR. Much.

ABB. An abundance of caution does no harm.

GIR. This is to abound not in caution, but in fatuous and ignorant superstition.

ABB. You would say that humbly obeying and submitting to the Pope is folly?

GIR. This would be no true but only an asinine humility under so unjust a burden.

ABB. For what reason?

GIR. But why do I conceal it any longer? Why do I hesitate? Why do I not say those things which are public and known to all?

ABB. Speak boldly: what do you fear under the protection of truth?

GIR. Tell me, I pray: what would follow from this humility and obedience?

ABB. I do not know.

GIR. Do you not know by whom this excommunication has been perpetrated and procured?

ABB. It is well known.

GIR. What, then, were they seeking from such obedience?

ABB. Away with you! say no more! I take your meaning, for the Pharisees had convened with the Herodians, as has been discovered, and had joined counsel to entangle you in their snares and to subvert divine and human affairs, but many of them fell into the pit which they had made [Prov. 26:27].

GIR. Therefore, if they were devising such things, should that sentence have been obeyed, resulting in such a great crisis in affairs and an evil outcome?

ABB. Certainly, it is no shame for me, now convinced by a better argument, to revoke bad advice, for you would have sinned grievously by obeying an unjust command, and since God has committed this burden to your shoulders, if, shaking it off, you were to dash it to the ground and shatter it, you would be the one responsible for an inexcusable crime.

GIR. Now you are headed in the right direction, for it is more fitting to obey God than men.

ABB. So do you want the truth? In these things we are deceived because we want to be deceived: there is no one, certainly, who does not recognize this injustice; nevertheless, some say that you have been justly interdicted because you did not want to unite the Congregation of your brothers to the other Tuscan Congregation.

GIR. One who wishes to desert a friend looks out for an occasion, for these Pharisees, finding no artful cause for a *just* interdict, at any rate, devised a certain trick in the new reformation of the other convents in Tuscany; while they, with great solicitude, pretended to desire to organize them properly under our discipline, they were studying how to insert these, as it were, defiled sheep into our flock, so that in this way either they might gradually introduce the plague of dissension and the venom of discord into the corrupted sheepfold and rend our sheep, or, when they saw that we utterly opposed this secret fraud (although they had already persuaded themselves of it), they would seem to have just provocation for hurling the thunderbolt. O Pharisees, you who always laid snares for Christ, who would not conclude that there is not even the tiniest bit of concern in you for reforming religion? Your life and your morals proclaim it, to be sure—what zeal for the house of God so suddenly consumes you? [Ps. 68:10; Ioh. 2:17] Or, rather, do not ambition, lust, and avarice burn you up? Would such a reformation seem good to you, friend?

ABB. On the contrary, it would be the worst *de*formation! But what have you answered them?

GIR. First, I have shown by multiple arguments that such a reformation would be irrational and impossible, as one can see in a certain little book published on this matter,[35] and because these arguments cannot be invalidated, they pretend, with exasperated indignation of mind, to disregard them. Besides, I have made it clear that what they seek is not in my power, but even if it were, because it is against God, I should not so much not *want* to carry it out as I *ought* not to.

ABB. Why do you say that this is not in your power?

GIR. Because the brothers dread it and reject it unanimously.

---

35. Savonarola, *Apologeticum fratrum Congregationis Sancti Marci* (Florence, 1497).

ABB. They must certainly be commended.

GIR. Commended, I say, and encouraged. But, briefly, so that you may better understand their every deception, there is nothing which offends our adversaries more than the mutual love, harmony, and charity of our brothers, because, these being present, it is impossible for them to gain control by their machinations against us; therefore, they have pried into every entrance by which they might introduce discord among them, but, when they have found them unshaken and steadfast in charity, turning to other arts, they have attempted to mingle goats with the sheep, so that once this mix-up had been made they might draw the sheep away together and scatter them in various places and thus finally gain possession of what they desired. But divine justice cannot give protection to crimes.

ABB. Oh, how well you have laid bare these hidden deceptions! And now I know truly that only the hand of God could have freed you from so many snares, nor, in fact, are you liable to any excommunication, but whoever with you honors truth ought to spurn human judgment when it violates divine precept.

GIR. You also have spoken very well.

ABB. I do not know what more could be desired beyond this. But in the last place this our most agreeable and noble elder remains, yearning wholeheartedly, as I see, with the desire to address you; his gray hair will perhaps draw from his breast something profound.

GIR. Let him proceed, for by his asking and my responding there will be mutual and shared delight.

Book Eight
Speakers: Saphtam and Girolamo

[Saphtam, eldest of the sages, summarizes the proofs Girolamo has adduced thus far: first, the divinely infused light he feels within himself; then, his rectitude of mind, the broadening of his intellect, and the deepening of his understanding of Scripture and spiritual life, all of which have enflamed his desire for God and zeal for good works; next, his own perseverance through great trials and the increase in piety of his disciples; and finally, the conformity of his teachings with Scripture and all things rational. All of these reasons persuade him of Girolamo's genuine prophetic gift; nonetheless, he asks to hear a simpler argument which he, in his limited capacity, might use to persuade others.

Under Girolamo's tutelage, Saphtam reasons that in judging the truth of what one hears one should believe neither everything nor nothing. Some things are more, some less worthy of belief. Among things worthy of belief are those which, to believe, are never harmful, but rather always beneficial, such as the Christian faith, which would tend to be beneficial even if it were not a religion. Some things it is better not to believe without proof, such as disparagement of one's neighbor, and some things are neither here nor there. In which category, Girolamo queries, would Saphtam place his prophecies? In the beneficial class, he replies, because of the good effects they have on those who follow his instructions, and because of the negativity of his detractors.

Second, Girolamo argues that upright living is the surest way to detect devilish deceptions, for God supplies greater grace to the just than to the unjust. Thus, were he a tool of the devil, he would be subverting his own aims with his strict moral teaching by providing his supposed dupes with the instruments for his own undoing.

Finally, in response to Girolamo's further questioning, Saphtam opines that a benefit, though wrapped in deception, would not give cause for condemning one's benefactor. A father who motivates his son to live uprightly by making him false promises of future wealth would nonetheless be worthy of his son's gratitude. All the more, then, Girolamo adds, ought a benefit conveyed with pure truth to be appreciated by those receiving it. Even were his prophecies fictitious, which they are not, they should not be condemned, because they persuade those who believe to live according to the Gospel. Because they might be from God (in that they agree with Christian doctrine), those who oppose them oppose themselves to God. If they remain in doubt, it would still be better to withhold judgment and leave the matter in God's hands.]

SAP. You certainly speak very wisely, nor is it right to doubt any further, much less to struggle or debate against [you].

GIR. And so, why do I suffer so many persecutions?

SAP. Because you are a servant of Christ.

GIR. I rejoice to suffer contumely and death for the sake of His name.

SAP. Blessed are you; it will be well for you.

GIR. Does anything else remain to be inquired into?

SAP. Indeed, I judge anyone who does not acquiesce in and believe these words to be either thoroughly obtuse or of very evil mind and diabolical obstinacy. But now the hour interrupts us, for while this most agreeable conversation has been prolonged, we have given no thought to the fleeting hours. And so, since enough has been said, we rightly end our disputation; be assured that we will be ever mindful of you and most loving toward you; moreover, if we can do anything [for you], we willingly offer to do it. Then, if it seems right to you, my companions, let us swiftly turn aside to the peak of that mountain, where that little cottage is visible.

Book Nine
Speakers: Girolamo and all the other interlocutors

GIR. Wait! wait! Most excellent fathers, why do you not fulfill your promises before you leave?

VRI. What promises?

GIR. Did you not promise at the beginning that you would tell me where you came from and the reason for your coming?

VRI. Do you still not recognize us?

GIR. Indeed, I do not know you at all.

VRI. We are the Seven Gifts of the Holy Spirit.

GIR. What? What am I hearing? I look at you and see mortal human likenesses, not gifts of the Holy Spirit.

VRI. This is the lot of humankind, to espy invisible things through things which are visible.

GIR. And so, you are signs of charisms, not men.

VRI. We confess it.

GIR. How could this be permitted? since the Holy Spirit can neither lie nor be ignorant of anything, but in the foregoing disputation, you questioned me, as though ignorant of many things and uncertain about the truth, and made many objections, which, in my judgment, are not appropriate to the Holy Spirit.

VRI. Do you not know that three men stood by Abraham at the entrance to his tent in the Mamre valley [Gen. 18:1–2] and that a stranger ap-

peared to the two disciples on the road to Emmaus, discussing
many things and pretending to go along with them? [Luc. 24:13 ff.]
And so we, on the point of reprehending the hardness of heart of
unbelievers, assumed the guise of explorers, to which our speech
likewise had to be accommodated; for this reason, we said that we
are from the East, that is, whence the Light arises "which enlightens
everyone coming into this world" [Ioh. 1:9], and that we were descended from the most ancient lineage, as being from the bosom of
the Eternal Father, retaining in our names the antiquity of the primeval language.

GIR. O most merciful God, how manifold the ways by which You draw
the minds of mortals to Yourself! How secretly and invisibly You often slip among them! How near You frequently approach, when You
are yet thought to be far away! Nor, truly, is it any wonder now if
you seven have appeared for the same number of charisms; hence
this joy was suddenly conceived in me, hence my spirit was scintil-
lating, set aflame by divine ardor, and though outwardly it had not
yet recognized the good, inwardly, melting with sweetness, it was
tasting it.[36]

VRI. Furthermore, if you consider the first letters of our names, you will
uncover the mystery.

GIR. So it is, for from the sum of them VERITAS [i.e., truth] resounds,
which you have come to make known not because of my merit
but by reason of the immense bounty of God. But I beseech you
likewise to deign to disclose the rationale of your [individual]
names.

VRI. I am the gift of understanding, by which supernatural things are
perceived to a certain degree; hence it is that when you were saying
that you are made certain by reason of supernatural light, I occupied
the chief part in the conversation so that I might more amply enlighten you for the sake of [your] greater assurance, which the name
assumed by me, "Vrias," correctly interpreted, makes clear, that is,
"My light of God," or "Lamp of the Lord," by which you were as-
serting that you are irradiated and made certain.

GIR. Now I certainly know that the Lord is with me, Whom I shall bless
at all times.

36. Cf. the disciples at Emmaus: "And they said one to another, 'Did not our heart
burn within us by the way, and while He opened to us the Scriptures?'" (Luc.
24:32).

ELI. The gift of wisdom is suitable for me under this name, "Eliphaz," which is "Gold of my God," for in the Holy Scriptures it is deservedly applied on account of the purity, effulgence, and perfection of His wisdom, which is more splendid than the sun and purer than all light and through which the purpose of human life is correctly perceived and loved. Therefore, since it is a wise man's duty to dispose things in good order, and, in the second place, you were adducing the rectitude of your mind toward God, by Whose grace you were saying that you do all things, I was with you, arranging and directing everything.

GIR. I give you what thanks I can, O glory and support of all things, you who proceed from the mouth of the Most High, asking that you always assist me, since in you is every grace of the way and the truth and every hope of life and virtue.

REC. I am the gift of knowledge, brightly pouring forth the radiance of all branches of learning, by which good men may come to know themselves fully, and through me natural and supernatural light have been augmented in you, as you were saying in the third place; therefore, I took upon myself the name "Rechma," that is, "One who sees much" or "One who sees perfectly," because by my power, perfection of teaching and of knowledge is drawn from the Lord.

GIR. Your treasure is a good for me beyond thousands in gold and silver, so that I am able to benefit both myself and others.

IEC. I am the gift of counsel, in the midst of doubts inspiring men toward those things which are righteous and pleasing to God. Therefore, for instructing and directing a wavering and endangered people in the faith, I have supplied you with many opportune and useful things; and so, I am called "Iechimham," which is "One who raises up" or "One who fortifies" or "One who encourages the people," for through sober admonitions they are raised up out of the murk of darkness and fortified in the good and, finally, encouraged heavenward, which we touched upon in the fourth place, when you were going on about your teaching and preaching.

GIR. Indeed, I know that by your guidance I have done many things beyond my powers; therefore, I ask you never to desert me.

THO. I encompass the laws of piety, aiming chiefly at divine worship and always roused to compassion for the wretched and for sinners; I also set the spirits of the just afire with charity, so that I might lead them to salvation with all my strength. And because I effect this primarily through the Sacred Scriptures, I am called "Thoralmed," that is,

"The Law teaches," for what do the Law itself and the whole of Sacred Scripture teach except piety? And who is able to understand the Scriptures unless he possesses piety? Therefore, I am rightly called "The Law teaches," because the Law itself teaches piety, and piety teaches the Law. And so, the fifth place of disputation was entrusted to me, when we strove to prove from the Sacred Scriptures those things which you have prophesied.

GIR. Oh, how often you have instilled in me, while contemplating, the ineffable sweetness of heavenly nectar! How often you have brought strength to me as I labored whether in reading or in preaching (for the best artist of all is love)! "What, then, shall I return to the Lord except to take up the cup of salvation?"[37] [Ps. 115:12–13] which I ask You to give me to drink in the service of Your name?

ABB. And I hold up the pillar of fortitude, by which the hearts of the faithful are strengthened so that they may powerfully resist their adversaries and defend the name of Christ and truth with great bravery. Up till now, by my guidance, you have prevailed against the conspiracies and snares of the impious and the lukewarm, and you will (no doubt) prevail in the future. For who will resist the powerful right hand of God? For this reason, I, disputing with you in the sixth place, selected the not inappropriate name "Abbacuc," that is, "Strong wrestler" or "Strength."

GIR. Truly, in the midst of so many struggles, your strength is always and everywhere indispensable, and so I pray that it will be an inseparable companion at my side, "lest my enemies prevail against me and say to me, 'Well, well! Where is his God?' " [cf. Pss. 69:4 and 70:9–10].

SAP. I, the gift of fear, come in the last place, warning the proud that they will be humbled under the powerful hand of God so that they may not despise things higher than themselves because they are not able to grasp them; therefore, I was smiling favorably on you, when, a little while ago in the seventh place, you were teaching that these things should be believed with humility, seeing that they can be in no way harmful, but rather very beneficial; hence, my name is "Saphtam," which is interpreted "Innocent, or humble, or simple investigator."

GIR. And would that your favor may always accompany me! Finally, you most sacred gifts, never leave me destitute of your protection.

---

37. *Nisi ut* is substituted for an omitted clause.

VERITAS [i.e., all seven speaking together]. If you humbly persevere, you will have what you ask.

Praise to God the Omnipotent
The End

Illustrations

Illustrations in the following gallery reproduce three categories of items associated with Savonarola. The first group (plates 1–5) consists of woodcuts published as illustrations for Savonarola's texts over which he could conceivably have had some control. The second (plates 6–8) contains depictions of scenes from Savonarola's sermons and prophecies, although he himself was not directly involved in their creation. The final cluster of illustrations represents art that has traditionally been seen as "Savonarolan" in inspiration and is included to give a sense of his legacy. This grouping is comprised of commissions by republican councilmen — and Savonarola's followers among them, including the Gonfaloniere — to adorn the Great Council Chamber (plates 9–11) and also of art commissioned by those seeking Savonarola's canonization (plates 12–13).

One of the great mysteries in the study of Renaissance Art is the extent of Savonarola's influence on the visual arts. Despite the rich testimony to Savonarola's charismatic effect on artists, art historians have never documented a fully convincing, direct connection between him and any single great work. Nonetheless, his impact was indisputably pervasive. Even as an old man, Michelangelo averred that he could still hear in his mind the voice of Savonarola preaching. Botticelli, in an act of contrition and repentance, placed his own art on the Bonfire of the Vanities. Fra Bartolommeo made a Dominican confession because of Savonarola and defended the convent of San Marco against its attackers.

We come tantalizingly close to seeing Savonarola's aesthetics incarnated in the service of his political thought in the plans for the Gran Consiglio chamber in the Palazzo Vecchio. Underneath the presently visible remodeling and Vasari's redecoration of the building at the command of the Medici, after their return to power in 1512, lies the space constructed during Savonarola's lifetime and designed with his input. Around 1503–04, Michelangelo and Leonardo da Vinci were commissioned by the Republic to paint epic moments in Florence's fight for freedom. Michelangelo's "Battle of Cascina" commemorates Florence's victory in 1364 over Pisa, ending five years of warfare (plate 9). Leonardo's "Battle of Anghiari" celebrates the Florentine triumph over Filippo Maria Visconti, Duke of Milan, in 1440 (plate 10). Unfortunately, neither mural survives today, but they are known to us in copies by admirers. The altarpiece for the Gran Consiglio chamber, originally commissioned from Filippino Lippi but finally executed by Fra Bartolommeo, depicts St. Anne, on whose feast day Florence regained its independence by driving out the Duke of Athens in 1343 (plate 11). The painting was never finished by Fra Bartolommeo because the Medici, upon their return to power in 1512, found its mixture of piety, policy, and nationalism too Savonarolan. When the Medici were expelled a third time, in 1527, the altarpiece was finally installed in the Council Chamber with much ceremony.

Because Savonarola was perceived as a divinely ordained prophet by many Florentines during his lifetime, his execution ignited a movement for his canonization. Despite the government's attempt to thwart all efforts to collect his charred remains, many of the faithful managed to gather them and retain them in reliquaries, some of which are in existence today. Throughout Tuscany, Savonarola's memory was preserved in the Observant monasteries and convents which implemented his reforms. They formed a nexus around which momentum for the cause of Savonarola's canonization gained force, a movement that continues today. Immediately after his death, popular images of Savonarola's martyrdom began to circulate, including prints, medals, and paintings (plate 12). One of the most historically and iconographically important of them is the now lost icon formerly in the Gerli collection (plate 13). Through the combination of images of Savonarola, his martyrdom, and his visions, explained in the banderoles that surround the image, it encapsulates the kernel of Savonarola's life, prophecies, and legacy.

The following abbreviations are used in the captions to indicate standard references:

BMC *Catalogue of Books Printed in the XVth Century Now in the British Museum,* vol. VI, ed. A. W. Pollard and V. Scholderer (London: British Museum, 1930)

Sander Max J. Sander, *Le livre à figures italiens depuis 1467 jusqu'à 1530,* 6 vols. (Milan: Ulrico Hoepli, 1942)

1. "Savonarola Preaching in the Pulpit of the Cathedral of Florence," woodcut, in Girolamo Savonarola, *Compendio di revelatione* (Florence: Piero Pacini da Pescia, 23 April 1496), fol. i recto. Inc 6316.10 (A), Department of Rare Books, Houghton Library, Harvard University; *BMC* VI 683; Sander 6761.

2. "Adoration of the Cross," woodcut, in Domenico Benivieni, *Tractato di Maestro Domenico Benivieni Prete Fiorentino in defensione et probatione della doctrina et profethie predicate da Frate Hieronimo da Ferrara nella citta di Firenze* (Florence: Ser Francesco Bonaccorsi for Piero Pacini, 28 May 1496), fol. f.iii verso. The Bridwell Library, Southern Methodist Universy, Dallas, Texas; *BMC* VI 675; Sander 896.

3. "Choice between Heaven and Hell," woodcut, in Girolamo Savonarola, *Predica dellarte del bene morire* (Florence: Bartolomeo de' Libri, 2 November 1496) fol. a6 verso. Houghton Library, Harvard University; *BMC* VI 662; Sander 6813.

4. "The Good Death," woodcut, in Girolamo Savonarola, *Predica dellarte del bene morire* (Florence: Bartolomeo de' Libri, 2 November 1496), fol. c.xiv recto. Typ Inc 6206, Department of Printing and Graphic Arts, Houghton Library, Harvard University; *BMC* VI 662; Sander 6813.

5. "Savonarola Debates with Wise Men," woodcut, in Girolamo Savonarola, *Dyalago della verita prophetica* (Florence: Antonio Tubini, Lorenzo d'Alopa and Andrea Ghirlandi, ca. 1498–1500), fol. i recto. Inc 6430, Department of Rare Books, Houghton Library, Harvard University; *BMC* VI 694; Sander 6771.

6. Sandro Botticelli, *Mystic Crucifixion*, tempera on canvas, ca. 1500. The Fogg Art Museum, Harvard University Museum, Gift of the Friends of the Fogg Museum of Art Fund, 1924.27.

7–8. Savonarolan medal, bronze, Florentine, ca. 1490s. Obverse: Profile of
Savonarola with Crucifix. Inscribed HIERONYMUS·SAV·FER·ORD·PRE·VIR·
DOCTISSIMUS (Girolamo Savonarola of Ferrara, Order of Preachers, most learned
man). Reverse Savonarolan visions. Two inscriptions: GLADIUS·DOMINI·SUP·TER·
CITO·ET VELOCITER (The sword of the Lord upon the earth swiftly and soon) and
SPIRITUS·DNI·SUP·TERRA·COPIOS·ET·HABUDAT (The Spirit of the Lord upon the
earth copiously and abundantly). Metropolitan Museum of Art, New York, Ann
and George Blumenthal Fund, 1950 (ex collection J. Pierpont Morgan) 50.58.5.

9. Michelangelo, *Battle of Cascina,* grisaille on panel, 1504–1506 (destroyed). Copy of central section by Aristotile da Sangallo, early sixteenth century. Collection of the Earl of Leicester, Holkham Hall, Norfolk/Bridgeman Art Library.

10. Leonardo da Vinci, *Battle of Anghiari,* pen and ink and chalk, 1503–1506 (destroyed). Copy of central section by Peter Paul Rubens, ca. 1615. The Louvre, Paris. Réunion des Musées Nationaux/Art Resource, New York.

11. Fra Bartolommeo, *Gran Consiglio Altarpiece,* oil underpainting on wood, 1510–1513 (unfinished). Museo di San Marco, Florence. Alinari/Art Resource, New York.

12. *Execution of Savonarola and His Two Companions in the Piazza della Signoria,* ca. 1498–1520. Museo di San Marco, Florence.

13. *Apotheosis of Girolamo Savonarola,* early sixteenth century, formerly in the Gerli Collection, Milan (lost). The banner at top reads: ECCE QUAM BONUM ET QUAM JOCUNDUM (Behold how good and how pleasant, Ps. 132 incipit). The banners underneath to the right and left respectively read: INSTA OROIBUS (Remain in prayer) and ROBORARE PATIENTIA (Be strong in patience). The border of Savonarola's portrait medallion reads: HI SUNT QUI VENERUNT EX MAGNA TRIBULATIONE ET LAVERUNT STOLAS SUAS IN SANGUINE AGNI (These are those who have come out from great tribulation and have washed their robes in the blood of the Lamb). Savonarola's halo reads: G. SAVON PROPHETA ET MARTYR. At the bottom of the composition, one city, labeled HIERUSALEM, is paired with a banderole that reads: CRUX MI DEI (Cross of the Mercy of God); the other, ROMA, is paired with another that reads: CRUX IRA DEI (Cross of the Wrath of God).

Politics

Aggeus, Sermon VII

First Sunday of Advent

28 November 1494

Benedictus Deus et Pater Domini nostri Iesu Christi, Pater misericordi-arum et Deus totius consolationis, qui consolatur nos, etc.[1] — II Cor. 1:3–4

Dearly beloved in Jesus Christ, since the whole of Christian religion consists in the knowledge of God and of oneself, we can therefore say that this Christian religion of ours consists in something small, although it seems so long and difficult.[2] This knowledge of God and of oneself resolves itself into love of God and hatred of one's own self, and Holy Scripture in its entirety tends toward this effect. And so, our teachers in sacred theology say that Holy Scripture has as its object God alone: thus it is short, though it seems long. Let us look at the Gospel, which is long in speaking and writing but is short, *nevertheless,* in substance, *which is,* to love God and to love one's neighbor, just as the Savior said: *"In his duobus mandatis universa lex pendet et prophetae"*[3] [Matt. 22:40], and *Plenitudo legis est dilectio*[4] [Rom. 13:10]. Now to our topic. Beloved, you recall that last year we treated again of the ark during both last Advent and Lent, but we could not finish it, since many other concerns got in the way. Now, in these past days, we have finished it, a little before the armies arrived here and your tribulations began. But though this matter of the ark was long and went on for a long time, it is short to repeat in substance what the ark means and its significance: to be in the ark is nothing other than to be in this world and out of this world. The blessed and the damned, who are out of this world, are not in the ark, the damned, because they are dead to God and to the world, and the blessed, though they may be dead, *vita eorum abscondita est cum Christo*[5] [Col. 3:3]. Those who are in the life of this world and live according to God are in the ark because, although they may be in this world, they do not live according to the world, but only according to God. In this way our ark is short: *Benedictus Deus et Pater Domini nostri Iesu Christi, Pater misericordiarum et*

---

1. "Blessed be the God and Father of our Lord Jesus Christ, the Father of mercies and God of all consolation, Who comforts us, etc."
2. Pseudo-Dionysius, *Mystical Theology,* chap. 1.
3. "On these two commandments depend the whole law and the prophets."
4. "The fullness of the law is love."
5. "Their life is hidden with Christ"; *eorum* ("their") substituted for *vestra* ("your").

Deus totius consolationis, qui consolatur nos in omnibus tribulationibus nostris[6] [II Cor. 1:3–4]. Let us, I say, bless our Lord, Who consoles us in all our tribulations.

You know that several times already we have told you that everyone ought to enter the ark and that we would close it and that the flood of tribulations would come. And you know that after the ark was closed and locked, we were in the greatest dangers, and that, by the grace of God, we have for now passed through these tribulations. But we should render thanks to God. Our Noe, the one who guides the ark, has called all those who are in the ark, and both says and cries out that we should take care not to incur the vice of ingratitude, which has three gradations: the first stage is not to know the favor one has received; the second is not to give thanks to the One Who has given it to us; the third, which is the worst, is to consider the favor an evil. Let us then acknowledge the favor from God, Who has allowed your city to pass safely through this ordeal, and let us give endless thanks to God and let us do all the good we can for His glory and for the salvation of His elect. And our Noe will sing a psalm, and by it we shall thank God, saying: *Alleluia, alleluia.* But first let us stop a little, and later we will continue with the psalm.

I was considering this past night how great was the simplicity and the goodness of our ancient fathers, such that, although they were learned and wise, still there was in them so much simplicity that they were quick to believe fully in the things of God; and then, when I considered that nowadays everything is the opposite with us, I was dumbstruck. Thus, turning this question and doubt over in my mind, I said, "Where does so much difference between us and our ancient fathers stem from?" I considered what is written about *the life of the Fathers;* I considered St. Jerome, St. Augustine, and St. Gregory, how learned they were and, on the other hand, how simple and believing they were in the things of God. And I tried to figure out whence such firm knowledge came to them.

These philosophers divide the types of knowledge into science, opinion, and faith, and they say that science has evidence and firmness; opinion has evidence and no firmness; faith has firmness and no evidence. The saints did not acquire their belief in the things of God by way of the senses, for one does not come to this knowledge through the senses, nor through first principles, which can be proved, nor through demonstration or any science. If, then, they did not acquire it through science, and you were to say that they acquired it through opinion, you would be greatly mistaken, for opinion has no firmness, and *yet* they were so firm in it that nothing, neither tribulation

6. "Blessed, therefore, be God the Father of our Lord, Jesus Christ, Who consoles us in all our tribulations."

nor martyrdom, could ever move them from it. If you say, "They believed through faith," I would reply to you, "We Christians have faith, and *yet* we are not as believing as they in these things of God." How, then, does it come about that those holy and ancient fathers of ours, being so very prudent and learned, had such a ready inclination toward and firm fixity in those things?

While I was thinking last night, as I say, this solution came to me. Consider the order of natural things, which, although they may be different from one another, nonetheless, each has its own instinct and natural inclination: heavy things, by their nature, tend toward the center; likewise, the animals, with regard to nourishing their offspring, are so inclined by nature; men have the natural light of reason, which inclines them toward natural things and to believe the first principles of the sciences, which cannot be denied; and those things which have the same form have the same inclination. Therefore, it seems to me that one can say that all God's saints and elect receive from God a special light that inclines them to believe firmly those things which God does or shows in His Church, in general as well as in particular. And this same light allows them to discern if they are to be believed or not. And in the same way that natural things, guided by an unerring intelligence, do not err, these holy ones, guided as they are by this special light God has given them, also do not err. And if you say to me, "How are you going to show me that they have this light and this unerring intelligence?" I answer, "Just as one cannot assign a reason for first principles because they are so obvious, so God gives these elect ones of His this ray of light which makes these things so obvious in their minds that they cannot believe the opposite, and what is more, this comes about through a special ray given by God to anyone who is upright in heart, as it is written: *Exortum est in tenebris lumen rectis corde*[7] [Ps. 111:4; *corde* added by Savonarola]; for the one who walks upright in heart, *even* if he should be in the dark, God enlightens him. Let your will be directed to God, and He will not allow you to go astray, just as happened to Nathaniel, who said: *"Tu es Filius Dei et Rex Israel"*[8] [Ioh. 1:49]; and to Peter, likewise, when he said: *"Tu es Filius Dei vivi"*[9] [Matt. 16:16]—there you have it! That was that ray which God had placed in the upright mind so that he might believe immediately. You see that Christ then said to Peter: *"Caro et sanguis non revelavit tibi, sed Pater meus qui est in coelis"*[10][Matt. 16:17]; our Savior wanted to show here that Peter believed because of the special light infused into his mind by God in

7. "A light has arisen in the darkness for those upright in heart."
8. "You are the Son of God and the King of Israel."
9. "You are the Son of the living God."
10. "Flesh and blood have not revealed this to you, but My Father, Who is in Heaven."

order that he might believe. I have said this to you so that you may believe and give thanks to God for such a favor, and know that it has not been in vain that you have been told so often and for so long, "Do penance, for tribulations are coming upon you."

I would like to be able to tell you this morning all the things I have said to you in the past about this, but it is not possible. For now I will say to you only this, which I have always had in my mind and have told you several times over the last year up to last Advent: do penance, do penance, and do not delay, for many then will not have time. Have you not already seen whether this was true? Have you not been next door to great danger? Do you not remember how often I said to you, "Though it looks like fair weather now, soon it will be cloudy," and that I used to say, *Qui habet aures audiendi audiat*[11] [e.g., Matt. 11:15], that is, "he who has ears to hear, let him hear." You have seen how it turned out for any who did not want to hear. You must recall how great a war the demons waged against us, and that God freed us from all those dangers, such that if I were to recount them all to you, you would be stupefied. I would like you to know that all my re-peated saying and crying out to you, "Do penance," was not in vain. Those who have light have recognized it, and those to whom God has given the light of His grace have shown signs of penitence. But know well that this penance was not sufficient; anyone who has thought it over in grace knows that it was not enough, but the merits of the blood of Christ and of the Virgin and our angels have made up the balance for your liberation from this danger. Know, Florence, that this happened because of the mercy of God and the ministry of His angels, and do not attribute anything to men, for it did not happen because of their virtues, but only by the power of God and His pity.

Anyone with half a brain, even if he has no faith, understands that what I say to you is true, but those who do not believe it, if you look carefully, either they are utterly lacking in reason, or they are obstinate and blinded by evildoing. They are ignorant of Holy Scripture, and when it says, *quod unus persequebatur mille et duo decem milia*[12] [Deut. 32:30], it seems strange, and they do not believe it and mock the things of God. These are the luke-warm, who do not believe and impede others from believing; but let them wait a while, for God has come to punish them *ut qui non vident videant, et qui vident caeci fiant*[13] [Ioh. 9:39]. Now! let us move on to our psalm.

Alleluia, alleluia: this is the title of the psalm, which is to say nothing

11. "He who has ears to hear, let him hear."
12. "One would chase a thousand, and two, ten thousand."
13. "So that those who do not see may see, and those who do see may be made blind."

other than this: give thanks to God for so great a favor, which He has done here through His mercy. *Confitemini Domino quoniam bonus, quoniam in saeculum misericordia eius*[14] [Pss. 106:1; 117:1, 29]. Confess that the Lord has freed you this time and that His mercy has been great toward you; the signs which you have, Florence, to make you recognize this favor (and which prove that God loves you), I am going to show to you. Love is separated into two types, namely, love from friendship and love from concupiscence. Love arises from friendship when one friend loves the other, not because of his usefulness, but only because he loves him and wishes him well. But love derives from concupiscence when one loves the other because of some usefulness to be got out of him or expected from him. Only God loves His creatures with the love of friendship because He is perfect in Himself and needs nothing from others; therefore, He alone is free in loving others. But man is not so, for in his love there is always some consideration of his own advantage; therefore, his love is more from concupiscence than friendship, and the angels *also* love from concupiscence, and, likewise, the blessed, who, loving God, derive from it contentment and advantage and pleasure in being with God and enjoying that divine essence.

Now to our topic. God has loved you, Florence, for He has shown you mercy, not for the sake of any advantage to Him, but solely on account of love from true friendship and in order to do you good, although He has no need of you. This, then, is the sign that proves to you how much you ought to love God in return, and render thanks to Him for the great love He has shown you and the great favor He has granted to you. It is right to call ungrateful one who sees himself loved and favored by another and yet does not render thanks to him. And because to be loved is by its nature most delightful to man, so, when he sees himself loved and is given something *gratis* by another, his heart must be stirred to love him who has granted him such a grace. Acknowledge, then, Florence, the grace that you have received. See, our psalm instructs you and says: *Dilexi, quoniam exaudiet Dominus vocem orationis meae*[15] [Ps. 114:1]: "because the Lord has heard me, I have loved Him" and given Him thanks. And then it continues and says: *Quia inclinavit aurem suam mihi, in diebus meis invocabo*[16] [Ps. 114:2], that is, "because the Lord has inclined His ear to my prayers, I shall forever call upon His mercy all the days of my life," for He has had compassion upon me and upon my sins, which merited every ill. Therefore, I shall remember this favor always and shall turn to God in all other tribulations which are to come.

14. "Confess to the Lord that He is good, that His mercy is forever."
15. "I have loved the Lord, for He has listened to my voice in prayer."
16. "Because He has inclined His ear to me, I will call upon Him all the days of my life."

And this is the first stage in recognizing the favor man has received. Let us proceed to the second.

When man has recognized the favor and the grace granted to him, he advances to the second stage: he praises and magnifies and exalts Him Who has granted such grace, and he never ceases to praise and magnify Him. Thus the Lord says: *Laude mea infrenabo te*[17] [Is. 48:9]: "I shall set my praise in your mouth like a bit,"[18] so that you will ruminate always on this bit and this praise. Oh, sweet bit, for him to whom God grants such grace that he praises Him and exalts Him always in his every utterance, and longs to praise Him always. Now, note that we say there are three types of attraction, namely, the natural, the animal, and the rational. Natural attraction has no knowledge within itself, but rather outside of itself, such that a heavy thing tends downward and does not know why, for knowledge of this is in God, Who has ordained it thus; nevertheless, this natural attraction never errs, for it is guided by Him Who cannot err. Animal attraction, although it has no reason within itself, follows the senses, which draw it to what pleases it, just as the little lamb does when she sees over there the food which delights her senses and follows after it and has her imagination fixed on it. And so, the movements of animals such as this are natural rather than free.

But as for man, who has intellect and free will and does not have his imagination fixed on one thing and can form within himself diverse imaginings however he likes, the attraction which characterizes him is called rational; it is free and follows freely whatever it wishes. Hence, the man who is in God's grace has imaginings which one who is without such grace does not have, and when the intellect of the man who is in a state of grace sets eternal life before him, the will follows this good which has been presented to him; the greater the good presented to him, the more he longs for it, and the more fervidly he follows after it. The will stands halfway between the knowledge given by grace and sensible perception, that is, between the natural light and the supernatural one. In this way, it stands as if between two magnets, one of which draws it upward and the other downward, and whichever is stronger in the man, that one wins, so that the point of victory is situated wherever the regard is more firmly affixed.

To our topic, then: if you want to praise God perfectly, it is necessary—especially in this initial stage—that you have your regard firmly fixed upon the knowledge of God and eternal life, and at the same time, it is necessary that you praise Him with your whole heart and mind, an interior conjunc-

---

17. "I will bridle you for the sake of my praise."
18. Savonarola construes the phrase *laude mea* as an ablative of means ("with My praise") rather than of cause ("for the sake of My praise"), which the context in Isaias requires. God is, in effect, issuing a threat of punishment.

tion which cannot take place without knowing God and His grace. That is, when you consider the favors which God has given you, you are moved to praise Him and say: *Benedic, anima mea, Dominum*[19] [Pss. 102:1, 2, 22; 103:1, 35]; "O my soul, bless and praise the Lord," Who has granted so many graces. The will follows in this praise and is reined in, as we have said above, for the Lord says: *Laude mea infrenabo te;* "I shall set my praise in your mouth like a bit." Read this psalm, and I would have you consider well all the verses that follow, and praise and bless God throughout all ages.

Beati qui habitant in domus Domini: in saecula saeculorum laudabunt te, Domine[20] [Ps. 83:5]; and for this reason—so that God may always be praised—the lauds and holy offices have been instituted in the Church. But nowadays we have converted these divine lauds into secular affairs, into music and songs, which may delight the sense and the ear but not the spirit, and this is no honor to God. Although these songs may be sweet to the ears, they do not rein in the soul, nor do they keep it tethered to the enjoyment of divine things, but that would require a return to that early simplicity and that the offices be recited without so much chanting, but only with devotion, with slight inflection of the voice, and with simplicity. I tell you that these songs of yours today have been invented out of ambition and avarice.

So then, Florence, praise God for the favor you have received, praise Him with heart and mind, and say with our psalm: *Circumdederunt me dolores mortis*[21] [Ps. 114:3], that is, "the sorrows of death have surrounded me." O Florence, remember the danger in which you stood so recently, the danger of death, I say, from which God, in His mercy, wanted to free you. Then it continues and says: *Et pericula inferni invenerunt me*[22] [Ps. 114:3], that is, "the dangers of Hell have found me out." O Florence, if things had ended badly, as they could have done, many, very likely, who had not confessed nor had a good intention to confess, would today be in Hell; therefore, thank God and give praise to Him, Florence, and continue and say with the psalm: *Tribulationem et dolorem inveni et nomen Domini invocavi*[23] [Ps. 114:3–4], that is, "I found tribulation and pain, but I called upon the name of the Lord" that He might come to my aid, and He aided me. See, then, that tribulation is good, in that it makes one turn to God, and He hears you. The words were not spoken in vain when I said to you, "Do penance, turn to God."

---

19. "Bless the Lord, my soul."
20. "Blessed are they who dwell in the house of the Lord; forever and ever they will praise You, Lord."
21. "The sorrows of death encircled me."
22. "And the dangers of Hell found me out."
23. "I found tribulation and sorrow and called upon the name of the Lord."

Go on then, Florence, and say, *O Domine, libera animam meam*[24] [Ps. 114:
4], "O Lord, free my soul" from sin. Note that it does not say, "free my
property, house, or other goods, nor dignities, nor honors." It says, "free
my soul."

He who is in the ark is as if out of this world; he always thinks about
and prays more for his soul than for any other thing; he commends himself
to God and says: *Misericors Dominus et iustus et Deus noster miseretur*[25] [Ps.
114:5], that is, "Our Lord is merciful," and, though just, He has more mercy
and exercises it more often than justice. "I see," says the one who is in the
ark, "that my sins have merited every punishment, yet the Lord has shown
mercy to me, and if He has taken away from me some property or any other
thing, because He is just I thank Him for it and say, *Omnia quaecumque
nobis fecisti, Domine, in vero iudicio fecisti, quia peccavimus tibi et mandatis tuis
non obedivimus*[26] [approximates Dan. 3:31, 29, 30], that is, 'what You have
done against us, O Lord, You have done it with true judgment and with
true justice, because we have sinned and have not obeyed Your commandments.' I am glad that You have taken away from me property and other
goods; to You alone I commend my soul." And in this manner, the good
man always praises God for everything. And this suffices for the second stage
we spoke of—to acknowledge favors from God and thank Him for them.
Let us now move on to the third stage.

The third stage is repayment, that is, to render thanks, by one's actions,
for favors received; yet we shall say with the psalm following the one we are
examining: *Quid retribuam Domino pro omnibus quae retribuit mihi?*[27] [Ps. 115:
12], that is, "what recompense shall I render unto the Lord for the great
favors that He has done and does for me every day?" What can man, the
sinner, render unto God? The sinner has nothing of his own but sins; nonetheless, the Lord is so good and so merciful that, in return for sins, He
bestows pity, mercy, and many blessings that are not merited except through
the mercy and grace of God. Therefore, O sinner, say with the psalm just
cited: *Calicem salutaris accipiam et nomen Domini invocabo*[28] [Ps. 115:13]. The
chalice is the Passion which our Lord suffered for you on the Cross, which
you cannot take up in actuality, but which you take up with your heart and
will, whenever it should be necessary to suffer for His love. God does not

24. "O Lord, free my soul."
25. "Merciful and just is the Lord; our God is compassionate."
26. "Anything whatsoever that You have done to us, O Lord, You have done in true
    judgment, for we have sinned against You and have not obeyed Your command-
    ments."
27. "What repayment shall I make to the Lord for all that He has given me?"
28. "I will take up the chalice of salvation, and call upon the name of the Lord."

need nor does He want our property; He wants only the heart of man and that man love Him above every other thing: *"Praebe, fili mi, cor tuum"*[29] [Ps. 23:26], says the Lord; "Give Me your heart, My son," for I want nothing else.

Let all of you, then, give your hearts to God, for this is the greatest repayment that you could possibly give and the greatest sacrifice; know, children, that living uprightly, which is pleasing to God, does not consist in external things, but in the knowledge of God and in loving Him with one's whole heart and inclining toward Him with all one's affection. This cannot be done except through continuous prayer, and it cannot be done well unless you devote yourself to simplicity, which today seems to be lost and extinguished among men, for everyone tries to be richer and more important, shunning any simplicity. I do not say that it is evil in itself to have property and honors, but one who seeks them enters into temptation, which often is the cause of the ruin and damnation of one who seeks such things and owns them, as is written: *Qui divitias quaerunt, incidunt in tentationem et in laqueum diaboli*[30] [approximates I Tim. 6:9]. Therefore, give yourselves, my sons and daughters, to simplicity and let go superfluous things, the pomp and the vanities, which I tell you are snares of the devil, which trap you without your realizing it. Slowly, slowly, little by little, they draw you at last to the dwelling-place of the devil. Let go of possessions, give them to the poor, and especially I say to you, priests: begin a little to live simply and be the first to begin, in order to show the way and give good example to others.

O clergy, clergy, *propter te orta est haec tempestas*[31] [approximates Ion. 1: 12]. Know that it was for the purpose of avoiding these tribulations, which today are seen coursing throughout Italy, that these prayers were made to which I have exhorted you for so long, and let us pray to God that they turn into plague rather than into war. But I hope to God that the Lord may free us of them, if not completely, at least in part, if you will do this which is the will of God.

O citizens, devote yourselves to living uprightly and to doing good deeds. Devote yourselves to simplicity; otherwise, God will be angry with you, should you be ungrateful and not acknowledge the favor which God has done for you. And you, women, I declare to you that, if you do not forgo your pomp and your superfluities and vanities and do not devote yourselves to simplicity, then if the plague comes, you will die like dogs. Devote yourselves, I say, to simplicity, and do not be ashamed to go dressed more simply than you do, for this is no shame whatsoever to you, if you

29. "Offer Me your heart, My son."
30. "Those who seek riches fall into temptation and into the snare of the devil."
31. "On account of you this tempest has arisen."

consider it well, but rather honor and usefulness. And you well-to-do women, who are among the first rank, start giving this good example to the others, and you will cause many others to follow you and do good, and you will have merit with God for this. Look, our psalm says: *Custodiens parvulos Dominus*[32] [Ps. 114:6], that is, "the Lord watches over little ones." The little ones are those who humble themselves and abase themselves and go about simply.

You know that the Lord says in the Gospel: *"Nisi conversi fueritis sicut parvuli, non intrabitis in regnum coelorum"*[33] [Matt. 18:3], that is, "if you do not become little ones, you will not enter into the kingdom of heaven," so devote yourselves, I say, to simplicity and humility, so that the Lord will be with you. Look at the psalm which follows and says: *Humiliatus sum et liberavit me*[34] [Ps. 114: 6)], "I was humbled and the Lord freed me." Know, furthermore, that from this simplicity peace of mind follows, for he who loves and delights in simplicity and having few things is less involved in the things of the world; a little is enough for him, and he lives very quietly. And thus the psalm continues: *Convertere anima mea in requiem tuam*[35] [Ps. 114: 7]: "turn, my soul," to this simplicity, to this which is restfulness and peace for you. *Quia Dominus benefecit tibi*[36] [Ps. 114:7]: "because the Lord has done good to you" and had mercy on you and will always do so, if you will do good. *Eripuit animam meam de morte*[37] [Ps. 114:8]: the Lord has freed you from death, for if the Lord had not held back His hand, things would perhaps have advanced to a point you cannot imagine, and yet, He freed many from death. *Oculos meos a lacrimis, pedes meos a lapsu*[38] [Ps. 114:8]; the feet signify the affections. How many are there who were filled with hatred and ill will, such that, if God had not held back, they would perhaps be in Hell today? And so, Florence, give thanks to God; repay this favor with works. Give yourself to God in repayment, and devote yourself to this simplicity, as I have told you. Now let us go to another repayment.

Another repayment which I want to tell you to make to God would be prayer, confession, and alms. Let everyone pray: *"Oportet semper orare"*[39] [Luc. 18:1], says the Lord, that is, "It is always necessary to pray *et nunquam*

---

32. "The Lord watches over little ones."
33. "Unless you should become like little ones, you will not enter into the kingdom of Heaven."
34. "I was humbled and He freed me."
35. "Turn to your rest, my soul."
36. "For the Lord has favored you."
37. "He has snatched my soul from death."
38. "My eyes from tears, my feet from a fall."
39. "It is necessary to pray always."

deficere"[40] [Luc. 18:1]. Let everyone pray, then; let everyone go to confession in this first week of Advent; and if someone cannot go now, let him at least prepare himself to do it as soon as possible, and let this be the first thing. Let the second be that you all prepare yourselves to make these forty days of Advent—I mean those who can, and not, it is understood, the sick and the weak, or those who are excused from fasting—and let the fast be at least three days a week, or at least two. The other is that you give consolation to these poor persons. It is necessary, I say, that some provision be made for them. Think of them this first week, and I, because I am feeling somewhat exhausted, will lay aside preaching this week. Think, I say, of provision for the poor. When Moses wanted to make the tabernacle to enclose the tablets of the law given to him by God, all the Hebrews, both men and women, everyone, promptly offered for such a work all the most precious things they had [Ex. 35:20–29]. So ought you to do to help Christ's poor. The tabernacle and the temple were the things of God; all the more so are these people, as it is written: *Templum Dei estis vos*[41] [I Cor. 3:16–17; II Cor. 6:16]. Do you want to see a beautiful temple and habitation of God? Gather all the poor and provide for all their needs, and be merciful toward them, as it is written: *Beati misericordes, quoniam ipsi misericordiam consequentur*[42] [Matt. 5:7]. I greatly desire that provision be made for these poor ones. So God inspires me, and so I give comfort to you.

The first Sunday coming up there will be two collections: one will be for the poor who are in the city, the other for those who are outside. And let there be sung that morning a solemn Mass of the Virgin, and let everyone offer according to his rank and means, and let the priests be urged to be foremost in this matter, and then all the others, if you want to avoid the tribulations and plague. And if you do this, helping the poor with your charity, your city will be rich and opulent.

The other provision which you have to make will be for the Feast of the Conception of the Virgin the next day [8 December]; let there be a solemn procession in her honor so that she may intercede for the city in every need. As for the other, I exhort the citizens and anyone who is concerned that at this time and for this charity for the poor, the money which you spend for the Studium [the University][43] be converted to relief for the

---

40. "And never to desist."
41. "You are the temple of God."
42. "Blessed are the merciful, for they shall receive mercy."
43. The Florentine Studium had been refounded in Pisa in 1472, largely at the instigation of Lorenzo de' Medici. All teaching in Pisa was suspended for a year after that city was lost to Florence in November 1494 as a result of the French invasion, though some subjects continued to be taught in Florence. See P. F.

poor, because this for now is more necessary and charitable than the other. And if this is still not enough, lay hands on the church vessels for the relief of the poor of Christ; the Pauline text is no obstacle in this case, because charity breaks through every law. The other good provision is that the shops be opened and that everyone, and especially the poor, be able to work and support himself with his labor. I would give comfort to those who still wait to lighten their burden and especially to those who are most in need. We will be able to talk about the other provisions that are necessary to living uprightly and to justice if the citizens will be content that I should make a few exhortations at the Palace. Above all, let everyone pray, for by this means all good works are always done. And if you will do this, you will be able to say along with the last verse of our psalm: *Placebo Domino in regione vivorum*[44] [Ps. 114:9], that is, "I shall please the Lord in the land of the living," *hoc est in vita aeterna,* where dwells the Lord of lords, *qui est benedictus in saecula saeculorum. Amen.*[45]

Grendler, *The Universities of the Italian Renaissance* (Baltimore: Johns Hopkins University Press, 2002), pp. 71–72.
44. "I shall please the Lord in the land of the living."
45. "Which is in life eternal . . . Who is blessed forever and ever. Amen."

Aggeus, Sermon XIII

Third Sunday of Advent

12 December 1494

Erudimini, qui iudicatis terram, et servite Domino in timore et exultate ei cum tremore.[1] — Ps. 2:10–11

Dearly beloved in Christ Jesus, granted that the soul of man belongs among spiritual creatures, yet, although his intellect has an infinite capacity, nonetheless, because he has so little natural light, he would not have been able to attain intellectual knowledge of things if God had not given him the body with its active feelings so that he might learn. Therefore, it was necessary to give him a body, through the senses of which the soul could acquire knowledge of things, and thus could have its natural perfection. Nor was it possible within the natural order to give him a sensible and yet immortal body in this life, because, where there are senses, there is a mixture of the four elements, and because everything composed of contraries is corruptible, therefore, it was necessary that he have a mortal body with its senses to learn, although the Lord could have provided against his mortality. And yet, this body of man is more delicate than the bodies of other animals, and of a more delicate character. Man does not remain alone, and he is called a social animal; he could not live as a solitary from birth to death, as other animals could do, for he needs so many things in order to live that one single man by himself cannot produce or provide for himself. God provides these things for the other animals, though they do not sow and do not labor. But to man, in order that he might provide for his own needs, God has given reason, and to the other animals, natural instinct, for they do not have an intellect.

Therefore, since man is a social animal, who does not know how and is not able to live alone, it was necessary that men join together and congregate in cities or castles or towns and form a community for the common need each had of the other, and so that they might be able to understand one another in these communities, nature has invented and given them language and speech in order that each might express his ideas to the other, according to his need. So then, every multitude of men living together is organized toward some end to which it can arrive by various paths, and it is necessary

---

1. "Be instructed, you who judge the earth, and serve the Lord in fear, and rejoice in Him with trembling."

to have one who directs and rules all the others. Every people and place, which tends toward its natural good, requires governance, and these types of government are distinct and different in several ways. Some are ruled by a single leader, others by several persons, still others are ruled by the whole people together. Regulation and governance by a single leader, when that leader is good, is better than any other government, or the very best, and more easily achieves unity. The reason is this: because it is more difficult to unify the many than the few, and, wherever power is more united, it has more strength, and because power is more easily concentrated and unified in one than in many, therefore, the government of one is better than that of many, when he who rules the others is good. But when that one leader is wicked, there is no worse government and form of rule, since the worst is the opposite of the best. Nonetheless, divers and various governments have been invented in accordance with the diversity of men and countries.

In the warm part of this hemisphere, men are more pusillanimous than in other places because they are less sanguine, and thus, in those places, the people easily let themselves be ruled by a single leader, and they readily obey him and willingly subject themselves to him. In the cold northern part, where people are more sanguine and less intellectual, they are likewise steadfast and submissive to their one lord and head. But in the middle part, such as Italy, where both the sanguine and the intellectual abound, men do not remain patiently under a single leader; rather, each of them would like to be the leader who governs and rules over others and can command and not be commanded. From this, then, arise the dissension and discord among the citizens of the city, where one wants to make himself great and dominate the others. Experience has repeatedly demonstrated this; both at the time of the Romans and every day since, one has seen and sees examples of this in the cities of Italy; even in your own city you have seen and experienced this many times in our own days. Therefore, it is the counsel of the holy Doctors that, in these places where it seems that the nature of man will not endure a superior, government by the majority is better than that of a single leader, and one could say that this is especially appropriate for the city of Florence, where the sanguine and intelligence aplenty abound in the nature of men.[2] But this government by the many must take care to be well regulated; other-wise, you would always be embroiled in dissension and partisanship, for in a few years restless men will divide themselves and become sectarian, and one faction will expel the other and make it rebel against the city, and so, it is nec-essary to think carefully about the form you have to choose, as the preceding words of our sermon declare: *Erudimini, qui iudicatis terram, et servite Domino*

---

2. Thomas Aquinas and Tolomeo da Lucca, *De regimine principum*, bk. IV, chap. 8.

in timore, that is, "Learn well, you who judge the earth, and serve God in great awe," which subject we would like to discuss this morning.

O Florence, I cannot tell you everything I feel within myself, because you are not prepared to bear it at present. Oh, if I could tell you all! You would see that I am like a new vessel full of must and sealed up; it boils every which way, but cannot issue forth. Many secrets are sealed in here that cannot issue forth, particularly since you would not believe them. O Florence, if you have not wanted to believe up to this point, at least believe now, and if you have believed, believe this morning more than ever. And do not consider me, poor little friar, inept little man full of sins. God has willed that you see and experience my ineptitude, so that you may see and consider so much the more that it is He, and not I, Who does everything and *qui incerta et occulta [. . .] manifestavit mihi*[3] [Ps. 50:6]. You know that during these past years in which I have preached to you, when it seemed that everything was at peace and that Florence remained quiet, I predicted to you then that much evil and many tribulations would be coming, and you did not believe it, because no sign of this was to be seen. Now you have seen them, and you see that they have commenced; you see the beginning of what I told you, and you cannot deny it.

And so, you ought now to believe all the more what I will tell you, since you have seen that what was said in the past has begun to prove true. If then I predicted some evil, and you have seen it, now that I tell you something good, you ought to believe it, because the prophet will not always be one who predicts evil. I say, Florence, hear what I am telling you this morning; hear what God has inspired in me. I confide myself solely to Christ, in that which I tell you; do it, for it will be well for you if you do. I tell you, do first those two things I told you another time, that is, that everyone go to confession and be purified of sins, and let everyone attend to the common good of the city; and if you will do this, your city will be glorious because in this way she will be reformed spiritually as well as temporally, that is, with regard to her people, and from you will issue the reform of all Italy. Florence will become richer and more powerful than she has ever been, and her empire will expand into many places. But if you will not do what I tell you, God will elect those who, as I said, want to see you divided, and this will be your final destruction.

If you would do what I have told you, here is the fire and here is the water: now do it! I have told you another time, and so know and hold to this most firmly, that God wants to renew His Church—do not doubt this at all—that He will renew it, and He will do so with the sword of tribulations—and soon! Likewise, do not doubt that Turks and pagans will have

3. "Who has revealed uncertain and hidden things to me."

to be baptized, and you can be certain that this is the time for them to come to baptism. This is the fifth stage of the Church,[4] and many who are here will see it. I have told you this secret, Florence, precisely so that you might be all the more encouraged to reform yourself in accordance with God's will and spread your wings to reform other people; blessed will he be who makes ready for these events. Remove from yourself then, Florence, the old habits, and wholly renew yourself according to God's will. Open your ears, Florence, and hear what I tell you: I wanted this morning to be held a fool, for God would have it so. Know this morning, Florence, that here in this church there is a greater multitude of angels than of men. Behold the Divine Majesty, to Whom I bow and say: "Divine Majesty, I beseech You and pray that this morning may be the beginning of the renewal of the Church. Open, Lord, the hearts of these people, so that they may understand those things which are in me and which You have revealed and shown to me. O angels, who are here present, offer your prayers to the Divine Majesty and implore Him that He may hear them." *Deus misereatur nobis et benedicat nobis, illuminet vultum suum super nos et misereatur nostri, ut cognoscamus in terra viam tuam, in omnibus gentibus salutare tuum*[5] [Ps. 66:1–3]: "Lord, have mercy on us, and give us Your holy blessing," and let us see the renewal of Your Church. O Florence, this is the third Sunday of Advent, on which the Church in the Introit of the Mass today begins by saying as follows: *Gaudete in Domino, iterum dico gaudete*[6] [Philip. 4:4], that is, "Rejoice, let all rejoice in the Lord"; therefore, chant these words and beseech the Lord that this may be the beginning of your renewal, so that you may be able to sing once more: *Ecce, quam bonum et quam iocundum habitare, fratres in unum*[7] [Ps. 132:1]. And returning to the words we took up at the start of our sermon, I say unto you: *Erudimini, qui iudicatis terram*; "learn, learn," I say, "you who judge the earth," how you must live and reform yourself and others.

There is a proverb, one among many, though it may be ill said, that

---

4. Savonarola briefly outlines his scheme of the ages of the world, based on the four horses of the Apocalypse (Apoc. 6:1–8), in the third sermon on the Psalms, above. There he says that "the pale [the fourth horse] signified the time of the lukewarm, which is today." The age of conversion, then, would be the following, fifth age. For another scheme, based on seven ages, see Bernard McGinn, ed. and trans., *Apocalyptic Spirituality* (New York: Paulist, 1979), pp. 190–191.
5. "May the Lord have mercy on us and bless us; may He let His face shine upon us and be merciful to us so that we may know Your way on the earth, Your salvation among all peoples."
6. "Rejoice in the Lord; again I say, rejoice!"
7. "Behold, how good and how delightful it is for brothers to live together in unity."

states are governed neither with prayer nor with "Our Fathers."[8] But I want to prove to you this proposition: that every government and every kingdom, the more spiritual it is, the stronger and more powerful it is, and the less spiritual it is, the weaker and more infirm it is. Regarding this, philosophers postulate two powers: one active, which is God; the other passive, which is prime matter. All other things, corporeal things, are in the middle between these two extremes, since they act by reason of their form, which is called "spirit." The name "spirit" was at first given to the wind, then to the air, and finally to the forms.[9] Bodies, as regards their forms, must have a spiritual part through which they operate; but as body only, they have a passive power and cannot act but can suffer. And whatever they have of an active and operative power, they derive from their form and, as we should say, spirit. Insofar as they are spiritual, they act, and the more spiritual they are, the more they act. If two bodies fight and struggle with each other — as, for example, water and fire — the one which has more spirit wins. If the fire were the stronger, it would remove the controlling form in the water and impart its own form to it and make it take on the form and power of the fire. Therefore, the more form predominates in a body, the stronger it is; from which it follows that the more spiritual bodies are, the stronger they are, and everything which is more spiritual is stronger. Simple [i.e., pure] spirits, which are elevated above matter, are very strong; hence angels, which are spirits, can move any large thing *at a nod*. And among the angels, since there are a number of hierarchical ranks, the closer they are to God, Who is the simplest pure act,[10] the simpler and stronger they are, from rank to rank, up to God, in Whom there is no passive power whatsoever. See then, how much the spirit can do. Now, to our topic: for the reason stated above, a kingdom, the more spiritual it is, the stronger and better it will be, for, being nearer to God, its spirit participating more fully in the divine, it must of necessity be better, more stable, and more perfect.

The spiritual is made known in two ways, through nature and through grace, nor is one greater than the other, for God bestows them both; grace is participation in the Divinity, because God through His grace attracts the soul of man, as the magnet does iron, and makes that soul partake of God and His friendship. Divinity spreads its light, called grace, and diffuses it in

---

8. Attributed to Cosimo de' Medici the Elder, d. 1464, in Niccolò Machiavelli's *Florentine Histories,* bk. VII, chap. 6.

9. Savonarola here refers to Aristotelian "form," or essence, that which makes a thing what it is.

10. *Actus purus:* God is all actuality, with no potentiality, because the latter indicates deficiency. See Thomas Aquinas, *Summa theologica,* part I.I, quest. 2, art. 3 and quest. 3, art. 2.

that soul which disposes itself to receive it and makes it partake of God. It follows, therefore, that the kingdom founded on the grace of God will be more spiritual than the one founded solely on and ruled by natural light; *consequently*, it will be stronger and more stable. Therefore, this proverb of yours, that states cannot be governed by prayer and "Our Fathers," is not true, but rather, quite the contrary; they would be much better governed by the spirit than by other human contrivances. You have the example in our Savior, Who has founded His kingdom on grace; see how powerful it was from the beginning, such that those poor little simple and barefoot followers, with only the grace which Christ lent them, overcame the might of the world with weakness, wealth with poverty, the wisdom of the world with the folly of the Cross. See now that the power of the spirit and of being spiritual avails more than anything else. See also and read in all the ancient histories that men, the more they were in a state of grace, the more they achieved and won. Look at Moses, look at Josue, look at Gedeon and the others, of whom Scripture and ancient histories are full. See now, it has been proved to you in this argument concerning the nature and property of the spirit and of being spiritual through nature or through grace, what effects it produces. Now we are getting a little more particular. I want to demonstrate to you by means of other reasons that my proposition is true. But first let us rest a little.

I have told you above in the first argument what the nature of spirit and of grace can do; second, one who is in God's grace has the sign of being among His elect, and because God has a more especial providence for His elect than for others, so also that government which governs itself by grace, for it God has a more especial providence; therefore, it is better and more stable. Third, that kingdom which has persons of special strength is safer, but one who is in God's grace is equipped with a more especial strength, and so, his government is safer. Fourth, where there is greater unity, there is greater strength, but one who is in grace and charity has greater unity, and, consequently, greater strength. Fifth, where there is more obedience, there is greater power and strength, but where there is grace, there is greater obedience, hence, there is greater strength. Sixth, where there is the grace of God, there one lives more frugally, and living so makes men more vigorous than gluttons are; therefore, such a government is stronger. Seven, where there are greater riches, that place and its government are stronger, but greater riches are amassed where God's grace is, so that kingdom is stronger because the common welfare and the public can be assisted in their needs. Eight, where one lives virtuously, there all the arts and business enterprises willingly convene, and so they always make that place nobler and more famous. Nine, in the needs of war, soldiers more willingly go to the assistance and to the pay of a loyal and respected city which keeps its faith in its payments, and so forth. Ten, neighboring cities fear more the city that is well regulated and united within itself; also, with such a city the surrounding neighbors willingly establish amity. Also, where the grace of God is, the angels guard that kingdom and especially defend it in its every need for the protection of God's elect who live there.

By contrast, you can now understand how that kingdom fares which is without grace and is carnal and voluptuous; it will always be weaker and more passive in its power. What is more, such a government does not have God's special providence, but only the general sort. *Also,* the citizens, where there is no charity, do not love one another. Where there is no obedience, they are divided and do not have nor can they have good counsel among themselves because of the disunity among them, and so, their kingdom becomes weak and fleeting, and, because of voluptuousness, men become effeminate and, consequently, weaker. Thus, because of their lasciviousness, riches are consumed, whence follows the infamy of the city among all its neighbors; virtuous men flee from it when they see the government heading down the road to evil, while murderers and wicked men flock there.

Now you see that your proverb is false, when you said that states ought not to be governed with prayers and living well. But, Florence, if you want your government to be stable and strong and to endure a long time, you must return to God and to living uprightly; otherwise, you will come to ruin: *Servite ergo*[11] *Domino in timore.* And the first thing required, as I have often said to you, is that you confess with true contrition for the past and with the firm intention of never again turning to mortal sin, and that you attend to the common good of your city. And if you do this, I will give you a very great promise: that your kingdom will be most blessed. And I do not say that you should go to confession and Communion once a year, but often, and accustom your children to these confessions and to simplicity, rather than to pomp and vanity.

Furthermore, it is necessary that the Magnificent Signory ordain that all those things contrary to godly religion be removed from the city, and in the first place, to act and ordain that the clergy must be good, because priests have to be a mirror to the people wherein everyone beholds and learns righteous living. But let the bad priests and religious be expelled; I do not say that you do it on your own—that you deprive them of their benefices—but with the authority of the Supreme Pontiff see to it that the clergy and the religious of your city are good. They should not puff themselves up with so much material wealth, but give it to the very poor for God's sake and let go their superfluities, and in this way they would gain Paradise. It is necessary, I say, to see that the clergy are good and everything is reformed.

Likewise, it is necessary that the Signory pass laws against that accursed

11. Savonarola's addition.

vice of sodomy, for which you know that Florence is infamous throughout the whole of Italy; this infamy arises perhaps from your talking and chattering about it so much, so that there is not so much in deeds, perhaps, as in words. Pass a law, I say, and let it be without mercy; that is, let these people be stoned and burned. On the other hand, it is necessary that you remove from among yourselves these poems and games and taverns and the evil fashion of women's clothes, and, likewise, we must throw out everything that is noxious to the health of the soul. Let everyone live for God and not for the world, all in simplicity and charity, so that we may all sing: *Ecce quam bonum et quam iocundum habitare fratres in unum*.

Apprehendite disciplinam, etc.[12] [Ps. 2:12]: learn to live righteously, purified in accordance with God's will. Let this be our first resolution. The second: attend to the common good. O citizens, if you band together and with a good will attend to the common welfare, each shall have more temporal and spiritual goods than if he alone attended to his own particular case. Attend, I say, to the common good of the city, and if anyone would elevate himself, let him be deprived of all his goods. The philosophers postulate that there are two goods in the universe. The first one they call *ab extra* [external], the other *ab intra* [internal]. By *extra*, they mean *ad quod omnia convertuntur*,[13] that is, the good toward which everything is turned or converted. By *ab intra* they mean the order of the universe, which is in itself so ordered that nothing can be added or subtracted; it is like a harmony, with all according well together. Such an order is tightly connected within itself: the things above have a wondrous inclination toward the things below, and also the reverse, those below toward those above. They also say that the good has these two properties, that is, it is desirable to everyone and is diffusive of itself by its very nature. God, Who is the highest good, is most attractive and desirable, and so, every creature turns toward Him as its highest good and as its very cause [of being] and naturally loves God more than itself; and God, as the highest, most desirable good, turns everything toward Himself and upon Him everything depends. In this way, He is loved by His creatures, both on account of this love and friendship and *also* because everything loves its own being. But because the being of creatures resides more perfectly in God than in themselves, it follows that the creature, loving its own being, loves God more than itself; it would naturally want its own destruction sooner than that of God, its own cause [of being], because if the creature is taken away, its being remains in its cause, but if God is taken away, every creature loses its being. Thus, the creature loves God more than itself because every good and every kindness it has depends on the first and

12. "Take hold of instruction . . ."
13. "To which all things are converted."

highest good, Who maintains His own good in them; and all the good they have is through participation in the highest good, God Omnipotent, to whatever degree the creature is capable of it.

It is the same within the order of the universe: the creatures do not want to upset it; rather, they would more readily act contrary to their nature than go against the order of the universe, in which order, among other things, is *quod non datur vacuum,*[14] for one sees that nature abhors it to such a degree that the creature acts contrary to its own nature in order not to go against the order of the universe and leave a vacuum. Thus, you see that the hand, which is a particular member of man's body, if it sees harm come to the head, extends itself in front and lets itself be cut off in order to conserve the whole [*l'universale*] of the body and its other members. O Florence, learn to conserve the whole and attend to the common good more readily than to the particular, and to him who will attend rather to the common good than his own, God will grant temporal, spiritual, and eternal goods. And one who has his love properly directed and not distorted will always love the common good more than his own, just as the love of creatures, instilled in them by God, makes them love their own cause [i.e., God] and the universal more than themselves.

And if you do not do this, trust me, your love is neither right nor well ordered. Citizen, if you want to be an upright citizen, do not seek status or offices, if they are not given to you. And if they are given to you, exercise them for the public and common good and not for yourself. Direct your love, I say, toward God, Who is the highest good, and do not distort your love onto vain things. Do it, first of all, for the honor of God; second, so that you might not upset the universal order, which requires that you love God more than yourselves and the common good more than your own. And God will pour forth every good upon you and will give you of His light, so that you may know how to rule well your city and yourselves. *Furthermore,* the good order of the city will give you this also: that you will be loved by everyone, proceeding righteously as you ought, and not only will you be loved within the city, but outside of it her good citizens will be loved and will enjoy good fame everywhere. And if the city will, in this way, be good and full of charity, God will make her abound in riches, and the citizens will be able to share in them when they have been bestowed upon her, and what is more, the rich will be able to come to the assistance of the poor.

This is the way of good government, if you want it to last and be stable and would have it be pleasing to God. It is also necessary in a well-regulated city that those who govern make sure that taxes paid throughout the city and its dominions are imposed on goods justly and not arbitrarily, as has

14. "That there is no such thing as a vacuum."

sometimes been done, so that men can exert themselves for the universal good. And furthermore, take care that those taxes paid on goods may be moderate, so that taxes may not be more than income. Similarly, let excises be moderate so that the public and the private have each their share; in fact, it is necessary to remove every tyranny and every wrongdoing. As to the dowries: it is good that they be apportioned with some measure, for often one sees that they impoverish households and families when they are excessive; for example, the larger dowries of citizens should not pass beyond five hundred ducats; those of the artisans, about three hundred, as it might seem best to whoever must settle these things. But let no one for this reason interfere with the endowments of the *Monte* [*comune;* the public debt], which belong to the common good in which everyone has a share.

Above all, you must be on guard lest anyone make himself a leader or master of others in the city. Such people are without the grace of God and His special providence, and ordinarily they are of the worst sort, without intellect and without faith; they rule and govern their affairs by astrology, which is contrary not only to Holy Scripture, but also to natural philosophy, because they cannot possibly know future contingencies nor the many particulars which can happen. *Moreover,* such people have no true friendship with anybody; they do not trust anybody. True and joyful friendship is necessary for human affairs and preserves the virtues, but such people do not have any good virtue, nor do they contract true friendship; they always feel hatred toward the good and toward those who are not like them in morals, and they fear them, nor can they bear to have just men near them because justice makes men magnanimous, and they do not want them near them. No one is intimate with them but people of bad to worse character, and they say, "You stand up for me, and I'll stand up for you." Often they do not trust even their nearest and dearest, many times not even their own wives or children. Constant fear does not allow them to enjoy unadulterated happiness even in pleasant matters; in fact, their kingdom cannot be long-lasting, because all the people, though they do not show it, hate their tyranny. It is said that people under a tyrant are like water restrained and held by force, which, when it finds a small outlet through which to escape, bursts forth impetuously, wreaking utter ruin. Yet, this is what divine justice wills, for these tyrants are given to the people on account of their sins, as the Scripture says: *Dabo tibi regem in furore meo*[15] [Osee 13:1]; and when punishment has been applied, since it cannot last forever, for God is merciful, then the tyrant is thrown out and the whole people rises up against him. Therefore, when God wants to show mercy, He expels the tyrant. Take care then that such people do not rear their heads in your city, and attend to the common good.

15. "I will give you a king in My fury."

And how this ought to be done, I shall tell you as God inspires me. I have told you in days past that, when a natural agent wants to do something, all its forethought centers on the form of that thing; therefore, I have told you that you ought to impose a good form on your new government, and above all, that no one should think to make himself a leader if you want to live in liberty. The form which you have initiated cannot endure unless you give it a better order. I believe none could be better than that of the Venetians; you should take example from them, cutting out, however, some things which are neither to our purpose nor necessary to us, such as that of the doge. And I also believe that it would be well, in order to encourage everyone to behave virtuously, that the artisans be in some way qualified for office [*beneficiati*] and induced to behave well for the sake of being so honored. Also, it would not be altogether off the mark to assign higher offices by election, and minor ones by lot. Beyond this, it is necessary, as I have told you before, to pass laws against the vice of sodomy and infamous persons, and that every vice be excluded from your city.

So, as I say, impose a good form at the beginning, and then, concerning other circumstances, we will talk about it, and you will provide whatever may be necessary; what I have told you is not, in the end, inconsistent with what you have begun here. I encourage you to do what you can as soon as possible, for thus has God inspired me. His Most Illustrious Lordship will take care that your crown will not be taken away from you. If you do with a good will all this which I have said to you, I promise you *in God's behalf* remission of all your sins and great glory in Paradise. You, citizen of another state, from what would you like to be secure? Behold, you will be secure. The form of another way of life which is being imposed here will make you secure; governing the city in accordance with the will of God will make you secure, since you want to remain at peace with others: *recedant vetera et nova sint omnia*[16] [II Cor. 5:17]; let everything be renewed, and the form which will be imposed will make everyone secure, because everyone will be given what is his and what is suitable for him. No one ought to fear, for the whole city will be everyone's, and it is better to have the whole than the part.

Come now, let us begin today; let today be the beginning of living uprightly. And first, the first thing you will have to accomplish will be universal peace among all the citizens;[17] let all old affairs be pardoned and

16. "Let the old pass away, and all things be new." The Vulgate reads: *vetera transierunt; ecce, facta sunt nova* ("the old things have passed away; behold, they are made new").

17. The Law on Peace and Amnesty was passed on 6 March 1495. In contrast to Cosimo de' Medici's banishment of all his enemies after his return from exile in

erased. And so, I say to you, and command you on behalf of God: pardon everyone, I tell you, and consider that what has been done by those others might have been done by anyone had he been hounded about it, and if you do what I have told you, you will be secure on all sides. If it is not so, seize me and do me all the harm you want. If you, all the citizens, make this peace together and are united, believe me, once this union has been heard of, all your enemies will fear you, and, in this way, you will be more secure and stronger then they. Now, if this universal peace is to be made among all the citizens, those of the old as well as the new state, it is necessary, first, to turn to God, from Whom come every grace and every gift; let prayers be said for three days continuously in every place, so that God may dispose the hearts of everyone to do it willingly.

In the meantime, in order to be able to impart a good form to your government, be ready to impose the necessary order, so as to take better counsel. You have in your city sixteen gonfaloniers of companies[18] — for so you call them — who place under themselves and encompass the whole city and all its citizens. Let the citizens gather together, each under his gonfalonier, and let them take counsel and consider what seems to them the better form to take for your government. Every gonfalonier advocates the form which his citizens advise; thus there will be sixteen forms; and then, let all the aforesaid gonfaloniers gather together and select from all these forms four which seem the best and most stable to them and take them to the great Signory. There, after singing the Mass of the Holy Spirit in the hall, let them choose one of the forms, and have no doubt that the one thus selected will come from God. I believe, as I have said above, that the Venetians' form of government is very good; let it seem no shame to you to learn from others, for the form they have was given them by God, and since they adopted it, there has never been civil dissension among them.

And know this also, Florence: God has made and instituted Himself your Physician [*medico*],[19] if you will observe what I have told you; have no fear of your enemies, for you will always be more powerful than they, and God will defend you, *qui est benedictus in saecula saeculorum. Amen.*[20]

1434, the Mediceans were to be absolved of all charges of criminality and allowed to participate in the new government.

18. The leaders of the citizen militia, four for each quarter of the city, under whom all able-bodied citizens were enrolled.

19. Savonarola employs an ancient trope, but its insertion here, with no prior referent, in a discussion of the best form of government for Florence gives it the force of a pun: Florence will recover her health (and wealth) if, in place of the malpractice of the Medici, she will submit herself to the governance of the divine *medico*, God Himself.

20. "Who is blessed forever and ever. Amen."

Aggeus, Sermon XXIII

28 December 1494

Quare fremuerunt gentes et populi meditati sunt inania?[1] — Ps. 2:1

We told you in the preceding sermon, dearly beloved in Christ Jesus, that every creature is finite in its being and has its own particular being distinct from the being of every other creature; although one may be worthier than and superior to another, *nevertheless,* all have a determinate being, and only God has an infinite and endless being. In the same vein, we told you that the virtue of every creature is similarly finite and cannot operate further than its limit extends. Similarly, man's intellect *also,* though very great, has its own limitation, and although the natural light of the human intellect may be quite capable of a great many things, nonetheless, it cannot by itself, without another and supernatural light, come to the vision of God, nor understand the Trinity, nor understand the Incarnation of Christ, nor the mysteries of the Sacrament of the Altar. There is one kind of knowledge derived from the senses, and another from the natural light of the intellect, and still another from the supernatural light of grace and glory. And just as one born blind can have no knowledge of colors and their differentiation *even* if they are spoken of, so one who does not have supernatural light, though he may speak of the Trinity and divine mysteries, he cannot understand them or grasp them as they are, or feel and taste them as does one who has the grace of God and the gift of supernatural light.

But I have told you that the Apostle Paul used to say: *Hoc sentite in vobis, quod in Christo Iesu*[2] [Philip. 2:5]; he did not say *"know,"* he said *"feel,"* that is, taste and savor that which Christ has felt in Himself, which cannot be felt and tasted without this grace and supernatural gift. This was the first foundation of our discussion in the preceding sermon; we exhorted you to seek this light and this gift from God, for it is worth more than all the things of the world. On this light rests the whole foundation of your city. The lukewarm do not have this light; therefore, their affairs and actions are imperfect, and they never make any advance in the spiritual life. They do not believe that this light is that which makes one believe in the things of God. Florence, seek this gift from God, and, having it, you will be blessed. This

---

1. "Why do the nations rage, and the peoples hatch pointless plots?" From the Introit for Midnight Mass on Christmas Day.
2. "Feel this within you, which [was] in Christ Jesus."

light unites all the hearts which have it; thus, in the primitive Church, full as it was of this light, *erat eis cor unum et anima una*[3] [Act. 4:32]. And just as the light of the intellect constrains man to believe those things which are proved to him by natural reason, so this light of grace and gift of God makes man believe those things which are above the human intellect. Thus, the Apostle, speaking of faith and belief in that which is above the natural light, has said: *Fides est substantia rerum sperandarum argumento non apparentium*[4] [Heb. 11:1]. Just as, through natural light, man is certain of those things which are knowable through natural reason, such as, for example, the first principles, so, one to whom God gives this light and this gift is certain and clear about those things which he believes to be above the light of the natural intellect and is in no way in doubt, for, if there were doubts, his belief would not be faithful, as in the case of one who doubts some article of faith and can no longer be numbered among the faithful, *quia dubius in fide infidelis est*.[5] And so, up to this point we spoke yesterday morning, by your leave, and we finished our prophet Aggeus, and at the end we said a few words about the flood of tribulations which are to come. But let everyone get into the ark, because those who are in it have to be the seed for reforming the world, and when everyone is in it, the flood will come, and everything then will be confirmed. But because many nowadays contradict these things, this morning we want to answer them a bit.

I recall that at other times, in our previous sermons, we have said that Florence is similar in name to Nazareth, which is to say, *"flowery."* In this garden of Florence many flowers have already sprung up which would bear fruit, if they were not impeded, but the weeds try to spoil them. I asked the Gardener which weed is most noxious in this garden, and He responded that couchgrass [*la gramigna*] is the weed that does the most damage. The couchgrasses of concern to us are those that always speak ill of everything and vituperate everything. Oh, how much couchgrass of this kind is in your city, as well as in every generation of men and [kind of] persons, whether religious or secular! But understand that the Gardener wants to extirpate it and set it in the fire of plague and of tribulations; much of it, however, will always remain to contradict the good and make them more perfect, but truth will always come out and cannot perish.

3. "There was one heart and one mind." In the Vulgate: *erat cor et anima una*.
4. "Faith is the substance of things to be hoped for, of things not made obvious by proof." Cf. the Vulgate: *est autem fides sperandorum substantia rerum argumentum non parentum* [*sic*] ("but faith is the substance of things to be hoped for, evidence of things unseen").
5. "For to be doubtful in faith is to be unfaithful"; Aquinas, *Summa theologica,* part 2.2, quest. 5, art. 3.

Among all the things in any category, there is always one of that category which holds the first place and is superior to the others.[6] Among corporeal things pleasurable to the senses, they say it is lust which most excites human hearts. Among the things of the intellect, if we speak of the active life, they say that kingdoms are the first and chief things which move [men] more than any other thing. If we speak of the contemplative life, we say that in this category it is truth which always has the greatest force. Truth has this nature: that in peace it is overcome if it sits idly and is not set in motion, but in war, where it is contradicted, it wakes up and in the end wins all.

From this we see that the truth of Christ, in the beginning when He was born in a manger, was minute; later, as He grew, it kept increasing. But then when He died, it seemed to be all but spent; nonetheless, afterward, through His Apostles, it grew so much, bit by bit, that it spread through all the world. Now, because of tepidity, it has become minute once again, but rest assured that it has to grow and increase through all the universe. *Quare ergo fremuerunt gentes?* Why, then, do you go about raging against and contradicting the truth? This couchgrass which I have spoken about wants to impede the good plants so that they do not grow. These are those wise of the world, that is, they seem to be wise to the world, and always it is from them that the contradiction against faith arises. O you mad and foolish wise ones, have you not seen that all the world and all those wise men and great potentates of that time opposed themselves to and set all their strength against those few Apostles and disciples of Christ, when in the beginning faith was small, and yet they were left the losers? And do you believe that now, although the faith is much greater, you can extinguish it with your contradictions? I warn you that you will not extinguish it. So, once again I say, concerning your new reform, which you seek to attack and ruin: you will see in the end that you fight in vain. But tell me something: is this reform good or evil? You cannot say that it is not good; why, then, do you attack it? If we try to build a heavenly city and a government like to that of Heaven, of the angels and of God, what can you add to it and on what point can you say that it would not be good? The heavenly city is ruled and governed with the utmost order and quiet and peace; so would I like your city to be. There in the heavenly city are the hierarchies of the angels, there are the blessed, and every creature which is placed there by God remains within its own limits, and each one is bounded, and every one has its own degree of supernatural light, and they are all different according to the greater or lesser degree of the light of grace and glory which the Lord has granted them. They do not all see the essence of God in the same way, and no one

6. Ibid., part 1.2, quest. 90, art. 2.

tries to see more than his power or capacity allows, nor does he desire more beyond what divine wisdom has ordained for him, and so, everything remains at peace and all are blessed. God is above all of them, the purest and most blessed, bright-shining and aflame, and He purifies, illuminates, and enflames His angels, and those above illuminate those who are below, and this heavenly city has marvelous unity and a marvelous ordering of all this universe, most especially because of the love of the elect of God.

Oh, great dignity of men, if they were to consider how much care God has for them! Oh, if only you wanted to make a government in your city that would be like to the heavenly one, blessed would you be, O Florence! There are in Heaven three hierarchies: the first stands in the presence of God *sicuti in valvis sanctissimae Trinitatis*[7] and sees within God and the Divine Essence all the things which ought to be done in the world. The second sees by means of the illumination of the first; the third sees things in their particular causes, and more particularly through the illumination of those above, and executes the things ordained by the second. And beginning again from the first, because every hierarchy has three choirs, this first one, comprised of Thrones, Cherubim, and Seraphim, sees the end purpose within the Divine Essence, since the end is what ought to be considered first. The Thrones, which are removed from any earthiness and are so transparent as to be apt to receive every illumination, can perceive within the Divine Essence what things have to be done. The Cherubim see the way things must ultimately be regulated to their end. And lastly, because one must come to love and to have a great desire in order to attain the end, this belongs to the Seraphim, who set themselves and others afire to pray for this end before the Divine Essence. Once this has been accomplished and this first hierarchy completed, one turns to the second, where there are three more choirs, the first of them being the Dominations, who are free from any servitude, yet strict with respect to their performance [of duties]. These are not sent down to this earth, but rather always stand before God together with the other three choirs discussed above; thus it is written: *Mille milia assistebant ei, etc.*[8] [Dan. 7:10]. These Dominations give commands to their inferiors, who execute them, and this execution consists in getting rid of, first of all, of evil, which appertains to the Virtues, who repress the demons and other evils which impede the good. Then there are the Powers, who organize every good in order to attain to the cherished and desired end. And because it is necessary

7. "As though within the very doorway of the most holy Trinity"; Pseudo-Dionysius, *Celestial Hierarchies,* chap. 7; quoted in Aquinas, *Summa,* part 1.1, quest. 108, art. 1.

8. "Thousands upon thousands were standing by Him." Cf. the Vulgate: *milia milium ministrabant ei et decies milies centena milia adsistebant ei.*

at this point to descend to particulars, this role appertains to the third hierarchy, in which are another three choirs. The Principalities are the first
choir; they are the leaders and captains over provinces, and every province
has its own leader in charge of it. These have under them the Archangels,
and under the latter are the Angels, who are sent to the world in accordance
with the mysteries which must be accomplished and in accordance with
whatever is the order and will of God, time after time. This is the order of
the heavenly government, and in this way, God and His angels govern all
this universe. Now, does this not seem to you a most beautiful order? This
is the way I would like, if I could, to make the government of your city be
like God's. What evil do you see in this? None. Why, then, do you attack
it? Why do you contradict it?

Now note that in this way and with this order God will renew His
Church both with the sword and with tribulations, and great are the things,
I tell you, which they have to do. The first hierarchy has seen this end,
namely, that God wants to renew the Church, and has communicated it to
the Dominations and to the second hierarchy. The Virtues have had the
power to bridle the evil spirits so that they cannot harm God's elect and the
power to order them for the good. The third hierarchy has moved now, and
the Principality who is the captain of the province has come into your city
and has considered what is needed for this outcome; he has sent the Archangels to the superiors and the Angels to the others, so that they will remove
the evil and then introduce the good in order to renew the Church.

O Florence, recall what I have told you so many times: to renew yourself
first. The first principle stands unchanged: that you fear God and observe
His law so that you may gain from Him the light of grace, and blessed
would you be should you do it, for then everything would go well. But
avarice and the love of honors and high rank, which you hunt after, do not
allow you to have this light, nor does it permit you to accord with the angels
who inspire you and summon you to the good; but once you have this light
that I am talking about, you will not care any longer about honors or possessions. And so, I have laid down this foundation for you first of all: that
you fear God and seek the light of His grace, and I have told you that no
citizen should seek to be first or superior to the others but [all] should be
content, each within his own degree and limit, as I have said above that the
angels and the blessed are in Paradise, each within the limits God has given
him, without seeking more beyond; in this way you would be an ordered
city like the celestial one. And next, I have exhorted you to love the common
good, and not your own, and to be united in charity; and toward this goal,
I have exhorted you to make a universal peace and that no one should want
to make himself the head of the city or to be above the others; yet you do
not believe this, and you say that cities and the state are not governed with

"Our Fathers"[9] nor with prayers. You are greatly deceived, and in the end you will find yourself deceived.

Tyrannies do not want to be governed with prayers nor with doing good, but the state of the people of God has always been governed with prayers and with living a good life. So you will find in the Old Testament that the people of God, while they were good and did good, were always directed by the divine light and by the prophets and holy men illuminated by God, and the king always had to have at hand near him the book of Deuteronomy, wherein is the law of God. O Florence, God will provide for you if you want to do good, and He will give you, if you want, in the likeness of the first hierarchy, the Thrones, the Cherubim, and the Seraphim, enlightened and learned men who are aflame with the knowledge and ability to govern you in accordance with the will of God, as well as good prelates and priests. However, you would have to make provision, in the first place, that within your city religious practice is holy and good, and that superfluities and polyphonic songs which are full of lasciviousness are removed, and that everything is done with simplicity and devotion, and [that you] have saintly preachers and saintly religious and abandon those who do not follow in the ways of God. So, we should pray to God to send the plague and the tribulations which He has to send, so that such evil and lukewarm men may be taken away.

Let us pray to God that His will may be done in His Church. You must see to it that in your city the good are raised up and the bad suppressed, and in this way, you will be similar to the second hierarchy; your lords would have to hold the place of the Dominations, that is, be free from every obligation to a superior and every personal preference and immovable in enforcing justice and show no favoritism, but rather punish equally anyone who has gone astray. And because in the city there are both good and bad, you must elect magistrates who are like the Virtues and celestial Powers, that is, they know how to expel evil and reward good, that is, punish the bad and protect the good so that they may not be attacked, for we are still in the gravest danger. Make yourselves also like the third hierarchy which oversees particularities; these magistrates will be in the place of the Principalities, Angels, and Archangels, whom you will elect for the city as your domain, and these ought to perform their offices with love and charity and not take gifts from people, but execute justice sincerely and for the love of God, Who commands them to do so. These magistrates and officers hold the place of Principalities, and next, their ministers and notaries and judges hold the place of the Archangels, who make known to the elders [of the city] the truth and

---

9. Attributed to Cosimo de' Medici the Elder, d. 1464, in Niccolò Machiavelli's *Florentine Histories,* bk. VII, chap. 6.

the good of justice, as well as the honor of the public. Finally, in place of the Angels will be the servitors and attendants of the said magistrates, so that they may be good and faithful. And let both the one and the other of these types of ministers be of good repute, of good morals, and of perfect life.

O Florence, if you will be well ordered in this way, you will be the City of God, and blessed will you be if you will acknowledge what I have told you. But you who are so argumentative, what do you oppose to this mode of government? If the city were as I have described it, for I seek and I preach nothing else if not that you might be a city well ruled in this way and that you might be governed and ruled in accordance with God's will, what can you say against this? Why do you rage so? *Quare fremuerunt gentes?* as the psalm we have chosen as our text this morning says.

Now to the psalm: this is the one about lions vociferously roaring. If we desire to do good in your city, why do you consider it evil and go about roaring and crying? Why do you speak ill and roar like a lion? Perhaps you would like to be a lion among other cubs, as I have said at other times.

This is the will of God, Florence: that you live uprightly. The angel has come into your city, and you neither can nor ought to contradict this good which he points out to you. You will not see anyone contradicting this good except proud, vicious, or foolish men. It says: *Quare fremuerunt gentes?* "why do these peoples rage?" as if to say: they are not really prudent men, but people who live like pagans, without any religion. And yet note that it says *quare,* that is, "why?" as if to say: they do this without cause and without any reason. Consider also the life, the lives of these who speak ill, and you will see if they are the people that I am telling you about. *Et populi meditati sunt inania;* these lukewarm people have contemplated vain things in wanting to contradict the things of God which He has ordained. Do as much as you know how to do, for God wants His work to go forward and take place, and your cunning will in the end turn against you, and the same will happen to you as did to the sons of Jacob when they contradicted and persecuted Joseph, their brother. *Astiterunt reges terrae*[10] [Ps. 2:2]; so the psalm says, and continues that they make alliance with the kings of the earth; the devils, the lukewarm, and the powerful of the earth wage this war, and because the lukewarm have neither virtue nor truth in them, they assist and support the powerful of the earth. But know that truth will conquer and, in the end, will prove the stronger; truth does not seek to attach itself to another power; rather, on its own, alone and naked, it wins always. David, when he had to fight, wanted no arms, but threw them to the ground and simply went into battle and won [I Reg. 17:39 ff.].

10. "The kings of the earth stood together."

Principes convenerunt in unum[11] [Ps. 2:2]; they have united, the philosophers, poets, and theologians of this time, and others like them, and they have made an agreement together. The wicked always agree on evil; do not suppose that they might ever agree on good. And even about evil sometimes, for some purpose, God does not allow them to agree. They have now gathered together *adversus Dominum et adversus Christum eius*[12] [Ps. 2:2]; O you lukewarm, you fight against God and against Christ. Tell them, because they do not know they fight against God and that, in the end, He will punish them. *Dirumpamus vincula eorum*[13] [Ps. 2:3]; hear what they say: "Let us break these bonds, let us break this reform; we do not want to abide by these laws we have." And they say, "Do we all, then, have to be brothers and religious if we do not want to be bound so tightly?" *Proiciamus a nobis vincula et iugum eorum*[14] [Ps. 2:3]; "let us throw off from our shoulders this yoke which this friar wants to lay upon us." Know, then, that He *qui habitat in caelis, irridebit eos et [Dominus] subsannavit eos*[15] [Ps. 2:4]. "The Lord, Who dwells in Heaven, will make a mockery of them," of their cunning and malice, and He will see to it that they will in the end be deluded, and He will punish them. *Tunc loquetur ad eos in ira sua*[16] [Ps. 2:5]; "then," that is, in His own time, "God will punish them *et conturbabit eos*[17] [Ps. 2:5], and He will disturb them when He speaks in His anger," that is, when He shows that He intends to take vengeance with the sword and the fire of great tribulation. God strikes in His wrath when He gives so many strokes that they are unbearable, and He strikes in His fury when the sinner cannot hold onto the grace of conversion and goes from sin to sin, from punishment to punishment, and from one hell to another. Oh, how great is this wrath and this fury, for which one can see no remedy! Be on guard not to fall into this snare.

Now our psalm continues and says: *Ego autem constitutus sum rex ab eo super Syon montem sanctum eius*[18] [Ps. 2:6]. Christ speaks here in this psalm and says: "I have been appointed King by My Father on the holy mountain of Sion." Christ is Lord and King of all, as He Himself says: *Omnis potestas est data mihi in caelo et in terra*[19] [Matt. 28:18]. Commend yourself to Him,

11. "The princes came together as one."
12. "Against the Lord and against His Anointed One."
13. "Let us break their chains in pieces."
14. "Let us throw off from us their chains and their yoke."
15. "He Who dwells in the heavens will laugh at them, and [the Lord] will mock at them."
16. "Then He shall speak to them in His wrath."
17. "And will disturb them."
18. "But I am appointed King by Him over Sion, His holy mountain."
19. "Every power has been given to Me in Heaven and on earth."

O Florence; I see that you would like someone to be your leader. It is true *quod in omni genere est dare unum primum*,[20] which is the rule and measure of all others. Among the colors, white is the foremost; among hot elements, the first is fire; among shining things, the first is the sun; among virtuous things, the major virtue is God's: He is the major good to be found, and the more a thing approximates to the highest good, the better and the more perfect it is. And because the government of God, which is concentrated in one, namely, in Him alone, is the most perfect, so, when a government is similarly concentrated in one leader who is good, then it can be called a good and perfect government. It cannot be denied that those governments which have only one leader may not be the best, but it is necessary that the leader be perfect. If you consider how this pertains to the soul, all its parts are focused on reason as its most perfect part.

Now, Florence, what would you have? What leader, what king can be given you so that you remain at peace? I have told you before that one leader ruling alone is better for every place and every country; St. Thomas [Aquinas] says that in Italy princes become tyrants because here the sanguine humor and intelligence abound, which is not the case in countries beyond the Alps.[21]

Now, Florence, God wants to make you happy and wants to give you a leader and a King to govern you, and this is Christ—see, here our psalm says so: *Ego autem constitutus sum rex.* The Lord wants to rule over you, if you would have it so, Florence. But let yourself be ruled by Him, and do not behave as did those Jews who demanded a king from Samuel, and God answered, "Give them a king, since they do not want Me, Who ruled over and governed them in the past; they have not despised you, but have despised Me" [I Reg. 8:7]. You, Florence, do not do as they did. Take Christ as your King and place yourself under His law, by which He governs you. Act in such a way as to be this Sion, of which the psalm speaks here. Sion means *"watchtower"*: that you may stand high up in matters divine in order to descry them and contemplate them. Let Christ be your Captain, the One Who gives you a new reform of holy living. That reform which has been preached to you is nothing other than unity, that is, the love of God and neighbor. This is nothing other than God's commandment: *Hoc est mandatum meum, ut diligatis invicem*[22] [Ioh. 15:12, with *mandatum* from 13:34]. For

---

20. "That in every class of things there is one which is foremost"; Aquinas, *Summa,* part 1.2, quest. 90, art. 2.
21. *De regimine principum,* bk. IV, chap. 8. This theory is more correctly attributed to Tolomeo da Lucca; see Donald Weinstein, *Savonarola and Florence: Prophecy and Patriotism in the Renaissance* (Princeton: Princeton University Press, 1970), p. 293.
22. "This is My commandment: that you love one another." John 15: 12 reads: *Hoc*

this reason, I have told you to make this universal peace, and if you will do these things I have told you, you will be a glorious city, and Christ, your Captain, will conduct all your affairs, and you will be the reform of all Italy and even outside of Italy.

Stand with Christ, Florence, and do not search for another leader; He is the Son of God, as the psalm says here: *Filius meus es tu; ego hodie genui te*[23] [Ps. 2:7]. *"Today"* means *"eternally,"*[24] for He is generated *from eternity* by the Father, Who can do whatever He wills. Look here at the psalm, for the Father says to Him: *Postula a me et dabo tibi gentes, hereditatem tuam*[25] [Ps. 2:8]. This means pray, because Christ is not to be considered solely in Himself, with regard to His own Person, but also mystically in relation to His members, and so, it would say: pray, you who are His members, and God will give the nations as an inheritance to Christ, His Son; that is, the infidels will be converted, and they will come to the faith of Christ, and His Church will be renewed. Pray, then, you members of Christ, and present to the Father the Passion of His Son, and faith will spread throughout the world *usque ad terminos terrae*[26] [Ps. 2:8], as the psalm says at this point: "to the utmost ends of the earth." *Et reges eos in virga ferrea*[27] [Ps. 2:9], and Christ will rule with great justice; *et confringes eos sicut vas figuli*[28] [Ps. 2:9]; Christ will strike the sinners, and they will break like vases, that is, they will be converted as Christ touches them and will be reformed into better vases, as the potter does when the vase he has made does not please him; he gives it a blow with his hand and makes another more beautiful and better than the first.

The rest of the psalm continues: *Nunc, reges, intelligite*[29] [Ps. 2:10], but let us first pause a while, and we shall soon resume with the rest.

On another occasion, dearly beloved, I told you that we were at sea, and in the ship, at a distance from the harbor, I stood keeping a lookout. I saw the harbor full of every good thing, but it was very far away. I encouraged and have always encouraged the sailors to row hard, because I saw corsairs and pirates pursuing us, and still I find myself up on the mast and

---

est praeceptum meum — ut diligatis invicem; 13: 34: *Mandatum novum do vobis ut diligatis invicem.*

23. "You are My Son; today I have begotten You."

24. *Hodie . . . aeternaliter:* since every day is today, i.e., God dwells in the eternal present.

25. "Ask of Me, and I will give the nations as your inheritance."

26. "Even to the ends of the earth." *Usque ad* inserted by Savonarola.

27. "And You shall rule them with an iron rod."

28. "And You shall break them like a potter's vessel." The words are in a different order from the Vulgate.

29. "Now, kings, understand."

on the yardarm, crying out and urging the rowers, and I see many who are negligent and do not want to row. I find myself exhausted in mind and body, exhausted, because it has already been four years since I began to wear myself ragged for you, Florence, and if it were not, I believe, for the prayers of good people, I do not know if I would have been able to bear so much. I have also been much afflicted by the constant remembrance of the scourge I see coming and by fear and trembling for your sake, that you might not perish in it. I have also been worn out with continual prayer and continual labors for your sake, to aid you so that you would not perish. And another thing: your sins have afflicted and perturbed me grievously, because I am always seeing you doing evil, and I fear your sins may put you in peril. I am exhausted, I say, for all these reasons. Everything I have done or am doing, everything is for your well-being. The religious from our convent who are present here all know that you are perhaps aware of only a small part of the labors which I bear for love of you; nonetheless, you have always murmured and continue in the same vein, but you should not do so, especially since I have deprived myself of every comfort for your sake. Now I am here and I find myself, as I have told you, utterly exhausted; I need to rest, if only for a little, and to seek some quiet. I am still at sea and I see the harbor very far away. I could, if I wanted to, turn back, but God does not want it. For this reason, I must stay, I must obey God; even so, I must have a bit of quiet for a few days and sleep a little on the yardarm. With the permission of these canons, our lords, another friar will come in my place for two or three sermons, and God will give him courage, although in himself he may not be worthy, and he will keep up the work of God in our midst. Then I will return on the feast of the Circumcision [1 January] or St. Sylvester's [31 December], or another day; things will work out for the best.

Nunc, reges, intelligite, the psalm goes on to say, and addresses these upper ranks, saying: you who rule, listen for a moment to My words. Therefore, turning to these government officers who have been appointed, the old and the new, we say: you, who have completed your duties and have carried out in your own time this new reform, you have done well, a thing pleasing to God, and have gained a great crown in heaven, because you have labored for the honor of God and for the well-being of your city. The greater the exertion and the greater the virtue, the greater the reward and the beatitude, for it takes greater exertion and greater virtue to rule others than to rule oneself. So you who have organized and directed the government will receive a great reward from those others and from the whole city, and in this, you have assimilated yourselves to God, Who rules the entire universe, since you have organized the government of your city. I say: the past officers have gained a great crown in Paradise, as well as a great crown among men. The angels have aided them, for this has been the work not only of men, but also of God. And so, these officers deserve to be held in reverence by you and to have their names inscribed in your chronicles to give example to those yet to come to conduct themselves well.

You others, the new officers, you must, at the very least, arrange this universal peace before you leave office. *Nunc, reges, intelligite*; I speak to you who must now rule and govern: heed what I say to you. This work which has been accomplished by the past officers has been accomplished by the will of God, and it has been the work of God more than of men, as you can recognize from the many signs you have seen. But you also can join in the work of God and be glad to assist in it. God wants you to pursue this work with fervor and charity, and those same angels who assisted the old officers will assist you also. Be diligent and solicitous about the common good and this universal peace. Christ is your King, and may you be His ministers. Be glad and thank Him for choosing you as His coadjutants. *Servite Domino in timore et exultate ei cum tremore*[30] [Ps. 2:11]: "serve God with fear and rejoice with trembling." *Apprehendite disciplinam, ne, quum irascatur Dominus, ne pereatis de via iusta*[31] [Ps. 2:12]; take care to do well, so that the Lord God may not be enraged against you, because, if you should not bring this reform to completion (since it will be completed with peace), and if the failure were to come from you either through negligence or some other thing, the Lord would be enraged against you and would make you lose your good fame, and contrariwise, He would give you punishment where He has given glory and fame to others. God wants to perfect this work in every way, so be sure to be good champions and good ministers. *Apprehendite disciplinam;* study well what you have to do because you have to labor in this work for the City of God. Confide all to God, not to men, and have no doubt that God will assist you.

Now our boat, as I have said, remains at sea and sails toward the harbor, that is, toward the peace which Florence must have after her tribulations. Officers old and new, all of you together, see to it that this universal peace is realized; make sure that good laws are passed in order to stabilize and strengthen your government. And let the first be this: that people no longer call themselves Bianchi ("whites") or Bigi ("grays"),[32] but that all together be united as one and the same. This partisanship and partiality in the city are not good. Pass sentence upon those who still speak in this way: Bianchi or Bigi. Oh, do it, because this is a matter of great moment that might return upon you one day to your ruin and destruction; the Guelph and

30. "Serve the Lord with fear and rejoice in Him with trembling."
31. "Take hold of instruction, lest, when the Lord is angered, you perish from the just way."
32. See the discussion of political affiliations in the Introduction.

Ghibelline factions[33] might be revived once again in your city, as in days gone by, and you know the consequences. Do what I have told you and have no fear if you do it. Truly, I say, do it, and on my conscience I assure you that it will be well done. Your enemies will be those you will make for yourselves. If you do not do it, you will make so many enemies that you will not be able to extinguish it as you would like. I tell you this for a good reason and as one inspired by God. Pass these good laws, and you will have no enemies. I would not speak to you with such resolution if I had not here touched upon the foundation of what I tell you. Make true peace, from the heart, and incline always toward mercy more than justice this time, for God has once again employed more mercy than justice toward you. O Florence, you were in need of great mercy, and God has shown it to you; do not be ungrateful. *Superexaltat misericordia iudicium*[34] [Ps. 2:13]. If you do what I tell you, and do it earnestly, Florence will enjoy great peace; otherwise, it will be the opposite. Keep this well in mind, and may all be in praise of Christ, *qui vivit et regnat in saecula saeculorum. Amen.*[35]

---

33. The two major parties in the ongoing struggle for supremacy between the Pope (Guelphs) and the German emperor (Ghibellines).
34. "Mercy is exalted above judgment." The Vulgate has *superexultat* ("exults over").
35. "Who lives and reigns forever and ever. Amen."

Treatise on the Rule and Government of the City of Florence

Written at the Request of the Most High Lords of the City during Giuliano Salviati's Term as Gonfalonier of Justice

Preface

O Magnificent and Eminent Lords, given that many excellent men of high intelligence and superior learning have written at great length and with great wisdom about the government of cities and realms, it appears to me superfluous to compose still more books on a similar matter, since it would serve no other purpose than the multiplication of books, lacking in all usefulness. Nonetheless, since Your Lordships have requested me to write treatises, not on the government of realms and cities *in general,* but about the new government of the city of Florence *in particular,* insofar as I am able, dispensing with all unsupported claims and superfluous words and with the utmost possible brevity, I cannot honestly refuse such a thing, since it would be most advantageous to your State, useful to all the people, and necessary to my office at the present.

For many years, by the grace of God, I have preached in this city of yours and have always followed four themes: I have exerted myself with all my skill, first, to prove that the faith is true; second, to demonstrate that the simplicity of the Christian life is the highest wisdom; third, to announce future things, some of which have already come to pass, while others will befall us shortly; and finally, I have spoken on the topic of the new government of this city of yours. And while I have already written about the first three things, although I have not yet published the third book, entitled *On Prophetic Truth,* I have yet to write about the fourth topic in such a way that all the world may see that I preach sound knowledge in accordance with both natural reason and the doctrines of the Church.

Although it was and is my intention to write about and discuss this matter in Latin, as I had already done in composing the first three books, and to explain how and how much and when one expects a religious [one in vows] to treat of and become involved in secular states, however, as Your Lordships have requested that I write succinctly in the vernacular for greater usefulness to common people, there being few of them who understand Latin in comparison with men of letters, it will be no trouble for me to produce this treatise first in Italian, and then, when I am more free from present occupations, I shall put my hand to the Latin with such grace as Almighty God will concede to me.

So then, I shall briefly treat, first, of the best form of government for the city of Florence, secondly, of the worst, because, although it is necessary first to exclude the bad and then to build up the good, nevertheless, because the bad is the privation of the good, one cannot understand the bad if one does not first understand the good. And so, it is necessary according to the order of argument, first, to treat of the best government, then the worst. Thirdly, I will make clear what may serve as the foundation for eradicating the worst form of government and for establishing, perfecting and preserving the present good form of government in the city of Florence, so that it may become the best.

First Treatise

Chapter One
That government is necessary in human affairs; what constitutes good, and what bad, government

Almighty God, He Who rules the entire universe, distributes the power of His government over creatures in two ways. On the one hand, into those creatures who have neither intellect nor free will, He infuses certain powers and perfections by which they are naturally inclined to progress through fitting means to their proper end, attained without flaw unless they are impeded by some contrary cause, a situation which rarely occurs. Therefore, such creatures do not govern themselves, but are governed and led to their own proper ends by God and by the nature He has given them. On the other hand, creatures who have the gift of intellect, such as humans, are governed by Him in such a way that they also need to govern themselves because they have been given the light of intellect by which they are able to distinguish between the useful and the useless, while the faculty of free will gives them the power to choose freely that which is agreeable to them. Because the light of intellect is debilitated, especially in childhood, a person cannot manage wholly for himself without the assistance of another, especially since virtually every individual person is insufficient in himself to provide single-handedly for all his needs, corporal as well as spiritual. Thus we see that nature has provided all the animals with those things of which they have need to sustain life, that is to say, with food, bodily covering, and weapons to defend themselves. Furthermore, when they are sick, through natural instinct they turn to seek out medicinal herbs, a state of affairs not natural to humans. But to humans God, Governor of all things, has given reason and the instrumentality of their own hands, by which they can prepare these things for themselves. And because, considering the fragility of the human body, an almost infinite number of things are necessary to nourish it, to make it grow and to preserve it, for provision of which so many skills are required that it would be impossible or at least very difficult to find them all together in one single person, it is necessary that people live together in order that each may help the other, some employed at one skill, others at another, and making together one complete corpus of all the sciences and arts.

For this reason, it is well said that he who lives alone is either God or a beast; that is to say, he is either a man so perfect that he is almost like a god on earth because, like God, he has no need of anything nor does he require the assistance of anyone else, as, for example, St. John the Baptist and St. Paul, the first hermit,[1] and many others; or he is like a beast, that is, he is completely deprived of reason, with no concern for clothing, nor shelter, nor cooked and prepared food, nor interchange with other humans; rather, he follows the instincts of his senses, deprived of every trace of reason. Because, therefore, so very few humans are to be found who would be either so perfect or so bestial, these being excepted, all the rest are constrained to live in communities, whether in cities, castles, villas, or other places.

Now, given that humankind is very prone to do evil, most especially when it is without law or fear, the invention of law is necessary to check the aggressiveness of evil people so that those who wish to live uprightly are safe, for there is no animal more evil than a man without law. Thus we see that the gluttonous are incomparably greedier and more insatiable than all other animals; neither all the food nor all the ways of cooking it to be found in the world suffice to satisfy them, since they seek to satisfy not nature, but rather their unregulated desire. Likewise such people surpass all other animals in the bestiality of lustfulness, because unlike the animals, they observe neither time nor appropriate manner; rather, they do things that are abominable to think about as well as to hear of, things which no animal does nor so much as imagines doing. In cruelty also humans outdo the animals in that the latter do not make cruel war against each other, more especially against their own species, as do humans, who seek out diverse weapons of assault and diverse means to torture and kill each other. Above and beyond these things, there are also among humankind pride, ambition, and envy, from which dissension and intolerable warfare arise among them. Nevertheless, since people must of necessity live in community with others and desire to live in peace, it has been necessary to establish laws by which the bad may be punished and the good rewarded.

But because it is not fitting that one make laws for others to whom he

---

1. Paul the Hermit (229?–342), not the Apostle Paul.

is not superior, and since one who has no power over other men would not be able to make them observe the laws, it is necessary to establish who may have responsibility for the common good and who may hold power over others. Because every individual looks after his own good, if no one had concern for the common good, human interchange would be unable to endure, and the whole world would fall into confusion. Some people, therefore, have convened to nominate a single leader who would have responsibility for the common good and whom everyone must obey; this form of government has been denominated a kingdom, and the ruler who governs it a king. Other people, either because they are not able to agree on a single person or because it seems better to them to do so, agree together on the principal and best and more prudent members of the community, desiring that such persons might govern them and distributing the magistracies among them for different terms; this form of government has been denominated an aristocracy [*governo delli ottimati,* i.e., "government of the best"]. Yet others want the government to remain in the hands of all the people, who would have to distribute the magistracies at different times to those who seemed best to them; this form of government has been called civil government, because it appertains to all the citizens.

Thus, since government of the community is established to maintain the common good so that people may live together peacefully, dedicate themselves to virtue, and more easily attain to eternal felicity, that government is good which diligently seeks to maintain and increase the common good and induces people to live uprightly and virtuously and, most importantly, to perform their religious duties. That government is bad which forsakes the common good and attends to its own particular benefit, heedless of human virtue or living uprightly if such is not useful to its own particular benefit; such a government is called a tyranny. And so we have seen the necessity of government among humankind, and what constitutes good and what bad government *in general.*

Chapter Two
That although government by a single ruler, when it is good, may be the very best by its nature, nevertheless, it is not good for all communities

And so, since that is good government which attends to the good, spiritual as well as temporal, of all its citizens, whether it may be administered by a single leader, or by the foremost among the people, or by all the people, one should understand that, speaking absolutely, civil government is good, that of the best citizens is better, and that of a king is the best. This is so because, given that the union and peace of the people is the purpose of government, this union and peace is easiest to accomplish and preserve under the authority of one than of several, and easier under the authority of a few than of a multitude. When everyone in a community looks to one person alone and obeys him, they do not divide into factions, but all are constrained by love or fear of that one person. But when there are several leaders, then this man chooses one leader and that man another, and what pleases one is pleasing or displeasing to another, and so the people do not stay so closely united as they do when only one person reigns; the more who govern, the less they remain united. It is an axiom that the power which is concentrated is stronger than that which is dispersed: for example, fire has more force when its materials are united and constrained together than when they are scattered and diffused.

Keeping in mind, then, that the power of government is more united and bound together in one than in many, it follows that by its very nature the government of one, when it is good, would be better and more effective than any other form. In the same way, given that the government of the world and of nature is the best government and given that art follows nature, the more human affairs assimilate themselves to the government of the world and of nature, the more perfect they become. Keeping in mind, too, that the world is governed by one Being, Who is God, and that all natural things in which one can see some form of government are governed by one ruler (for example, the bees by one queen, the powers of the mind by reason, the members of the body by the heart, etc.), it follows that that government of human affairs which is administered by one governor would be by its nature the very best of all governments. And so, our Savior, desiring to establish the best government for His Church, made Peter the head of all the faithful; furthermore, He desired that every diocese, as well as every parish and monastery, should be governed by one person, and that, finally, all of these lesser leaders should be under the authority of one head, His [earthly] vicar.

Since, positively speaking, the government of one person, when it is good, surpasses all other good governments, such a government should be established in every community, if possible; all the people should act in agreement to select one good, just, and prudent prince to whom all would owe obedience. But it should be noted that this form of government is neither good nor possible nor even to be attempted in every community, because many times it happens that that which is best absolutely may not be good, and may even be bad, in some places or for some peoples, just as the state of perfection of the spiritual life, that is, the religious state, is the best state in and of itself, but such a state is, nevertheless, not to be imposed on all Christians. Indeed, such a thing should not even be attempted, nor would it be a good thing, because many would not be able to bear it, thus causing dissension in the Church, for, as our Savior says in the Gospel, "No one sews new cloth to an old garment; otherwise, the old will tear away and create a worse rent. Neither is new wine put into old wineskins lest the skins burst and the wine be spilled"[2] [Marc. 2:21–22; Luc. 5:36–37]. Thus, we see that some food is good and indeed excellent in and of itself, and yet to some people, when they eat it, it would be poison; likewise, fresh air, perfect in itself, is bad for some constitutions. And so, while government by a single person is the most perfect in and of itself, it would, nevertheless, be bad and indeed the worst form of rule for the sort of people inclined to dissension, because it would often lead to the persecution and death of the prince, from which infinite ills would befall the community. The prince being dead, the people would divide themselves into factions, and civil war would follow, creating divers leaders; among these, he who conquered the others would become a tyrant and so despoil the city of all good, as will be demonstrated below. And so, if the prince wants to make himself secure and form a stable government over such a people, he would of necessity become a tyrant and drive out all other powerful people, plunder the possessions of the rich, and weigh the people down with many afflictions; otherwise, he will never be able to secure his power.

There are, then, some peoples whose nature is such that it will not tolerate the rule of one without great and unbearable difficulties; they are like those people who by custom and constitution are habituated to the brisk air and to living in camps, so that if someone should make them remain in nice warm rooms and wear fine clothes and eat delicate food, they would instantly take sick and die. When wise and prudent leaders are faced with the responsibility of establishing a government, they first consider the nature of the people to be governed; if their nature and customs easily lend themselves to the rule of one, then this form of government should be selected in preference to any other. However, if this form of government does not suit them, then the leaders are forced to choose the second option, government by preeminent citizens. And if the people will not submit to this either, then they must be given a civil government with laws agreeable to their nature. Now let us see which of these three good governments is most suitable for the people of Florence.

Chapter Three
That civil government is best for the city of Florence

For anyone who diligently considers what we have said above, there is no doubt that if the Florentine people were to submit to the government of one individual, they would appoint for themselves a prudent, good, and just

2. In keeping with his intention to make this treatise accessible to all, Savonarola gives most biblical quotations in the vernacular.

prince rather than a tyrant. But if we examine well the opinions and arguments of the wise, of natural philosophers as well as theologians, we will clearly perceive that, considering the nature of this people, this form of government would not be agreeable. For they say that such a government is best suited to people who are of a servile nature, such as those who lack courage or intelligence, or both the one and the other. However, although people who abound in courage and are strong in body may be audacious in war, nevertheless, should they lack intelligence, it is an easy thing to make them subject to a prince, because it would not be easy for them to machinate against him on account of the weakness of their intelligence; rather, they follow their ruler just like the bees, as one sees among the northern peoples. On the other hand, those who have intelligence but lack courage, being cowardly, easily yield submission to a single prince and live peacefully under him, as do the eastern peoples and more besides who lack either one quality or the other. But peoples who are intelligent, who abound in courage and are bold in war, cannot easily be ruled by one lord if he does not tyrannize over them, because, by virtue of their intelligence, they machinate against the prince continually, and, because of their daring, they easily put their plots into execution, as is seen all the time in Italy, which as we know through the experience of times past up to the present has never been able to persevere under the regime of one prince; on the contrary, although it is a small province, it is divided up among almost as many princes as there are cities, which are virtually never at peace with each other.

It is a given, then, that the Florentines are the most intelligent of all the peoples of Italy and the most sagacious in their undertakings, as well as spirited and bold, as has appeared many times through experience. Although they seem dedicated to the mercantile trade and appear to be a quiet people, nonetheless, when they commence any undertaking, whether of civil war or against external enemies, they are most terrible and fierce. As one may read in their chronicles of war, they have taken arms against many great princes and tyrants and have never willingly surrendered to any such; rather, they have defended themselves to the end and carried off the victory. Thus, it is not in the nature of these people to support the government of a single prince, even were it good and perfect, because, given that the bad are always more numerous than the good, through the shrewdness and hostility of evil-minded citizens (who are primarily motivated by ambition), either the prince would be betrayed and killed or he would be forced to become a tyrant. The more diligently we consider the matter, we perceive that not only is the government of a single ruler ill suited to the Florentine people, but even less so is the rule of preeminent citizens [*ottimati*], because custom is second nature. Just as nature is inclined in one direction and cannot be diverted from it—rocks, for example, are inclined to fall down and are not able to rise except under force—in the same way, custom becomes converted into nature, and it is extremely difficult, if not impossible, to change a person's habits, much less a people's, even when they are bad ones, because they have become second nature.

Now, the people of Florence, having selected a civil regime since antiquity, have invested so much habit into it that for them it is more natural and agreeable than any other form of government, since through habit it is so deeply impressed in the minds of the citizens that it would be difficult and indeed almost impossible for them to do away with such a government. Although it happens that we have been governed by tyrants [the Medici] for many years, nonetheless, those citizens who usurped authority during this time did not tyrannize over the city by boldly arrogating to themselves absolute authority, but more astutely governed the people in a way that did not divide them from their nature or their customs. And so, they retained the form of the city's government and the customary magistracies, all the time keeping an eye out so that no one should become a magistrate who was not their ally. And so, since the form of civil government by the people has remained intact, it has become so natural to them that to try to alter it and give them another form of government would be nothing less than to make them go against their nature and against ancient custom; to do so would generate such perturbation and dissension in this community that it would be put in danger of losing all its liberty, to which experience, the master of all arts, best attests. Furthermore, every time that a government of leading citizens has taken control in the city of Florence, there has been great dissension, and it is never pacified until one faction has driven out the other and one citizen becomes a tyrant. As soon as that man has been installed, he has usurped liberty and the communal property with the result that the people are always malcontent and restless. And if Florence has been divided and full of discord in the past on account of the ambition and hatred of leading citizens, so much greater would such disturbances be in the present—if God in His grace and mercy had not provided for the Florentines [at the time Piero de' Medici was deposed]—because of the return of the citizens who had been exiled at divers times by previous governments, especially by the regime of 1434, at which time so much hatred was nourished by the injuries done to many households and kinfolk.[3] Had God not stretched forth His hand, there would have been spilling of much blood, destruction of many houses, and discord and civil war would have followed within as well as without. Things being what they were because of the coming of the king of France [Charles VIII], anyone who found himself in the city at that time and had any judgment would have had no doubt that this

3. At the recall of Cosimo de' Medici from exile, who in turn exiled his enemies.

was its final destruction. But, through the prayers of the good men and women who inhabit the city, the council and civil government, framed not by men but by God Himself, have been the instruments of divine power in maintaining its liberty. Certainly, anyone who has not entirely lost his natural judgment on account of his sins, considering in what dangers the city has been during the past three years, cannot deny that it has been governed and preserved by the grace of God.

And so we may conclude that, by reason of the divine authority from which the present civil government proceeds and the foregoing arguments, civil government is best for the city of Florence although it may not be the best in and of itself. Government by a single ruler, although it may be best in and of itself, is nevertheless not good nor the best for the Florentine people, just as the state of perfection in the spiritual life is the best in itself but may not be the best or even good for many faithful Christians for whom some other state of life would be the best, although that state in and of itself would not be the best. And so, we have proved our first point, that is, what would be the best form of government for the city of Florence; now it is time to demonstrate the second, which is, what would be the worst form of government for it.

Second Treatise

Chapter One
That government by a single person, when it is bad, would be the worst, especially that of one from among the citizens who becomes a tyrant

The rule of a single leader is the best among all the forms of government when it is good, since it is more stable and is less easily converted into tyranny than is the case when many people share power, because the more that power is decentralized, the easier it becomes to generate discord. Nonetheless, just as it is the most perfect and stable when it is good, when it is unjust and bad it is the worst of its kind among all the forms of bad government. In the first place, this is so because, as evil is contrary to goodness, so is the worst contrary to the best; therefore, it follows that while government by a single leader is the best when it is good, it would be the worst when it is bad. For, as we have said, power is stronger when it is united than when it is dispersed; thus, when a tyrant reigns, the power of such an evil government is united in one person, and because there are always more evil people than good ones and because like is attracted to like, all the bad people seek to unite themselves to him, especially those who desire to be rewarded and honored, but also many more unite themselves to him from fear, as do those people who are not totally depraved but who nevertheless love the things of this world and either through fear or love of what they desire fawn on him. Those who are good but not entirely perfect follow him out of fear and do not have enough daring to resist him, and since there are so few perfect men, so that it is as though there were none, all the power of the government unites itself into one. Moreover, since that tyrant is wicked and unjust, he brings every evil to perfection and easily corrupts every good thing. But when there are many bad people who hold authority, one impedes the other, since the power of government is dispersed among many; they do not have as much force to do the bad things which they desire to do as does a single tyrant. Likewise, a government is so much the more evil the more it divides itself from the common good, because, given that the common good is the end of every good government, the closer it approaches to this, the more perfect it is, and the further it removes itself from this, the more imperfect it is; everything achieves its perfection by approaching its end, but by distancing itself from it becomes less perfect. But it is certainly true that a bad government of many leaders distances itself from the good less than a bad government presided over by one leader, because, although those many usurp the common good, such as revenues and honors, and divide it among themselves, nevertheless, insofar as it remains divided among many, to a certain degree such a good remains communal. But when all of the commonweal is resolved in one person, nothing remains in any way common; rather, all becomes the particular property of one person; therefore, the bad government of one ruler is the worst of all forms of government because it departs most from the common good and is the most destructive of it. Also, these qualities increase its longevity because the government of one is by its nature more stable than that of many, and even though it may be bad, the former is not so easily impeded or overthrown as the latter, because the members report directly to the chief and only with great difficulty raise an insurrection against him. Within the government of a tyrant it is very difficult to make one person a chief of the opposition against him, because he keeps an eye out continually to extinguish those who could become chiefs and is very careful to act in such a way that his subjects are unable to unite against him; he remains ever vigilant in this matter. But when many people govern, it is an easy thing to disrupt their bad government because it is easier for good people to gather together with others who seek the public good and to create dissension among the bad citizens in order that they might not band together; this is easily accomplished, because each of them seeks his own particular good, from which dissension soon arises among them. The bad government of a single person is the worst of them all for the very reason that it is so much more difficult to impede and overthrow. We must note, however, that although the bad government of one ruler is by its nature the worst, nonetheless, sometimes greater mishaps occur within a bad government of the many than in that of a single ruler, especially as it comes to an end, because when a government of many is bad, it is divided unrestrainedly into many parts, and in this way it begins to rip apart the commonweal and the peace, and finally, if no remedy is found, one group will of necessity remain superior and drive the other one out. From this follow infinite evils, temporal, corporal, and spiritual; among these, the worst is that government of the many resolves itself into a government of one because the one person who finds most favor with the people is transformed from a citizen into a tyrant. Given that the government of a single leader, when it is bad (as we have said), would be the worst form of rule, nonetheless, there is a great difference between the government of one who, from a natural and true master [*signore*], becomes a tyrant, and that of one who is transformed from a citizen into a tyrant, because from the latter arise many more misfortunes than from the former. If such a one wants to reign, he must put down, whether by death or exile or other means, not only his enemies but also those citizens who are his equal, whether in noble station or riches or fame, and he must effect their undoing before the eyes of all who could threaten him; from these atrocities proceed an infinite number of woes. But such does not befall the ruler who is a master by nature, because none would be his equal, and the citizens, being accustomed to subjection, would hatch no plots against his position; therefore, he does not live in suspicion as does the citizen who was made a tyrant.

Because among those peoples who live under governments of preeminent citizens or under civil governments it is easy to create divisions through those discords among men which occur every day and through the multitudes of wicked people and murmurers and swearers, and to fall prey to tyranny, such peoples ought, with all precaution and diligence, to provide themselves with very strong and severe laws so that none may become a tyrant, punishing with the supreme penalty not only those who talk about it but even those who hint at it; for every other failing they should have compassion toward the sinner, but in this case they should have no compassion on him whatsoever, other than the assistance owed to the soul.[4] The penalty for plotting tyranny should never be decreased, but rather increased to give an example to all, in order that everyone may be on his guard not only, I say, not to hint at such a thing, but not even to think about it. He who is compassionate in this matter or neglects to punish it sins most grievously before God, because from the very beginning infinite misfortunes follow from the government of a tyrant, as we shall demonstrate below. When evil people see that punishments are light, they take the dare, and little by little tyranny wedges its way in just as drops of water little by little erode

4. Last rites.

rock. Therefore, one who does not punish such an offense heavily is the cause of all the evils that follow from the tyranny of such citizens; every people which governs itself civilly ought, rather, to tolerate more readily every other evil and mishap that follows from a civil government, when it is imperfect, than to allow a tyrant to rise up. So that everyone may better understand how great are the evils which follow from the government of a tyrant, although I have already discussed that elsewhere, nevertheless, for a greater understanding, we will describe the tyrant himself in the following chapter, what are his principal characteristics, for to try to tell all of tyranny's failings and abuses and grave sins and all the evils which follow from it would be impossible, they being infinite.

Chapter Two
Of the malice and worst qualities of the tyrant

Tyrant is the name for a man of evil life, the worst among all those people who want to rule above all others through force, especially if he becomes a tyrant from among the citizenry.[5] First, it must be said that he will be proud, vaunting himself above his equals as well as his superiors, to whom he ought to be subjected. Furthermore, he is envious and always saddened by the glory of others, especially other citizens of his own city; he cannot bear to hear the praises of others, although many times he dissimulates and hates with an agonized heart; he rejoices in the shame of his neighbor to such a degree that he would prefer that everyone were calumniated in order that he alone might remain glorious. On account of the fantasies of greatness and sorrows and fears which gnaw him within, he searches for delights as a medicine for his afflictions, and so, one rarely—or perhaps never—finds a tyrant who is not lustful and given to the delights of the flesh.[6] Because he cannot maintain himself in state nor afford the pleasures which he desires without abundant wealth, it follows that he nourishes an inordinate appetite for possessions, for which reason every tyrant, insofar as he is tyrannical, is avaricious and thieving, not only stealing the principality,

---

5. Though some scholars contend that Savonarola did not have Lorenzo de' Medici specifically in mind when he characterized a tyrant, one has only to compare Francesco Guicciardini's sketch of the man to see that he provided many of the details, though not the entire portrait (*History of Florence*, ed. and trans. M. Domandi [New York: Harper, 1970], chap. 9). Guicciardini's assessment: "In fact, we must conclude that under him the city was not free, even though it could not have had a better tyrant or a more pleasant one" (p. 76).

6. "He was very libidinous, completely carnal, and persistent in his love affairs, which lasted many years. Many thought that this so weakened his body that it caused him to die quite young [at forty-three]" (ibid., p. 74).

which belongs to all of the people, but also usurping what belongs to the community council,[7] besides the things which he covets and takes from individual citizens by his wariness and hidden ways, and sometimes he even does it openly. It follows then that the tyrant commits virtually all the sins in the world. First, because he has pride, luxury, and avarice, which are the roots of all evils. Second, because he has set his entire raison d'être in the position which he holds, there is nothing he will not do to maintain it; indeed, there is no evil he is not prepared to do with regard to his position, as experience demonstrates, because the tyrant will stop at nothing to maintain his state; therefore, he has either planned to do or is accustomed to committing all the sins in the world. Third, because from his perverted government derive all the sins of the people he governs, and so he is accountable for all of them, just as if he had committed them himself; from this it follows that every part of his soul becomes depraved. His memory always records every injury and seeks to avenge itself, while forgetting benefits from friends; his intellect is always working to devise frauds, deceptions, and other ills; his will is full of hatreds and perverse desires, his imagination of false and caitiff representations, while all his exterior senses are used for evil ends, whether for concupiscence itself, or to the detriment and derision of his neighbor, because he is full of wrath and disdain. All of these afflictions attend him because he has set his raison d'être in such a position of power, which is difficult, even impossible to maintain for a long time, because nothing violent can last forever; wherefore, seeking to maintain by force that which destroys itself, he needs to be very vigilant.[8] The end being evil, everything arranged to support it must of necessity be evil, and so the tyrant cannot but think of, remember, imagine, and do things which are evil; if he should do something good, he does not do it in order to do good but rather to acquire fame and make friends for himself to be able to maintain himself all the better in this perverse state. Thus he is like the devil, king of the proud, who never thinks of anything but evil; if he should say something true or do something that has the semblance of good, he organizes it all for a bad purpose and especially for [the gratification of] his great pride. So, the tyrant orders all the good things he does for [the gratification of] his pride, which he seeks to preserve in every way possible; the more moral the tyrant appears to be on the outside, so much the more is he cunning and evil, mastered by a greater and wilier devil, who transforms himself into an angel of light so that he may strike a harder blow.

Moreover, the tyrant is immeasurably bad for the government, for in

7. Lorenzo raided public funds on a number of occasions to avoid bankruptcy for himself (ibid., p. 73).
8. "His gravest and most troublesome fault was his suspiciousness" (ibid., p. 74).

conducting it he attends principally to three matters. First, that the subjects might not know anything about the government, or very little and nothing of importance, so that they might not perceive his treacheries. Second, he seeks to stir up discord among the citizens, not only within the city but also within the fortresses, towns, and houses, among his own ministers of government, and even among his counselors and his own servitors, because, just as the kingdom of a true and just king is preserved by the amity of the subjects, so is a tyranny preserved by general discord, because the tyrant favors one of the parties, which holds the other down and makes the tyrant strong. Third, he seeks always to abase the powerful in order to secure his own position; he kills or causes misfortunes to befall those most distinguished for their possessions or nobility or intellect or other virtues; the wise he considers without reputation and makes mock of them to destroy their fame so that they will not be followed. He wants to have the citizens for his servants, not his partners; he prohibits them from convening and gathering together so that they will not make alliances together for fear that they might plot against him; he contrives that the citizens might become more unsociable together than one can be alone, disrupting their friendships, dissolving marriages and family relationships, wanting to make them do everything his way. When these things have been accomplished, he seeks to instill discord within families; he has scouts and spies everywhere, who report to him whatever anyone does or says, men as well as women, priests and religious as well as laymen; to this end, he instructs his wife, daughters, sisters, and womenfolk to strike up friendships and conversations with other women so that they might elicit the secrets of the citizens from them and all that they do and say at home.

He takes care that the people may be occupied with the necessities of life; when he can, he keeps them poor with duties and taxes. Many times, especially when there is peace and abundance, he distracts the citizenry with spectacles and holidays so that they might concentrate on themselves rather than on him;[9] similarly, he wants the citizens to think about governing their own homes rather than concerning themselves with state secrets, in order that they might be inexpert and imprudent in governing the city and that he alone might remain the governor and appear most prudent of all. He honors flatterers so that everyone is forced to flatter him and to support him; he despises anyone who speaks the truth because he does not want to allow anyone to oppose him, and so he disdains those who speak freely and does not want them near him. He does not often banquet with his own

9. "He was mourned by the populace and by the lower classes, who had constantly enjoyed abundance, pleasures, entertainments, and many feasts in his time" (ibid., p. 76).

citizens but would sooner dine with foreigners. He has the friendship of lords and great foreign dignitaries because he considers his own citizens to be his adversaries and is always afraid of them; therefore, he seeks to fortify himself against them by means of these foreigners. He wants his own government to be behind the scenes, seeming outwardly not to govern at all,[10] saying and making his accomplices say that he does not want to alter the city government but to preserve it; therefore, he seeks to be trusted as the protector of the common good and shows mercy in small matters, sometimes giving audience to boys and girls or to poor people, many times defending them from even the slightest injury. Of all the honors and dignities that are bestowed upon the citizens, he shows himself to be the originator and looks to make sure that everyone acknowledges him for them; but the punishment of those who go astray or who are charged by his accomplices in order to bring them down, or when bad things happen, these he blames on the magistrates and excuses himself for his impotence to assist them in order to acquire fame and the goodwill of the people and to make those who are magistrates hated by those who do not see through his fraud.

Likewise, he seeks to appear religious and dedicated to divine worship, but he performs only certain exterior actions such as going to church, giving alms, building temples and chapels, or donating paramenta for the sake of ostentation. He also converses with religious people and feignedly makes confession to one who is truly religious in order to appear genuine, but, on the other hand, he despoils the Church, usurping benefices and giving them to his satellites and accomplices and hunting them up for his own sons; in this way he usurps goods both temporal and spiritual. He does not want any citizen to design anything remarkable, such as grand palaces or feasts or churches, or to accomplish any great deeds in government or in war, so that he alone might appear wholly singular. Many times he abases great men through his secret devices and then, when he has brought them low, openly exalts them higher than they were before so that they might consider themselves obligated to him and so that the people might consider him clement and magnanimous, as a means to acquire still more favor.

The tyrant does not leave justice in the hands of ordinary judges in order to favor and to kill or abase whomever he pleases. He usurps the funds of the community[11] and discovers new ways to burden and oppress them to pile up money from which he supplies his satellites, and with it he also puts in his pay princes and military leaders, at times when they are of no use to

10. The *modus operandi* of the Medici.
11. A stab at Lorenzo for "borrowing" from the *Monte di doti* (a dowry fund), thereby leaving many poor girls with little choice but a convent (if they could find one to take them) or prostitution.

the community, to give them some income and make them his allies; by this means, he is able to burden the people more respectably, saying that it is necessary to pay the soldiers. With this excuse he plans and incites wars without cause, through which he does not seek or desire to obtain victory nor even to pillage the possessions of others, but only to keep the people impoverished and the better to stabilize his own position. From public moneys he frequently erects grand palaces and temples and hangs his family crest everywhere. He also patronizes singers and songstresses because he seeks to be glorious above all others. To those he has raised up, who are themselves of low condition, he gives the daughters of noble citizens as wives in order to abase and destroy the reputation of the nobility and to exalt such base persons as he knows will be faithful to him, not because they have generosity of spirit, but because they have need of him; such persons being generally very proud, they consider the tyrant's friendship to be the greatest blessing.[12]

The tyrant willingly receives presents in his thirst for acquiring things; on rare occasions he gives things to the citizens, but more often to princes and foreigners to make them his friends. And when he sees something belonging to a citizen which pleases him, he praises it and regards it and makes gestures that demonstrate his desire for it, so that out of either embarrassment or fear the owner will give it to him; he retains near him his flatterers, who encourage and exhort the citizen to make him a present of it, or else he asks to borrow things which please him and then just never returns them. He despoils widows and wards, pretending that he wants to protect them; he takes the possessions and fields and houses of the poor to make parks or gardens or palaces or other things for his own pleasure, promising to pay them a fair price, and then he does not even reimburse them at half the value. Neither does he pay wages to those who serve in his house as they deserve, but rather prefers that they wait on him for nothing. He seeks ways to pay his satellites with things that belong to others, giving them offices and benefices which they do not deserve, taking from others the offices of the city and giving them to his own. And if some merchant has a great deal of credit, he schemes to make him go bankrupt, so that no one else might have the extent of credit that he has.

He raises up evil men who would be punished by justice without his

12. "He strove to keep down as much as possible those citizens whose nobility, wealth, power, or reputation he thought would cause them to be highly esteemed. . . . He chose . . . men whom he had raised to reputation, men who would have had no power whatever without his support. . . . This same suspiciousness made him see to it that powerful families did not become related through marriage. . . . At times, to avoid the marriages he feared, he would force some young man of quality to marry a woman who would normally have been unacceptable" (Guicciardini, *History*, pp. 74–75).

protection so that in defending him they defend themselves, but if perchance he should elevate some good and wise man, he does so to show the people that he is a lover of virtue; nonetheless, he always keeps an eye on such good and wise men and does not place any trust in them but handles them in such a way that they cannot do him any harm.

Whoever fails to do the tyrant courtesies in public or to present himself at his house or in the piazza is considered an enemy. He has his minions everywhere, who go about leading youths astray and inciting them to evil even against their own fathers; they lead them to him, seeking to implicate all the youths in the land in their wicked counsels and to make them enemies of all those whom he considers his adversaries, even their own fathers. He endeavors to make them consume their substance in carousing and other wantonness, so that they become impoverished and he alone remains rich.

No one can fill any office unless he knows about it or rather approves it; even the cooks in the palace or the servants of magistrates he does not want appointed without his consent. Many times he raises to office the younger brother or the least person in the house, or someone who lacks every virtue and goodness, in order to incite the eldest and best to envy and hatred and to create discord among them. No one can give censure or praise or make any peace without him, because he always seeks to favor one party and degrade another according to his will alone.

All good laws he cunningly seeks to corrupt because they are contrary to his unjust government, and he constantly makes new laws to suit his own aims. In every office and magistracy, within the city as well as without, he has someone who watches and reports to him everything that is said and done, and who, on his own part, gives directions to certain officials as to how they are to act;[13] thus he is the refuge of all evildoers and the exterminator of the just. Above all else he is vindictive, to such a degree that even the slightest injuries he seeks to avenge with the greatest cruelty in order to put fear into all the others, because he fears everyone.

Whoever disparages the tyrant must abscond, because he will be hounded even to the ends of the earth, and by treachery or poison or other means the tyrant will have his revenge; he is a great homicide, because he always desires to remove obstacles to his government, although he always pretends to be otherwise and to regret the deaths of others. He often acts as though he wants to punish the perpetrator of such murder, but then he

13. "This same distrust caused him to place a permanent chancellor in Rome, Naples, and Milan, to ensure that the ambassadors there would never depart from his wishes. The chancellor, a salaried public official, was to be at the service of the resident ambassador, but in direct touch with Lorenzo to keep him informed about what was going on" (ibid., p. 76).

secretly helps him escape; some time later, when such a one pretends to ask for pardon, he recalls him and keeps him close to him.

The tyrant always wants to be superior in everything, no matter how trivial, such as in playing games, in public speaking, in jousting, in racing horses, in learning, and in every other area in which there is competition, he always seeks to be in first place; when he cannot be so by virtue of his own ability, he asserts his superiority through fraud and deception.[14]

To uphold his reputation he rarely gives audiences, and many times he attends to his own pleasures and makes the citizens stand outside waiting for him, and when he does come, he gives them short shrift and ambiguous responses. He wants to be understood by gestures, because it seems that he is ashamed to want and to ask for things which are evil in and of themselves or to reject the good, and so he speaks in clipped phrases which have the appearance of good, but he wants their underlying meaning to be understood.[15] Often he sneers at respectable people both with words and actions and laughs at them with his cronies.

He carries on secret correspondence with other princes, and then he convenes a council to decide what is to be done, not telling the secret which he knows, so that everyone else hazards a guess, and [the tyrant] alone appears to be prudent, wise, and well informed of the secrets of [other] leaders; by this means, he wants to arrange it so that he alone lays down the law for everyone. The least little note from him or a word from one of his retainers is worth more before any judge or magistrate than any justice.

In short, nothing is stable under a tyrant, because he rules everything in accordance with his will, which is directed not by reason but rather by passion; therefore, every citizen under him hangs by the thread of his pride, every asset is vulnerable to his avarice, all the chastity and modesty of women are endangered by his lustfulness. He has pimps and procuresses who drive the wives and daughters of others to him by force, especially during great banquets, where, many times, they have secret passageways to the rooms through which the women are led against their will, and there they remain, taken in the snare. He tolerates sodomy, to which he is sometimes addicted to such a degree that no well-favored boy is safe. It would be an interminable affair to run through all the sins and evils which the tyrant commits, but

14. "He desired glory and excellence more than any man, but he can be criticized for having carried this desire even into unimportant matters. In versifying, in games, and in other pursuits he got very angry with anyone who equalled or imitated him" (ibid., p. 72).

15. "Lorenzo was by nature very haughty. Not only did he not want anyone to contradict him, he wanted people to understand him almost instinctively, so that in important matters his words would be few and vague" (ibid., pp. 73–74).

these suffice for the present tract. Now let us come to the city of Florence in particular.

Chapter Three
Of the good things of the city which the tyrant impedes; and that tyranny is most especially noxious to the city of Florence

If tyranny is the worst form of government for every city and province, then it seems to me that this must be especially true for the city of Florence, speaking here as Christians. Because all governments of Christian people ought to be directed finally toward the beatitude promised to us by Christ, and because one does not arrive at such an end except through the medium of holy Christian living, than which (as we have shown before elsewhere) nothing can be better, Christians ought to frame their governments, both particular and universal, in such a way that this good Christian living is its principal result, above all else. And because this living uprightly is nourished and increased by the practice of true divine worship, every effort ought to be made to maintain and preserve and augment this worship, not so much with ceremony as with truth, and with good and holy and learned ministers of the Church, as well as religious, and in every city (as much as they are able and allowed) they should remove bad priests and religious, because they will find no men who are worse than these, whom they call holy, nor who do more harm to godly religion and to holy Christian living and to every good government. It is much better to have few and good ministers than enough but bad ones, because the bad provoke the anger of God against the city, and since all good government proceeds from Him, they are the reason that God withdraws His guiding hand from the city and lets the grace of good government run to ruin because of the gravity and multiplication of their sins, through which they draw behind them the majority of the citizens and relentlessly persecute good and just men. Just so, in the Old and New Testaments we read and discover over and over that all the persecutions of the just proceed principally from such people, that on account of their sins the scourges of God have come among the people, and that they have invariably destroyed every good government, corrupting the minds of the king and princes and other leaders.

It is necessary, therefore, to take great care that within the city everyone lives a good life so that it may be filled with good men, especially the ministers of the altar, because, as godly religion and holy living increase, the government is necessarily perfected. In the first place, because God and His angels take special care concerning this: as we read frequently in the Old Testament, when godly religion stood firm or grew, the kingdom of the Jews went from good to better; we read the same thing in the New Testament and [the histories] concerning Constantine the Great, Theodosius, and other deeply religious leaders. Second, through the prayers which those who are deputed to the worship of God make continually, and of the good people within the city, and also the communal prayers of all the citizens on great solemnities: thus we read in the Old and New Testaments that cities have been extricated from the greatest dangers through prayer and provided by God with innumerable spiritual and temporal benefits. Third, through good counsel, through which kingdoms preserve and augment themselves: when the citizens are good, they are specially illuminated by God, as it is written: *Exortum est in tenebris lumen rectis corde* [Ps. 111:4], that is, "in the darkness of the difficulties of this world, the righteous in heart have been illuminated by God."[16] Fourth, through their unity, because where the holy Christian life is lived, there can be no discord, in that all the roots of discord, namely pride, ambition, avarice, and lustfulness, have been removed, and where there is unity, there is power; and so it has been proved in times past that minor kings, through unity, have became great, and great ones, through discord, have been laid waste. Fifth, through justice and good laws, which good Christians love: thus Solomon says: *Iustitia firmatur solium*[17] [Prov. 16: 12], that is, "Through justice the kingdom is strengthened." The kingdom will grow in wealth on account of righteous living as well, because the people, not spending their money superfluously, accumulate an infinite sum in the public treasury, with which they pay soldiers and officials, feed the poor, and make their enemies stand in awe of them. Even more so will it grow because merchants and other rich men, hearing of this good government, will flock willingly to the city, and their neighbors, who have been badly governed by others, will also desire their government. Because of their unity and the goodwill of their friends, they will have need of only a few soldiers, and all the arts and sciences and virtues will come to the city, and there they will gather together an infinite treasure and will expand the realm in many directions. This expansion will be good, not only for the city but also for other peoples, because they will be well governed, and godly religion will spread, and the faith and holy Christian living will increase; this will render great glory to God and to our Savior, Jesus Christ, King of kings and Lord of lords [I Tim. 6:15; Apoc. 19:16; see also Apoc. 17:14].

Now all of these good things tyrannical government impedes and undermines, because nothing is held in greater detestation by tyranny than the worship of Christ and righteous Christian living, because it is its direct opposite, and opposites seek to cancel each other out; therefore, the tyrant tries

16. More literally, "light has arisen in the darkness for the righteous in heart." The Vulgate has *iustis* rather than *rectis corde*.
17. "The throne is made secure with justice."

as hard as he is able to diminish true worship of Christ in the city, although he must do it secretly. If he finds some good bishop or priest or religious, especially one who speaks the truth freely, he cautiously endeavors to remove him from the city or else to corrupt his mind with adulation and presents. He gives benefices to evil priests and to his own ministers and cronies, and he bestows favor on corrupt religious and those who praise him. He is always scheming to corrupt the youth and all righteous living in the city as the thing preeminently contrary to him. If this is a serious matter, or rather the greatest possible evil, in any city or kingdom, it is all the more grievous in those of Christians, among which, it seems to me, there is none greater than the city of Florence. First, because this people is very much inclined toward the practice of Christian worship, as anyone knows who has been here; therefore, it would be the easiest matter to establish in it a most perfect worship and the holiest Christian living if [the city] were under a good government. It is certain, as we see every day, that if there were no wicked priests or religious, Florence might return to the manner of living of the first Christians and would be like a mirror of religion to all the world; thus, as we see at present, despite such great persecution directed against the righteous living of the just and so many impediments both within and without, despite excommunications and evil propaganda, the city lives in such a fashion among the cities of the godly that (it may be said with peace toward all others) no one can name, nor is there, any other city where there might be a greater number of greater perfection of life than in the city of Florence. If then, among such great persecutions and impediments, the city grows and prospers through the Word of God, what might it accomplish if peace were to live within it, undisturbed by the contradictions of tepid and wicked priests, religious, and citizens?

This is even more strongly confirmed by the keenness of intellect found in them, for it is known to all the world that the Florentines have a subtle spirit; we know also that this quality is a very dangerous thing when it is turned to evil, especially when this happens to children, because then they are harder to cure and more apt to multiply the evils of this world. On the other hand, if they are turned to good, it will be difficult to pervert them, and they will be apt to multiply such good in many ways. Therefore, it is necessary to make sure that the city of Florence has a good government and that there is no way for a tyrant to gain control, knowing as we do how much evil tyrannical government has done in this and other cities, because so great has been the cunning [of Florentine tyrants] that they have often deceived the princes of Italy and kept divided not only neighboring cities but also those far away. The wealthier and more industrious the city, the easier it has been to do this, for which reason all Italy has many times been thrown into confusion.

What we have said—that a tyrannical government cannot endure for long—is further confirmed because (as we have said) nothing violent can last forever, and because, speaking as a Christian, tyrannical government is permitted by God to punish and purge the sins of the people, and so, when they have been purged, such a government must necessarily cease, because once the cause is removed, so must be the effect. If then such a government cannot last for long in other cities and kingdoms, so much the more is it unable to endure at peace in Florence, because the genius of Florence is such that it cannot remain at rest; we know through experience that there have often been uprisings here against those who govern, and from these uprisings and civil wars sometimes follows the disturbance of all Italy, which causes many evils.

For these reasons, then, and others which for brevity's sake I pass over, it manifestly appears that if in every city tyrannical government ought to be removed and any other sort of imperfect government ought to be more readily endured than tyranny, from which follow so many truly evil consequences, such that one can find neither more nor more grievous ones elsewhere, then how much more ought this to be done in the city of Florence? Anyone who will digest the preceding discussion well will understand without difficulty that there is in this world no punishment nor scourge so burdensome that it would be proportionate to the seriousness of the sin of the one who would seek or attempt or so much as desire to be or to make a tyrant over the city of Florence, because every punishment conceivable in the present life is minute in comparison to such an offense. But Almighty God, the just Judge, will know how to punish it as it deserves both in this life and in the next.

Third Treatise

Chapter One
Of the establishment and practice of civil government

Now that we have determined that for the city of Florence the best form of government is civil government and that tyranny, bad for any city, is the worst for it, we next must consider how to take precautions so that no tyrant might establish himself in it and how to introduce the said civil government. Since tyrants sometimes rise to power by force of arms, and such force cannot be resisted with reason, we cannot give any instructions concerning this; but we intend to make clear how to prevent a citizen from making himself tyrant over the city little by little by seizing control of it, not by force of arms, but with cunning and with allies, as has been done in the past. But because some might believe that it is necessary to make sure that no citizen becomes excessively rich, expecting that his money will draw the people to him, and that excessively rich citizens easily make themselves tyrants, and because trying to prevent this occasions many misfortunes, in that it is very dangerous to try to strip possessions from the rich or to place a limit on the wealth of the citizenry, we therefore declare that riches are not the principal cause that a citizen becomes a tyrant. If a rich citizen has nothing but riches, the majority of the other citizens, on whom the government of the city depends, will not congregate around him, they being little able to trust a rich man of this sort, because the citizens would never allow someone to make himself a tyrant for the cost of a few dollars; in a city as large as Florence, let a citizen be as rich as he likes, he will never be able to buy off as many citizens as he would need, given that each would want a great deal of money and that the greater part of the citizens are rich themselves and so would naturally disdain to take service under one whom they consider merely equal to themselves.

Because, then, the citizens seek dignity and reputation within the city more than money, knowing that reputation helps one to grow wealthy, it is necessary to prevent any citizen from acquiring the authority, by any means, to distribute the benefits, offices, and honors of the city, because this is precisely the foundation upon which a tyrant is established in the city, since citizens love honors and want to be esteemed. When they see that they cannot otherwise obtain the city's benefits and honors, they submit to whoever they believe can distribute them. Thus, as the number of citizens who submit themselves to the one who has the greater authority increases little by little, he makes himself a tyrant; when more than one person usurps such authority, the people are necessarily divided and finally combat one another, and the person who has the larger following or who emerges victorious becomes the tyrant. Therefore, it is necessary to establish that the authority to distribute offices and honors is invested in all the people, in order that one citizen might not have greater respect than another, and that each might consider himself equal to the others, and that no one can turn himself into an overlord.

Because it would be very difficult to gather all the people together every day, it is necessary that some number of citizens be invested with this authority of all the people; but because a small number could be corrupted by friends, family ties, and money, it is necessary that the number of citizens invested be large. And because everyone might perhaps want to be one of this number, and this would generate confusion, because the common people might also want to meddle in the government, which would soon produce disorder, it is necessary to limit this number of citizens by some method so that no one could get in who might be dangerously disruptive, and yet no citizen could complain. Once the number of citizens has been decided upon, this body should be called the Grand Council, and since it would possess the power to bestow all government honors, there is no doubt that it would be the governor of the city; then, when it has been created, it will be necessary for it to do three things.

First, it must establish itself by due procedure and very strong laws, so that the state cannot be subverted. And because some citizens, their affections for the city being misdirected, are more solicitous of their own special preserve than of the common good, so that they will fail to assemble in the Council (by which negligence the Council might lose its authority and therefore be dissolved), one will need to make provision that anyone who fails to assemble at the proper time without a legitimate excuse must pay so much the first time, and the penalty must be a heavy one, the second time even heavier, and the third time he should be removed from the Council, so that what one will not do for love, he will do to avoid a debt, for one ought to love the common good more than one's own self-interest. For this common good, one ought to risk both one's possessions and one's life, especially considering what great benefits proceed from a good government, and from a bad one what great evil, as we have said. It is also necessary to set up other similar laws, penalties, and provisions, as experience continually demonstrates always and everywhere, in order to secure the Council and stabilize its authority in the city, because if this is taken away, everything will degenerate.

Second, provisions should be made to ensure that such authority cannot become a tyranny, because just as one who is a natural leader sometimes allows himself to be corrupted by bad men and to become a tyrant, so can a good Council, through the malice of the evil, become wicked and tyrannical; and because vicious and foolish men, when they increase in number, are the cause of many ills in government, it is necessary to exclude such men from the Council as much as possible. Likewise, make certain, with the weightiest penalties, that they cannot make agreements [with each other] nor ask for favors or votes; whoever is found to be at fault on this point should be punished without mercy, because a government which does not punish severely cannot preserve itself. And so, it is necessary to work diligently to remove all imperfections and roots of evil through which the Council, or a majority of it, might be corrupted and come into the hands of the unscrupulous, because it would be utterly destroyed instantly, and tyranny would take control of the city.

Third, it is necessary to ensure that the Council not be overburdened by having to assemble a certain number of citizens for every minor issue; rather, let the leaders attend to important matters, and let them entrust the lesser to their subordinates, always reserving to themselves the authority to bestow offices and benefits, so that everyone must pass through their sieve in order to remove the grounds for tyranny, as we have said. Also, it is necessary to make provision that they meet at a certain time, not inconvenient to the citizens, and that many items of business are brought together at once and dealt with at the time they meet. They must find a way to make elections brief and to expedite them as much as possible. We could say many more things concerning this and go into particulars, but if the citizens of Florence will attend to what we have already said and to what we will say in the following chapter, they will have no need of my instructions, because they themselves, if they want, know how, with the help of God, to provide for every concern bit by bit, learning better every day through experience. I do not wish to exceed the limits of my station, so as not to give our adversaries cause for complaining.

Chapter Two
What citizens must do to perfect a civil government

Every Florentine citizen who wants to be a good member of his city and to lend his support to it, as everyone should, must believe that this Council and civil government have been mandated by God, as is indeed true, not only insomuch as every good government proceeds from Him, but also through the special providence God has at present for the city of Florence; concerning this, anyone who has been here for the past three years and who is not blind and totally without judgment clearly understands that if it had not been for the hand of God, there would never have been such a government in the face of so much and such strong opposition, nor would it be able to maintain itself up to this day against so many traitors and so few champions. But because God wants us to exercise our intellect and free will, which He has given us, He makes those matters appertaining to human government imperfect at first so that we with His help might make them perfect. Since, then, this government is still imperfect and lacking in many parts, having little more than a foundation, every citizen should desire and work, as much as he is able, to bring it to its perfection; in order to accomplish this, it will be necessary for all, or at least the majority, to have the four following qualities.

First, the fear of God, because it is a certainty that every kingdom and government proceeds from God, just as everything does, He being the First Cause which governs everything. We see that the government of the natural world is perfect and stable because nature is subject to Him and does not rebel against His authority; likewise, if the citizens were to fear God and subject themselves to His commandments, without a doubt He would guide them to the perfection of this government and would enlighten them as to all that they must do.

Second, it is necessary that they love the common good of the city and that, when they are appointed to the magistracy and to other honors, they leave aside all concerns for their own property and the special interests of their family and friends and have an eye directed solely to the common good, because this affection for the common good first illumines the eye of their intellect; and so, being stripped of private interests, they no longer see through false spectacles, in that, regarding the true end of government, they cannot easily err in matters ordained to it. Furthermore, they will merit that the commonweal should be increased by God, just as, among other reasons that the Romans greatly expanded their empire, this one may be assigned: because they loved the common good of the city so much. God, wanting to reward this good work (since He does not want any good to be unremunerated, and yet this work did not merit eternal life because it was without grace), repaid it with temporal goods corresponding to their works, that is, He augmented the commonweal of the city and expanded its empire throughout all the world.

Third, it is necessary that the citizens love each other and forsake all hatreds and forget all the injuries of times past, because hatreds and disaffection and envy blind the eye of the intellect and do not let one see the truth; indeed, whoever in the Councils and magistracies is not purified in this regard makes many mistakes, and God allows him to incur punishment for his own sins and those of others, but He will enlighten him when he has been well purged of such disorders. On the other hand, when the citizens live together in peace and mutual love, God will reward their goodwill, giving them a perfect government which will prosper and increase; this is another reason why God gave such great power to the Romans, because they loved each other and remained at peace with each other in the beginning, and although this was not a supernatural charity, it was nonetheless good and natural, and God therefore rewarded it with temporal goods. If, then, the citizens of Florence will love each other with charity both natural and supernatural, God will multiply both their spiritual and temporal goods.

Fourth, it is necessary that the citizens enact justice, because justice either purges the city of evil men or else puts them in fear, while the good and just remain superior in authority because they are elected to honor willingly by those who love justice; these officials are enlightened ultimately by God concerning all good laws, and they are the cause of all the good in the city, which for this reason is filled with virtue, virtue being always the reward of justice. The number of good people multiplies because they willingly congregate where justice resides, and God, for this reason, then further increases the realm, just as He did for the Romans; for this reason also, that is, because they were strict in exacting justice, He gave them universal power, desiring that His people should be directed by justice.

If, then, Florentine citizens would consider diligently and with justice the reason that no other form of government is suited to them than this we have spoken of [i.e., civil government], and if they would believe with faith that it has been given to them by God, and if they put into practice the four things listed above, there is no doubt that in a brief time such a government would be perfected through the good counsel which they would take together, in which God would illuminate them concerning that which they were seeking to accomplish, and also because they would have been specially enlightened, by virtue of being His servants, concerning many particularities which they would not know how to discover on their own. Truly, they will have constructed a government of Paradise, and they will have attained many graces, spiritual as well as temporal. But if they do not want to believe that this government is given to them by God, nor that it is necessary for them, nor to fear God, nor to love the common good but to attend to their own personal desires, nor to love each other but to remain forever divided, nor to execute justice, the government given by God will remain, while they will consume each other, and little by little they will be consumed by God, and to their children will be given the grace of this perfect government. Already God has shown signs of His wrath, but they do not want to open their ears, and so God will punish them in this world and the next, since in this world they will always have unquiet minds and be full of passions and woes, and in the next they will abide in eternal fire, because they have no will to follow the natural light, which shows this to be their true government, nor the supernatural, of which they have received signs. Already at present one part of those who would not put themselves under the rule of this government and were always restive in it suffer the punishments of Hell. And so, Florence, having seen by many signs that God wills this government to stand, unchanged as it is in the face of such great opposition against it both within and without, and its assailants threatened by God with dire punishment, I pray you from the depths of the pity of our Lord, Jesus Christ, that you be content now to keep calm, because if you do not, He will send a greater scourge upon you than He has done over any peoples of the past, and you will lose both this world and the next. But if you do this, you will attain felicity, which I will describe in the next chapter.

Chapter Three
Of the happiness of the one who rules well, and of the misery of tyrants and their followers

Given, then, that the present government derives more from God than from man, those citizens who, motivated by great zeal for the honor of God and for the common good to observe the things mentioned above, will strive as much as they are able to restore it to perfection, will acquire earthly, spiritual, and eternal happiness.

First, they will liberate themselves from the slavery of tyranny, whose potentially vast reach we have discussed above, and they will live in true liberty, which is more precious than gold and silver; they will rest secure in their city, attending to the governance of their own houses, to honest profits, and to their farms, with joy and tranquility of mind. When God multiplies their possessions and honors, they will have no fear that they might be taken away. They will be free to go to the country or anywhere they like without asking leave from a tyrant, to give their sons and daughters in marriage as they please, to celebrate weddings and rejoice and have such company as is pleasing to them, to devote themselves to virtue or to the study of the sciences or the arts, which will be earthly happiness to a certainty.

From this will follow spiritual happiness, because everyone will be able to devote himself to holy Christian living without anyone impeding him. There will be no coercion by threats to act unjustly while in office, because everyone will be free, nor by reason of poverty to make unfair contracts because, the government of the city being a good one, wealth will abound, and everyone will find work, and the poor will earn a living, and they will be able to rear their sons and daughters holily, because they will make good laws concerning the honor of women and children. Through this especially godly religion will flourish because God, seeing their good intentions, will send them good pastors as Scripture says: "God gives pastors suited to the people" [Ier. 3:15?],[18] and such pastors will be able to guide their sheep without impediment, and good priests and religious will multiply even more so, since the wicked will not be able to live there, because one opposite chases away the other. And so, in a very short time, the city shall return to such devotion that it will be like a terrestrial paradise, and will live in jubilation and in songs and psalms; boys and girls will be like angels, and they will be brought up to live both as Christians and as good citizens. In time, through these practices, the government of the city will become more heavenly than earthly, and the happiness of the good will be so great that they will enjoy a kind of spiritual felicity even in this world.

Third, through this they will not only merit eternal happiness, but they will greatly augment their merit, and their crowns will increase in Heaven, because God gives the greatest reward to those who govern their cities well. Since blessedness is the reward of virtue, the greater a man is in virtue and the greater the things he does, the more he merits a greater reward; inasmuch as greater virtue is required to rule oneself and others, and especially a community and a realm, than to rule oneself only, it follows that one who rules

18. Savonarola here gives his "scriptural" quotation in Italian only. Jeremias 3:15 reads: *et dabo vobis pastores iuxta cor meum* ("I will give you pastors after My own heart").

a community well deserves the greatest reward in eternal life. And so we may see that in all the arts greater reward is given to the master who directs all the things that pertain to the art than to the servants who obey the master; certainly, in the military arts, greater reward is given to the captain of the army than to the soldiers; likewise, in the art of building, greater reward is given to the master builder and the architect than to the manual laborers; and so it is in the other arts. In the same way, the more a man's works are excellent, and the more he honors God, and the more useful what he does is to his neighbors, the more meritorious he is. Considering, then, that to govern a community well, especially such a one as Florence, would be an excellent work, and that it would result especially in honor to God, and would be of the greatest utility to the spirits and bodies and temporal good of men, as one can easily understand from what we have said above, there is no doubt that it merits an excellent reward and the greatest glory. Likewise, we may see that one who gives alms or feeds the poor is greatly rewarded by God, as our Savior says that in the Day of Judgment He will turn to the just and say, "Come, blessed of the Father, inherit the Kingdom prepared for you from the foundation of the world; for when I was hungry and thirsty and naked or a stranger, you fed me and clothed me and welcomed me and visited me when I was sick, for that which you have done for one of My least ones, you have also done for Me" [Matt. 25:34–40].[19] If, then, God greatly rewards anyone for individual acts of charity, how much more will He reward those who govern a great city well, those who through their good government feed an infinite number of poor people, provide for many of the wretched, defend widows and wards, draw from the hands of the powerful and iniquitous those who cannot otherwise defend themselves against their force, liberate the countryside from thieves and assassins, protect the good, and uphold righteous living and holy worship, and perform an infinite number of other good deeds? Like loves like, and the more it is loved by it, the more it becomes assimilated to it; since, then, all creatures are similar to God, all are loved by Him, but because some are more like Him than others, these are also loved by Him more. Inasmuch then as the one who governs is much more similar to God than the one who is governed, it logically follows that if he governs justly, he is loved and rewarded by God more then than for the personal actions [he performs] when he is not governing, especially since the one who governs is in greater danger and expends greater efforts of mind and body than the one who does not govern; therefore, he merits greater reward.

19. Again, Savonarola does not quote the Latin, but condenses Matthew to give the essence of Christ's message.

By contrast, whoever wants to be a tyrant is unhappy in this world, first, with earthly unhappiness, because, however much he may have in riches, he cannot enjoy it on account of many afflictions of spirit and fears and continual worries and above all because it is necessary to spend much of it to maintain himself in power; desiring to hold everyone subject to him, he is more subjected to all of them, because he must serve them all in order to make everyone feel benevolent toward him. Then, he is deprived of friendship, which is one of the greatest and sweetest goods that anyone can have in this world, because he does not want anyone equal to himself but keeps everyone in fear of him, and especially because the tyrant is hated almost always by everyone for the evil which he does; and if he is loved by the wicked, it is not because they wish him well, but because they love that which they want to extract from him, for among such thieves there can be no true friendship. Furthermore, he is deprived of good fame and honor by reason either of the evil which he does or the perpetual hatred and envy of others. He can never have true comfort without sorrow, because he always has to think about and fear the enmity he has occasioned; therefore, he lives in fear and does not trust even to the loyalty of his own guards. Second, he suffers spiritual unhappiness, because he is deprived of the grace of God and all knowledge of Him, surrounded by his sins and encompassed by perverse men who follow him every hour of the day and cause him to fall into many errors, as we have discussed above. Last of all, he will suffer eternal unhappiness, because the tyrant is almost always incorrigible on account of the multitude of sins he sees he has done, of which he has made such a habit that it is very difficult to abandon them, and because he would have to return so many things that he has pilfered and replace so many gifts that he has given that he would be left with nothing but the shirt on his back; how difficult this would be for someone accustomed to live in such pride and pleasures, anyone can easily understand. The flatterers around him also make light of his sins, or rather give him to understand that that which is evil is good, and tepid religious confess and absolve him, showing him that black is white, and so, he is miserable in this world and then goes to Hell in the next, where he has punishments more grievous than other people both by reason of the multitude of the sins he has committed and made others do and also on account of the office which he has usurped, because, just as the one who rules well is most highly rewarded by God, so is the one who rules badly punished most severely.

All citizens who follow the tyrant also participate in his misery, in temporal matters as well as in spiritual and eternal; therefore, they lose their liberty, which is a treasure above all others, besides the fact that their possessions and honor and children and wives are all in the power of the tyrant; their sins continually imitate his because they are forced to do everything to please him and to assimilate themselves to him as much as they can, and so, they will be partakers of his most grievous punishment in Hell.

All citizens who are not content with civil government, although they are not tyrants because they are unable, lacking wealth, honors, reputation, and friendships, also participate in this same unhappiness because they gather to themselves all the lean and hungry citizens wanting to get even, as well as all the evil men; for this they need to spend money, but they have severed themselves from the good and so have no true friendship, and everyone who follows them plots to rob them. In the company of the wicked they commit thousands of sins, which they might not have done, and they are disturbed at heart and always full of hatred, envy, and grumbling, and so are in Hell both in this world and in the next.

Given, then, as we have proved, that the one who rules well is happy and like to God, and that the one who rules badly is unhappy and like to the devil, every citizen ought to forsake his sins and selfish concerns and make the effort to rule well and to preserve and augment and make perfect this civil government for the honor of God and the salvation of souls (all the more so considering that He has especially given us this government on account of the love He bears for this city), in order that he may be happy in this world and the next, through the grace of our Savior, Jesus Christ, King of kings and Lord of lords, Who with the Father and the Holy Ghost lives and reigns for ever and ever. Amen.

Praise be to God.

Moral Reform I

Carnival:[1] 16 February 1496

Luca Landucci,[2] *A Florentine Diary*

16th February. The Carnival. Fra Girolamo had preached a few days before that the boys, instead of committing follies, such as throwing stones and making huts of twigs, should collect alms for the *poveri vergognosi;*[3] and as it pleased the divine grace, such a change took place that instead of [indulging in] senseless games, they began to collect alms several days beforehand; and instead of barriers in the streets, there were crucifixes at each corner, in the hands of holy innocents. On this last day of Carnival, after vespers, these troops of boys assembled in the four quarters of Florence, each quarter having its special banner. The first was a crucifix; the second was an image of our Lady, and so on; and with them went the drummers and pipers, the mace-bearers and serving-men of the *Palagio,* the boys singing praises to Heaven, and crying, *"Viva Cristo e la Vergine Maria nostra regina!"* [Christ and the Virgin Mary our Queen!], all with olive branches in their hands, so that good and thoughtful people were moved to tears, saying: "Truly this change is the work of God. These lads are those who will enjoy the good things which the *Frate* promised." And we seemed to see the crowds of Jerusalem who preceded and followed Christ on Palm Sunday, saying: *"Blessed art thou who comest in the name of the Lord"* [Matt. 21:9]. And one may well repeat the words of Scripture: *Infanzium e lattenzium* [sic] *perfecisti la[u]dem*[4] [Matt. 21:16, quoting Ps. 8:3]. And observe that there were said to be 6 thousand boys or more, all of them between five or six and sixteen years of age. All the four troops united at the *Servi,* in the portico (i.e., under the colonnade of the *Innocenti* — the Foundling Hospital), and in the *Piazza* (of *SS. Annunziata*); and then they all went into the church of the *Nunziata,*

---

1. A last fling of revelry before Ash Wednesday, the beginning of Lent.
2. Landucci was a Florentine apothecary (1436–1516) and devotee of Savonarola until the excommunication of 1497. His sons were among the *fanciulli* participating in the processions described here.
3. The "embarrassed poor," members of good families in straitened circumstances and too ashamed to be seen begging. For brief discussion of Piagnone involvement in charitable activities and additional bibliography, see Lorenzo Polizzotto, *The Elect Nation: The Savonarolan Movement in Florence, 1494–1545* (Oxford: Clarendon Press, 1994), pp. 32–33.
4. "[Out of the mouths] of infants and sucklings You have perfected praise."

and after that to *San Marco*. Then they took the way of all processions; they crossed the *Ponte a Santa Trinità* (and went round over the *Ponte Vecchio*) into the *Piazza (della Signoria)*, and so to *Santa Maria del Fiore*, the church being crowded with men and women, divided, the women on one side and the men on the other; and there the offering was made, with such devotion and tears of holy emotion as was never seen. It was estimated that there were several hundred florins. Many gold florins were put into their collecting-bowls, but the greater part consisted in *grossi* (copper coins) and silver. Some women gave their veilholders, some their silver spoons, kerchiefs, towels, and many other things. All was given without grudging. It seemed as if everyone wished to make an offering to Christ and His Mother. I have written these things which are true, and which I saw with my own eyes, and felt with so much emotion; and some of my sons were amongst those blessed and pure-minded troops of boys.

17th February. This was the first day of Lent, and an immense number of boys came to hear Fra Girolamo's sermon in *Santa Maria del Fiore*. Certain steps were erected along the walls, opposite the chancel, for these boys, behind the women; and there were also many boys amongst the women; and all those who stood on the steps sang sweet praises to God before the sermon began. And then the clergy came into the chancel and sang Litanies and the children responded. It was so beautiful that everyone wept, and mostly healthy-minded men, saying: "this is a thing of the Lord's." And this went on each morning of Lent, before the *Frate* came. And note this wonder: not a boy could be kept in bed in the morning, but all ran to church before their mothers. . . .

27th February. The boys were encouraged by the *Frate* to take away the baskets of *berlingozzi* [sweet cakes], and the gambling-tables, and many vain things used by women, so that no sooner did the gamblers hear that the boys of the *Frate* were coming than they fled, nor was there a single woman who dared go out not modestly dressed. . . .

29th February. The said boys went about everywhere, along the walls of the city and to the taverns, etc., wherever they saw gatherings of people; this they did in each quarter, and if anyone had rebelled against them, he would have been in danger of his life, whoever he was. At this time the plague was increasing.

Letter from Paolo de Somenzi, Orator,[5] to Lodovico Sforza, Duke of Milan

My most illustrious, excellent, and distinguished Lord:

Today, that is, the day of Carnival, there was celebrated here such a festival that there is no record of the like ever having been celebrated in Florence before, and it was carried out through the work of Fra Girolamo of Ferrara in the manner described below. For about the past twenty days this friar has exhorted the whole populace to try to get their children to make altars in the streets, setting up an image of the Crucifix on them, and then begging for alms for the embarrassed poor; for this reason, on virtually every corner of the street, there was an altar where a crowd of children hung about with basins in hand, asking for *denarii* for the embarrassed poor. They were so importunate that it was difficult to pass down the street unless one gave them some coins, and especially for women, [it being even] worse for the young than the old, for the friar had proposed and ordered it so. They held long sticks in their hands so that they could not pass without first paying something. By resorting to such devices, they collected about three hundred ducats, and then today this friar has had a procession of these children, who numbered about ten thousand, and most of them have not attained fourteen years of age; of six- to nine-year-olds there were some four thousand. First they had a Mass said in the main church with great solemnity, and then these children, separated by quarters, with trumpets before them and crying out, "Long live Christ," went in procession to the Nuntiata and many other churches, and finally to San Martino to hand over the money, that is, to dispense it to the embarrassed poor. Such has been the feast celebrated today in Florence, which all the people attended to watch.

This friar has made it public that he intends to preach all this Lent because he says he has leave from the Supreme Pontiff.

I commend myself humbly to Your Illustrious Lordship, whom I pray God may maintain in happiness for a long time.

16 February 1496

The humble servant of Your Most Illustrious Lordship,

Paolo de Somenzi de Cremona, Chancellor

[On the outside:] To the Most Illustrious and Excellent Prince, D. D. Lodovico Marie Sforza, Duke of Milan, my Most Distinguished Lord

Milan

Urgent

---

5. Somenzi served as ambassador to Florence for the Duke of Milan and thus held a negative view of Savonarola.

La vita del Beato Ieronimo Savonarola,

previously attributed to Fra Pacifico Burlamacchi[6]
    Chapter XXXVIII
    Concerning the conversion of the Florentine children and their fruits and works

Oftentimes the eye, while taking delight in the shining globe flying across the sky, intends, for a contrary reason, to regard that light with reverence, for although it feels the sharpness of its sight to be an inadequate match for the flying rocket's glare, it nonetheless sets its desire on the beauty of so beautiful a light in order to strengthen its sight. Just so it seems to be for me, seeing before the eyes of my mind the rays of celestial doctrine shining in an inaccessible light; the more furiously I strain [after it] with the intellect, the more I am confounded and lower my eyes. But because such great virtue and fruits cannot be concentrated inward, a sun and inaccessible light and splendor certainly was our servant of Jesus Christ, Fra Girolamo, who with the splendor of his celestial doctrine has encompassed the whole territory of Holy Church, and with the ardent heat of his charity has fired the land of cold and frozen hearts, not only of the wise and those old in years, but also of young and tender children, gathering and numbering them within the province of Holy Church, who, in the words of her Spouse, says: *"Sinite parvulos venire ad me, talium est enim regnum celorum"*[7] [Matt. 19:14; Marc. 10:14; Luc. 18:16]. The conversion and harvest of such as these this servant of God has accomplished. If all the powers of the body were converted into tongues, and these flaming tongues sparked fire, they would not be sufficient to recount what God has miraculously accomplished in these childish youngsters through the preaching of His servant, such that one might say with the prophet: *A Domino factum est istud, et est mirabile in oculis nostris*[8] [Ps. 117:23]. He, then, like a good shepherd, raised the eyes of a pure mind to the guardianship of a wandering flock of tender, ill-cared-for lambs, that is, the lascivious children of the city of Florence, in order to snatch them from the jaws of rapacious wolves. However, such work was at first (as is well known) derided by the sages of this world and was considered impossible by everyone because they [the children] had been nourished in many bad habits for a long time, having broad license and liberty to be enveloped

---

6. Roberto Ridolfi identifies the actual author as Fra Timoteo Bottonio; *Life of Girolamo Savonarola*, trans. Cecil Grayson (New York: Knopf, 1959), p. 307.
7. "Let the little children come to me, for of such is the kingdom of heaven."
8. "By God has this been done, and it is marvelous in our eyes."

in all the vices (they looked like girls in all their ornaments and coiffures, or rather, like public prostitutes, shameless in word and deed), and especially in that unspeakable vice—a thing abominable to name—and were gamblers, gluttons, vainglorious, and lascivious, and enveloped in many other sins besides. The servant of God, fortified with divine assistance, led them back in the briefest space of time to such perfection that this was deemed by every devout and well-disposed person to be the work of God, as the servant of God had affirmed many times when preaching in public. And so, in a short time, despite great opposition, he easily converted an innumerable multitude of children from one extreme to another; that is, from gambling, vanity, and other vices, they turned to the purity and simplicity of Christian living. This could not have been anything but the work of the Most High God, in that they were made mirror, measure, and example of goodly living to their parents and others of their elders. The lascivious became chaste, the light-minded serious, and the wicked good: who can do this but God? By the sermons of the holy prophet, then, they were transformed, abandoning the superfluous vanities of dress, purses, coiffures, and other vanities; they were cleansed of all the vices and became so perfect and fervent that they were an example to the whole city. Divine grace shone in them in such a way that one could say what is said of St. Stephen [Act. 6:15]. There was in their countenances a certain splendor of grace such that they seemed the faces of angels.

There was in the city of Florence an age-old custom of playing with rocks, against which, since it had endured for so many centuries, no Florentine lords or other magistrates, with their proclamations and penalties and with all their forces, or innumerable preachers had ever been able to enforce the prohibition that on the days of Carnival there would be no rock-throwing, in which game many were killed every year. The servant of God, with the word of his preaching alone, removed this pestiferous and deadly abuse.

It is impossible to say how solicitous they [the children] were to hear the divine word, so much so that they always arrived first for the preaching with all their childish enthusiasm and would persist for two or three hours before the preacher came in prayer and singing the divine praises, such as litanies or other [hymns] composed in Tuscan and adapted for the occasion or with a few verses aimed at the renewal of the Church, such as *Tempus faciendi, Domine, dissipaverunt legem tuam*[9] [Ps. 118:126] and *Tu exsurgens misereberis Syon, quia tempus miserendi eius, quia venit tempus*[10] [Ps. 101:14] or

9. "It is time, O Lord, to act; they have dissipated Your law."
10. "When You arise, may You have mercy on Sion, since the time to pity her, the time has come."

Accelera, Domine, ut eruas nos[11] [Ps. 39:14?] or *Benefac, Domine, bonis et rectis corde*[12] [Ps. 124:4], and similar ecclesiastical material. And while they sang, they would sit there with such sweetness that it seemed as if Paradise had opened, and they went on till the servant of God entered the pulpit, and as soon as they saw him, they would intone: *Benedictus Dominus Deus Israel, etc.*[13] [Luc. 1:68; canticle of Zacharias] or *Nunc dimittis servum tuum, Domine*[14] [Luc. 2:29; canticle of Simeon]. The place where they sat was arranged in the manner of a theater, although it was square in length: there were large and long beams set with one end on the ground, and on the other end they leaned against the wall inside the church in such a way that every beam, in height, reached to the glass windows; on top of these, other beams were placed in seventeen tiers, and they went round from the column of the blessed water which gives entrance from the canon house over to the other column of blessed water which goes to the Annuntiata, and from the wall of the Annuntiata door over to that of the via del Cocomero [now via Ricasoli], and from that which goes to the via del Cocomero over to the column of blessed water at the door which goes to the Compagnia of Santo Zenobi.[15] They were arranged in this manner: between the pulpit and this [last] column were the benches where the women sat; between the pulpit and the holy water [column] which goes to the canon house were the benches where the men sat; the first and second rows facing the dome were reserved for the men; the third and fourth rows, in the direction of the via del Cocomero, were given to the children alone because there were several thousands [of them]. It was a marvelous thing to see such an ornament, never again arranged and constructed for any other preacher. And these rows and these benches described above are those which the Compagnacci[16] wanted to burn.

Their obedience was great; not only toward their parents, but toward everyone else, they were reverent, mild-mannered in their conversation, prudent in their speech without any affectation or hypocrisy, but rather they spoke with the utmost sincerity. In divine worship they acted so fervent that everyone was amazed; at the masses, offices, and their own devotions and prayers, they were innumerable; at confession and Communion they were

11. "Hasten, Lord, to rescue us."
12. "Bless, O Lord, those good and upright in heart."
13. "Blessed be the Lord God of Israel."
14. "Now You can dismiss Your servant, Lord."
15. The corners of the square are marked by columns bearing holy-water stoups at four points of egress from the church.
16. "The [bad] companions," a gang of aristocratic young men of the Arrabbiati ("the rabid" or "the enraged") faction, led by Doffo Spini and violently opposed to Savonarola's reforms.

fervent and careful, assiduous and attentive at divine lauds, within the city as well as without. And in order to satisfy their desires more fully, schools and shops remained closed at the hour of the sermons so that they would be able to hear the word of God.

Considering, then, the great fruit perfected in these children, he planned to lay out for them a certain order and manner of living, through which they might persevere in living uprightly as they had begun. But because he was continually occupied with matters of greater importance, he committed them to the care of the priest Fra Domenico da Pescia, his single faithful companion up till his death on the holy cross; [the latter] accepted [the charge] gladly, giving thanks to God, and, gathering them together several times, with exhortations from the Divine Scriptures he pastured the little flock. And like a good shepherd, so that they would not go astray, he began to inquire into the desires and inclinations of their pure minds, finding them prudently disposed to every sort of good work and [filled] with a sincere and ardent desire to advance from virtue to virtue. Although they had already cut their hair and removed their Frenchified purses and—since once the [old] dress was taken off, the vices would also be drawn out—abandoned their [old] clothes and reclothed themselves in various virtues and had accomplished many good works throughout the city, nonetheless, he decided to compile and compose a fine and suitable reform, which, furnished with laws and duties, would be like a constitution and rule for them, and, so that it might have a greater authority and value, it would need to be ratified by the great and illustrious Florentine lords. The proposal was pleasing to everyone, and each wrote his consent, and since it pleased them, they willed and desired to put it into execution immediately. They wrote a model for this reform as follows:

> Each child who wants to be a child of Jesus Christ and a devout
> follower of the servant of God, Fra Girolamo, and of his teaching,
> will diligently observe the commandments of God and of the
> Holy Roman Church; at confession and Communion they will be
> as attentive and fervent as their spiritual fathers consider appropri-
> ate so that they might not become lukewarm. They will be assidu-
> ous in attending the sermons, not like the lukewarm, but like the
> saints, with humility, so that they will be enlightened by a celestial
> light and inspiration to live uprightly. They will not be found at
> the public spectacles of the pagans, such as the *palio* [a horse race]
> and tilts, or masques, or suchlike things. Let their clothes be sim-
> ple, according to the status of each, without purses, and with their
> hair cut short up above the ear. Let them flee gambling and bad
> companions and all the vices as though they were serpents. Dis-

graceful books, whether in the vernacular or in Latin, and lascivious poets, let them not only not read them or hear them read,
but flee them as a poisonous pestilence and hold them in abomination. On feast days let them be continuously occupied in holy
practices with chaste modesty, meekness, and reverence, and not
in jaunts to Fiesole or Santo Gaggio, for example, to engage in
playacting or other festivities. Let them not seek instruction in
fencing, or dancing, or playing instruments; let them not be
found at musical performances; and, finally, let them not go to
hear those who sing on stage.

And so that these [rules] might be observed and many other
good works be put into execution, we want appointed in every
quarter of the city, that is, in each of the four parts of the city, a
leader over these children, to be called guardians, of whom there
will be four, one for each quarter. These, by their authority and
power as their leaders, will see that all these rules are observed
and will direct them toward [even] better works. Let each guardian have four counselors with whose counsel everything will have
to be approved, and without it nothing will be valid. Under these
guardians there will be appointed more magistrates. First are the
peacemakers [*paciali*], whose first [responsibility] is composing
and maintaining the peace within among themselves and without
among the other children of their quarter so that they might not
come into any discord, and second, to set up agreements.

The second type of magistrates were the organizers [*ordinatori*], who
were to make the arrangements when there was a procession, how they were
to be organized, and to seat them according to each one's status in the rows
at the church when there was preaching or when they gathered elsewhere.
They had the authority to expel adults who did not belong in their association and to make sure that [their charges] kept silent during the preaching,
and when they went in procession, and when they heard the religious services
in church. The third group of magistrates were the correctors [*correttori*],
who had to apply fraternal correction in accordance with the Gospel model
to all delinquents, to any, male or female, who engaged in vanity, in the
name of the King and Queen of Florence, [namely] blessed Jesus Christ and
His Mother Mary, ever virgin, Whom they had accepted as their King and
Queen. These [magistrates] also selected the almoners, who, when there was
to be a procession, would carry around basins to receive alms for the benefit
of the embarrassed poor; at Carnival time and on all the feast days throughout the year, they would erect altars with a Crucifix and lighted lamps on
the corners of the principal roads, where the children would stand with all

modesty, waiting for persons of means to pass along the way, and then they would snatch up a lovely dish placed on the altar and, bowing with gracious reverence, ask alms for the poor, and each citizen would offer whatever he wished.

They did all this in order to extirpate the abuses and perverse customs of Carnival, for in those days they were accustomed to go about in masks, to hold dinners and banquets with great immodesty and drunkenness, to gamble, throw stones, and make barricades and *capannucci*.[17] These were the barricades: they would take a long piece of wood and set it across the public roads where people would pass, and especially newly married women, and not allow them to pass on unless they gave them money, which they would then spend on their sensual and vain pleasures. The *capannucci* they made were large trees set on the public roads, against which leaned a large multitude of faggots and logs and pieces of wood, to be burned on the evening of Carnival. It happened more often than not that on the day of Carnival many battles would be fought near these *capannucci*, sometimes with rocks and sometimes with arms, so that one [group] might burn down the *capannuccio* of the other, and one party would fight so furiously against the other that often some would die; all were inventions of the devil and snares set to catch souls. So, in place of these wretched abuses, the servant of God instituted good customs and removed the ancient and diabolical ones; therefore, the devil was enraged with him and together with his members rose up all the more against him. These were very exemplary works, not only among the Florentines but also for foreigners, such that pilgrims and merchants who entered the city and saw the altars on every street and the noble children begging for alms would marvel and say, "What is this?" *The citizens would reply,* "Our children, in place of the vanities they used to engage in, have been led to do what you see through the preaching of the servant of God." Because of this great example, many were edified, and the good odor and fame of the holy prophet spread and circulated everywhere.

[Next] was the magistracy of the purifiers [*lustrelatori*], who went seeking out any place where they might find the Cross or [statues of] saints put in places where by necessity it is customary to pour out water; all these they would whitewash and remove so that they might not be kept irreverently in such places. They would also find themselves in the role of investigators, who on feast days throughout the year, after either dinner or vespers, would

17. *Capannuccio:* diminutive of *capànna,* meaning a hut constructed of branches and straw. This dialect word is used by all the Florentine writers to describe the impromptu bonfires constructed by competing gangs of youths to celebrate Carnival. The Savonarolan bonfires were in the same form, shaped something like a tepee, but elaborately engineered to display the items collected for burning.

surround the gambling places all over the city within and without and con-
fiscate their cards and dice, [gaming] tables, and other implements of gambling, and sometimes money, which they would give to the poor, all this
being accomplished with benign and sweet words.

So great was the terror and fright aroused by these children that gamblers, when they heard them approach, would flee, leaving everything behind; nonetheless, sometimes someone would speak evil words to them and
beat them, but they would bear everything with patience. Their parents,
hearing about this, took it very ill and demanded that the Office of the
Eight[18] assign in each quarter an official attendant as their companion and
protector; seeing this, the enemies of truth became frightened. In this way
the whole city, inside and out, was purged of gambling. These were children
of well-to-do and noble persons, and for this reason, they aroused the
greatest fear. They would also go around the city, and when they found a
girl or a married woman adorned with much pomp and vanity, they would
correct her and say, "On behalf of Jesus Christ, King of our city, and of the
Virgin Mary, we ask you to lay aside and abandon these vanities; otherwise,
sickness will fall on you." But they uttered these words with such gentleness
that the women would be stung with remorse by their warning and with
many tears remove those vanities from their heads and give them over to be
burned. While they were engaged in such pursuits, it happened that an old
man inveterate in every sort of misdeed, seeing the works of these children,
called some of them to him and, instigated by the devil, said to them, "Whatever are you doing? Since you are children from well-to-do families, why do
you degenerate from them and go around begging like paupers? What vile-
ness is this? Go along to your games, your rock-throwing, and worldly pleasures while you are young." To these words one of the children, filled with
the Holy Spirit, responded, "We thought that you would have praised us
for doing all this good and that you would have reproached us severely if
we threw stones or committed some disgrace, and yet, you do the opposite."
To this the old man, thoroughly enraged, said, "You are a sorry lot," and
ran off like a fugitive.

These children suffered the greatest disapproval from their parents, relatives, and friends, who would say many rude and injurious things to them,
but they, like gentle little lambs, would bear everything with patience for
love of Jesus Christ. They would go from house to house with such gentleness and grace, asking for their vanities and disgraceful pictures, and if these
things were given to them freely, they would pay them back by invoking on
them all the blessings which Moses, the greatest of prophets, said over the

18. *Gli Otto di guardia e balià:* the Eight of Watch and Ward, the tribunal charged
    with trying criminal and political cases.

people of God in the desert. So great was the grace poured out on their lips that all were moved to tears, and even those who were their enemies would give them everything, weeping, men as well as women, diligently searching out everything such as cards, [gaming] tables, chessboards, harps, lutes, citterns, cymbals, bagpipes, dulcimers, wigs, veils (which at the time were very lascivious ornaments for women's heads), disgraceful and lascivious paintings and sculptures, mirrors, powder and other cosmetics and lascivious perfumes, hats, masks, poetry books in the vernacular as well as Latin, and every other disgraceful reading material, and books of music. These children inspired fear in any place where they were seen, and when they came down one street, the wicked fled down another. Their works were such that they were deemed impossible by men, and I believe that in the future no one will believe this. And yet it happened, for these deeds were not performed by children but by God, and although they did these things for a long time and against much opposition, nonetheless, no one was ever able to discover— which is a miracle in itself—that it ever caused any scandal. These were the offices and ranks of the children in which they carried out the above-mentioned works. None of those who were in a magistracy could do anything without the permission of the guardian and his counselors, for whom they had the greatest reverence. Likewise, those who belonged to a magistracy were all obeyed with great love in their operations, because they proceeded in their actions with great order, peace, discretion, and unity, and without any discord or scandal.

And so that their reform might have a greater authority and stability, they arranged along with their father, Fra Domenico, that it should be strengthened and confirmed by the authority of the Magnificent Signory, and [so] they organized solemn embassies to their Excellencies of the Signory; these, together with a great company and multitude of children, took to the road toward the palace and, having climbed the stairs, asked for an audience. When at last they were admitted, the one who was charged to speak began in this fashion:

> Magnificent and excellent Lords, and all you other counselors and magistrates, the Omnipotent God, our Lord and Savior Jesus Christ, *Rex regum et Dominus dominantium*[19] [I Tim. 6:15; Apoc. 19:16; see also 17:14], because of His kindness and clemency, wants to be the especial King of the city of Florence, and His Mother, Mary ever virgin, wants to be Queen of this our city, freed from a harsh and tyrannical slavery. They have given her liberty so that she might be reformed for the better both in her

---

19. "King of kings and Lord of lords."

mode of living and in her customs, and so, They have sent us
Their prophets, who, through their preaching and sermons, come
to purify and enlighten us; thus, on the one hand, with their
prayers they take care to purify and enlighten us, while, on the
other, with their exhortations they enflame us with love for our
King, so that, leaving behind our ancient, diabolical, and perverse
customs and pleasures, we may be reformed for the better. For
this reason, moved by the Divine Spirit and by the exhortations of
His prophet, we come humbly supplicating your exalted Lordships and devoutly ask you to satisfy our finest and godly desires,
from which will follow honor to God [and] salvation for your
souls and those of your children, who, holding you in greater
honor and reverence, will come to give you perpetual consolation,
and their good repute will be an example of goodly living to all
Christian people. For this purpose, we have drawn up our reform
and set it in writing, that is, our customs, and dress, and other
suitable matters, and we pray your exalted Lordships that they
might be strengthened and confirmed in writing and signed and
secured with your public seal so that, with your authority, we
might be able to pursue the sodomites, remove roadhouses, gambling dens, and taverns, and purge our whole city of vices and fill
her with the splendor of virtue, showing thereby that this is the
will of the Most High God, as He says to us and shows us daily
through His prophets. For this reason, once again, with all our
power and as much as we are able and know how to do, we pray
your Lordships, for the love of our King, blessed Jesus Christ,
and of our Queen, Mary ever virgin, that you satisfy our desires
and just requests so that together we can reach that immense and
exalted glory of the blessed and so, made glorious, rejoice with
the Father, the Son, and the Holy Spirit, Who lives and reigns for
ever and ever. Amen.

So great an abundance of spirit and grace overflowed and poured forth
from the lips of the youth that the Signory and all those standing about were
moved to tears so that they could not contain themselves, and because of
the sweetness of a great consolation, they could scarcely speak; nonetheless,
the Provost of the Signory with effort attempted to speak and highly commended the children and praised their laudable proposal; he encouraged
them to persevere and to advance from virtue to virtue, and from good to
better, and although they intended to satisfy thoroughly their holy and just
petition and desired nothing more than that their children might be true
Christians both in name and in deed, and because for this reason they desired

to take mature counsel together, they would give their reply to the holy prophets, Fra Girolamo and Fra Domenico, but for now, the children should depart in peace and pray to God that He might inspire them to act in accordance with His honor and His will. And so, with fair promises, they dismissed them. Two members of the Council commissioned by the Signory came to speak with Fra Girolamo and Fra Domenico, saying that this work had to be arranged so that it might be carried out with mature judgment, and under what conditions they would consider the reforms approved by the people, both the children and the women, and in this way the matter was left hanging.

Palm Sunday Procession/*Monte di Pietà:*[1] 27 March 1496

Amos and Zacharias, Sermon XL

Palm Sunday

> *Hosanna filio David! Benedictus qui venit in nomine Domini! Hosanna in altissimis!*[2] — Matt. 21:9

As the time of the Passion of our Savior approached, dearly beloved in Christ Jesus, in order to show that He was willingly going to suffer, He Himself drew near to the place of the Passion, as this morning's Gospel relates: *Cum appropinquasset Hierosolymis et venisset Bethphage ad montem Oliveti*[3] [Matt. 21: 1], that is, Jesus approached Jerusalem and came to the Mount of Olives within the boundaries of Bethphage, which belonged to the priests. From here He sent two disciples to Jerusalem, saying: *"Ite in castellum quod contra vos est"*[4] [Matt. 21:2], *that is,* "go to the castle opposite you" (He called Jerusalem a castle because it was built with many towers). *"Et invenietis asinam alligatam et pullum cum ea: solvite et adducite mihi"*[5] [Matt. 21:2]; "you will find an ass tied up and, along with it, a colt; untie them and bring them here to Me." This ass was there for the poor who had need of it, and anyone who needed it took it; "and so," He added, "if anyone should ask you anything, tell him *quia Dominus hic opus habet*[6] [Matt. 21:3], tell him that the Lord has need of it." Note that He said absolutely "the Lord," as if to say, "Say that the Lord of the world wants it, and no one will say anything to you." So, they led the ass and the colt, and the Lord rode and came into Jerusalem. It was a short way from the Mount of Olives to Jerusalem, and,

1. A lending institution meant to undercut the exorbitant interest rates of Jewish moneylenders. See s.v. *"Montes pietatis,"* in *The Catholic Encyclopedia,* vol. X (n. p., Appleton, 1911; online edition: Kevin Knight [www.newadvent.org/cathen], 1999).
2. "Hosanna to the Son of David; blessed is He Who comes in the name of the Lord; hosanna in the highest." The *venit* is imported from Ioh. 12:13, perhaps under the influence of the Sanctus of the Mass; Matthew has *venturus est,* as does Psalm 117:26, the text being quoted.
3. "When He had approached Jerusalem and had come to Bethphage at Mount Olivet"; the verbs are plural in Matthew.
4. "Go into the citadel which is opposite you."
5. "And you will find an ass tied up and a colt with it; untie them and bring them to Me."
6. "That the Lord has work to do here."

222

nonetheless, the Lord wanted to go mounted this time, although at other times He was used to going a longer way on foot. It is necessary to stress that He did this as in a mystery, so that the ninth chapter of Zacharias' prophecy might be fulfilled: *Exulta satis, filia Sion; iubila, filia Ierusalem: ecce Rex tuus veniet tibi iustus et salvator: ipse pauper et ascendens super asinam et super pullum filium asinae*[7] [Zach. 9:9]; "rejoice, daughter of Sion (which was Jerusalem); behold your King, Who comes meekly on an ass and her colt."

Ask the Jews how this prophecy has been borne out and which of their kings ever went this way, with such triumph, into Jerusalem under these two conditions: the first, that he would ride on an ass and a colt; the second, that he would come in such triumph. I say "with triumph" because the men of Jerusalem, on hearing that Jesus was coming and remembering that He had raised Lazarus, went forth and took the cloaks off their backs and spread them along the way, while others cut down branches of olive trees and laid them on the ground [Matt. 21:8]. The people went along with Him, part ahead, part behind, crying out with the greatest triumph: *"Hosanna filio David! Benedictus qui venit in nomine Domini, Rex Israel!"*[8] [conflation of Matt. 21:9 and Ioh. 12:13] Ask the Jews which one of their kings ever came into Jerusalem in this way, and you will see them left confounded. Some ask how He rode on the colt, which was not tamed; one answer is that the Lord Himself could have tamed it. *Hosanna* is a Hebrew interjection, which cannot be exactly interpreted in Latin; *hosanna* means, in effect, *o Domine, salva!*[9] So, the people around the Savior cried out, "Blessed is He Who comes in the name of the Lord: *hosanna in excelsis:*[10] save us [You Who are] on high!"

This is the holy Gospel, which I will show you is meant for Florence and to signify that the Lord has come to you. And then we shall make a quick run through the psalm *Domine, Dominus noster*[11] [Ps. 8:2], and we shall end there because we want to preach briefly this morning. This sermon is for the children, and we do it for them, but it will also be for those adults who want to become like children in purity, as the Lord says: *Nisi conversi fueritis et efficiamini sicut parvuli, non intrabitis in regnum caelorum*[12]

---

7. "Exult your fill, daughter Sion; rejoice, daughter Jerusalem: behold your King shall come to you, the Just One and Savior; He [shall be] poor and mounted on an ass and the colt of an ass."
8. "Hosanna to the Son of David! Blessed is He Who comes in the name of the Lord, King of Israel!"
9. "O Lord, save!"
10. "Hosanna in the highest"; *in excelsis* is found in Marc. 11:10, as well as the Sanctus of the Mass.
11. "Lord, our Lord."
12. "Unless you are converted and become like children, you will not enter into the kingdom of heaven."

[Matt. 18:3]. So, it will be a sermon for those who are children in age and in purity.

Now then, this mystery is expounded as follows: by the ass is signified the Synagogue of the Jews, and by the colt, which was as yet untamed, is to be understood the Gentiles, to whom Christ came later in the person of His Apostles. And because that which is said of the whole Church can also be said of the part, we shall speak this morning about the city of Florence with respect to this Gospel.

God created Adam and gave him a native righteousness, but because he sinned, he lost the grace God had given him, and so the whole human race was infected by his sin. Therefore, all men who are born have original sin, and if they die without baptism, they go not to Hell but to Limbo, where they will never see the face of God, and this is their penalty. Our Savior, having come to suffer, has, thereby, provided against such errancy and has given us baptism, which, first, removes the stain of original sin and, second, gives man God's grace, so that, if he should die before he arrives at [the age of] free will, he goes to Paradise by the merit of Christ's Passion.

Free will is said to be given to a child at the age of seven; *however,* I believe that nowadays, on account of the great wickedness which has proliferated, we can say that a great many begin to exercise free will by the age of six, and perhaps even earlier. One reads of that five-year-old child who, as St. Gregory says, blasphemed against God, as his father taught him; he was snatched away before his father's eyes and was carried off by devils, and both St. Thomas and St. Gregory maintain that he is damned.[13] Likewise, when a child attains free will, if he keeps himself in a state of innocence and sinlessness, he acquires so great a purity of mind and heart that the angels often converse with him. One reads in the Old Testament that the angels used to hold much converse with those who lived in the first age because of their simplicity and purity. So, my child, if you were to keep yourself pure and without sin and to do good, your angel would be with you and would converse with you, sometimes visibly and sometimes invisibly. But when a child begins to commit some mortal sin, he loses baptismal grace; however, if by five or older the child sins, a penance is appointed by which he can remove the stain of sin and return to grace. And so, child, if you have fallen into sin, rouse yourself, confess, and do penance. Let go games and lasciviousness and remove yourself from wicked company; let go childish things; learn the lauds and prayers; join the confraternity.[14]

I say the same to the girls, also, who must be brought up in purity. This

13. Gregory the Great, *Dialogues,* bk. IV, chap. 19.
14. The company of children described in Pseudo-Burlamacchi, *Vita,* chap. XXXVIII, above. On Ridolfi's reattribution of authorship, see page 212, note 6, above.

means dressing in white, as you children must do today for the procession. But through the failings of their spiritual fathers and their fathers according to the flesh, who have not taken care of their little lambs, boys and girls have fallen from their purity because they have raised them according to the world and not God.

But you, Florence, had become the ass, as regards the adults, and the colt, as regards the boys and girls, and you used to live as if [you were] in the dark concerning the faith. The ass is an animal which is indelicate in its ability to judge and obtuse in its thinking, and it is a lascivious animal, and a beast of burden; that is, it carries weights, and is full of bestiality. So was Florence, which used to live obtusely, *that is,* blindly with respect to the faith, full of lasciviousness, and which voluntarily bore the weight of sins, so that nothing worse could be said than "Go to Florence." The women were all full of lasciviousness, and the children were the same. So, the adults were the ass, the children the colt.

The Lord, then, wanting to come once again to enlighten the world, deigned in His mercy to begin at Florence and was drawing near to Jerusalem, as the Gospel says: *Cum appropinquasset Hierosolymis et venisset Bethphage.* He was drawing near to Florence, a new city, and came to Bethphage, which is interpreted as *domus maxillae vel domus buccae,*[15] that is, He drew near and came through the mouths of the preachers whom He had enlightened. And He came to the Mount of Olives, *that is,* to those who contemplate the Scriptures, which are signified by the mount where there are olive trees, *that is,* which is full of the oil of the Holy Spirit. Now, when the Lord was here on the Mount of Olives, He sent two of his disciples to Jerusalem and said to them: *"Ite in castellum quod contra vos est,"* that is, go to the city which will be against you, which will persecute you and do you much harm; you will find an ass tied up, *that is,* the adults of that city bound up in lasciviousness and sins; *item,* the ass is one who bears a heavy weight, that is, they bear the weight of bad government, under which liberty has perished, and all the citizens are slaves and asses. "You will also find," Jesus said, "the colt"; this signifies your children who were all lascivious. "Untie them," said the Lord, *that is,* preach the faith to them, preach how to live uprightly to them, and let them be converted to simplicity, and lead them to Me, that is, to honor Me and to the faith; dress them in white, that is, have them purify their consciences, and let them leave their lasciviousness and their rock[-throwing]; let the girls leave their vanities and attend to living uprightly. And because living uprightly *est bene facere et mala pati,*[16] put the red cross

15. "House of the jaw or house of the mouth." This "etymology" mixes Hebrew (*beth,* "house") with Greek (*–phage* ("one who eats").
16. "Is to do good and to suffer evil."

in their hands, which means that you will be given tribulations aplenty by friars, priests, soldiers, your fathers and mothers. Put an olive branch in their hands, which means that the Lord will enlighten you, if you do good, with the oil of the Holy Spirit. Then the Lord said, "Bring both to Me," *that is,* convert them for the sake of My honor and convert them to Me.

Come here, you wise men and unbelievers: does it seem to you that the children have come to the Lord? Tell me something: how is it that the children never before came to hear the sermon in this fashion? You have not been able to restrain them with your laws from rock[-throwing] and to correct them of other vices, and now you see how on their own, by divine inspiration, they enter on the good way. The Lord also said to the disciples who went for the ass and the colt, "If anyone should say anything to you, tell them that the Lord needs them, because He wants to reform His Church, and, therefore, He wants this youngling." The Lord, I say, wants these children. He will take but a few of these elders. The others will be dealt with, because they are inveterate in evildoing. So, say that the Lord needs them.

Does this not seem a miracle to you? Does this not seem a thing from God? O Florence, the prophecy of Zacharias has been fulfilled in you. *Exulta, filia Sion: ecce Rex tuus venit tibi mansuetus, sedens super asinam, etc.* [Matt. 21: 5; cf. Zach. 9:9]. Here is your King, Who has come down to you. Have no doubt at all about what I tell you, that the angels will come with you today. Florence, your gentle King will sit upon the ass and the colt, *that is,* on the adults and on the young. The garments laid on the ass signify the Sacred Scriptures, or, to be more precise, the virtues which have been preached to you and of which you are full. These are the garments on which the Savior sat; that is, He sits within the intellect of both the small and the great, those who have understood this light of these Scriptures, and Christ governs them all. Tell me: who governs the children in this work if not Christ? You have tried your best with your laws, but you have never been able to restrain them. And it was reported to me yesterday, Florence, that your children came together to weave garlands of olive branches in order to have them at the feast today, and they were spread out in choir upon choir, and they wove garlands and chanted lauds so that it seemed a paradise. See how it is, Florence! The cloaks and the garments which they threw on the ground when Jesus passed by signify the good works which they have thrown down on the ground; that is, they have given good example. The olive trees signify the Scriptures (as above) with which they have given good example and drawn others to living uprightly. The people who walked ahead and behind signify those who have been converted earlier or later, and they all sang: *"Hosanna in excelsis";* this signifies that they have called upon Jesus and asked Him to be their King.

This is the holy Gospel in brief, which will all be borne out in you, Florence. Now, one word on the psalm, and we will make an end.

Today at the procession, everyone, men, women, and children, great and small: the children will go first holding red crosses, then the tabernacle, then the religious, then laymen, who will all carry olive branches, and also it would be good to carry your little cross. Next, the women with the girls, but do not let the women who are not girls carry the garlands, because this would be a sign of levity in the women. Everyone will praise the Lord and pray for the city and for the wicked ones that they may be converted. Come now, the Virgin has given you fine weather for your prayers, but see to it that you do not grow cold in prayer, for she says she wants you to pray. *Furthermore,* let everyone make an offering—this is what throwing the vestments on the ground means; let everyone assist in and augment this offering which is made for the *Monte di Pietà.* Most important, let the procession start off in good time; do not wait till the nineteenth hour [noon] to begin.

Hosanna: benedictus qui venit in nomine Domini! Let us praise Him Who has come in the name of the Lord! Let us praise Jesus, Who has come in His own name! Let us praise the Savior Who has come to save us!

Domine, Dominus noster, quam admirabile est nomen tuum in universa terra![17] [Ps. 8:2] O Lord of the universe, O our especial Lord, how marvelous is Your name! I have found in the Scriptures that Your name is marvelous in two ways: first, for its power; second, for its mercy. *Sanctum et terribile nomen eius*[18] [Ps. 110:9]: Your name is holy on account of Your mercy, and it is terrible on account of Your power. Lord, You created the world and poured out Your power upon all creatures. This power came to the nose of the philosophers, who went sniffing for so long that, because of the power which they saw dispersed among creatures, they came to the knowledge of You as Creator, and they said that You were the prime cause and the first principle, and they attributed to You all the names of power, but they did not find Your mercy. Afterward, You gave the Mosaic law in which You pronounce all the names of power and always say: *"Ego Dominus, Ego Dominus"*[19] [Ex. 20:2, 5]. Up to now Your name, Lord, has not exactly been marvelous through *all* the earth, because at that time You were worshipped only by the Hebrew people. But Your name began to be marvelous through all the earth when You poured out the name of Your mercy in the Virgin and became man and when You shed Your name on the wood of the Cross. Then was Your name marvelous; then, Lord, You gathered the oil of the Holy Spirit, and You went above and sent the Holy Spirit down to Your

17. "Lord, our Lord, how marvelous is Your name through all the earth!"
18. "Holy and terrible is His name."
19. "I am the Lord, I am the Lord.'"

Apostles, who went preaching Your name through all the earth and made Your name marvelous and glorious all over the world, as they said: *In nomine Iesu omne genu flectatur caelestium, terrestrium et infernorum et omnis lingua confiteatur quia Dominus noster Iesus Christus Dei filius est in gloria Patris*[20] [Philip. 2:10–11]. This was most wonderful, this is a great marvel, that God should be man and that He should have such great goodness that He wanted to die for man. *Quoniam elevata est magnificentia tua super caelos*[21] [Ps. 8:2]: my Lord, "Your magnificence," that is, Your Christ, Who is Your magnificence, "has been elevated above the heavens"; You have made Him magnificent and glorious; He has ascended to Paradise; He has drawn human hearts to Himself, and everyone has blessed and magnified Him. Let us praise Him, then, and say again: *Benedictus qui venit in nomine Domini: hosanna in excelsis!*

O Lord, how marvelous is Your name! Come now, children, all praise the Lord joyfully. Wise men have not known how to praise Him, the philosophers have not known how to praise Him, but children have praised You, our Lord. *Ex ore infantium et lactantium perfecisti laudem*[22] [Ps. 8:3]. There are some, O Lord, who have debased Your name because they consider themselves such geniuses that they never render praise to Your name for anything. But the children who carry Your cross have praised You and always do praise You. The philosophers have praised You through their own natural light, these praise You through a supernatural light; the philosophers did it for their own honor, these do it in simplicity for Your honor; the philosophers praised You with their tongues, these praise You with their works; the philosophers praised You within the confines of their schools, these children praise You through all the streets singing: *"Benedictus qui venit in nomine Domini: hosanna in excelsis!"* These are the ones who truly praise Your name. *Ut destruas inimicum et ultorem*[23] [Ps. 8:3], that is, in order to confound Your enemies, to confound the pagans, to confound the usurers, to confound the ambitious, to confound the lascivious, to throw to the ground the enemy who contradicts this work and those who want to defend their own sect. Lord, these You will drive out and cast down to the ground. O you elders, learn from these children to praise the Lord and say: *"Benedictus qui venit in nomine Domini: hosanna in excelsis!"*

Quoniam videbo coelos tuos, opera digitorum tuorum, lunam et stellas quae

---

20. "At the name of Jesus every knee must be bent of those in the heavens, on the earth, and under the earth, and every tongue confess that our Lord, Jesus Christ, is the Son of God in the glory of the Father." The Vulgate has *quia Dominus Iesus Christus in gloria est Dei Patris* ("that the Lord Jesus Christ is in the glory of God the Father").

21. "For Your magnificence is elevated above the heavens."

22. "Out of the mouths of infants and sucklings You have perfected praise."

23. "In order to destroy the enemy and the avenger."

tu fundasti[24] [Ps. 8:4]: that is, "I shall see Your heavens, the moon, and Your stars." Certainly, my Lord, I see clearly and manifestly, not only by an inner light, but *also* from outside, through these works, that You have led this colt to Yourself. I see, I say, Your heavens, that is, good prelates, Your preachers, and those whom You have enlightened, those who will bear fruit on this earth. Lord, I see the works of Your fingers, *that is,* I see the works of the Holy Spirit, which You have begun to pour out. I see the moon, *that is,* the city of Florence, which has received its light from the sun, that is, from You, Jesus Christ, Sun of justice. I see the stars, that is, that you have enlightened people of every station: the great, the small, religious and lay, and those of every sort, just as the stars are large and small and more or less luminous.

Quid est homo, quod memor es eius?[25] [Ps. 8:5] O Lord, who is this man? Who are we that you remember our doings? What merit is in us, Lord, that You should have come to visit us? Why have you done this for us? *Aut filius hominis, quoniam visitas eum?*[26] [Ps. 8:5] Lord, who is the son of man? He is our Jesus Christ; You have made this Man King of the angels, You have made Him King of the universe. Angels, you cannot pride yourselves that your God is an angel, but we can well pride ourselves that our God and yours is a man. Angels, worship that Man; O cherubim, O seraphim, worship that Man; O thrones, O powers, O dominations, all kneel down and adore this Man.

Minuisti eum paulo minus ab angelis[27] [Ps. 8:6]; my Lord, it is true that You have made this Man a little less than the angels in one respect, that is, that He was passible, and the angels are not passible. *Gloria et honore coronasti eum, et constituisti eum super opera manuum tuarum*[28] [Ps. 8:6–7], but after He had suffered, You made Him glorious and crowned Him with Your glory and set Him over all Your works, over the heavens and over the angels. *Omnia subiecisti sub pedibus eius, oves et boves universas, insuper et pecora campi*[29] [Ps. 8:8]; You have placed everything under His power; You have made Him Lord of all; You have made subject to Him the little sheep and lambs, who are good men and good children. *Et boves:* these are the good preachers whom You have made subject to this King. *Et pecora campi:* You have also made subject to this Man the beasts of the field, that is, those who walk

24. "For I shall look upon Your heavens, the works of Your fingers, the moon and the stars which You have established."
25. "What is man that You are mindful of him?"
26. "Or the son of man that You visit him?"
27. "You have made him little less than the angels."
28. "You have crowned him with glory and honor and have established him over the works of Your hands."
29. "You have subjected all things under his feet, all sheep and cattle, as well as the beasts of the field."

along the way which is broad like a field, *that is,* wicked sinners, the lustful, the avaricious, and all other wicked men are made subject to this King. *Volucres coeli et pisces maris qui perambulant semitas maris*[30] [Ps. 8:9]; the birds and the fish of the sea You have also made subject to this Man. The birds are the prideful who fly through the air like birds; the fish of the sea are the avaricious who go around every which way to acquire property and money; all of these You have made subject to this King. You have also made subject to Him all of Hell.

Benedictus igitur qui venit in nomine Domini: hosanna in excelsis; blessed are You, our King and Lord, blessed are the bowels of Your mercy, blessed be Your Mother,[31] our Queen. Lord, I commend to You Your city; I commend to You these children; I pray You that this work may be commended to You and that Your hand may be upon them today in this holy procession.

Florence, this is the King of the universe; He now wants to become your especial King: Florence, do you not want Him for your King?
[Transcriber's comment: "Note that the sermon did not go any further because to the last question all the people responded as loudly as they could, 'Yes,' they wanted Him for their King, and everyone cried out, 'Long live Christ!' and 'Mercy!' Then the preacher gave the blessing and everyone left."]

---

30. "The birds of the sky and the fish of the sea who go along the paths of the sea."
31. Savonarola uses the affectionate form, *Mamma*.

Girolamo Benivieni,[32] *"Viva ne nostri cuori, o Florentia"*

A Song

about the graces promised to the city of Florence, composed for use in the prescribed solemnity and procession [Palm Sunday], and sung publicly on that occasion in the year of our salvation 1496[33]

Long live Christ, your King, O Florence,
may He live in our hearts; long live the Bride,
His Daughter and Mother, your Guide and Queen,
for by Their goodness, by Their clemency,
you will become richer, more powerful and glorious
than you ever were. The day draws near,
nor can such a promise
or priceless gift prove empty,
because no human tongue proclaims it,
but divine goodness.

O you who are fortunate above every city,
more fortunate, indeed, than anyone would believe [possible],
and than even you perhaps think or hope,
although every virtue is dead in you,
and every honor seems to go to whoever has nothing to do with it
    [virtue],
yet in you lives that glorious seed
on which our every hope
surely depends, from which must issue the fruit
which through You, O sweet Jesus,
will nourish the whole world with Your true blessings.

---

32. The poet Girolamo Benivieni (1453–1542) was a close friend of Giovanni Pico della Mirandola and, at one time, a disciple of Marsilio Ficino. First drawn to Savonarola's sermons out of curiosity, he became a regular participant in the Academia Marciana disputations, translated Savonarola's works into either Latin or the vernacular as needed, wrote hymns (such as the two included here) for religious festivals, and defended Savonarola as a true prophet till the end of his long life. Though his loyalty is uncontested, he became a great friend of Giulio de' Medici, later Pope Clement VII, after that family's restoration to power in Florence. His brother Domenico was also in the forefront of apologists for the friar. For an account of his career, see Donald Weinstein, *Savonarola and Florence: Prophecy and Patriotism in the Renaissance* (Princeton: Princeton University Press, 1970), pp. 205–208, 216–220; and Lorenzo Polizzotto, *The Elect Nation: The Savonarolan Movement in Florence, 1494–1545* (Oxford: Clarendon Press, 1994), esp. pp. 141–146, 153–158, 165–167, 248–250, 302.
33. Benivieni published his poems with commentary in 1500.

Amidst your afflictions, my happy Florence,
you can rightly anticipate your salvation
more than any other [city looks for] joy amidst its greatest pomps,
for you alone have built your foundations
and your holy gates on the holy mountains.
Your Lord loves [you] more than any other [city].
Of you—oh, [what] immense love—
of you alone are said on earth
things more exalted and glorious
than were ever before seen in you by anyone.

Do you not know that when you were chosen
for such a grace, these words were said in heaven
by your kindly and heavenly Queen?
"O Florence, city beloved by God,
by my Son and by me, keep strong and lively
your faith, prayer and patience,
for by them the power is given
to make you ever blessed in heaven with God
and honored here on earth
among other [cities] like a sun among stars."

Rise, O new Jerusalem, and see,
see your glory. Acknowledge, adore
your Queen and her beloved Son.
In you, city of God, who now sit weeping,
such joy and splendor will yet be born
that not only you but the whole world shall be adorned.
In those happy days
you will see coming to you from the ends [of the earth]
a devout and pilgrim people,
[coming] to the fragrance of your consecrated lily,

Of your noble lily, whose leaves
will extend so far beyond your kingdom
that they will put your ungrateful neighbors in the shade.
Blessed by God are those gathered within you,
and cursed be anyone who has disdain
for your welfare, your glory, and your peace.
You, while it pleases your King,
anticipate that in the blink of an eye,
miraculously,
the veil may be torn which now shadows your glory.

Song, I do not rightly know if perhaps silence might be
more honorable than speech amidst so many doubts,
or if it is advisable for you to show yourself in public.
If the gifts of God were not mentioned in you,
this would be the fault of an ingrate, yet if you speak
or sing of them along with me, they may be ridiculed.
So, then, either you rejoice alone within my breast,
or if you would rather go elsewhere,
never show yourself where
there is no one who at least sees with our eyes.

Commentary

Long live: through faith and love. *In our hearts:* in our souls. *Christ, your King:* for Christ, even though He is a man, is the King of the whole universe. Wherefore, He says of Himself in the words of the prophet: *Ego aut[em] constitutus sum Rex ab eo super syon montem s[an]c[t]um eius*[34] [Ps. 2:6]. According to this servant and prophet of His [i.e., Savonarola], He wants to be at this time—in a certain more restricted and personal and special way— King and Lord of the city of Florence. Consequently, His ever virgin Mother is also the special Lady and Queen of that city. *The Bride:* that is, the Virgin herself, Bride and Daughter of God. *Mother:* Genetrix of Christ. *By Their goodness:* and not for any previous merit of ours. *Richer:* in eternal spiritual things, as well as in temporal and material. *More powerful:* by the expansion of her [Florence's] empire. *And glorious:* before both God and men. *But divine goodness:* which cannot in any way lie.

Above every city: not only in Italy, but in the whole world at this time. *Fortunate:* note that I do not say only that no greater felicity could possibly be enjoyed, but that none [greater] can even be imagined than that which is promised to the city of Florence, that is, eternal felicity. *Seems:* not only with respect to the evil life of many and your present tribulations and discords, but also, and much more, for the correction of your true and legitimate citizens and children, that is, for the sake of their simple faith and for the belief instilled [in them] by God alone concerning things divinely predicted to you, for which reason you are now derided and vilified by all the people of Italy. *To those who do not see:* that is, to all those who have already closed their ears to the words of God; it is no wonder that they have also closed the eyes of the intellect, and since they do not see, they do not believe in and do not know the secret judgment of God and what He intends to do at this time with the city of Florence, and this may be the ruin which

34. "But I have been appointed King by Him over Sion, His holy mountain."

hangs over the heads of all the incredulous and worldly-wise. *That glorious seed:* that is, the grace of God and the true root of good Christian living, which, before the preaching of this servant and prophet of God, was almost completely lost even among many of those who are reputed to be and give the impression of being teachers of the law. *On which:* from that seed, that is, from that grace and true root of good Christian living, as if from the very best seed, we know indubitably, or rather, we are certain that there must *Issue:* according to the promises made to us, *That fruit:* that admirable light and virtue, which, through You, O most sweet Jesus, that is, through Your grace and benignity, *Nourish:* in these our times *With Your true blessings:* that is, with the true light of Your faith and Your love, which are the true blessings of the human soul, *Nourish:* I mean with Your true blessings, *The whole world:* that is, all the people and all nations, by leading them back to Your worship and Your one true religion: *et fiat unum ovile et unus pastor*[35] [Ioh. 10:16].

You can rightly: with respect to a firm hope of your marvelous and fast approaching felicity. *Amidst your afflictions:* in your present tribulations. *Alone:* for we know of no other city which has set, as Florence has, the foundations of its hope in God and in *His holy* ones [the saints]. *His mountains:* that is, in His blessed spirits. *And your holy gates:* that is, the souls of the elect, through which, as through gates, your graces and your future felicity will descend upon you, O Florence. *Your Lord:* the blessed Christ Jesus, *Rex regu[m] et dominus dominantium*[36] [I Tim. 6:15; Apoc. 19:16; see also 17:14]. *About you—oh, immense love:* of your King and God. *Of you alone:* I say, and of no other city *Are [these] things said:* by this servant and prophet of God. *More exalted and glorious:* as appears in the *Compendium* of his previously cited revelations. *Than were ever before seen in you by anyone:* for you will be raised up by your King and Lord, Jesus Christ, to an excellence so great, with respect to the expansion of your temporal empire, as well as grace and fervor of spirit, such as you have never even approached from the day of your first foundation up to the present day.

Do you not know? O most fortunate city of Florence. *That when [you were chosen] for such a grace:* how greatly you are favored to have been made worthy of the blessings and felicity promised to you *By your kindly and heavenly Queen:* that is, by the Virgin herself, glorious Queen, who is, as is said, the Alumna and Protectress of the city of Florence. *"O Florence, city, etc.":* these are the formal words spoken by the glorious Virgin herself to this true prophet of God and recorded by him in the Latin tongue, just as he used

35. "And let there be one sheepfold and one shepherd." *Fiat* has been substituted for the Vulgate's *fiet*.
36. "King of kings and Lord of lords."

them in the *Compendium* of his revelations: *"Florentia, Deo Domino Iesu Christo filio meo et mihi dilecta, tene fidem; insta orationibus; roborare patientia: his [e]n[im] et sempiternam salutem apud Deum et apud homines gloriam persequeris."*[37]

I call Florence a *new Jerusalem* because, just as from Jerusalem issued that light and virtue which spread and disseminated the faith of Christ everywhere, so out of Florence will issue that light by which the whole world has to be reformed and led back to the true worship and original simplicity of the primitive Church of Christ. *[You] who now sit weeping:* on account of your present tribulations. *Not only you,* O Florence, *but the whole world will be adorned:* with the true worship of God, as we said a while ago, and with the true light of Christ. *In those happy days:* when you will have arrived at the summit of your felicity both temporal and spiritual. *From the ends [of the earth]:* from every region and part of the world. *To the fragrance:* to the fame. *Of your consecrated lily:* for so great will your glory be that, as the fragrance of your sanctity is wafted everywhere, people will come to you from every part of the world, drawn by its sweetness, some to see your felicity, some to receive from you your then most holy laws and the true way of governing and of living, some also to live and dwell under the rational measures of your then most just restraint, whence chiefly will arise the expansion of your power and of your jurisdiction.

Of your noble lily: of your noble ensign and, through it, of your state and your temporal rule. *Whose leaves:* that is, its borders. *Will extend so far:* and expand. *Beyond your kingdom:* and of your present jurisdiction and power. *That they put your ungrateful neighbors in the shade:* since you have not inflicted any injury on them nor given them any occasion to harm you, even after you regained your freedom, but, on the contrary, you have done good to everyone, surely, what they do against you now, they do most ungratefully. However, it will be a thing neither surprising nor inequitable if, after your lily has regained its vigor, it should spread out its at present badly weakened leaves, which will naturally cast shade on them, subduing your ungrateful and ill-wishing neighbors under the branches of its up till now all-too-tame Lion. *Blessed:* are they *By God:* in the blessings of the spirit as well as in temporal goods. *Who are gathered within you:* whatever person or people will come voluntarily under the restraint of your then most just government, directed and administered solely by God. And so also, on the contrary, *Cursed be anyone who disdains your welfare:* whether temporal or spiri-

---

37. "O Florence, beloved by God, the Lord Jesus Christ, my Son, and me, keep the faith, be constant in prayer and steadfast in patience, for with these you will win through to both eternal salvation with God and glory among men"; Bernard McGinn, ed. and trans., *Apocalyptic Spirituality* (New York: Paulist, 1979), p. 266.

tual. *Your glory and your* future *peace:* and inestimable tranquility and repose. *You, while to your King:* the blessed Jesus Christ, *It is pleasing:* and thus He maintains this stability within His eternal plan for the sake of your greater welfare. *Anticipate:* just so, O Florence, and be patient in these your present anxieties, just as in those which have been given by God as a test to your elect in order to make them better able to receive your felicity. Anticipate, I say, because *In the blink of an eye:* that is, in the briefest space of time, and when you are not thinking about it, *May be torn:* by God, and torn to shreds, *The veil:* that is, all your vices and defects, private as well as public, by which, as if by a soiled and very thick veil, the path to your future felicity is now closed off from you, O Florence, and obstructed, and which likewise conceals and withdraws from the eyes of everyone who lies within the obscure night of this world your present favors, your future *Glory:* and your true joys, and that peace which the blind world with all its pleasures can never itself possess.

    Song: O song. *I do not rightly know:* on my own and by my own ability to distinguish. *If perhaps [silence might be more] honorable:* advantageous and appropriate. *More than speech:* about this grace and felicity promised to the city of Florence. *Silence would be:* that is, silently enjoying the hope of those things within the bosom of our consciences. *Amidst so many doubts:* contradictions and difficulties. *If it is advisable for you to show yourself in public:* indiscriminately, to anyone whether a believer or unbeliever, and, I might add, by arguing up one side and down the other. *If the gifts of God:* that is, the promises made to the city of Florence and the graces which she has already actually received, such as living uprightly by the true light of the Scriptures and of the faith, as well as the recovery of at least some small part of her lost liberty, and the other gifts and graces divinely granted to us in these times—if such gifts *In you,* O song, *were not mentioned:* as pointless matters and little appreciated by us. *This:* your keeping silent about such graces, gifts, and marvelous works of God. *Would be the fault of an ingrate:* and not only, I say, of ingratitude, but of an impiety little short of apostasy and unbelief. *And if:* on the other hand. *You speak or sing of them:* publishing them before everyone indiscriminately. *Along with me:* that is, with your author. *And they:* the gifts, graces, and works of God. *Should be:* what is even worse and much more execrable. *Derided:* sneered at and vilified by beastly people who do not understand the things of God, but consider them (as the Apostle says) foolishness, and consequently laugh at those who believe them, who love and seek after and desire them. It would be an ill thing, then, to be silent about the gifts and favors and marvelous works of God in order to avoid the danger of incurring the fault of ingratitude, but worse to speak of them to everyone without making any distinction in order to avoid doubts about giving holy things to dogs and casting the pearls of heaven before swine and [so] subjecting them to the opprobrium and derision of the beasts of the earth. *So then:* O song, since these things *Either within my breast:* that is, in the secret place of my heart. *Alone:* together with me and without any other witness of our felicity. *You rejoice:* and take delight. *Or if you would rather go elsewhere:* outside of me. *Never show yourself where there is no one who sees:* the truth of these things, and if not with that living, pure, and infallible vision with which this servant of God has seen it, that is, with the light of prophecy, *At least with our eyes:* that is, with the light of faith with which, although in another mode [from prophecy], the things of God are seen, understood, and recognized.

Luca Landucci, *A Florentine Diary*

27th March (Palm Sunday). Fra Girolamo caused a procession to be made by all the boys, with a wreath of olive on their head and a branch of olive in their hand, each carrying a red cross, about a span high or more. There were said to be five thousand boys, and also a great number of girls, dressed in white like the boys, with the cross and the olive branch in their hands, and the olive wreath on their heads. Following them came all the city officials and the heads of the guilds; and after these the rest of the men, and then the women. I do not believe that there was a single man or woman who did not go to make this offering on the altar of *Santa Maria del Fiore*, the proceeds of which were to set up the *Monte della Pietà*. Very large sums were given. At the head of this procession there was a tabernacle with a painted Christ upon the ass, as He rode through the street of Jerusalem on Palm Sunday; and over it the umbrella was carried, whilst all cried: *"Viva Cristo ch'è 'l nostro Re!* (Christ our King!),"* through the whole city.

Piero Parenti,[38] *Storia fiorentina*

Although it had been suggested before by other preachers that it would be well to expel the Jews from Florence and set up the *Monte di Pietà,* now especially this idea took fire, supported by the preacher at Santa Croce and not contradicted by Fra Girolamo. Because it was customary to have a procession and solemn celebration at the inauguration of such an undertaking, they combined the procession meant to carry out the *Monte* [*di Pietà*] and the children organized by Fra Girolamo for Palm Sunday, and the children, in their new habits, prayed to God to remove His anger against this land and to free us from plague and from all other imminent adversities. Their habit was such that on top of their everyday clothes they had put on shirts or smocks, so that they appeared dressed in white. Moreover, they had olive garlands on their heads and red crosses each measuring a palm and a half. They were divided into quarters [of the city], according to the custom of the city.

Each quarter had its own standard and chief with the ensign of his quarter. Behind them followed the children, three by three, holding hands. After the four quarters, estimated at six to seven thousand children, there followed under a canopy a panel on which was painted our Lord on the ass, and facing him were the Jews laying down their robes and spreading them before the ass along with olive branches and palms, in accordance with what is reenacted on such a holy Sunday. Also depicted on the said panel was a crown, in accordance with the vision of the aforementioned Fra Girolamo,[39] but before the panel were carried two real crowns dedicated to the King and Queen of life eternal. Behind these followed little girls wearing the same habit. And all were chanting litanies, often crying out: "Long live, long live Christ the King and the Queen of life eternal." Then there followed on a pole the ensign of the *Monte di Pietà,* and [next], according to rank, all the orders of religious and at the end the priests with the bishop. Close behind came all the magistrates of the land, starting with the Colleges, since the

---

38. Son of Marco Parenti, an affluent Florentine merchant, and the aristocratic Caterina Strozzi (1450–1519), Piero Parenti was a chronicler and a student of Marsilio Ficino, renowned as a Latin translator. Like Ficino, he was initially attracted to Savonarola, but later disapproved of his exaggerated idealism. He was among the irregularly appointed Eight (April 1498) and, consequently, an examiner at Savonarola's trials (Roberto Ridolfi, *Life of Girolamo Savonarola,* trans. Cecil Grayson [New York: Knopf, 1959], pp. 266, 288). This excerpt is from the edition of Andrea Matucci (Florence: Olschki, 1994).

39. Described in the *Compendium of Revelations; McGinn, Apocalyptic Spirituality,* pp. 242 ff.

Signory remained at the Palace; finally, all the people, men and women, in vast numbers, swelled the crowd.

When the usual routes had been completed, each [group] returned to Santa Maria del Fiore, where a huge altar had been prepared with four containers and ministers. They received all the offerings which were to be used for the foundation of the *Monte di Pietà*. Above the said altar stood the ensign of the *Monte,* and each one going by it made an offering. Also, through the streets were carried baskets and tubs, in which were collected all the people gave: coins, cloths for a number of purposes, and other things of value, such as embroidered cushions, rings, belts, silver spoons and forks. But because the land was poor and in disarray, it was calculated that the entire sum amounted to about fifteen hundred ducats.

This was the beginning of the *Monte di Pietà,* over which was placed at first a public magistracy of men who would execute this commission, and this subsidy and loan would be supervised from the house of Piero de' Medici, since formerly he had obstructed this laudable work, so that he might get the payback he deserved.

La vita del Beato Ieronimo Savonarola,

previously attributed to Fra Pacifico Burlamacchi
>   Chapter XXXIX
>   *Concerning a procession arranged by the servant of God*

In the year of our Lord 1496, the servant of God decided to arrange a procession with great popular devotion and exuberance on Palm Sunday, when palms are distributed, in order to honor and reverence this day, for which everyone had to assemble in this way: early in the morning, several thousand people—both men and women—received Communion from the hands of the servant of God and took up palms; then they listened to the sermon in the cathedral, which was given by the servant of God for the sake of the children, who that morning, on account of their great number, occupied all four rows of benches; after dinner, all gathered at the Church of the Nuntiata, and, departing from there, they went to the gate of the first cloister of San Marco and through the cloister to the church, where a red cross was put in the hand of each of them in accordance with the mystery which the servant of God had seen and described in the first chapter of his *Compendium* of his revelations.[40] Leaving San Marco, they went up the via Larga and entered the temple of San Giovanni Baptista. They went two by two, according to the order of the quarters of the city, with their magistrates and followed a humble and devout tabernacle, on which was painted with admirable beauty the image of our Savior sitting on a docile ass; all around Him was a great multitude of every age, each laying his robe on the ground, and it seemed that they exclaimed: "Hosanna to the Son of David!" On the other side was a painting of Mary with that crown which had been presented to the glorious Virgin, Queen of Florence, when [as described in the *Compendium*] the servant of God went as an ambassador, which was held aloft by courteous angels. This mystery of the Savior was preceded and followed by many couples of children in dress and form like angels, shining with such grace and chasteness that they seemed to have descended from Paradise. There were more than eight thousand children, as those who counted them affirmed; it was a marvelous thing and behavior not typical of children of such tender age, to see their order and equal spacing, the devotion and concentration and silence and fervor, and the grace of their gestures, saying the [divine] offices and lauds, such that one could not deny that in this work they were directed and accompanied by the angelic spirits. The officers had ordered the children to carry silver basins which they had filled with a great deal of money collected for alms in order to set up the *Monte di Pietà*. After

40. Ibid., p. 200.

the tabernacle came all the other religious orders according to their rank, with the clergy last, then the friars and the laity with blessed olive branches and red crosses, and after them were girls dressed in white with garlands on their heads, and, at the end of the procession, all the other women. So great was the fervor of that day that not only women and children, but also men known for their intelligence and prudence, laying aside all human wisdom, dressed in white like the children, and in the presence of the mystery of our Savior, danced and knelt and sang in the manner of David before the Ark [II Reg. 6:14], so that out of the mouths of pure and suckling infants, praise for our Savior and King might be perfected [Ps. 8:3]; wherefore, many, as if taken out of themselves, despising and spurning every pomp and dignity of the world, carried olive branches and red crosses and sang loudly along with the children: "Long live Jesus Christ, our King!" There was so much jubilation and gladness in their hearts that the glory of Paradise seemed to have descended on earth, and because of the fullness of their spirits, they could not contain their tears.

In this manner they went around a great part of the city till they came to the Piazza della Signoria, where they sang several lauds newly composed for the occasion by the noble, learned, and devout citizen Girolamo Benivieni, which began "Long live in our hearts, long live, Florence" [*Viva ne nostri cuori, o Florentia*]. Having left this place in song and jubilation, they went round the city and came to the Cathedral Church of Santa Maria del Fiore, where, after offering their hearts and souls to our Savior and commending the whole city to our King and Queen, each offered all they had collected from their quarter, not only on that day of the procession, but also on other days, in order to set up the *Monte di Pietà,* which, if the servant of God had not recommended and assisted in establishing it from the pulpit, would never have been effected, as is apparent from his sermons on the prophet Amos. Not only were the children's basins full of money, rings, gems, and precious objects, but many other basins were full, which were placed on an altar of wonderful size built under the dome of the church in front of the choir, where precious garments and gifts of gold and silver were offered. It might be compared to the people of Israel, who voluntarily offered precious objects to Moses and Aaron in order to build the tabernacle of the Lord [Ex. 35:20 ff.]. A great deal of money was collected there from which four *monti di pietà* were established, one in each quarter of the city, and certainly, if this work of the servant of God had not received assistance, the Jews would never have been expelled from the city of Florence.[41] After

---

41. Legislation was enacted to this end (28 December 1495) but never put into effect. The law was rescinded less than a year later (13 November 1496), possibly with Savonarola's compliance. See Polizzotto, *Elect Nation,* pp. 35–37.

making the offering and giving thanks to God, they returned to the Piazza of San Marco, where all the friars issued from the convent without their hoods, and not only the little novices, but also the young and old friars, each with a garland on his head, made a round dance as large as the piazza, singing and psalming before the Lord, without any regard for human concerns, for where the spirit is, there is freedom, and this spirit of the angels, which does not derive from law, prevails here on account of the great sweetness and piety. Everyone shed tears and, so, went home.[42] Certainly, that was a marvelous day, made full by the Lord of exultation and joy, in which the whole populace went mad for the love of Jesus and could say to the wise of the world: *"We fools are the Christian people; you who are wise are the people of this world."* The truly spiritual could well consider the prophet's dictum: *Beatus populus qui scit iubilationem*[43] [Ps. 88:16]. Certainly, at that time Florence was happy and blessed and seemed a new Jerusalem.

42. The Latin version of the *Life* reads: "Those who act in accordance with the Spirit of God are not under the law. Then, weeping because of the great sweetness and devotion, everyone returned to his own [home]." See Pseudo-Burlamacchi, *Vita*, p. 129, n. 1.
43. "Blessed the people who know jubilation."

Bonfire of Vanities I: 7 February 1497

Girolamo Benivieni, *"Da che tu ci hai, Signore"*
Prayer to God
  for the promises made by Him to the city of Florence

  Since You, Lord Jesus,
  have chosen us through Your grace,
  inflame our hearts now with Your love.

  Rouse up, my Lord,
  Your power and come;
  show that You are God.
  Lord, why do You still forbear?
  Why do You not bind and bridle
  that incorrigible set
  which upsets[1] the welfare
  of the city of the flower?

  Since You, Lord Jesus, etc.

  You know, sweet Jesus,
  that our city
  no longer has an earthly king
  other than Your goodness.
  So then, may that piety
  which makes us worthy, Lord,
  to have You reign in us
  overcome our error.

  Who does not know that, because of the sin
  of Your rebellious people,
  You have prepared as a revenge
  famine, plague, and sword?
  Oh, make Your flail
  turn to gladness for the good,
  for transgressors into justice,
  that is, wrath and fury.

  If evil nourishes the mind
  of some proud one or fool,

1. *Turba / ch'el ben disturba.*

he disdains Your government
because he is enwrapped in vices.
May the reward be taken from him
of Your promised gifts,
which are life for the good,
for the bad, death and sorrow.

Open Your fount and rain down,
generous Jesus, that grace
which may restore to You
Your beautiful Florence.
We in this new age,
having made a gift
of body and of mind,
now give to You our hearts.

Since You, Lord Jesus,
have chosen us through Your grace,
inflame our hearts now with Your love.

Commentary

Having already reformed our city in great part, as we saw in the argument of the preceding song, not only with respect to living uprightly and the things of the spirit, but also with respect to those things which are necessary for the public and civil government thereof, and considering the marvelous reward which God had granted him also for his ministry to the young, as discussed in the previously mentioned argument, the servant of God and true prophet, Fra Girolamo Savonarola, thought, perhaps being inspired by God in this, of bringing them under some order, rule, and law for living and acting, according to the manner and prescription of which they would be ruled and governed in all their actions. Since he could not take upon himself the execution of this affair because of his innumerable commitments, he assigned it to his most faithful fellow servant in Christ Jesus, Fra Domenico da Pescia. The latter, being as fervent and vigilant as his [superior] in every work of Christ, quickly gathered those youths most expert in and best suited to this effort (not so much in years as in purity of life and natural judgment) and began, as a most diligent pastor, to investigate [what] the desire, inclination, and opinion of each of them [might be] about their new reform. Because of the consensus of all and because of their maturity of opinion, incredible promptitude, and favorable disposition toward this affair, he concluded that the hand of God was in it, and so he frequently kept them near him. Having examined all that could be done about this, they finally hammered out a reform, no less useful and suitable than beautiful and wide-ranging, regarding the modesty of dress and the observance of all moral laws, especially pertaining to the true worship and true root of Christian living, as well as the creation, term, and organization of several ministries, and the offices necessary to effect them.

Among these (for it would be too long and beyond our purpose to speak of all of them here), they decreed that for each quarter [of the city] some of these youths should be elected for a certain time and within certain rules and restrictions, whose office would be to go all through the city, each within his own quarter, on certain days set aside for this and, while going about, to investigate where gambling was still carried on or where other things less than honest or not permitted were being done, and when they found anything, they were, with all humility and gentleness, to admonish anyone who had been found by them in such acts, denouncing him, when this was necessary, to those public magistrates of the city, who held the power to punish such crimes. Whenever they might find women or girls dressed immodestly and without their proper decorum on the public streets or in the churches, they would admonish them in the same way, that is, with all humility, gentleness, and reverence, on God's behalf and exhort them to lay aside such vanities for the public good of the city and of their private souls. They would also search their own homes and the homes of our other citizens and encourage anyone found to have vain or lascivious things or things scarcely suitable to a Christian profession to strip themselves of such vanities and curses provoking God's wrath, and if they found anyone who did not want to let them in or who even mocked them in some way or did them any other injury or rudeness, they would (as they have done faithfully from the beginning up to now) bear patiently, for the love of Christ, all opprobrium, every persecution, and every scourge, never even answering with anything less than gracious and most modest words, but to those willing to strip themselves of such things, they would promise on God's behalf many personal graces and special blessings.

It would take a long time to describe all the circumstances, even for what concerns only this office, [or to tell] with what modesty and with what good effects for the whole city, they have executed it [their office] up to the present time such that, solely through their encouragement and gentle persuasion, the people have many times been compelled to deprive themselves of their dearest (in sensual terms) and most precious things. Sometimes it happened that when these youths came to the houses of those who were most unbendingly opposed to their work and exhorted them as they had others, that is, by blessing them modestly and reverently in the name of Jesus Christ, their King, to lay aside such things if perchance they had any in their possession, suddenly, transforming from ferocious wolves into humble and gentle lambs, they would scrupulously search over their houses along with these youths and hand over all that had been demanded of them, even the most ferocious among them being unable to restrain his tears for sheer emotion at such a time. Such was the grace, such the authority that God had granted them in this work! It sometimes happened that when suddenly they came upon some gamblers, men otherwise beastly and full of rage, and besides [delivering] their usual grave and most modest warning, tried to take away their dice or cards, not only would they not offer any resistance or even utter an injurious word, but they would go off as if they had become drunk and dumbstruck or at least allow what they wanted to be taken away without saying a word, which shows, beyond all ambiguity, that there was in these [youths] a force and a virtue other than their own.

I could add here many other examples, especially concerning the admonitions they made to many most noble young women and girls of our city, through the admirable results of which anyone with discernment can recognize that this is the work of God, but in order not to provide fresh opportunity and furnish new material to the incredulous for slandering the works of God once again, I will not for now continue any further than may be necessary for the argument of the song under examination. And if perhaps what has already been said should seem to anyone superfluous or puerile and ridiculous, let it not be burdensome to such a one, I pray, if he is a Christian, to lay aside at least for a while the lenses of Satan's pride and put on those of Christ's humility, and then he may legitimately form that judgment which the testimony of his conscience dictates to him. I say, then, that these youths, by the power of God and in the manner described, cleansed a goodly number of the houses of our citizens from the aforesaid lascivious, vain, and detestable things, and when all these things had been gathered in a place deputed for this purpose and the licentious days of Carnival approached, these servants of God decided to convert the usual licentiousness and ill-bred dissolution of them into purity and sanctification of spirit. And so, in place of the masques of indecent games and abominable speeches, they ordered that on the very day of Carnival the youths would have a procession similar to the one about which we have spoken at length in the preceding argument, however without changing their usual clothes as in that one; thus they wanted to make a sacrifice to God *in odorem suavitatis*[2] [Eph. 5:2; Philip. 4:18; cf. Ex. 29:18], instead of those other execrable festivities, fires, and *capannucci*[3] of the devil, but with the same means, that is, with all those vain, lascivious, and indecent things which the youths had gathered. To this end, it was ordered that an edifice of wood, capacious enough to contain the

2. "In an odor of sweetness."
3. *Capannuccio:* see page 217, note 17, above.

above-mentioned objects, should be erected in the Piazza della Signoria by the hands of certain engineers. The structure so built rose from the earth with eight sides which narrowed toward the summit in the manner of a pyramid, reaching to a height of about thirty cubits, and each of its sides, at the lowest part, was fifteen cubits wide. Surrounding the entire structure were seven tiers, [ascending] one above the other at equal intervals, on which were set all the aforesaid objects with a not disagreeable artfulness; a part of these tiers was decked out with a variety of panels and canvases of precious, though lascivious, pictures; part with castings and sculptures of no middling beauty; part with musical instruments, such as harps, lutes, citterns, and other such; part with a great many women's ornaments and vanities, such as mirrors, veils, wigs, cosmetics, perfumes, and other such things, vanities without number, more than one would have believed could be in the city. Also hanging from these tiers was no small quantity of chessboards, of [printers'] forms for making cards and gaming boards, and a numberless number of dice, tables, cards, and similar instruments of Satan.

Above these seven tiers representing the seven deadly sins, seated on a wide chair as if he were their prince or captain, was Carnival himself in the form of a monster as filthy and abominable as anyone could imagine he would be in the eyes of God, composed of so many and such vices as those which are wont to occupy the unhappy souls of our mendacious Christians. The aforesaid items were set out in such an overall order, and yet so separated as to make each distinct, that this edifice, which was as decorative as it was appropriate, was rendered pleasing and delightful to the eyes of everyone in its entirety no less than in each of its parts. I will mention some of its parts, for among its other ornaments, there were some paintings, some bas-reliefs, and some other things of such worth and beauty that those who saw them generally estimated them to amount altogether to the value of many thousands of ducats. Leaving aside objects more highly valued, I myself held in my hand the painting of a head for which the person who had purchased it had paid ten ducats, and among other things, there was a chessboard worked with jewels and ivory which some said would cost forty ducats by itself and without the chess pieces.

I wanted to recount all this so that anyone who did not see them might more easily believe the value of the whole and, consequently, understand what God can do even through the agency of small children. But to return to our topic: I say that when the procession had come to Santa Maria del Fiore, and the laud or song which I composed solely for this purpose had been sung [*Da che tu ci hai, Signore*], and all those things which the youths had gathered for Christ's poor, which amounted to not a few hundred ducats, had been offered, they returned at last with all the people to the Piazza della Signoria. Here, after these same youths with equal enthusiasm had sung a song reportedly fashioned in the manner of a mocking invective against Carnival,[4] they set the edifice on fire in a number of places; the festivity, delight, and joy of all the people was as great as required by the burning of so many varied instruments, arts, snares, and engines of the devil and the purification of the city of God from so execrable and evil a plague, cultivated up to this very day in the bosom of Christ. On account of all this, not only the men, women, and children, but also inanimate objects, such as the public bells, pipes, and trumpets seemed in that hour to exult miraculously in the exuberance of so much joy and public gladness, and so, with a remarkably clear sound, along with a great outcry from all the people and the crackling [of the] flames, they rang out, rising all the way up to Heaven, to the glory and honor of God and the confusion and ignominy of Satan and his members.

When the licentious days of Carnival had passed in this way, with this public joy and spiritual consolation of the whole city, and those of Lent followed, a time of compunction and penitence, the youths began once again to search the houses of our citizens in accordance with the aforesaid order, induced to do so not only by the successful outcome of their first search, but equally by the opportune occasion of the season, which tends on its own to incline the minds of men to fast and abstain not only from the food for the body, but also from all those illicit things which are pernicious to the purity of our Christian profession. And so, through the grace of God and the exhortations of His servant and prophet, who was then preaching publicly in Santa Maria del Fiore, they collected in a very short time more things and of greater value and beauty than those of which we have spoken above. Because they wanted to make of these things a public and grateful sacrifice to God, as they had done with those others before, they decided to arrange once again a procession and an edifice or triumph in a manner and form which was more in accordance with what these servants of God intended to represent mystically through this new spectacle, according to the dictates of those times. To this end, being required by duty to think out something appropriate to this device, of which there has already been some discussion, I composed the following song [*Venite, ecco el Signore*]. But because, by the envy of Satan, a means is never lacking to hinder the works of Christ, when He allows it, there occurred — and by the hidden judgment of God there continues to occur — such circumstances that this affair has not undeservedly been deferred up till now, and will be deferred as long as God wills it,

---

4. *Canzona che fa uno Fiorentino a Carnasciale,* ed. Isidoro del Lungo, in *Canzona d'un Piagnone pel bruciamento delle vanità nel Carnevale del 1498* [*sic*] (Florence: Grazzini, 1864), pp. 1–21; see Patrick Macey, *Bonfire Songs: Savonarola's Musical Legacy* (Oxford: Clarendon Press, 1998), p. 75, n. 40.

perhaps till His elect may be so disposed and strengthened through persecutions and the virtue of patience that even under the sword they may be
ready and able to offer themselves and their very souls to God along with
these objects, or till God rouses up His power and—as the song below
says—comes at last to see how things stand with His city and, consequently,
to cleanse this otherwise flowery and beautiful garden of all those weeds and
evil plants, cultivated up to now, which not only bear no fruit themselves,
but—what is even worse—overshadow and hinder with their noxious shade
many of those which could either make themselves or cause some others to
change from sterile and fruitless to useful and fertile.

Now, because when the matter changes, the form is also changed, I
suppose that the mood of those times [to come] would have to be very
different from that of the present; I also think that, because the offering of
such a sacrifice must serve and be accommodated to the conditions of future
times, it will be necessary to change the order, manner, and device, and that,
consequently, this present song of ours remains, with regard to such a sacrifice, defrauded of its purpose. However, since I wished that it might achieve
the effect for which it was first intended by some other way, it has pleased
me to pair it here with its preceding sister in the hope that what has been
withheld from it in one way, solely through the envy of Satan, it might
achieve perhaps even more abundantly by God's benignity: and this is to
invite and, by inviting, to move those souls pre-elected by God to progress
through the purification of the intellect and the ardor of their affections
toward their Spouse, Jesus Christ, and, in a certain way, to press Him to
hasten His ardently desired advent and, consequently, the graces and the
felicity divinely promised to us through His servant and prophet.

Piero Parenti, *Storia fiorentina*[5]

IV.cxxv

However, this malaise, being discovered little by little, now caused concern to the partisans of the [French] king, who, insofar as it was possible for them, aided each other, and though they trusted each other more than the friar, who bent a good part of the people to his will under the cover of doing good and fleeing vanity so that they gave him too much credit, they agreed to the following: that on account of their detestation and abomination of vanity, and of gambling, and of all vices and sins, there was to be built on the Piazza della Signoria a certain round structure of wood, in the manner of a hut or pyramid, in tiers going up to a good height, on the summit of which was the figure of Satan, with other devils at its foot, and on it were to be burnt lascivious pictures, vanities such as ladies' wigs, mirrors, cosmetics, dolls, perfumes, panel paintings, sculptures, gods of love, playing cards, dicing tables, chessboards, lutes and other musical instruments, books by different poets, and other similar things appertaining to ostentation or lasciviousness. After this, it was ordered that a multitude of children would go forth in procession from San Marco, quarter by quarter, each with its own ensign before it, make a complete circuit through Florence, and, finally, return to the piazza, where, taking up a position around the *ringhiera* [a raised platform in front of the Palazzo Vecchio] and loggia of the Signory,[6] they would sing a certain laud composed to disparage Carnival and in honor and praise of Jesus Christ, King of Florence.[7] After the trumpets and pipes of the Signory had been sounded, they would come with lighted torches to set fire to the aforesaid structure, which was packed full of broom and logs, and, with the greatest rejoicing, burn everything which was piled on top in the presence of almost all the people and with the windows all around full of women.

Such was the day of Carnival, which concluded with no other festivities. What a marvel! that *capannucci*,[8] daggers, and rocks should be abandoned, and that in exchange they should devote themselves to begging on behalf of the poor, to having processions and burning vanities. And although such a spectacle appeared to be a celebration, nonetheless, it was remarked partly

5. This excerpt is from Joseph Schnitzer's edition, in his *Savonarola nach den Aufzeich-nungen des Florentiners Piero Parenti*, vol. IV of *Quellen und Forschungen zur Geschichte Savonarolas* (Leipzig: Verlag von Duncker und Humblot, 1910).
6. The contemporary layout of the piazza is to be seen in an anonymous painting of Savonarola's execution, reproduced here in plate 12.
7. *Canzona*, pp. 1–21. See page 249, note 4 above.
8. *Capannuccio:* see page 217, note 17, above.

in jest and partly from hypocrisy that only the partisans of the friar praised these things as well done, another faction reproved them, and the friar's credit varied so much throughout Florence that fathers were divided from their sons, wives from their husbands, brothers from brothers over it, and not only the citizens of the government [the enfranchised] exhibited these differences, but even the young men between eighteen and thirty years of age. One faction took for their leader a son of Bernardo Nasi,[9] whom they titled "king," and another chose the son of Girolamo Martelli, whom they acclaimed "duke," and it was their intention to battle each other in a game of football and for one faction to overcome the other. But the Eight, considering this a dangerous thing, laid down the law and so removed such matter for scandal.

Once again the Signory, judging it dangerous for the Franciscan friars to preach, especially since these did not fall in with the agenda of their sect and party, ordered that they completely abstain from preaching. Apparently, the first authorization [allowing them to preach] came out without the consent of the Gonfalonier,[10] or rather, without the advice and consent of the friar [Savonarola]. Since he then disapproved of it, the Signory reversed itself and made a new ordinance. For this reason, the aforesaid preachers were completely alienated from then on.

9. A Piagnone, supporter of Savonarola.
10. See page 162, note 18, above.

Iacopo Nardi,[11] *Istorie della città di Firenze*

I.xxi

On account of the favorable outcome of the aforementioned affair, the belief accorded to the prophecies of the friar mushroomed on the one hand, but on the other, the opposition and great contention which were made against him by his adversaries of every condition increased. But he, proceeding none-theless with his preaching, continually augmented his following of auditors of every age and profession to such a degree that on the day of Christ's Nativity a procession and devotion were made by the people, worthy for this reason alone not to be passed over in silence, for the example of those who are to come. And so, that morning, at the Cathedral, a great number convened of more than thirteen hundred children or youths, aged eighteen or less, that is, those who had been given permission or had been counseled by their own confessors to receive Communion; when the dawn Mass, sol-emnly sung by the priests, had been heard, and all the clergy had first taken Communion, according to the dignity of their rank, then the said children devoutly received Communion from the hands of two canons with such great modesty and remarkable devotion that the spectators, and especially the foreigners, could not restrain their tears on account of their great amaze-ment that that age, which is so frail and so little inclined to divine contem-plation, should be so well motivated and trained to so good a disposition.

After this time, since Fra Girolamo refrained from preaching in order to reduce the antagonism of his adversaries and persecutors, his companion, Fra Domenico da Pescia, succeeded him (as he had been accustomed to do), preaching on all the Sundays up till Lent with such spirit and devotion — although apparently he had not been considered very learned (though I do not know how anyone could think this) — that within this space of time, brief as it was, he persuaded the people to remove from their homes all lascivious and disgraceful books, whether in Latin or the vernacular, and all the statues and paintings of every sort which could incite people to wicked or disgraceful thoughts. And for this purpose, he commissioned the children, organized under custodians or masters or lords or officials made and deputed from among these same children, that each should go through the houses of the citizens of their quarter and ask sweetly and with all humility for every anathema (for so they denominated such lascivious and disgraceful things), as under excommunication and malediction by God and the canons of Holy

---

11. Nardi (1476–1563), a Piagnone writer and historian, was banished from Florence at the return of the Medici in 1530. His *Istorie della città di Firenze* was written late in life, during his years in exile. He died in Venice.

Church. So they went everywhere, seeking and begging, and at every house where they received some such thing, they gave a certain very devout but brief blessing, either in Latin or the vernacular, which had been prescribed for them by the said friar; indeed, from the beginning of the forty days of Advent up to Carnival, they were given or collected an amazing multitude of such disgraceful statues and paintings, and also wigs and women's hair ornaments, bits of silk, cosmetics, orangeflower water [for the complexion], musk, perfumes of many sorts, and similar vanities, and then beautiful and expensive gaming tables, chessboards, playing cards and dice, harps and lutes and citterns and similar musical instruments, the works of Boccaccio and Morganti,[12] and books of all sorts, and an amazing quantity of books of magic and superstition.

On the day of Carnival, all such things were carried to and placed in an orderly fashion on a great and elevated platform, raised in the piazza the day before; this edifice, which formed a very wide circle at the base, rose to its top little by little in the form of a round pyramid and was surrounded by steps in the manner of seats, and on these steps or seats, all those things were disposed in an orderly arrangement, along with brooms and logs and other flammable materials. On the day of Carnival, all the people converged on this spectacle to see, leaving their savage and beastly rock-throwing, as had been done the previous year, and instead of masquerades and similar Carnival festivities, the company of children heard, in the morning, a solemn Mass of the Angels devoutly chanted in the cathedral by the order of this Fra Domenico. After dining, all the children gathered with their guardians, each in his own quarter, and went to the church of San Marco, all dressed in white and with olive garlands on their heads and little red crosses in their hands, and then, when they had returned to the cathedral, they offered such alms as they had begged for that day to the embarrassed poor. And having done this, they went to the piazza, where they assembled around the *ringhiera* and loggia of the Signory, continually chanting psalms and ecclesiastical hymns and vernacular lauds; finally, descending from this place, the four guardians and leaders of the quarters with burning torches set fire to the

---

12. The *Morgante maggiore* of Luigi Pulci (1432–1484), companion of Lorenzo de' Medici, is described by Pasquale Villari as "a spirited, graceful medley of strange and sparkling fancies, in which an invocation to the Virgin is followed by another to Venus, and this again by a satire on the immortality of the soul" (Villari, *Life and Times of Girolamo Savonarola*, trans. Linda Villari [London: Unwin, 1888], p. 48). Morgante, a giant, serves Orlando (Roland) as squire in this mock-epic rendition of the Matter of Spain (the deeds of Charlemagne and his Twelve Peers).

aforesaid edifice, or *capannuccio*[13] as we would say here, and so, at the sound of a trumpet, they burned all the things mentioned before.

Indeed, through the agency of children, a quite splendid and devout Carnival feast was celebrated on that occasion, contrary to the ancient custom of the day, in which the common folk engaged in beastly rock-throwing all day and other activities even more damnable [yet typical] of our corrupt age. Nonetheless, this affair gave rise to a great murmuring and scandal among the people, as commonly happens with all new things, even when they are good, since anything can easily be interpreted in a negative way; indeed, there was no lack then of those who censured the waste and destruction of so many things of such great value, which, being sold, would bring in a good sum of money to give to the poor for the love of God, as those complainers said in times past of the precious ointment which that devout woman poured over the feet of Christ [Ioh. 12:3 ff.; see also Matt. 26:7 ff., Marc. 14:3 ff., Luc. 7:37 ff.], neither noticing nor considering that the pagan philosophers and makers of policy, whether real or imaginary and invented by people of the past, and Plato especially [in his *Republic*], banished all those things which today are most severely prohibited by Christian philosophy.

13. *Capannuccio:* see page 217, note 17, above.

La vita del Beato Ieronimo Savonarola,

previously attributed to Fra Pacifico Burlamacchi
    Chapter XLa
    How he set fire to all the vanities

The following year, 1497, when the diabolical and scandalous days of Carnival drew near, the servant of God, wanting to convert the day from one
of dissolution into a day of wisdom and sanctification and usefulness to
souls, in place of the masques and games and disgraceful deeds and abominable discords which were customarily engaged in by the young people
during these days of Carnival, ordered a procession full of mysteries, similar
to the first one, with appropriate dress. Instead of the execrable festivities of
the devil, that is, of barricades and *capannucci*,[14] he ordered the following to
be carried out at the twenty-first hour [about two P.M.] of that accursed day
of Carnival: that a great *capannuccio* be built in the Piazza della Signoria of
all the devil's instruments, that is, all the vanities and lascivious and disgraceful things collected by the children in that year as a sacrifice to God and in
the odor of sanctity.[15] It was to be built by the craftsmen, smiths, and wood-
cutters who would come together for this work in this shape: they took a
tree and erected it in the middle of the Piazza della Signoria, rising thirty
Florentine yards from the ground, and on its summit they nailed some
beams, whose bases they fastened to the ground in the manner of a pyramid,
covering an area of one hundred twenty yards. On these beams, from the
foot up to the summit, they placed fifteen steps, under which, in the empty
space, were great bundles of faggots and broom and other timber for burning with gunpowder, so that it would burn more quickly. This structure had
eight sides, forming a circle, and each side had fifteen steps; upon these
fifteen steps were set and arranged all the vanities and lascivious objects of
women, disgraceful pictures and sculptures, gambling implements, books of
poetry in Latin as well as the vernacular and all kinds of disgraceful reading
materials, musical instruments together with their books, masks and all the
accursed [trappings] of Carnival, divided up with marvelous artistry and variety in this way: near the steps precious foreign cloths painted with very
beautiful but shameless figures were arranged in such a way that it looked
like the workshop of a painter; above those cloths there were sculpted figures
of the most beautiful women of antiquity and of the most excellent proportion, both Roman and Florentine, portrayed by the great masters of sculp-

---

14. *Capannuccio:* see page 217, note 17, above.
15. The text has *in odore di santità,* but more probably *di soavità* is meant, for *in
    odorem suavitatis* (Eph. 5:2; Philip. 4:18; cf. Ex. 29:18).

ture, such as Donatello and the like. On another step there were gaming tables, blocks for printing cards, dice, and trumps; on another there were musical instruments, such as harps, lutes, citterns, accordions, dulcimers, pipes, cymbals, batons, and horns, together with their books; on another were the vanities of women: wigs, veils, ampules of rouge, cosmetics, mirrors, perfumes, face powder, musk, hats, and suchlike; on another were the books of poets and all sorts of lasciviousness, both Latin and vernacular: Morganti,[16] the Matter of Spain,[17] Petrarch, Dante, the *Centonovelle* [*Decameron*] of Boccaccio, and similar disgraceful things. On still another, there were beards, masks, hats, and every diabolical instrument suited to the occasion [i.e., for Carnival masquing]. All these things were disposed in a varied and distinctive way in order to appear delectable to the eye, and it is no wonder, for there were sculptures of great value and paintings of admirable beauty; there was an ivory chessboard worth forty ducats, and those of alabaster and porphyry were worth even more, so much so that a Venetian merchant went to the Signory and offered twenty thousand ducats for the whole edifice and triumph, if they wanted to sell it to him; he was repaid for his offer by having his portrait placed at the top of this structure on an open seat, as if he were the prince of all these devices. And there was also set up there a figure of Carnival so monstrous and deformed that it would be difficult to imagine.

Once the edifice had been constructed and adorned in this way, on the morning of Carnival many thousands of people, men and women alike, received Communion from the hands of the servant of God, singing hymns and spiritual canticles in such a way that one might believe that the angels had come down to dwell with human beings, and so it certainly was. The servant of God celebrated a solemn Mass, and after he gave the benediction, all went home to eat; after dinner, a solemn procession began that circumambulated the city as was the custom, and for this procession, the children were given a most beautiful child representing the Infant Jesus, white and rosy, and with the brilliance of glistening snow, standing on a base of gold. With His right hand He gave a blessing, and in His left He held the crown of thorns with the nails of His Passion and the Cross, and He showed to the people His pierced feet and hands and side. It was stupendous in its beauty, made by that great sculptor, Donatello. The statue was carried by four children, angelic in appearance and dress, on a portable altar heavily ornamented with gold and silk, and this they carried on their shoulders; over these four, twelve [other] children carried a silk canopy of marvelous beauty, painted with great variety, on poles elevated on high. Ahead of this Baby

16. The *Morgante maggiore* of Luigi Pulci; see note 12, page 254 above.
17. Charlemagne romances, such as Boiardo's *Orlando innamorato*.

Jesus went an innumerable multitude of children, arranged two by two, according to the order of the quarters of the city. Around the Infant Jesus were child cantors, who sang psalms and spiritual hymns, praying to God with their hearts and voices for the Florentine people; these were musical pieces newly composed for and suited to that occasion. After the Savior, the guardians with their officers and almoners carried silver vessels to receive alms for the poor of St. Martin, besides those which they collected on such days and begged for on festival days throughout the year. After these came our [children] with red crosses, and after them the girls and women, and when they had made the circuit according to the custom of the city, they came to the Cathedral, where, after singing most beautiful lauds, the whole populace offered itself to the glorious Queen of the city of Florence. Afterward they offered a great quantity of money to the officers of St. Martin to subvent the embarrassed poor, and once the prayers and lauds were finished, they came to the Piazza della Signoria, where half of them were lined up on the *ringhiera* before the Palazzo [Vecchio]; the other half were put in the loggia of the Signory, according to the order of the four quarters. Here they sang a witty invective against Carnival,[18] newly composed, and then the four guardians with a lighted torch in hand set fire to the *capannuccio* with as much gladness and rejoicing among all the people as such a conflagration of so many vanities and snares of the devil required. Not only the men, women, and children, but also the insensible creatures held festival: the bells of the palace, the trumpets of the Signory, the pipes and the cymbals sounded for the glory of so great a triumph offered to God. At that moment, one could see everything wondrously exultant because of the abundance of joy, and so, as the flame ascended to Heaven with great praise from all the people to the honor of God and the ignominy of Satan and the confusion of his members, the whole of that triumph was consumed.

These were the works of the servant of God which flourished in the city of Florence. Look, lift up your heads, and consider that the prophets of the Lord are known by their fruits. Who ever heard of such things or who ever saw the like? *Non factum est tale opus in universis regnis*[19] [III Reg. 10:20].

---

18. *Canzona,* pp. 1–21. See page 249, note 4 above.
19. "Such a work has not been done in all the kingdoms of the earth."

Silencing and Excommunication

Silencing

Letter from Pope Alexander VI[1] to Savonarola

Rome, 21 July 1495

Beloved son, greeting and apostolic blessing:

We perceive by the account of many that, among other servants of the vineyard of the Lord of Sabbaoth, you perform the greatest labors, concerning which we most heartily rejoice and return praises to the Omnipotent God, Who has supplied such grace to human understanding. We do not doubt that it is by that same divine Spirit Who distributes grace among mortals that you are able both to sow the word of God among Christian people and to increase the fruit a hundredfold. As in recent days, through your letter about this, we have come to understand your resolve and intention, which is to disclose to the people in your preachings those things which you know to be in God's service, and since people have recently related to us that you subsequently have said in public sermons that those things which you announce are to come you say not from you yourself or from human wisdom but by divine revelation, for that reason, desiring, as is befitting to our pastoral office, to speak with you about these things and to hear them from your own mouth, so that understanding these things better from you yourself, we might carry out what is pleasing to God, we exhort and command by virtue of holy obedience that you come to us as soon as possible. For we shall see you with paternal love and charity.

Dated at Rome at St. Peter's, under the seal of the Fisherman, the twenty-first day of July 1495, in the fourth year of our pontificate.

B. Floridus

[On the outside:] To our dear son, Brother Girolamo of the Order of Preachers of the Observance, living in Florence

---

1. Rodrigo Borgia (1431–1503), elected Pope on the death of Innocent VIII (d. 1492).

Letter from Savonarola to Pope Alexander VI

Florence, 31 July 1495

Most Blessed Father, after kissing your blessed feet:

Although I know that the commands of one's elders should always be obeyed, for, as Scripture says: "Whoever hears you, hears Me" [Luc. 10:16], I know, nevertheless, that the meaning of the words rather than the words themselves ought to be considered. Whence, in the capitulum *"Si quando extra," De rescriptis,*[2] as Your Holiness well knows, the reply of Alexander III, your ancient predecessor, to the Archbishop of Ravenna, runs thus: "Considering carefully the nature of the matter on account of which we wrote to you, you may either reverently carry out our command or set forth in your letters a reasonable cause why you could not carry it out, because we will patiently hold back if you have not done what has been suggested by distorted insinuation." Therefore, I, who desire now to visit Rome, which I have never seen, so that I might be able to venerate at firsthand the dwelling of the Apostles Peter and Paul and the relics of the other saints and Your Beatitude, I am now inflamed with greater desire on account of the command of Your Holiness, who has deigned to call to yourself this minute worm. Nevertheless, because many things stand in the way, I shall attempt to set forth reasonable causes to you, so that you will know that I am detained by necessity, not by my will, so that I cannot appear in your presence, although I have received your commands most readily and reverently.

First, then, infirmity of the body prohibits me, indeed with fevers and dysentery, which I have suffered lately. Next, on account of the continual agitations of the body and spirit undertaken this year especially for the welfare of this city, to such an extent that I have been debilitated in the stomach and other vital members, so that I cannot bear any additional labor; indeed, it is necessary to abstain from preaching and even my studies by the counsel of my doctors, the common opinion of whom and of everyone else being that unless I submit my cure to opportune remedies, I shall run the hazard of a sudden death.

Moreover, since, by my efforts, the Lord has liberated this city from an immoderate effusion of blood and from many other crimes and recalled it to concord and the holy laws, I have made enemies, both within the city and without, disgruntled men, not only citizens, but also foreigners, thirsting for human blood, who, to exalt their own horn,[3] have sought ardently to hand this city over to looting and slavery; and so, their expectation having

2. Pope Gregory IX, *Decretals,* bk. I, tit. 3 *De rescriptis,* cap. 5 *"Si quando aliqua."*
3. A common expression in the book of Psalms.

been frustrated, they are vehemently angry with me and hold enmity toward me for no reason; often, also, they plot my destruction, now with poison, now with the sword, so that without bodyguards I cannot safely set foot outside my door. And so, when I betook myself to the king of France [Charles VIII], although protected by a most faithful guard, these citizens, who desired the republic for themselves, did not allow me to cross the borders of their jurisdiction. And although I trust in the Lord, nonetheless, lest I seem to tempt God, I have decided that necessary precautions ought not to be despised; as it is written: "If you are persecuted in one city, flee to another" [Matt. 10:23].

Furthermore, this new reformation of the city, which God has effected, has had feeble roots up till now, and unless it be daily strengthened and perfected, as the worst people pant and slaver over it, it will easily fall into harm and overthrow. Since, therefore, by the judgment of prudent and honest men, my departure would be of the greatest harm to this people and of little use now there with you, I trust that Your Holiness will not take ill a postponement for a brief time, until this work I have undertaken is completed, for the sake of which I am truly certain that these impediments have befallen by divine command, so that I might not set out on a journey, for it is not the will of God that I absent myself from this place at present.

However, I hope that soon the time may come when I may be able, by reason of this pledge of Your Holiness, to come to Rome with a fuller explanation of this apostolate. Since Your Holiness perhaps wishes to be more informed now about the future matters concerning the destruction of Italy and the renovation of the Church, preached publicly by me, you can learn these things plainly from a little book [the *Compendium of Revelations*] which I have had printed in a certain quantity, and as soon as it has been completed, I shall hand a copy over to Your Holiness' ambassador to be sent to you, from which you shall receive most fully whatever it would be possible to hear from me. For it is not allowed to me to utter things other than those contained in it, for I have expounded only those things which have been taught before; however, those things which ought to be held in secret, it is not lawful to disclose to any mortal. However, I have managed to put the former things forth in writing, so that it might be established before the whole world, if these things fall out otherwise, that I have been a false prophet; if, to the contrary, they come to pass in accordance with my predictions, thanks are due to God our Savior, Who shows that He takes this trouble for the sake of our salvation, because if it is possible, He wants no one to perish eternally.

Finally, I ask Your Beatitude to receive my truest and sincerest excuses in such a way that you are persuaded that I desire nothing more than to obey you and to comply with your commands, and that you might not burden me beyond my powers. I, for my part, shall be a goad to myself, as soon as, once these ordained impediments have been removed, I shall be able to give satisfaction to Your Beatitude yourself, to whom I commend myself most humbly.

From the convent of St. Mark in Florence, the last day of July 1495.

Most devoted son and servant of Your Beatitude,

Brother Girolamo of Ferrara, of the Order of Preachers.

Letter from Pope Alexander VI to the Brothers of Santa Croce[4]

Rome, 8 September 1495

Beloved sons, greeting and apostolic blessing:

Since the inscrutable profundity of the divine plan has determined that we, as the successor of Peter, though unworthy, should be the head of the administration of the universal Church at this time, we intend, by the perpetual exercise of diligence, as much as it is given to us by [our] divine office, to see to these things by which religion, salvation, and peace are preserved, flourish, and are enlarged among the Christian people; indeed, let the novelty of dogmas, covered with a veil of false simplicity, by which schisms, heresies, and the subversion of morals frequently arise in the people and the clergy, be routed from the Church with the whip of correction, so that it might not be able to disturb the peaceful state of the Church in the present time, nor by such evil example become a power of doing wrong to others in the future. To be sure, we have heard that a certain Girolamo Savonarola from Ferrara, of the Order of Preachers, is delighted with the novelty of a perverse dogma and in this same insanity of mind is misled by the shift in affairs in Italy, so that without any canonical authority he attests among the people that he has been sent by God and speaks with God, against the canonical decrees. (It does not suffice for anyone barely to assert so much, that he himself has been sent by God, since any heretic can assert this, but he must add to that invisible commission by the working of a miracle, or by special testimony of Scripture.) Moreover, [he asserts] that Christ Jesus crucified and God lie if he lies (indeed, a horrifying and execrable kind of adjuration), that anyone not believing his vain assertions puts himself outside the state of salvation; finally, he does, says, and writes other things no less improper, which, if they are passed over unpunished, there is

4. Instead of replying to the offending party, the Pope fired off a directive to the Franciscan convent of Santa Croce, archcompetitors of San Marco, incorrectly addressing them as Dominicans. (Perhaps the Pope meant to address the Dominicans at Santa Maria Novella?) Since Savonarola was Prior of San Marco, if it had been correctly addressed, he would have been in the perplexing position of being put in charge of handling his own condemnation and correction. By misdirecting it, however, the Pope assured that it would become public. In this missive, the Pontiff expresses anything but satisfaction with the friar's activities and answers, and his remedy for this incipient rebellion is a reunification of San Marco with the Lombard Congregation, from which he had so recently separated it. Demoting Savonarola in this way would make him subject to removal to another convent, should his superiors so order, an easy circumvention of his refusal to come before the Holy See.

nothing that the boldness of false religious will not dare, and in the body of the Church, which ought to be reverenced, vices would enter under the guise of virtues.

We have thought by long delay and our long-suffering patience to bring it about that he might recognize that his own prophetic claim is foolish, turn aside to the way of solid truth, and deliberately and faithfully renounce his rashly and injuriously published words, which had been the cause of perturbation in the Church. We used to believe, some time ago, that the day had already come when we would have to think better of this person, and that the sorrow, which up to then we had suffered patiently from his unbridled arrogance and scandalous separation from his own fathers of Lombardy—which has been brought about, as we learned afterward, by the subtle cunning of certain perverse friars—we might, from his humble adherence, in the future change into joy. But, as we sorrowfully repeat, we have been deceived in our hope. For although through our letters we have admonished him by virtue of holy obedience to come to us so that we might understand the truth from him and from his own mouth, nevertheless, he has not only refused to come and to obey us, but even, on a day of great sorrow, furnished cause even more bitter to us, impudently putting forth things to be read by the eyes of the faithful, which he had previously spouted rashly to be imbibed in a single hearing. On account of these things, since we are detained by the grand and laborious work of bringing back a universal Italian peace, we have committed the examination, judgment, and punishment of this same case, according to the statutes of your Order, to Fra Sebastiano of Maggi from Brescia, Vicar General of the Lombard Congregation of the Order of Preachers, through our letters in the form of a brief. The aforesaid Girolamo Savonarola, being strictly ordered in virtue of holy obedience under pain of automatic excommunication, we command to acknowledge, with prompt and sincere obedience, the aforesaid Vicar as judge, deputed by us for the investigation of this case, and to betake himself, with ready submission, anywhere in this country at the commands of this man, setting aside any delay or appeal. Meanwhile, indeed until this case is discussed in the presence of the aforesaid Vicar, we decree through the present letters that the aforesaid Girolamo shall be suspended from any office of declaiming among the people and of reading publicly.

Furthermore, so that opportunity may not be given by the evil example of this same Girolamo, so taken with his own outspokenness, to any other among your brothers to err and to play the fool, this very place of the Order of Preachers of San Marco in Florence and of San Domenico at Fiesole, we reunite, incorporate, and annex from now on to the aforesaid Congregation of Lombardy, commanding all the brothers of the aforesaid places of San Marco and San Domenico under pain of automatic excommunication to submit to and obey the Vicar of the aforesaid Lombard Congregation as their own legitimate pastor, and we recall from now on and decree to be revoked whatsoever of authority, of command, or of any other power that may have been granted even by apostolic authority. We enjoin also, under pain of automatic excommunication, Fra Domenico da Pescia and Fra Tommaso Busini and Fra Silvestro of Florence to proceed to Bologna within the space of nine days from the present notice, of which we assign three days for the first term, three for the second, and three for the third, in order to be relocated by the authority of the aforesaid Vicar of Lombardy at one of the convents of the Congregation anywhere except in the dominion of the Florentines. Whosoever opposing notwithstanding.

Dated at Saint Peter's, Rome, under the seal of the Fisherman, the eighth day of September 1495, in the fourth year of our pontificate.

B. Floridus

[On the outside:] To the beloved Brothers of the Priory and Conventual Monastery of the Holy Cross, of the Order of Preachers [*sic*],[5] in the city of Florence.

5. See previous note.

Letter from Savonarola to Pope Alexander VI

Florence, 29 (?) September 1495

Most Blessed Father, after kissing your blessed feet:

The letters of Your Holiness in the form of a brief were made public yesterday in our convent, by which Your Holiness announced that you have reunited this convent and the convent of San Domenico at Fiesole with the Lombard Congregation, and ordered that Fra Domenico da Pescia and Fra Tommaso Busini of Florence and Fra Silvestro of Florence are to proceed to Bologna—and for this reason this is to be done, because I myself, Girolamo, had said and written and preached publicly to the people many foolish things against the sacred canons and [moreover] things which could easily create scandal in the Church of God—and committed my case to the prosecution and punishment of the Vicar General of the said Lombard Congregation through other letters of yours. Which letters we received with a good spirit and that reverence which is fitting, insofar as they show Your Holiness concerned about the condition of the Holy Church and about the health of our souls. But we grieved and we shall grieve exceedingly, because the malice of men has advanced even to this degree that there are those who have not been terrified to suggest things so false and so perversely interpreted even to the highest Pontiff and Vicar of Christ on earth. And since it is well known from the series of foregoing letters that the outcome of this whole affair has sprung, on account of my asserted fault, from me, Your Holiness will kindly bear with me, if I, the one, as it were, by whose agency this tempest is said to have arisen, should go on with a superabundance of words to you who are occupied with the greatest matters, through which my simple innocence, truth of action, and sincerity, the good effects which have followed and which it is hoped will follow, may be defended from false interpretations, assertions, and suggestions. Nor will this be difficult, since "I have spoken publicly to the world and have always taught in the church and in the temple, where all Christians assemble, and I have said nothing in secret"[6] [Ioh. 18:20]. Here I have so many thousands of witnesses of my simplicity and approved doctrine that I have no doubt that I shall defend my cause before Your Holiness with no difficulty whatsoever, for as the Philosopher says: "The true agrees with the true, but everything disagrees with the false."[7]

And, so, they have suggested in the first place to Your Holiness, as is

---

6. Savonarola uses the words of Christ as his own, substituting *ecclesia* for *synagoga* and *christiani* for *Iudaei*.
7. Aristotle, *Nicomachean Ethics* I(A).viii.1 (1098b, ll. 10–11).

evident in this letter: "that I have delighted in the novelties of perverse dogma, etc.," which is obviously false. For it is publicly known that I follow no depraved dogma, nor preach anything but the Holy Scriptures and the holy Doctors; also, in public preaching, I have often said and have left a written record that I submit myself and everything of mine to the correction of the Holy Roman Church. And this same thing, if I am not mistaken, I have said in certain letters of mine to Your Holiness, concerning which you even make mention in a certain brief Your Holiness sent to me. However, if anyone should say that to preach future events is new dogma, it is false, because this has always been present in the Church of the Lord God, as is clear from a run through the Scriptures and church histories. For there is no harm to the Christian religion in preaching things to come, as long as they are not against the faith or good morals or natural reason, nor was this ever prohibited by any law, nor can it be prohibited. For this would be to impose a law on God, Who says in Amos, chapter three: "The Lord God shall not perform His word, unless He shall have revealed His secret to His own servants, the prophets" [Amos 3:7].

Secondly, seeing that it is said in the aforesaid letter: "and in this same insanity of mind is misled by the shift of affairs in Italy, etc.": this also is manifestly false, and it is known by all that five years have passed during which I have preached these things, or rather, even more than ten already. Therefore, I am not misled to do this on account of the shift in Italian affairs.

Thirdly, it is said: "and that he is sent by God, etc.": this also all who have heard me know to be false, because I never said this. Rather, in my writings, which can be read by all, I have written that I was sent by my superiors in the same way as almost all other preachers, but I have never said that I have been sent by God alone, as many thousands of people can attest.

Fourthly, it is said: "and that he speaks with God, etc.": this also I have never expressly said, nor do I ever use such a manner of speaking, as the whole Florentine populace can attest. But even if I had said this, I ought not to incur any punishment on account of it, for it is not to be found in any place in Scripture nor in the whole body of canon law, or civil, nor in any authentic book, that anyone who says that he speaks with God may be punished. Besides, it would be foolish and impious to make such a law, since no one can impose a law on God, for He Himself can speak with whomever He wishes, and give orders to them, so that they might say: "The Lord says these things, etc.," as the prophets used to do.

Likewise they have suggested that I have said: "Jesus Christ crucified and God lie, if I lie," when I have absolutely not said this, as though I want to equate myself with God, but if by chance anyone should say some great thing, such as, for example: "There shall be signs in the sun and moon and stars" [Luc. 21:25], he may then add: "If I lie, Christ also lies." Is this "an execrable kind of adjuration"? Thus, sometimes when I have said any truth which Christ has spoken, I have subjoined: "If I lie, Christ also, etc."

Moreover, it follows in the brief: "that anyone not believing his vain assertions puts himself outside the state of salvation, etc."; this also I have never said, but truly I have said only this: that since I know that many things which I have said are from God, whoever, with an obstinate spirit, does not want to believe them, but resolves utterly to contradict them, this is a sign that he is outside the state of grace, since, as I have said, grace, the light of faith, always inclines to truth. Therefore, anyone who is in grace cannot be against the truth, which is established by God. Indeed, those who do not believe our assertions, but do not, even so, contradict them with an obstinate spirit, I have said often and publicly written that they could be in a state of grace and be saved. Therefore, I have not said that those who contradict me were sinners, but that, in the manner aforesaid, the contradiction of the former sort of persons [those of obstinate spirit] was a sign of the absence of God's grace in them.

Moreover, it is said in the same place: "that he does, says, and writes other things no less improper, which if they are passed over unpunished, etc." This entire populace is witness that I neither say nor do improper or scandalous things, but things which are of great virtue and necessity in their many fruits and of healthfulness for souls and tending both toward peace in the city of Florence and toward reformation. And when it is written: "Every word shall stand in the mouth of two or three witnesses" [Deut. 19:15; Matt. 18:16], I might adduce in public not only two or three, but two or three or even ten thousand witnesses, with whom also these same works, done not by me but by God through me, shall cry out and give proof that I have never said such things or even anything like those which base persons have devised against me.

Furthermore, in this same brief it goes on: "We have thought by long delay and by our long-suffering patience to bring it about that [he might recognize] that his own prophetic claim is foolish, etc." I testify that no one could be found in the world, who has ever heard so arrogant a word from my mouth, namely, that I have said that I am a prophet. Indeed, on the contrary, many, yes, thousands, could justly testify that I have often said that I am not a prophet nor the son of a prophet. Which, even if I had said it, I do not see why I ought to be punished. For no law condemns any person who says that he predicts things to come by the divine spirit, unless under this veil he solicits the people to evil or disseminates heresy or does any other evil, as it is written in Deuteronomy 13, which, concerning me, no one can say, as is very well known. Otherwise, no prophet might be able to rise up in the Church, and so this gift of prophecy might be banished from the

Church, which would be contrary to Amos 3, cited above: "The Lord God shall not perform His word, etc." [Amos 3:7], and Proverbs 29: "Since prophecy has departed, the people are scattered" [Prov. 29:18]. But if it should be said that in Deuteronomy 18 it has been said that "The prophet who, depraved with arrogance, has wanted to speak in My name things which I had not taught him to say, or in the name of other gods, shall be destroyed, etc."[8] [Deut. 18:20], I respond that the sign of a true prophet comes somewhat after the fact, since, if what has been said should come to pass, the prophet was true, but if not, false. It is not to be understood thus either: namely that unless what he has predicted comes about immediately, he should be destroyed; otherwise, Isaias and Jeremias and many other prophets and Christ the Lord Himself would have been put to death, since they lived many years before those things came about which had been predicted by them; on the contrary, they actually predicted many things which did not come to pass in their lifetime. And therefore, it ought to be understood that if anyone says that he predicts things to come from the Spirit of God, and he predicts things which are not against the faith nor against the canonical Scriptures, nor against the doctrine of the Catholic Church, their outcome ought to be patiently awaited, nor ought such a one to be scorned, especially when a good life has been his companion, because God has many hidden servants. Thus the Apostle says: "Do not scorn prophecies" [I Thes. 5:20]. If, however, at the time fixed beforehand by the prophet, those things which he predicted have not come about, then he ought to be severely denounced, and thus this same law may be understood. Since, therefore, many things which I have predicted have already come about, to which very many are witnesses, so I ought not yet to be denounced nor punished, because I have foretold those future events. If, however, other things do not come to pass in their own time, I ought deservedly to be denounced; however, I am certain that they shall come to pass, nor shall a single long mark [apex] pass away from them [Matt. 5:18].

Furthermore, it follows: "and his words, which had been the cause of perturbation in the Church, etc." Assuredly, Most Blessed Father, it is very well known not only in Florence, but also in divers parts of Italy, that in the city of Florence peace has followed upon my words, which, if it had not followed, all Italy would have been perturbed, because the city of Florence, agitated by sedition and massacres, as much intestine as external, would have collapsed. Truly, the king of France with his entire army would then have set alight a conflagration big enough to consume the whole of Italy. But if credence had been given to my words, Italy today would not be shaken in this way, for, foreseeing her afflictions, although I was derided by many, I

---

8. *Aliorum* ("other") is substituted for *alienorum* ("foreign").

announced the sword to come and gave a ready remedy for peace, saying that it was penance alone. Whence the whole of Italy ought to give thanks to God on my account. For I have taught this remedy of tranquility, observing which, in fact, Florence already has what she had not, and if all Italy were similarly doing this, the sword would by no means pass through her. Truly, what can be harmed by penance? And so, indeed, no one can testify that I have sown any scandal in the Church; moreover, I have innumerable witnesses that I have sown good seed. Yet "the enemy has sown it over with weeds" [Matt. 13:25], and "he has fallen into the pit which he made" [Ps. 7: 16].

Next, it is subjoined: that "by the subtle cunning of certain perverse friars," the separation of our convent from the Lombard fathers was effected. First, that those of whom absolutely no infamy is known, who on the contrary are of the very best reputation among this whole people, should be called perverse friars could not have been suggested to Your Holiness except by wicked men. Let Your Holiness send anyone from among your most trustworthy [advisers], who might interrogate the citizens and populace concerning the reputation of the brothers of San Marco and San Domenico at Fiesole, and he shall prove and come to know very clearly how obvious was this lie of theirs. Secondly, it is false that this separation was obtained only by a certain few and not by all, as is clear in the public record. Thirdly, it was obtained so that we might live not more laxly and in license, but more strictly, as the outcome itself demonstrates. Furthermore, it was not obtained slyly, since this case was discussed for a long time and maturely examined, as our most reverend Protector, the Cardinal of Naples, is a witness, who obtained this separation by his own prudence. For according to the tenor[9] of our constitutions, this province is distinct from the province of Lombardy, and one ought not to take precedence of the other. Moreover, when the number of brothers in this province had been diminished on account of some sort of plague, the convent of San Marco was, through letters of this same most reverend Master General, united or entrusted to the Lombard Congregation. Then a certain prior, without summoning the other brothers, obtained a brief, so that the aforesaid convents of San Marco and San Domenico at Fiesole and San Domenico at San Gimignano might be united to the aforesaid Congregation by apostolic authority also; no one can doubt that this brief, because it was surreptitious, had no force. And, therefore, when the brothers had increased in number, if, by the authority of Your Holiness, they have been returned to their natural situation, it cannot be said that this was fraudulently done, but rather according to the tenor of our constitutions.

Furthermore, it follows in the same place: "for although . . ." and further

9. A legal term meaning "the exact wording."

down: "nevertheless he has not only refused to come and to obey us, etc.";
this also is false. For, although Your Holiness may have ordered me to come
to you, nevertheless, I sent letters to you, adducing the reasonable causes for
which I could not then come to you, in accordance with that capitulum, *"Si
quando extra," De rescriptis.*[10] The first was that I was infirm and invalid, and
that I would have exposed myself to danger of death. Second, that I have
mortal enemies of such a kind that, by the judgment of all citizens who
know this, I could not have reached Rome, and this is, as it were, public
knowledge in the city, for which reason I cannot leave home without a
diligent and faithful guard. The third reason was on account of danger to
the city, whose government still was weak and only by our admonitions thus
far sustained and carried out. In the final line of the letter I asked Your
Holiness to excuse me this time, so that I can come another time with greater
satisfaction. However, I marvel that Your Holiness has not [received] my
letters, a copy of which we have, for this reason, adjoined to letters of our
convent sent to Your Holiness yesterday, so that you yourself might see how
falsely they have spoken who have said that I refused obedience. Furthermore, since Your Holiness is occupied in most important affairs, you cannot
take notice concerning those things which in your absence may have been
pushed aside by [other] minutiae; perverse men, understanding this, have
suggested to you to commit this case of mine to be decided, judged, and
punished by the Vicar General of the Order of Preachers of the reformed
convents of Lombardy, a judge who is exceedingly suspect to us for just
cause. For it is notorious that between the Congregation of Lombardy and
ours, on account of the aforesaid separation, the greatest controversy has
arisen, and that that Vicar, along with his brothers, fails not to attack us
daily. And so to constitute the enemy of someone his judge, Your Holiness
knows how much this is against all laws both divine and human.

Moreover, when anyone has mortal enemies, all laws concede to him
that he may not be bound personally to contest with them, when danger to
his life is imminent, because here fear disheartens even the steadfast man.
"For who would venture, or for what reason might someone be bound, to
submit to the judgment of such a consistory, which would result in placing
himself in the bosom of his enemies and offering himself voluntarily to death
through violent injury, not through justice being carried out?"[11] as it is written [also] in Clement's *De re iudicata,* the reason given in the text below:
"Seeing that these things are indeed justly feared, they are avoided by custom: reason flees this, nature abhors it."[12] This also is adjoined: "One who

10. Pope Gregory IX, *Decretals,* bk. I, tit. 3 *De rescriptis,* cap. 5 *"Si quando aliqua."*
11. Ibid.
12. Pope Clement VI, *Constitutions,* bk. II, tit. 11 *De sententia de re iudicata,* cap. 2.

is mindful of a citation of this sort would therefore be out of his mind to abridge the thing cited";[13] by which law, together with many others, not only in the Clementine *dicta* but in the previously cited capitulum *"Si quando,"* in the opinion of many doctors [of canon law] and especially the distinguished pupil of Your Holiness, Lord Felinus [Sandei of Ferrara], we are protected, and our noncompliance with Your Holiness is unpunishable, since we have assigned very many just reasons [for it]. For I have mortal enemies, as I have written to Your Holiness, so many and of such a sort that I cannot depart from here, nor without the greatest caution leave home, on account of multiple ambushes.

How then can it be said in the aforesaid brief that I ought to submit to this Vicar of Lombardy wherever in the country he might call for me, especially when there are many places in Italy to which I could not in any way transport myself without danger to my life? Whence therefore come these things, if not that perverse men have craftily suggested these things which are false to Your Holiness, and our letters to you have not been responded to at all? Indeed, I have such enemies because of the truth I have preached, for truth gives birth to hatred.

[For a great many wicked citizens, who had driven out one faction not so much on account of zeal for the republic as for the sake of fulfilling their own ambition, aiming at the highest position, used to stir up other new and numerous factions and feuds here, and as it is said of the hydra, one head having been cut off, more were regenerated. From which it followed that when the city went over to a new government and the license of the people was in a tumult, discords, brawls, retaliations, seditions, murders, and destruction of the whole city were imminent, greatly assisted by the most powerful king [Charles VIII of France], in whose company fomenters of hatred were not lacking, inciting him to the overthrow of this country. Thus this city, on the verge of collapse, agitated as much by internal as by external hatreds, would easily have provided a spark to ignite the whole of Italy, if God had not intervened. I, with a view to near-present danger, averted the anger and sword of the king as much as I could and exhorted him to clemency, piety and religion, admonishing him to restrain his men from plundering and atrocities, not only here but everywhere, and to have the fear of God always before his eyes. Then this city, unharmed, by the gift of God, was rescued from the midst of the fire, and into it, concord of the citizens, public peace, and fear of God have been introduced. What else could I have done for the advantage and peace of the people and especially for the divine honor, slaving by day and by night for all the people, or what more necessary

13. There is a pun at work here: *saperet* (from *sapere,* "to be wise") vs. *desiperet* (from *de-sapere,* "to be foolish").

thing ought I to have done at that time? Finally, for [all] my labors, I win this reward from the ingrates, which still causes me no regret, since our reward shall be abundant in heaven. "For lying and vain are the sons of men and vain is the hope of them". [Ps. 61:10][14] And although I do not fear them, since I know that it is written: "You will be hated by all men on account of My name" [Matt. 10:22], nevertheless, I do not want to tempt God, since it is also written: "If you are persecuted in one city, flee to another" [Matt. 10:23]. And the Lord Jesus frequently gave this example to us, and the Apostle Paul often made use of human defenses.

Moreover, the divine law and all the canons and doctors maintain that any religious can transfer from a laxer rule to a stricter, and he ought to do this even more within the same order, since he is bound to do what he promises to God: "to strive for perfection," as St. Thomas says.[15] However, he cannot, on the contrary, transfer from a stricter to a laxer,[16] unless perchance he were not able to live in the stricter on account of infirmity. If, therefore, Your Holiness knew that the brothers of our congregation live more strictly than the brothers of Lombardy, assuredly, since you desire that religious strive for perfection, you would not have ordered us to be reunited to the Congregation of Lombardy, for we cannot be reunited to them unless we are conformed to them. That, moreover, we live more strictly than the brothers of Lombardy, we, who know the inner workings of both congregations, are certain, and this is also extrinsically apparent from many signs; for it is written: "By their fruits you will know them" [Matt. 7:16]. First, we do not hold possessions [i.e., estates, landholdings] even in common, nor do we want to hold them; they, however, do not observe this. Also in food and vesture we are more sparing, as can be discerned by the eyes; also, we are more frequent in periods of silence and prayer, as those who have been among us testify. The whole city is also a witness that there is a great difference in the way of life of our brothers in these times, and in their lives when they were united to the Lombard Congregation. For all acknowledge with a single voice that our brothers have gone over to a stricter life, nor could they be easily deceived in this, especially for so long a time, since we always are and live before their eyes. This also is a sign, that although the Lombard Congregation has obtained a papal excommunication against its

14. The questionable authenticity of this bracketed passage is discussed by the editor of the critical edition of the letters, Roberto Ridolfi, *Le lettere di Girolamo Savonarola* (Florence: Olschki, 1933); and in revised form in *Lettere e scritti apologetici*, ed. Roberto Ridolfi, Vincenzo Romano, and Armando Verdi, Edizione Nazionale delle Opere di Girolamo Savonarola (Rome: Belardetti, 1984).
15. Thomas Aquinas, *Summa theologica,* part 2.2, quest. 186, arts. 2, 3, 5.
16. Ibid., quest. 184, art. 7.

own brothers who withdraw from it without a license, our Congregation, however, is free; thus, anyone who wants to withdraw can. Nevertheless, the Lombard Congregation is scarcely able to retain its own good brothers from transferring over to us, and already some praiseworthy men have come from them to us. From among us, indeed, who are free, no one worthy of approval has transferred over to them up to the present, nor wants to transfer. So it is obvious from this that, hearing the tenor of this brief, all have been greatly disturbed, and determined to defend themselves in the presence of Your Holiness, all saying unanimously that they want to observe what they have promised to God, nor do they want to relax their life on any grounds, but, confiding in God, to bind themselves more tightly. Moreover, we know that it is not the intention of Your Holiness to give command to pastors who detest the sheep, for they do not tend the sheep, but ravage and kill them. Therefore, let it be known to Your Holiness that on account of the vexations which the brothers of Lombardy, who often used to perturb our peace, have imposed upon our brothers, this reunion cannot be without effects seriously distressing and hateful to the brothers, from which might follow perturbations of the sheep and scandals, rather than advantage to souls. Which is also clear from this, that when in past times they were united to the brothers of Lombardy, they never had true peace with them, since they did not conform in customs; whence also our constitutions have divided these two provinces from each other. Moreover, if Your Holiness reunites our convents to the Lombard convents, there will be injury to the most reverend Master General of the Order, to whom these convents of ours are subordinate by full right, while the convents of Lombardy are not; thus, the Master General would be punished without fault [on his part]. Moreover, when Your Holiness says in your letters that these convents and brothers must reunite themselves to the Lombard Congregation lest they, charmed by their own freedom, follow my errors, and orders three of our brothers to go to Bologna by the end of nine days, and when it is already known that I have not erred in any of those things which are thrown up at me by my adversaries, we can confidently say that these things are not your intention, because "where the cause is lacking, the effect ought to be lacking."[17]

Since, therefore, Most Blessed Father, it is established that all those things which have been suggested to Your Holiness are false and are and have been falsely invented by perverse persons who seek my life, who with their cunning desire to draw me out of this city, not so that I might come to the feet of Your Holiness, in whose presence they know I would easily defend all our affairs, but so that they, aspiring to tyranny by their own ambition or for other reasons, might kill me on the way, Your Holiness will

17. Aristotle, *Physics* III(ß), 195b, 16–18.

not disdain dutifully to admit our defenses and, as I believe, call us prudent rather than disobedient, while in the meantime, we shall desist, so that we might come to know our Father and Lord's kind response and absolution free from such weighty accusations. For we were taught this doctrine by your predecessors and holy doctors, namely theologians and experts in canon law, whence, among many other things which could be mentioned, it is especially clear, as Your Holiness knows, in the previously cited *"Si quando extra," De rescriptis,* and through glosses and doctors writing about this same capitulum, and most especially through the Lord Felinus of Ferrara, the well-deserving student of Your Holiness yourself, to whom, if these things were not known, we would write them at the bottom of these present letters. Moreover, that all those things which we have written above are true, when it might be fitting, it will not be difficult to prove. Let Your Holiness send a man from among your most trustworthy, just, and above suspicion, and it will be clearly certified by almost the entire populace. And I am prepared in all things to correct myself, wherever I err, privately and publicly in the presence of the whole populace, and to revoke all my errors, if any have been found in me. Let Your Holiness deign to signify to me what from all the things which I have said or written ought to be renounced by me, and I shall very willingly do it. For both now and always, as I have often said and written, I submit myself and all my sayings and writings to the correction of the Holy Roman Church and of Your Holiness. To whom I, prostrate at your feet, commend myself and my brothers.

Son and servant of Your Holiness.

Letter from Pope Alexander VI to Savonarola

Rome, 16 October 1495

Beloved son, greeting and apostolic blessing:

Granted that we have explained more fully through our other writings in the form of a brief how much these disturbances, especially that of the Florentine populace, have displeased us, and all the more in that they have had their origin in your preachings, because, laying aside the extirpation of vices and the praises of virtues,[18] you have ventured to preach future events in public sermons and to affirm that you knew those things by the Light of eternity and the inspiration of the Holy Spirit; by means of these and similar things, simple people can often deviate from the way of salvation and obedience to the Holy Roman Church. You ought rather to have attended in your preachings to union and peace than to preach such things as the vulgar call your prophecies and divinations; you ought also to have considered that the conditions of the times are vehemently opposed to the sort of doctrine which you put forward in public, a doctrine which would be sufficient to create discord even where there is the greatest peace—how much more so where such feuds and factions flourish! And so, the peril to many souls and our desire for peace for that people [the Florentines]—and so that we might satisfy our pastoral duties—have induced us to write to you. Nor, to be sure, without mature counsel would we have decided to call you to us, so that you might purge yourself from the charges against you, which, really, if they were true, ought not to pass unpunished. However, when we learned recently from some of our brothers, cardinals of the Holy Roman Church, and through your letters and messages, that you were prepared on your own account in all your words and deeds to submit yourself to the correction of the Holy Roman Church (which is the duty of every good Christian and religious), we rejoiced exceedingly, and we began to persuade ourselves that these things had been preached not in an evil spirit but rather with a certain simplicity and zeal for being of service in the vineyard of the Lord, although, indeed, experience might teach the contrary. Indeed, lest we seem to neglect entirely such things which ought not to be neglected in any way, we decided to write to you again. And responding to your letters, we command you, by virtue of holy obedience, to abstain entirely from any preaching, whether public or private, so that in ceasing from public sermons, you might not be charged with resorting to conventicles. Fully maintain the manner we desire until you are able safely, properly, and with that seemliness which becomes a religious—not, as we understand, accompanied by troops—to convey

18. The proper themes for a sermon.

yourself into our presence (for we shall see you with a cheerful and paternal spirit), or until we either decide in good time what manner you ought to adhere to in future, or, if it pleases us, to appoint some suitable and upright man.[19] Because if you do as we hope, from that point we suspend the briefs and what is contained in them, which we have written to you, and whatever clauses are contained in them, so that you may be able to clear your conscience peacefully.

Dated at Rome at St. Peter's, under the seal of the Fisherman, on the sixteenth day of October 1495, in the fourth year of our pontificate.

B. Floridus

[On the outside:] To our beloved son, Girolamo Savonarola of Ferrara, of the Order of Preachers

19. In place of the previously appointed Fra Sebastiano.

Open *Letter to a Friend*

Florence, end of 1495

Dearly beloved in Jesus Christ:

I am quite surprised that you, on account of the contradictions of perverse men and calumnies made against me, have somewhat weakened in the
way of truth, as if you did not know that it is nothing new that the truth
of the Gospel has always elicited great contradiction because, this being the
only way leading to salvation, the adversary of Christ, Satan, although he is
the enemy of *every* truth, incites all the world against *this* Gospel [in partic-
ular] because he, spurred on by his envy, does not want man to acquire that
glory of which he has been deprived through his pride. However, he does
not persecute the truth of philosophy or any other truth, because, without
faith, they are of little use. Go through the histories of the Old and New
Testaments, and you will find that in times past there were much greater
contradictions against the truth which leads to salvation and against its
preachers than at present. And although every man who has heard me is or
may be certain that the calumnies made against me are manifestly false—and
I have shown this in part in my writings—nonetheless, since you are away
and hear many evils said every day without any defense of the truth, I am
impelled by the charity which I bear you to defend the truth in this letter
and to demonstrate to you how frivolous are the calumnies of our adversaries.

To begin with, some say that I am a heretic. They speak with little
prudence and consideration, since I have publicly stated and written many
times that I submit myself to the correction of the Holy Roman Church on
all points where I may have erred, and I have asked the Supreme Pontiff
and the whole Roman court to write to me or advise me in what part I err
against the faith, offering to retract [it] publicly in the presence of all the
people. Nonetheless, after narrowly investigating both my sayings and writings, they have found nothing contrary to Sacred Scripture or the doctrines
of the Holy Roman Church. Therefore, you must surmise that those who
accuse me as a heretic are either perverse or ignorant; understand that many
of those who slander me would not know how to tell you what heresy is if
you asked them because they do not even know if they are alive or dead,
and since you say that many good and learned religious go about openly
accusing me of heresy, saying that they do so out of zeal for truth, I answer
you that if you were to believe that all those who wear a religious habit are
religious, you would be greatly mistaken. Do you not know that it is written:
"They will come to you in sheep's clothing, but underneath they will be
ravening wolves" [Matt. 7:15]? If you knew how great a multitude of these

are to be found today, you would be astonished. I would not want you to trail along behind the opinion of the ignorant crowd, which believes that as soon as a man puts on a mean religious habit, he becomes holy and learned, and they adore him as a saint and listen to his words as the words of a wise and learned man. All the arts are learned over a long time; the art of living uprightly and the study and knowledge of sacred theology, which are the most difficult of all and to the perfection of which few attain, the foolish crowd believes are learned in a day or by a change of dress. Believe me that the doctrine of the Scriptures and holiness of life require continual exertion over a long time; to acquire these two in an instant is an apostolic privilege which is granted to very few men. Do not believe, then, that every man who calls himself religious is good or learned; rather, believe this, not as coming from me, but from St. Augustine: that just as better men cannot be found in the world than those who have progressed in the monastery, likewise, worse men cannot be found than those who have failed in monasteries. The priests, the scribes, and the Pharisees, not the people, contradicted Christ. Pride and envy, much more than every other vice, oppose the truth. You find in the father of lies, Satan, who is the adversary of truth, no other sin than that of pride and of envy. Exterior works, mean clothing, and the ornament of ceremony do not make a man religious, but rather humility and charity do, which such men show themselves not to have, because slandering one's neighbor so irreligiously and without any basis in fact and laying on him such grave calumny cannot be without the guilt of mortal sin, as one with even a modicum of instruction in questions of conscience easily understands, and it is so much the more serious the more great malice is adjoined to it, since everyone knows, or easily could know if he has no desire to malign me, what I have publicly said and written.

You also say that I am defamed as being schismatic and disobedient to Holy Church. To these [charges] I would have you reply that, if this is true, it will certainly not go unpunished; however, His Holiness, having heard my reasons, has, like a wise man, been left thoroughly satisfied, and although many malignant men of different ranks and conditions have tried to turn him away from the truth, his prudence has been such that he has not been moved to any unjust act by the power of these detractors' tongues. These, lacking any argument, have finally tried to persuade him that I have spoken ill of him in particular and of some of his most reverend cardinals; this also was of no avail to them because, as the proverb says, lies have short legs, especially when they go contrary to a truth evident to many thousands of people, as mine is, because I do not preach in corners or organize conventicles in houses, as do our lukewarm friends; rather, I preach in churches, where all the people can convene [Ioh. 18:20].

You also say that this prediction of future events which I do is much contradicted and that many make mock of it, but you should not be surprised at such a thing, because, if you go through the Old and New Testaments, you will find that this very thing happened to past prophets. But it is well to be amazed at those who make mock of it, since the Apostle Paul commanded us not to despise prophecies when he said: *Prophetias nolite spernere, omnia probate, quod bonum est tenete*[20] [I Thes. 5:20–21]. That is, "do not despise prophecies, test everything, and hold on to what is good." It is not becoming to a wise man to burst suddenly into disapprobation or derision of what he has no reason to reprove, such as future contingencies, because if he, reproving, were asked the reason for his reproof and derision, he would either have to be silent or reply without any reason as madmen do. Therefore, wise men, if they do not believe, still do not disapprove; rather, they bide their time, committing everything to God, especially since they know that God has sent prophets in every age to fulfill the needs of His Church, as St. Thomas declares in his *Secunda secundae*.[21] But tell me: what does it mean that many years ago, and also in the present time, many have prophesied and are prophesying, both men and women, and many preachers have publicly preached visions and predicted events which have been altogether contrary to what has happened, and yet they have not suffered, nor do they suffer, any contradiction such as I have suffered and do suffer, especially since I have never yet told one lie, and the things I have predicted are continually seen to be proved true? Truly, truly, the devil would not excite such contradiction against this truth which I preach if it were not so opposed to his kingdom. Clearly, one can see that this persecution comes from him, because no one can be seen to work in this but his members, that is, wicked men who have no other part of a Christian than the name.

You also say that many, even including citizens of Florence, calumniate me, saying that I have ruined the city and that this government introduced by me is a government of madmen. You would better understand how ridiculous this calumny is if you had certain information about past governments of this city, and about the condition of its citizens, and about the nature of its people, and you would clearly understand that those who speak ill of this government are either ambitious men, or disreputable, or utterly lacking in judgment; but all those who have judgment and are dispassionate understand that no government better for this people or more salutary for the city of Florence could possibly be found. This is the judgment of all the people, excepting only a few who are nicknamed "the rabid"[22] by the people because they do nothing all day long but bark and say such absurd things

20. "Do not scorn prophecies; test everything; retain what is good."
21. *Summa*, part 2.2, quest. 174, art. 6.
22. *Arrabbiati*.

that even the children laugh at their foolishness. But I, in order to satisfy every man, have publicly said many times that those who are not happy with this state should find a better one, proffering my services, with God's help, to set it up and establish it, and yet, no one has known how to find one. Rather, on the many occasions when I have debated privately about this matter with certain ingenious people, they themselves conclude in the end that a better government than this could not be given to the city of Florence, and those who are so critical, because they are constrained by the reason of good citizens, do not know what to say or what they themselves want; it is clear that their intention would be either to be tyrants or servants of tyrants. But because some say that this government is rooted in the lowly masses, I want you to know that this is false, because this is a single government, completely civil and political, and the major part consists of noble persons, and this would be even more the case if well-to-do citizens would show themselves to be lovers of the common welfare. And if on some occasion a member of the nobility has been demoted, it was not done to inflict an injury on him or for any revenge, but only out of a suspicion which the people had either that he did not tend in the direction of the common good or that he wanted to make himself a tyrant. And if the elders of the city had been united in love for this government, it would already be so honed and trim that few things would be needed and the city would be happy. But because many consider it odious, they have exerted all their ingenuity and power to ruin it and have hampered many good works and have allowed into the Grand Council many low and foolish persons of little judgment, along with some others who would not be fit to live on earth, for the sole purpose of ruining every good thing. And although God has permitted them to do this, He will not allow this government to run completely into ruin, but He will in the end make their machinations rebound on their own heads, as the prophet says: *Incidit in foveam quam fecit*[23] [Ps. 7:16]. That is, "the sinner has fallen into the ditch he has dug to trap his companion."

Surely, if God had not provided such a government for this city, considering present conditions, so great would the discord of its citizens have been that the city would have been ruined not only by them, but also by others, and she would have lost her true liberty and become a den of thieves. However, after the departure of Piero de' Medici, there converged on the city citizens of different factions who had committed many grievous injuries against one another from 1433 to 1494; each of these aimed to avenge himself and to make himself great within the city, it seeming a just cause to them that they should have satisfaction for the injuries and the damages done to them in the past, and since they had been suppressed for such a long time,

23. "He has fallen into the pit he made."

it seemed to them that they should at present be exalted. On account of this, many new factions began to proliferate in the city, and if some precautions had not been taken for this by the present government through a universal peace, these discords would necessarily have generated much bloodshed, banishment, and destruction of the citizens. So all those who complain about this government are very ungrateful to God and His instrument, through which He has operated: first, those citizens who were intimate friends of the past state, because, if they consider carefully, [they will see that] from the present government they have possessions and honor and life; second, those who were banished, because they have been readmitted into their own *patria* with honor, for although while they were away in exile, they might have been able to be repatriated by means of a pardon and live by their occupations, [it would have been] without honor or favors from the city; third, the citizens who remained in the city, though humiliated and without dignity, because now they are free from such oppression and can live in peace with honor and the favors of the city, if they choose to comport themselves well; fourth, the citizens who have striven for this liberty, who were extricated by God from the great danger they were in on the day of the city's changeover, because, if they will consider it correctly, they were not able, especially in such an extraordinary case, to scotch their adversary by either their own ingenuity or their own might, but God alone, on account of the penance and prayers of good men and women, drove him out of the city so that there would be no bloodshed, but on the other hand, if it were not for this government, these foes would have destroyed each other because of the discord among them; fifth, and most of all, those citizens who aspired to govern this city but have neither brains nor goodness, because, if it were not for this government, they would have made such fools of themselves that the people would have been impelled to hand them over as sport for the children. Thus, all these citizens must render thanks to God, Who has provided for them with a favor beyond their understanding. But there is no doubt that anyone who speaks ill of this government or attempts to ruin it deserves to be severely punished by God and by men. Truly, if you were in this city and knew those who speak ill of this government, you would conclude, without any other examination of witnesses, that their lives should be forfeit, and that it would be more honorable for anyone to be censured by them than praised. And when they say that I have usurped this state like a tyrant, you can imagine how great is their foolishness, for it is not possible for these two things, namely, a tyrant and the Grand Council, to coexist. Understanding this to be the case, those who are more astute seek to undermine the Council in order to make themselves tyrants, knowing that this Council is the opposite and destroyer of tyranny.

If the city of Florence goes from bad to worse, this does not proceed from the failure of truth in the promises that were made, but from a lack of faith and justice. In all the arts and sciences the first thing that matters is belief, as the philosopher states: *Oportet eum qui addiscit credere,*[24] and anyone who does not believe never learns. If this is true in the human arts and sciences, how much more is it so in the art of living uprightly and in divine science, which revolves around supernatural matters, and so, one who goes to read or learn Sacred Scripture and does not believe firmly that it was effected by God often stumbles because he finds in it many things which seem contradictory and many which seem without reason or childish, which were deliberately set down and written in this way by the Holy Spirit so as to hide them from the unworthy, and when he finds them, he falls into some error and into deriding the Scripture. But if one believes that it comes from God, when he finds such passages he says, "Since this has been said by God, it cannot be false, nor without reason, nor childish, although it may seem so to me because I do not understand it." Seeking to understand, with many prayers and investigations, he is enlightened by truth, as is manifestly to be seen in the saints of old, who found the hidden senses of Scripture and resolved their doubts through faith. So also in those things which I have predicted, it necessarily follows, since they proceed from the same light, that anyone who believes is not tripped up by them, but one who does not believe is always finding new obstacles, wherefore it is written in the prophet Isaias: *Nisi credideritis, non intelligetis*[25] [Is. 7:9].

If the citizens of Florence had diligently attended to my words and believed them, they would have understood that they would suffer more or less great tribulations, the more or less they practiced justice. And since they did not act with any justice, and they still do not, what wonder is it if they still suffer tribulations? The city is full of ribalds, infamous for their many vices, who have such boldness in disparaging upright living and the present government effected by God that they compose catchy tunes [*belle canzone*] about it and openly slander the good, and there is no one who will say anything to them. They are well known, those who seek to ruin the Council and who have made agreements with many [others] for this purpose, which is a *crime* of *lèse majesté* and opposed to that which God has created. But no one dares to say anything; rather, many pretend not to know about such things, and they have [deliberately] misunderstood them for fear of having to pass judgment on them, while even the good citizens have been enveloped in this negligence because they are not truly good, since they do not have a zeal for justice. No one wants to be unpleasant, and everyone seeks favor

24. "To advance in knowledge it is necessary to believe."
25. "Unless you believe, you will not understand." The Vulgate has *permanebitis* ("endure"); Isaias is to say this to Achaz concerning the continuance of his kingdom.

from the people so that, in effect: *Dilexerunt magis gloriam hominum quam Dei*[26] [Ioh. 12:43]. For this reason, God is angry with them. Not that the promised graces are lost; rather, they will be fulfilled in our lifetime, but God forbid that what happened to the Hebrew people should happen to them, for they were taken out of slavery in Egypt, and to them was promised the Land of Promise, which they could have reached in a few days, but because of their unbelief and because of their murmuring against the favors of God, they remained in the desert for forty years, so that all those murmurers and unbelievers would die, and none escaped [this fate] but two, namely Josue and Caleb, and thus, the land promised to them was given to their children [Num. 14:20–35].

I want you to know this secret: that if Florence had acted justly and purged herself of wicked men, the tribulations would not have come about at this time; rather, she would now begin to flourish; but since she acts in such a way that no justice is done, if she does not amend, not only will these tribulations not end, but they will start all over again from the beginning. But if they should amend and perform some notable act of justice, they would placate God and free themselves of tribulations, but if they do not amend, not only will the wicked be afflicted, but also the good because they have not dared to punish those who deserve to be punished. They have such little faith that they do not think that when they lay hands on those who are infamous and destroyers of the common good, God will help them, and that from this would come nothing but well-being and peace for the city and a reputation to the honor of God. The wicked who are in the magistracy have more daring to carry on their own vendettas under the guise of justice, in criminal as well as civil cases, against someone who may have spit in church and committed a venial sin than the good have against the destroyers of the common good and infamous men; and if you were to say that they actually have effected some justice, I would answer that it was so little and done with so little zeal that it was little pleasing to God. They believe that with their clemency, which is a *dementia* and not a *clementia,* they please God, but they do not consider how unbending God is in punishing, as is apparent in Holy Scripture, especially when it is a sin against the common good.

And when you say that it seems to you that I am in great danger, you speak like one who does not fully believe that this is the work of God. First of all, I want you to know that there are more with us than with our adversaries, as Eliseus [*sic*] said to his disciple: *Et si Deus pro nobis, quis contra nos?*[27] [Rom. 8:31] Second, since this is the work of God, if I should fail,

26. "They have delighted more in the glory of men than of God."
27. "If God is for us, who can be against us?"

God will not fail of instruments to lead it on, for this work can be wounded, but not destroyed or killed. *Besides,* if I should die for this, I will be happy to die for the love of God; would that God in His grace might grant this to me.

You also say that many mock me because I have written that I have been in Paradise. To this objection I respond that to make a marvel or a mock of this is something only a stupid or a malicious man would do, for if they were to examine carefully the circumstances of what I have written [in the *Compendium of Revelations*], they would easily find that it is not to be understood that I have been bodily in Paradise, but that it was a wholly imaginary vision. In Paradise there are no waters, nor animals, nor trees, nor walls, nor gates, nor ladders, nor seats, nor precious stones; and since I have explained all these things in a spiritual sense, they could easily have understood, if they were not grossly ignorant and thickheaded, or if they were not so very malicious, that all those things which I saw were formed in the imagination through angelic ministration in the manner which I stated at the beginning of the book and by which the understanding of all these things was given to me. In the same way, the prophets saw many things; Ezechiel especially says often that in this manner he was in different places to which it is certain that he went with his spirit and not with his body, and he says this explicitly in many passages of his book.[28]

You also say that many make mock of these visions. To which I respond that I am much amazed at this, since all the Scriptures, and almost all ecclesiastical books, are full of them, and yet many preachers in our own day do nothing but preach about their brothers. If, then, they make mock at present, it is a sign either that they have preached falsehoods and deceived the people, or that they believe that no one can have visions if they do not.

You also say that to some what I have said seems to be in error, that is, that Rome has to be reproved and Jerusalem [will be] the chosen one and preferred to her, to which I respond that this is not an error, because it does not mean that the Roman Church has to change form on account of this, but that the present Rome, that is the wicked of Rome, will be reproved and snuffed out, while the flower of the Christians will be in the region of Jerusalem. I am not saying, then, that the Roman Church will collapse, or that there has to be a change of faith, or that there are to be two Popes, but that under one Pope Jerusalem will flourish in good Christian living more than our part [of the world], and all parts of the world where there are Christians will humble themselves to the Roman Church because they will all be governed by the Roman faith under a holy Pope, the successor of Peter, the first Roman bishop, and his see and principal diocese will be

28. E.g., chap. 37, the valley of dry bones.

Rome, although he will also have plenary power over all the churches, as do all the Popes. And even if the Pope did not remain in Rome, he would still not lose his jurisdiction, for he is always the Roman bishop, and in him the whole Roman Church, or rather the universal Church, is united.

I could respond to many of your other objections, but I believe you will easily resolve them on your own, especially if you will go back and read my *Compendium of Revelations*. Nonetheless, to answer all of these together, I want to give you this sign about the doctrine which I have preached, that it is from God, because one sees from experience that everyone who believes in it, the more he believes in it and the more he aligns himself with it, the more he rests in it and delights in it and seeks to live uprightly, content with little and happy in adversity and tribulations. But anyone who departs from this doctrine, either through the persuasion of the wicked or through some temptation, incontinently loses the joy and quietude of his heart and becomes enraged and curses and runs about every which way, disquieting both himself and others. On the contrary, you will find that those who do not believe this doctrine and contradict it are either among the lukewarm, of whom we have spoken above, or they are vicious and infamous men without discernment, or they are men made desperate through their impoverishment, and, being unable to make up for their loss from [the resources of] the commune, they speak ill of this teaching, which has tied their hands, and are thoroughly restless men; they do nothing but run about and speak ill wherever they find themselves. Nonetheless, if such men, through the persuasion of good people or for some other reason, separate themselves from this foolishness and error and come over to this truth, they are quickly changed, and become quiet and sweet-tempered, and confess their past sins, and begin to live in a Christian way, and become defenders of this doctrine. And this experience has already been seen in many, not only among the lowly, but also among men well trained and capable in every branch of learning, whether in the secular state or the religious. All this is so obvious that even those who are wicked know it, though they say that those others have become melancholy and mad. As Isaias the prophet says: *Impii quasi mare fervens quod quiescere non potest et redundant fluctus eius in conculcationem et lutum. Non est pax impiis, dicit dominus Deus*[29] [Is. 57:20–21]. That is, "the impious are like a raging sea, which cannot rest, and its currents and waves surge with silt and mud. The impious never have peace, says the Lord God." On the other hand, the prophet David says: *Pax multa diligentibus legem*

29. "The impious are like the raging sea, which is unable to lie still, and its waves surge with conculcations and mud. There is no peace for the impious, says the Lord God."

tuam[30] [Ps. 118:165]; that is, "Lord, those who love Your law possess great peace."

If, then, those who follow the doctrine I preach acquire peace, as experience proves, it is a sign that it is the divine law, and that I preach nothing but the Gospel law or a doctrine which proceeds from God; and if its adversaries are always restless, it is a sign that they follow the error of the impious and the doctrine of the lukewarm, which is both bestial and diabolical.

So, do not let yourself be drawn out of the way of truth because of the contradictions we face, so that you might not be [accounted] one of those of whom our Savior says: *"Ad tempus credunt et in tempore tentationis recedunt"*[31] [Luc. 8:13]; that is, "they believe when they have no opposition." He who will persevere till the end will be saved [Matt. 10:22].

May the grace of our Lord Jesus Christ be with your spirit. Amen.

30. "Great is the peace among those who love Your law."
31. "They believe for a time, and in the time of temptation they fall away."

Excommunication

Open *Letter to All the Elect of God and Faithful Christians*
Florence, 8 May 1497

Fra Girolamo of Ferrara, useless servant of Jesus Christ, to all the elect of God and children of the Eternal Father, wishes grace, peace, and the consolation of the Holy Spirit:

Because we want, dearly beloved, to imitate our Savior, Who yielded many times to the great wrath and intense fury of the scribes and Pharisees, we have given up preaching until such time as is pleasing to Him. But knowing that the devil does not care about bodies but desires souls and that he goes about inciting this persecution so that while the word of God is held in check, he may be better able to deceive men, I think that he will incite the lukewarm, who will not cease to turn souls aside from the truth, and fearing lest you allow yourselves to be deceived and being solicitous about your salvation, I will do by letter what at present cannot be done verbally, and perhaps this will be so much the more useful as it is the more universal, since a letter can be received by those who cannot hear the words. I beg you, then, dearly beloved, not to be perturbed about my tribulations and persecutions, which I suffer for you; rather, congratulate me, because the Lord has made us worthy to suffer for His love and for the love of truth, especially since you know that I have continually predicted to you that we have to suffer great persecutions, waging battle against a double power and a double wisdom and a double malice, and so you must stand firm in the truth we have preached as you see gradually fulfilled all which we have predicted and believe that the promised graces and consolation will also come.

Diligently consider the Scriptures and the works done in the Church in times past, and you will find that the Church has always grown under persecution, so that from being small and next to nothing at her beginning, she spread, because of the great persecutions, all over the world, and when the persecutions lessened, the Church also lessened both in number and in merit. Now, since God wants to renew her and make her grow, it is no wonder if once again the persecutions begin, under which she is made perfect in every part. But think how good and benevolent is our Savior, and how sweetly He leads us, since He has not sent us all at once into great persecutions but has nursed us through them little by little, for at first, by His permission, reprobate men made mock of us; then they added many calumnies against us, saying that we are deceivers, hypocrites, heretics, and other similar cal-

umnies, but not finding these things in us in truth, they tried in many con-
voluted ways to have us excommunicated or interdicted without cause. Unable to achieve even this, they made many plots against our person and
threatened us, and then they openly showed themselves attempting to kill
me; nonetheless, we have not yet shed a drop of blood, because our Lord,
Who knows our frailty, does not allow us to be tested beyond our strength.
But as our tribulations grow, little by little, He makes our faith and virtue
and courage grow so as to sustain us in greater ordeals, and in this way He
prepares us for much greater persecutions, so that men, seeing us unmoved
from the way of truth in spite of so many tribulations, may be stirred to
wonder at our constancy and begin to think that we would not endure so
many things if our faith were not true and if there were not another better
life than this, and because of this, they might begin to be induced to live
uprightly and to follow this truth also. In this way, because of tribulations
this light will spread, and from it will ensue the opposite of what the enemies
of the Cross of Christ desire; these, desiring to extinguish it, cause it to burn
more brightly, for the more one pokes a great fire or the more one blows
on it, the more brightly it burns. Therefore, you should not fear that these
persecutions may extinguish or diminish the work begun by God; rather,
believe that on this account it will grow.

Great indeed has God's mercy been toward us, since He has chosen us
to partake of so great a light, not some light other than that which the
Church has always received from God, as some go about saying foolishly,
but the light of faith, which the Christian faithful have always had, while
others are deprived of it, and, therefore, they never cease saying and doing
evil, following their father, Satan. And that those who persecute you are the
congregation of Satan, you have most explicit signs in their lives and words
and works, since their ministers, with great impudence, without the restraint
of either fear or shame, go on profaning the temple of God, making mock
of the words of Christ, and in the place of truth, sanctified many a time by
the word of God, they have committed obscenities and have mangled the
titles of the praises of Christ with derision and blasphemy, so that the word
of God might be held in odium, exerting themselves to impede it so that all
virtues might be extinguished and so that they can sin all the more freely,
opening the way to gambling and all the vices and sins. Consider, then, what
this generation of men—if indeed they are men!—is, which does what pagans and infidels would not, for they hold their temples in the highest reverence and punish injuries to God most seriously. But these care nothing
about performing justice for injuries done against God, but for those even
justly done to some evil man, they seek revenge, not justice, and they would
have done it already, if they had not been hindered by good and just citizens.
Consider, also, who are those who are happy about this state of affairs, such

as the lukewarm and those who incite them or advise or go along with them. For this reason, then, you can be certain that the way which I have preached to you is the way of truth, since among yourselves you do not see similar excesses, but rather, all the virtues and good works, and since we would not be persecuted but by the synagogue of Satan. However, since you are and dwell in the midst of a depraved and perverse generation, in which you shine like stars in the darkness of the night [Philip. 2:15], you must follow our Savior and His disciples and the martyrs, who did not turn back because of the persecutions they suffered; rather, they stood ever firmer, with patience and with joy in the truth, and encouraged others to do likewise. Do not be ashamed of the Cross of Christ, but rather, glory in it [Gal. 6:14], for if perverse men glory in doing evil, how much more ought we not to be ashamed of living uprightly and being persecuted by the members of the devil!

Now is the time, dearly beloved, to earn the victory, because the judgment of God always begins first among His elect, whom He troubles and tests in many ways, as gold is tested by fire [I Pet. 1:7]; later it will come upon the reprobate. Consider, then, if God gives so many tribulations to His elect, how many will He give to the reprobate, for the judgment of the elect purifies with mercy, but the judgment of the reprobate will be without mercy. Do not marvel that God allows wicked men to do so much evil and impiety without present punishment, and that He does not give evidence of any revenge, for God can loose no greater wrath against them than to let them prosper in their sins and make them instruments of Satan, and exercise the good in the virtue of patience. Just as God reserves a great multitude of demons in this caliginous air of ours and does not make them stay in Hell, as they deserve, in order to test His elect in the faith, so does He allow reprobate men to live and prosper for the same purpose which the demons have; at the last, their judgment will be extremely severe and everlasting. But we await a great inheritance in Heaven, which will never fail, for we shall be children of God, by Whom, as by a father, we have been chastised and mortified in this life, as He has done with all His children. Certainly, the martyrs and saints of the past suffered much greater persecutions and passions than we have so far, and so, we should not grieve nor lament nor believe that, because of these tribulations, we have been abandoned by God; rather, we must believe we are His children, chosen for an eternal glory prepared in Heaven for all those who will suffer persecution for His love. We ought, therefore, to be joyful and show worldly men that the inheritance and the glory which we await is so great that we do not hold anything in this present life to be of value, and the world being come to so great a degree of blindness as you see at present, we must suppose that this which is found at present among this generation of lukewarm and villainous men is no less than it was at the time of the Apostles among the scribes and Pharisees, and among the pagans and idolaters; and so we must arm ourselves against their wickedness with faith, prayer, and patience, persevering in living uprightly and always growing in it, because there is nothing better able to combat and rout them than your good life, seeing which, they are left overwhelmed and confused. And do not complain that the word of God has been taken from you, for this was [done] not by human counsel, but divine, so that you might know how evilly such men would act if they had the power, and that because of this, you might clearly understand that they are not Christians and that they believe in the faith not at all, since, exactly on that day on which the Savior enjoined His disciples to go and preach the Gospel to every creature,[1] they exerted themselves to remove the word of God from the city and to open up profane places, singing on stage, and gaming, and all those things of the devil, who is the enemy of Christ. But pray to the Omnipotent God that He might deign to open up the fount of His word, for when God commands that the mouth be opened, there is no man who can resist, and if these evil men want to be pagans, we will show ourselves to be Christians, and we shall act as did the Apostles and martyrs of old when they were commanded not to preach [Act. 5:17 ff.]; they said that it was necessary to obey God rather than men [Act. 5:29], and they would willingly suffer every tribulation for the love of Him Who was crucified for our salvation [Rom. 8:35–39].

I beg you, then, by the bowels of the mercy of Jesus Christ, that on this holy solemnity of the Holy Spirit [i.e., Pentecost] you prepare yourselves for the most sacred Communion with true confession of your sins and purification of your heart so that the Eternal Father, by the merits of the Passion of our Savior, may send you the gifts of the Holy Spirit, through which you will bear up under these tribulations and many greater, not only with patience but with joy, and you will attain a perpetual crown in life eternal with the angelic hierarchies. Remain calm in mind, meek, humble, chaste, pure, sincere, charitable, constant in prayer, lively, without anger or hatred, defending the truth and showing the foolishness of impious men, who approach their death beaten down by sin without redemption. On this sweetest of solemnities prepare your hearts in confidence for the coming of the Holy Spirit, invoking Him with faith and longing, so that, through the gift of

---

1. Ascension Thursday, 4 May 1497. An Arrabbiati-controlled Signory, determined to silence Savonarola, issued an edict banning all preaching (ostensibly as a preventive measure against the plague), effective from 5 May. Though the ban was not yet in effect, Savonarola's sermon on the feast day was disrupted by a riot in the church, instigated by the Compagnacci.

understanding,[2] He may give you knowledge of things invisible and eternal; through the gift of wisdom may He make you love and ardently desire them; through the gift of knowledge may He make you despise earthly things, which pass away in a moment; through the gift of counsel may He direct you into the way of truth and justice in everything you have to do; through the gift of piety may He make you pious and benevolent toward your neighbor, especially toward the wretched, and, even more, toward sinners, having compassion for their blindness, and bestirring yourself to pray fervently for your enemies; through the gift of fortitude may He make you strong to endure with joy all your tribulations for the love of Him and of truth; through the gift of fear [of the Lord] may He preserve you in the right way in all humility and obedience, so that you may live joyfully and happily, neither desiring nor fearing anything of this world, knowing that time passes in a flash, and once what is to be has passed, we shall find ourselves in that immense and eternal felicity, and we shall rejoice with our Lord God and His blessed, relishing what eye has never seen, nor ear heard, nor human heart ascended to, that which God has prepared for those who love Him [I Cor. 2:9; Is. 64:4]. May the grace of the Father, the peace of the Son, and the consolation of the Holy Spirit be always with all of you. Amen.

Given at San Marco in Florence, on the Feast of the Apparition of St. Michael the Archangel, 1497.

2. A list of the Seven Gifts of the Holy Spirit follows.

Letter from Savonarola to Pope Alexander VI

Florence, 20 May 1497

Most Blessed Father, after kissing your blessed feet:

For what reason is my Lord angry with his servant? What have I done, or what crime [marks] my hand? If the sons of iniquity unjustly disparage me, why does my Lord not first interrogate his servant and hear that which he may believe? For it is difficult to persuade the mind already inclined to an adverse view. "Many dogs surrounded me; the council of malignant men besieged me, and they say to me: 'So! so! there is no salvation for him in his God'" [Pss. 21:17; 39:16; 3:3]. For Your Holiness stands in the place of God on earth, to whom they accuse me of the crime of *lèse majesté,* by feigning that I will not cease to slander and to attack you with maledictions, and they twist my words tortuously and sacrilegiously pervert them. The same has been done repeatedly during the last two years, but a thousand auditors stand forth with testimony of my innocence; the words pronounced from my mouth also are on record, accurately excerpted — as I believe — and published everywhere [in the] works of copyists and of printers. Let them be brought forward, read, examined, if anything is there which might offend the Holiness of my Lord, which they so often falsely denounce to you. Is there anything said by me publicly? or anything written? Let me ask to be convicted by open contradiction.

What private interest? what expediency? what kind of insane mind devises such things? I marvel, how does Your Holiness not detect their wickedness and madness? With what countenance, with what conscience does that certain illustrious and elevated orator of whom you speak[3] taunt innocent me with a crime of which he himself is most especially a perpetrator? For necessity now compels me to make it public. They are here — I repeat — the most reliable of witnesses, who have heard him at another time very openly raging against Your Holiness from the pulpit; and lest I be thought to lie, if it should be proper, I will add the guarantee of a shorthand-writer in producing worthy witnesses. And, in fact, I recall that I argued against and condemned his insolence, since one is not permitted to inveigh against the smallest person, much less against a Prince and Pastor of sheep. Who, indeed, is so demented not to know such things? I am not as yet, God granting, so far gone that I would forget myself; by no intention, by no activity on any occasion would I dare to provoke voluntarily and contemn the Vicar of Christ on earth, who is especially to be revered.

For the rest, moreover, nothing beyond the Catholic faith and whatever

---

3. Fra Mariano da Genazzanno, Vicar General of the Augustinians.

the Holy Roman Church approves has been set forth by me, that I know of, because I have subjected myself always to her every reproof, and, so far as it might be appropriate, I do subject myself again and again. What except the penitence of sinners and the improvement of morals, drawn from the faith of our Lord Jesus Christ, do I declare to all men, as long as I strive to recall to the hearts of men that nearly extinct faith? And very soon, God granting, the work *The Triumph of Christ* (*De triumpho Christi*) shall be published by me in assertion of the faith, from which it shall manifestly appear whether I am a disseminator of heresies — God forbid — or of Catholic truth. Therefore, let Your Holiness not want to put faith in envious and abusive men, unless trial of the matter has already been made, since they can be convicted publicly already of so many lies. Because if human assistance fails, so that the iniquity of the impious prevails, I shall hope in God, my Savior, and I shall make their wickedness known to all the world in such a way that perhaps someday they shall repent them of the purpose they have undertaken. I commend myself most humbly to Your Blessedness.

From the convent of San Marco at Florence, the twentieth of May 1497. The humble little son and servant of Your Blessedness,
Brother Girolamo of Ferrara, of the Order of Preachers.

Open *Letter to All Christians and Those Beloved of God, against the Surreptitious Excommunication Newly Made*

Florence, 19 June 1497

To all Christians and those beloved of God, Fra Girolamo Savonarola of Ferrara, servant of Jesus Christ, writes in charity and wishes them well-being and joy in all tribulations, he having been sent by Christ to the city of Florence to announce the great scourge which is to come upon Italy, and especially Rome, and spread well-nigh all over the world in our own day and soon, so that the elect of God may find themselves prepared for all these many tribulations and escape the great wrath of God, Who wants by this means to weed out the bad plants and renew His Church and the whole universe. May thanks, therefore, be always rendered for His goodness, which has elected us to the ministry of this truth, on account of which we willingly suffer many persecutions and struggle night and day, God desiring that in this way the fame of this prophecy might fly through all the regions inhabited by Christian people or, rather, through all the world, so that no one might have an excuse for his errors, and so that the minds of those whom He will deign to choose for this renewal, both within the Church and among the infidels, may be disposed to receive the grace of the Holy Spirit, Who is the model for such a renewal.

Now the wicked men, who are kept in the world in order to inflict persecution on the just, believing that they extinguish this truth and annihilate the prophecies, [in fact] fulfill them, just as Joseph's brothers believed that by selling him to the Midianites he would not become their master, and, nonetheless, that sale fulfilled the prophecy [Gen. 37]. Herod, believing that he was extinguishing the truth of the prophecy of Christ by massacring the children [Matt. 2], fulfilled the prophecy of Jeremias [31:15] and that of Osee [11:1], and the Jews, persecuting and then killing our Savior, fulfilled all the prophecies written of Him, and the persecutions inflicted on the Apostles and martyrs have fulfilled the prophecies of the New and Old Testaments. In the same way, up to the present, the prophecies preached by me are being fulfilled, among which you see expressly fulfilled the one about excommunications, concerning which many years ago, when no one thought anything about it, I preached to you many times, saying that we had to fight against a double power and wisdom and malice, so that from this and from many other [prophecies] which your eyes see already fulfilled, you can firmly believe that all those not yet fulfilled will be fulfilled and that God will extricate us from every danger and will give us in the end a great victory: *Quia non relinquet Dominus virgam peccatorum super sortem iustorum. . . . Declinantes autem in obligationes adducet Dominus cum operantibus iniquitatem.*

Pax super Israel![4] [Ps. 124:3, 5] Remember that I told you that a great favor would not be repaid except with great ingratitude, and that for so much effort I expected nothing else from Florence but tribulation, and that for Rome and the adversaries of truth nothing was lacking to top it off but this, namely, to persecute the servants of Christ. But because the lukewarm never cease to scurry about everywhere and to deceive simple people, making out to be evil things which are not, and raising scruples in the ignorant and in simple women concerning whatever suits their purposes, rather than about speaking evil and persecuting good people and the truth, I would not want you on this account to go astray and abandon the way of truth. Remember our Lord Jesus Christ, the prophets, the Apostles, and the saints of the past! Keep in mind what I have told you about St. John Chrysostom, Athanasius, St. Jerome, and Hilary, and many others who have suffered worse things than we have. Do not believe, then, dearly beloved, that such excommunications have any validity either with God or with the Church, when they have been imposed because of the false suggestions of men in order to do evil and to work against God and against truth. But because they could not find a just cause to excommunicate me, they have suggested falsehoods to the Pope in place of truths, saying that I disseminate pernicious doctrine and heresies, even though the whole world bears witness that I preach only the doctrine of Christ, not in corners but in churches where all Christians can gather [Ioh. 18:20]. And if this doctrine preached by me, or rather by the Holy Spirit, is, as my adversaries have suggested, a perverse dogma, let them stay with that which pleases them, for we are determined to die for this one.

And because they accuse me of disobedience, know that I have never been disobedient to the Holy Roman Church, nor to the Pope, nor to any of my superiors up to this present moment. I say this not in self-praise but as the truth, and so I propose and vow to do for the future in this writing, which I am content that, if I do not speak the truth, it may be counted against me on the day of judgment in the tribunal of Christ. It is true that in the opinion of some, when a man does not obey [even] in those matters which are expressly contrary to God, that this is disobedience; however, it is unreasonable to believe that we are obligated to obey our superiors in everything; rather, we ought to be obedient to a superior insofar as he represents God, but he does not represent God and is not our superior when he commands what is contrary to God.[5] Therefore, on occasion, when such

---

4. "For the Lord will not leave the rod of sinners upon the lot of the just. . . . But those turning aside into bondage, He will lead away with the workers of iniquity. Peace be on Israel!"

5. Savonarola's invocation of a suprapapal power bore strange fruit: in a *pratica* held

was the case, I have not obeyed, knowing that neither God nor the Church wanted me to be obedient in opposition to their commandments; I have treated of this matter many times and preached about it, knowing that this had to come about, so that you might be armed with replies. Read in the first sermon of Lent of 1495 and in the sermons of the Monday and Wednesday after the fourth Sunday, and you will find the solution to all these issues.

And because our adversaries have held it against me that I did not want to obey and to consent to unite the congregation of friars of San Marco with the rest of the Tuscan [Congregation], I have answered many times that those who persuaded the Pope [to agree] to this union were doing it not out of zeal for religion, but only to persecute me and to find occasion in this way to proceed against me, believing that I would never consent to a thing which it would be evil to do, for their consciences told them that, this being a pernicious thing, I would not do it. But because of twelve reasons to which they have never been able to reply because they convince every intellect and lead them to reach the same conclusions by showing this union to be contrary to the honor of God and the salvation of souls, I responded that they required of me a thing not in my power, because the consent of all our friars was necessary, and they were all opposed to it as a most pernicious thing. Besides, it seemed to us the honest thing to call together the relatives of these youths who have come under our protection in order to live an upright life and to make clear to them the conditions of such a union so that they, with the whole city, would not be able to complain that we had deceived their children, who certainly would have been deceived by us if we had consented to this union, because their mode of living would be less strict, and they would become like those lukewarm ones whom we have proved to be the worst men in the world, so that it would have been better that they had stayed at home with their relatives. Indeed, I responded that, since I am a foreigner here [being from Ferrara], should our fathers and brothers want to consent, I could not oppose them, but if they did not want to, I could not oppose them [either], and if they did not want to, I could not force them, and so I sent the case back to them. Now they have written that they do not want to consent to this; rather, they would suffer excommunication and prison and martyrdom. If this, then, is so, why do they impute this disobedience to me, if not that these adversaries seek after

on 5 July 1497 to deal with the excommunication, opposing sides in the debate argued whether Christ's or God the Father's authority was the greater (as though They might have differing agendas). See the discussion in Alison Brown, "Ideology and Faction in Savonarolan Florence," in *The World of Savonarola: Italian Elites and Perceptions of Crisis,* ed. Stella Fletcher and Christine Shaw (Aldershot: Ashgate, 2000), pp. 29–30.

one man alone, whom they hate because of the truth? So you see, dearly beloved, how great is the audacity of our adversaries, who are not ashamed to suggest manifest lies to the Pope. Therefore, such excommunications are worthless, nor are they what Holy Church intends, and if they say that the sentence of a pastor, whether just or unjust, ought to be feared,[6] you have the answer to this in that sermon for the Wednesday above-mentioned.

But I beg you to pray to our Lord that He might now deign to set His hand to something other than reason, because men have arrived at such wickedness that they openly, and without shame, contradict truth and reason; but see to it that you live cheerfully, for, if these reasons are not to be heard, and if they try to proceed any further, we shall make this truth understood all over the world in such a way that no one will be able to deny it, for when the time is right, God, to the confusion of those Christians who do not want to use their reason, will cause irrational creatures to show reverence to the truth which the rational creature shuns. Pray that it may be soon. The grace of Jesus be with you. Amen.

Given at San Marco in Florence on the nineteenth of June 1497.

6. Gregory the Great, *Homilia XXVI in Evang.;* see *A Dialogue concerning Prophetic Truth,* bk. VII, page 125, note 33, above; and the Open *Letter against the Recently Imposed Sentence of Excommunication,* page 304, note 18, below.

Letter from Savonarola to Pope Alexander VI

Florence, 25 June 1497[7]

Most Blessed Father, after kissing your blessed feet:

Faith, supported by innumerable miracles and the divine works of the most famous men, by prophecies as well as arguments and doctrines, and continually strengthened by the blood of countless martyrs, is the one and only true peace and consolation of the human heart. For in that it transcends sense and reason and rests on the divine power and goodness, bearing the soul away to things invisible, it makes us be not in this world and imparts to us a greatness of soul. By it we can not only bear patiently all adversities, but even glory in tribulations. Certainly it is written: "Whatever befalls the just man will not sadden him" [Prov. 12:21]. The just man, indeed, is one who lives in faith, as the Lord attests, Who says: "My just one shall live in his faith" [Abac. 2:4]. Blessed, therefore, is the one who is called by the Lord to this grace of faith, without which no one can have peace, as Isaias says: "There is no peace for the wicked, says the Lord, my God" [Is. 48:22]. And so, let Your Holiness, Most Blessed Father, respond to this, because suddenly "sorrow may be converted into joy" [Ioh. 16:20]; for sweet is the Lord, Who in the immeasurableness of His kindness passes over our sins. Every other consolation is trivial and false, because time is short and we transmigrate to eternity; faith alone brings joy from a distant land. What I have heard and seen with my eyes and touched, these things I speak [I Ioh. 1:1–3], for the sake of which I willingly suffer persecutions so that I might merit Christ and escape eternal punishment, knowing that "it is terrifying to fall into the hands of the living God" [Heb. 10:31]. Therefore, let Your Blessedness encourage the work of the faith for all men, "on account of which I labor unceasingly even to the point of imprisonment" [II Tim. 2:9], but lend no ear to the impious, and the Lord will give you "the oil of gladness [. . .] in return for the spirit of mourning" [Is. 61:3], for the things which I have prophesied and prophesy are true and from God. "But who has opposed God and had peace?" [Iob 9:4] These things, Most Blessed Father, I humbly write to you — a few words to the wise — with charity as my guide, desiring Your Blessedness may be truly and not falsely consoled in the Lord, because "when His anger is enflamed suddenly, blessed are all they who trust in Him" [Ps. 2:13]. And so "may the God of all consolation" [II Cor. 1:3], "Who has led forth from the dead our Lord Jesus Christ, the great Shepherd of sheep,

7. Written in response to the murder of the Pope's eldest son, Juan, Duke of Gandia, very probably by his brother, Cesare Borgia.

in the blood of His everlasting covenant" [Heb. 13:20], "console you in your every tribulation"[8] [II Cor. 1:4]. Farewell.

From Florence, the seventh Kalends of July 1497.
The son and servant of Your Blessedness,
Brother Girolamo Savonarola, of the Order of Preachers,
by his own hand.

8. Pronouns and verbs are adapted to a singular addressee.

Open *Letter against the Recently Imposed Sentence of Excommunication*

Florence, end of June 1497[9]

You ask me, N., dearest brother, whether an excommunication such as that which in recent days we have shown to be unjust ought to be observed at least in public. Concerning this matter, Peter Lombard[10] in the fourth [book] of his *Sentences,* distinction 18, article 1, conclusion 2, and, likewise, [St. Antoninus] the Archbishop of Florence,[11] in the third part [of his *Summa theologica*] respond, in the plainest words, as follows:

> An unjust excommunication is not to be feared with respect to the punishment of the law, since, in truth, one who does not observe a judgment which is nothing incurs no punishment at law, but with respect to blame, it is to be feared for reasons of scandal. But, as Boethius says, some concepts are common to all, some [only] to the wise.[12] When, therefore, a judgment is known to the wise to be null, although among the common populace it may not be known, one is allowed not to observe it in secret, but ought to observe it in public, until scandal has been reasonably allayed. Thus, when someone is publicly excommunicated and publicly denounced, let him, in his own defense, make public a reason why the judgment is not valid, an appeal, or other just cause. When this has been done, any scandal [alleged] will be that of the Pharisees rather than of the little ones.[13] In such a case, it is to be disregarded.

Also, in the *Decretals* [of Gratian[14]] 11, question 3 [cap. 46], Pelasgius [*sic;* Pope Gelasius I[15]] says: "Let anyone against whom a judgment has been issued set aside his error, and it will be void; but if it is unjust, he ought to pay no attention to it, inasmuch as an unfair sentence cannot oppress anyone

9. The excommunication was issued on 13 May 1497 but, because of the courier's pusillanimity and other mishaps, not formally proclaimed in Florence until 18 June.
10. 1100?–1160?; *magister* at the Cathedral School of Notre Dame.
11. St. Antonio Pierozzi, Archbishop of Florence from 1446 to 1459.
12. Paraphrased (from *De hebdomada*) in Aquinas, *Summa theologica,* part. 1.2, quest. 94, art. 2.
13. In other words, any claims of being scandalized will be disingenuous.
14. Twelfth century.
15. D. 496.

before God and His Church; thus, one may feel no compulsion to be absolved from that by which he considers himself in no way obligated."[16]

And, therefore, since even before, concerning the same matter, it was well known to everyone that this excommunication had been extorted by impious and false suggestions and excessive importunity, seeing that they had easy access to the perpetration of many evils, and since, through the letter recently published by me in public, I also showed the truth of this same matter to the people in order to allay scandal and point out a reasonable case for [considering it an] injustice, I am not bound even in public to observe it, nor can anyone be scandalized, unless he would obstinately profess himself a Pharisee. This can be even better understood in the words of Jean Gerson,[17] a very learned and religious man, who is acclaimed as a most Christian doctor by the Parisians, for in his tractate *Concerning Excommunications and Irregularities,* among other things, he puts it eloquently as follows:

> [The charge of] contempt for the keys [of Peter, hence papal and episcopal power] ought to be investigated with regard to legitimate authority and the legitimate use of that authority, who it is that excommunicates by his command or threatens irregularity. Otherwise prelates would be able to introduce whatever servitude they might wish on others, if obedience is always owed to their unjust and erroneous judgments. And thus it is clear that this common saying—"The judgment of a prelate or judge, even if unjust, is to be feared"[18]—requires a gloss. In any event, the statement is not generally true, even supposing a sentence may be called fearful, seeing that it ought to be upheld, not repelled; indeed, in such a case, it would be a donkeylike patience and harelike and fatuous timidity to endure it.
>
> Contempt for the keys is more dangerous in relation to the person of the Supreme Pontiff than in relation to inferiors, since from inferior abuses recourse to the Pope is accessible through the relief of an appeal. And if it is said that an appeal can be made

---

16. *PL* 187, col. 857.
17. 1363–1429; Chancellor of the University of Paris.
18. *Sententia praelati, vel iudicis, etiam iniusta, timenda est.* Gerson paraphrases Gregory the Great, *Homilia XXVI in Evang.* (quoted by Aquinas in his *Summa,* suppl., quest. 21, art. 4). More accurately: *Sed utrum juste an injuste obliget pastor, pastoris tamen sententia gregi timenda est (PL* 76, col. 1201; i.e., "But whether the pastor binds [one] justly or unjustly, the judgment of a pastor ought to be feared by his flock)." See the discussion also in *A Dialogue concerning Prophetic Truth,* bk. VII, at page 125, note 33, above; and Exodus, Sermon III, at page 317, note 4, below.

from the Pope to a General Council, they said in the past, before
the General Council at Pisa and Constance, that this was in no
way allowed, and they adduced in their support their own laws
expressed very strongly, as it seemed to them; but now it is
stoutly asserted that this is a heresy condemned through a most
explicit constitution effected at the aforesaid Council of Constance,[19] just as elsewhere it has been shown more diffusely.
Therefore, this is to be answered differently: that, when it is even
allowed, the Council cannot or ought not to be randomly resorted
to for prosecuting appeals in minor cases, just as recourse is had
to the Pope.

Contempt for the keys is not incurred in many cases in which
obedience is not given to the command of the Pope, as long as he
is obviously abusing his power irregularly and scandalously for destruction and not edification, inasmuch as the Apostle says that
the power has been given for that reason [II Cor. 13:10]. Example:
If the Pope should want to seize the treasures of the churches, or
to usurp hereditary properties, or to reduce the clergy with their
possessions to abject servitude, or to despoil them of their rights
without cause, who would say that these things ought to be tolerated? Who would not think that one could say to the Pope: Why
are you doing this? Who will not assent in resisting him to his
face?

Contempt for the keys is not always found even in those who
do not obey the sentences of excommunication promulgated by
the Pope or his [representatives], but also it ought not to be ad-
judged to be [found] in those who take care to protect themselves
through the secular power against such pretended sentences; for
natural law says that force may be repelled with force. It is agreed,
moreover, that such excommunications ought to be called not law,
but force and violence, against which the free man or spirit has
the sanction of divine law to protect himself.

Contempt for the keys, and consequently excommunication or
irregularity, is not incurred when, in cases such as those premised,
a jurist or theologian says in accordance with his conscience that
such sentences are not to be feared *or upheld*,[20] and this especially
if due form or caution is observed, lest scandal to little ones, who

19. Held during the schism of three rival Popes. Conciliar superiority to the Pope
was later firmly rejected.
20. This phrase is not in the edited texts of Gerson and, so, is presumably Savonarola's addition.

think that the Pope is the one God, Who holds every power in heaven and on earth, might follow; nevertheless, the stupidity of such persons ought to be driven out with proper information. And if they do not wish to acquiesce, these same persons indeed ought to be examined for scandal not given [to them] but received [from them], that is, for the scandal of the Pharisees, arising from malice, not of the little ones, arising from simplicity or ignorance.

Contempt for the keys ought to be said to be fomented rather than abolished as long as those who ought to resist abuse of the keys are divided among themselves and impede themselves, whether through stupidity or laziness, so that a procession in the house of God might not be made by common consent, some supporting abuses, others wanting to remove them. The truth is that every favorable and humble way ought to be attempted with the Supreme Pontiff, as long as he, being badly informed, issues unjust sentences, either on his own or through his [subordinates], because he might desist and reform. But if humble diligence produces nothing, a manly and courageous freedom ought to be assumed.[21]

Behold how well to our purpose Jean Gerson speaks! To believe, therefore, that all censures ought to be observed proceeds from ignorance, which is especially inappropriate and injurious in priests and religious who have undertaken the office of reading and teaching in public. And such [ignorance] even today has grown to such a degree that many blind and rash persons affirm that all those coming to our convent or speaking to us are, *ipso facto,* excommunicated; although this at any rate is very doubtful, since this is not expressly stated in the words of the aforesaid brief, but in fact the Pontiff only warns them under similar pain of excommunication. However, doctors [of canon law] commonly hold that when it is said: "I warn you under pain of excommunication," unless it is added: "which you, acting contrarily, incur *ipso facto,*" he has not *been* excommunicated but may in future *be* excommunicated, and today this usage has commonly been maintained everywhere. Indeed, to assert a doubtful thing as certain in this case proceeds either from malignity and presumption or from ignorance, especially because penalties ought to be used sparingly, nor can anyone be condemned by law in a doubtful case. And in this also their blindness and

---

21. Considerations 7–12. The full text of Gerson's "Considerations" can be found in *Oeuvres complètes,* ed. Msgr. Glorieux, vol. 6: *L'oeuvre ecclésiologique* (Paris: Descle, 1965), pp. 294–296; and in *Opera omnia,* ed. Louis Ellies du Pin, vol. 2, part 3 (Hildesheim: Georg Olms, 1987), cols. 422–424.

ignorance are made fully manifest, that they preach that those who converse with me or come to our convent ought to be shunned, not knowing that it was ordained by Pope Martin V at the Council of Constance and thereafter that the faithful are scarcely bound to shun the excommunicated, whether in divine services or outside them, unless their names have been expressly made public and denounced, and also at the Council of Basel it was reaffirmed, except in cases of physical assault against ecclesiastical persons. Whence, even if it were posited that the aforesaid excommunication is valid, it would not necessitate that such persons be shunned. But because our priests and religious, devoting their time all day to prayers and readings, rarely or never rest, they are so troubled by [this] crass ignorance and blindness, that I may make no mention of more serious matters. Pray, indeed, for the Church, so that God may finally deign to illumine her, as [He has] from the beginning. Farewell in Christ.

Letter from Savonarola to Pope Alexander VI
Florence, 13 October 1497

Most Blessed Father, after kissing your blessed feet:

As a son sorrowing over the displeasure of his father importunes and seeks out every pathway and avenue to placate him, nor despairs on account of any repulse of his customary filial reverence, as it is written: "Ask and it shall be given to you, knock and it shall be opened to you" [Matt. 7:7], thus also I, troubled more on account of Your Holiness' interdicted favor than on account of any other loss, repeatedly fly to your feet, entreating that my outcry may be heard at last in your presence, and that you not desire that I be any longer torn from your bosom. For to whom but to the Shepherd as one of his sheep should I go, whose voice and blessing I implore and am eager to hear, and whose saving presence I desire? Already I would have fallen at your feet, if a route safe from the injuries and plots of my enemies had been known to me. Which, indeed, when it may be possible without misgiving, I intend to do, and I desire with my whole mind to be able to absolve myself at last from every calumny. Meanwhile in everything, as I have always done, I humbly subject myself to Your Majesty, and if anything has been mistaken through foolishness or inadvertency, I supplicate your forgiveness, for no jot of malice shall you ever discover in me. I beg, therefore, that Your Holiness deign not to withdraw the fount of your kindness and mercy from me, whom, if once you have acknowledged me your own, you shall find me no less devoted to you than sincere, and your most obedient servant at all times. I commend myself humbly to Your Blessedness.

From the convent of San Marco in Florence, on the thirteenth of October 1497.

The most devoted son and little servant of Your Blessedness,

Brother Girolamo of Ferrara, of the Order of Preachers.

Letter from Savonarola to Pope Alexander VI

Florence, 13 [3] March 1498[22]

Most Blessed Father:

Since the duty of a Christian is to defend the honor of God, the faith of our Lord Jesus Christ, and rectitude of life, for my part, seeing that, on account of the example of many pastors, the sheep of Christ wander utterly from the way, I, preaching the truth of the Gospels, invigorating the faith, teaching the Christian life, and prophesying future evils, by the inspiration of God so that I might provoke people to penance, busying myself to nourish the peace in this city, and, on account of all of these things, suffering persecution from the wicked, merited from Your Blessedness at least not such contradiction, but every assistance. You, however, on the contrary, although you have heard and perused my very clear excuses and justifications and have understood the whole truth of my preaching [*predicationum*],[23] which only the wicked and enemies of the Cross of Christ boldly lie that they know nothing of and cease not to impugn, you, I say, Most Blessed Father, have given ear to all my detractors, and withdrawing from me all assistance, which you ought to offer not only as a Christian but by reason of the office you hold, you have given authority and power to wolves. Truly the Lord, "Who chooses the weak of the world so that He might confound the strong" [I Cor. 1:27], has heard the prayers of His poor; therefore, it has been arranged that this truth—on account of which we suffer evils from you—shall be proved against you and against all His other adversaries by natural causes and divine signs; these things truly shall come about openly, and they shall be proved with causes and signs such as all those who impede this work of God shall regret to hear, for the praise of men we do not seek in these things, who look forward to death for the sake of Christ with the greatest desire. And so, Most Blessed Father, do not delay to take thought for your salvation. Farewell.

At Florence, on the third Ides of March 1498.
The useless servant of Jesus Christ,
Brother Girolamo Savonarola of Ferrara,
by his own hand.

22. Though the date is clearly given as the third Ides of March (hence, the thirteenth), Ridolfi, the editor of the letters, postulates that this is an error (*Le lettere di Girolamo Savonarola* [Florence: Olschki, 1933], p. clxxiii). The papal brief to which it responds was received in Florence on 28 February, and the Signory sent its reply on 3 March (Roberto Ridolfi, *Life of Girolamo Savonarola*, trans. Cecil Grayson [New York: Knopf, 1959], pp. 223–226).
23. Savonarola may here be playing (subconsciously?) on the one-letter difference between preaching (*predicationum*) and prophecy (*predictionum*).

Letter from Savonarola to Pope Alexander VI

Florence, 13 [3] March 1498
Alternate Version[24]

Most Blessed Father:

After I had seen that other pastors of the Church by their depraved example, as well as unwholesome doctrine, were sending the sheep committed to their care into error and through many outrages leading the way to Hell, I used to consider that the function of my office was sometimes to defend the truth of Catholic doctrine, sometimes to correct [and] denounce corrupt morals and to recall [the strayed] to Christian discipline, for the honor of God and the exaltation of the sacred faith. Indeed, while I did this and had my hands full leading the people into the narrow way through the proclamation of scourges soon to come to sinners, tribulation and difficulty found me, in which there is no one who consoles or helps me. And it is true I used to hope that Your Holiness would rise up to my aid and for my sake fight against the enemies of the faith; I see that things have turned out otherwise for me. Since Your Holiness seems to have rejected so many defenses of my innocence and so many reasons set forth by me, not to plead excuses for sins but to demonstrate the integrity of the doctrine which I preach and to show my humility, with which I revere Your Holiness and the Holy Roman Church, and to give ear to my adversaries, just so I suppose in the future I ought to expect in vain any assistance from Your Holiness, which I ought rightly to receive from you both as a Christian and as the Supreme Pastor. Thus, the power to savage me has been given to feral wolves. But for all that, in Him "Who chooses the weak of the world so that He might confound the strong" [I Cor. 1:27] I trust that I will be heard by Him on account of this truth, for the sake of which I suffer and sustain all these things, and that all those who hound and hinder the work of God which I have attempted to carry out will pay the penalty, seeing that I, by the example of Christ, have never sought my own glory, nor do I seek it;

---

24. This second version of Savonarola's last letter to Alexander was not delivered. No evidence indicates which was composed first. Ridolfi, in his *Vita*, alternates between theories that this "cruder" version was written first in a burst of passion and that it was written later as Savonarola brooded in increasing bitterness. The editors of the most recent edition of this correspondence opt for the latter view. See Roberto Ridolfi, *Vita di Girolamo Savonarola* (Rome: Belardetti, 1952), p. 634, n. 35 (the notes are omitted from the English translation); and *Lettere e scritti apologetici,* ed. Roberto Ridolfi, Vincenzo Romano, and Armando Verdi, Edizione Nazionale delle Opere di Girolamo Savonarola (Rome: Belardetti, 1984), p. 403.

and I look forward with the greatest desire to death. Let Your Holiness not delay to take thought for your own salvation.

Dated from Florence, the third Ides of March, in the Roman style, 1498. The useless servant of Jesus Christ,
Brother Girolamo Savonarola,
by his own hand.

Moral Reform II

Bonfire of Vanities II:
27 February 1498

Exodus, Sermon III

Quinquagesima Sunday[1]

    Sermon . . . delivered on 25 February 1497[8], Carnival Sunday, in the Church of Santa Maria del Fiore, recorded by . . . Lorenzo Violi from the living voice of [Fra Girolamo] while he was preaching.

    In exitu Israel de Aegypto domus Iacob de populo barbaro. Facta est Iudaea santificatio eius, Israel potestas eius, etc.[2] — Ps. 113:1–2

Because we, dearly beloved in Christ Jesus, are on the battlefield to fight against the lukewarm, who go about sowing much evil to the ruin and destruction of souls, for this reason, in previous sermons, we have demonstrated their errors. In the first sermon we showed how the excommunication has no validity for many reasons, which I told you at that time.[3] In the second we entered upon a further point, that is, who it was who clearly understood the purpose for which this excommunication had been imposed, and, more particularly, who brought it about; and since the inferences which I had proposed to you had been certified as true, we said and proved to you that anyone who obstinately maintained that it was valid was a heretic. Rest assured that if they believe otherwise, they are not Christians. The first inference concerned the variation in the letters coming from Rome, and you saw that they contained such variation that it could be demonstrated that they were executed by a pea-brain. The second was that this excommunication was enacted in order to undermine the public good of this city, and this is manifest not only all over Italy but even outside of Italy. The third was that we have presented justification for everything we have done, as is evident both in our books and writings published openly and in the letters sent to Rome. The fourth was that this doctrine which I have preached to you increases the kingdom of Christ and diminishes the kingdom of the devil. Furthermore, I showed you by natural reasoning that it was the teach-

---

1. The Sunday immediately preceding the beginning of Lent.
2. "When Israel went forth out of Egypt, the house of Jacob from a barbaric people, Judea was made His sanctification [means of making holy], Israel His dominion [means of governance]."
3. Discussion of the following points can be found in the letters included in this volume.

ing of Christ because it had the same effect as the teaching of Christ. Hold this for certain, that from the Ascension to today, while this preaching was held in abeyance, in this country more sins and greater were committed, and more frequently, than had ever been done before in times past since this mode of living commenced among the people. Therefore, I tell you that God is greatly enraged against you. I speak, I say, about the wicked. The fifth was that the reform of those who wanted us to join the Tuscan Congregation was irrational. The sixth was that I saw no one come to take on this work; rather, I saw many seeking to ruin it, and, nevertheless, I could not nor did I want to abandon it, since it is the work of God.

Having made these inferences, I proved with many reasons that anyone who obstinately upheld that this excommunication was valid was a heretic. I said, first, that since this excommunication forbade our preaching, which was the cause of increase in the kingdom of Christ and decrease in that of the devil, anyone who maintained its validity maintained also that the kingdom of Christ was not increasing and that that of the devil was growing, and, therefore, was a heretic. *Item,* I showed that, since this teaching had already been publicized in writing all over the world and had been approved by many worthy men, if it were now destroyed, it would cause great detriment to our faith, and, therefore, that anyone who maintained that the excommunication ought to prohibit it was a heretic. *Item,* anyone who did not want fraternal correction to be effected opposed the law of the Gospel, and, because this excommunication prohibited preaching and, consequently, fraternal correction, I said that anyone who obstinately upheld it was a heretic. *Item,* I showed you through the statement of St. Thomas that God (much less any man) could not dispense with the commandment which contains the aim of every law. *Ergo,* much less could one be commanded [to dispense with it]. Therefore, this excommunication, being contrary to charity, which is the aim of every law, was not valid, and so, anyone who obstinately upheld it was against charity and, so, also against Christ and, therefore, was a heretic. *Item,* I said that the commandment of charity is greater than that of marriage, and so, *if it should happen* that a woman had promised faith to one man and then had been married to another, had she then been excommunicated for her unwillingness to go with the second man, such an excommunication, which entails staying with the second, ought not to be observed, and anyone who maintained that such an excommunication should be observed in this way is a heretic. And so, I told you that, charity being much greater than marriage, anyone who maintained that this excommunication (which is against charity) was valid is a heretic. *Item,* I told you and showed that a turning toward the grace of the Holy Spirit accompanies this teaching, and that anyone who wants to resist the grace of the Holy Spirit (as does this excommunication) is a heretic, and so, I said that anyone who upholds it is a heretic. Then I showed you how that saying, *sententia pastoris sive iusta sive iniusta timenda est*,[4] was to be understood. I showed you that you ought not to give credence to the opinions of the learned, except insofar as they adduce reasons for them, and that many ignorant people do not understand what they say and have written as their [the learned's] opinions many false things and false books. I could point out to you more than a hundred most manifest errors. I do not want to say more; this was, in brief, the last sermon I gave. Now let us come to what I want to tell you this morning.

These reasons which I have outlined here go to the root and are not taken from up in the treetops. There are many who go rather to the leaves and branches than to the root of the matter. When you want to understand the laws clearly, look at the root and reason for which they are made. You, canon lawyers, have not made the laws; rather, they have proceeded directly from the theologians, and every time that the law does not accord with reason or with the law of the grace of Christ, especially in those things which concern the soul, it has no validity. And every time that reason does not accord with it, it does not come from the root of the tree, but is a dried-up branch. But do you know who is deceiving you? They are the lukewarm, especially those who appear to be so morally upright. These little women are deceived by them, and they believe that if one wears a cape, he must be learned and he must be a saint. I do not know how these others are formed [in their novitiate], but ours spend quite a few years and study for a long time before they are finished. The cape, I say, does not make one learned and does not make one saintly. Go and see: in religious orders there are many who understand nothing of grammar, and yet they preach, and they learn their sermons from the manuals (it is necessary to uncover the truth). I must tell you about one [of my experiences]: I myself, also, was once deceived, but I made the best of it. There was a religious who would say to me, "Give me some argument in logic and philosophy," and I would give it to him; he even requested that it be in the vulgar tongue. Then he would go and preach, and he would seem to be a capable man; sometimes he would err, but one would not notice it unless he were learned. It would be the same as for one who plays music; although he might not strike the notes exactly so, to anyone who was not in the know or was not a maestro, he would seem to play well. For this reason, I tell you that they know nothing, and it is necessary to uncover the truth. Anyone who wants to know needs

4. "The judgment of a pastor, just or unjust, ought to be feared"; Gregory the Great, *Homilia XXVI in Evang.*; see *A Dialogue concerning Prophetic Truth*, bk. VII, at page 125, note 33, above; and the Open *Letter against the Recently Imposed Sentence of Excommunication*, at page 304, note 18, above.

to study both in books and by living a good life, not to go visiting all day long with the little women, persuading them not to attend the sermon.

Now, against these lukewarm I want to expound the psalm we have chosen this morning. Come forward, you lukewarm, for I have taken you by the arm this morning, be you a priest or a friar or whatever you will. I speak particularly of those who seem to be so morally upright and stand there like sacred images. I want to show you that you have nothing good within, but that you are [merely] a painted image. I will show it to you through this psalm. "O Father, don't you want us to begin reading the book [Exodus] this morning? Haven't you chosen it?" "Yes, we have chosen it, but this morning we shall expound this psalm: *In exitu Israel de Aegypto*. And because we have been taken out of Egypt, we want to sing *alleluia, alleluia,* and we want to rejoice." "Oh," you will say, "the Church does not sing *alleluia* now, in Septuagesima,[5] but says: *Circumdederunt me dolores mortis*"[6] [Ps. 17:5]. Go, tell the lukewarm to sing this, and let them say that they are surrounded by the pains of death. We want to sing *alleluia* and to rejoice with our Lord, Who has taken us out of Egypt. And then this Lent we shall explain to you the book of Exodus, wherein you will see the tribulations and persecutions that were inflicted by the Pharaoh on the people of God. But have no doubt that we, too, want to cross the Red Sea, and Pharaoh will not be able to do anything to us. Now let me make a brief pause.

We need to arrange it so that all those who are engaged in study come to hear the sermon, and that they listen for a little to the law of Christ, and they know for what purpose the laws were made, and how they are to be understood. It is a shame that they stretch the laws, each as he wants, and they engage in lengthy disputes; it is necessary, I tell you, to get outside of the subtlety of the law sometimes. Come now, I have told you to rejoice and sing *alleluia* in order that you might know what the law of Christ is and have clear consciences. Let us first see what law is. According to the theologians, *lex est ordinatio rationis a principe promulgata propter bonum commune.*[7] That is: "A law is nothing other than an ordinance of reason promulgated by a prince for the preservation of the common good." It says "an ordinance of reason" because the law is made in order to live uprightly according to reason. Second, it says "made by a prince" because it needs to have compulsory force. Third, it says "promulgated" because, if it were not public and

---

5. The third Sunday before the beginning of Lent and, hence, the whole of the brief season (two and a half weeks: Septuagesima, Sexagesima, and Quinquagesima) before. The season of Lent itself is Quadragesima, meaning "fortieth" (forty days).
6. "The pains of death encompassed me"; from the Introit for Septuagesima Sunday.
7. "A law is an ordinance of reason promulgated by a prince for the common good"; Thomas Aquinas, *Summa theologica*, part 1.2, quest. 90, art. 4.

known, men would not know how to uphold and observe it. Fourth, it says "for the common good" because otherwise it would not be law, if it had not been made for the universal welfare. So God, Prince of the universe, makes His laws for the welfare of creatures, in other words, the law of nature, the promulgation of which is nothing other than the impression by which it follows some inclination.[8] For instance, the inclination which the stone has to go down is given to it by natural law; the fire's inclination to go up is given to it by natural law. The inclination of the vine to make grapes comes from natural law. Man also has his own law of natural light given to him by God, but because of the reluctance of the flesh, he needs another law, that is, the law of grace, and this is the law of Christ, which, the more it enfolds a man, the more it draws him to God. It becomes almost a second natural law, inclined toward living uprightly and impelled toward eternal things, especially when perfect and moral men are completely absorbed in that grace. When this law is perfected in them—as it is in the blessed—they cannot turn back, because they are fixed on their goal, like the stone, which by reason of its own law has the inclination to go down—if you were to throw it up a hundred times, it would always return to its inclination and its law.

This law of Christ and His grace, He wrote it first in the hearts of the Apostles and then, through them, in the hearts of others. He never wrote it in a book or on paper. Consider what kind of law this is which Christ introduced all over the world, and yet He never wrote a book of laws. Know, then, that anyone who does not have this law of Christ within him cannot very well understand any other law. But you who have this law of Christ will well understand the purpose of these other laws. Wherefore, I will exult this morning that you are the epistle of Christ, wherein through our ministry His law is written; you do not have it written in any book, but in your hearts. There is a very great difference between having it written in the heart and having it written in books, as great as that between grace and ink, between the pen and the Holy Spirit, between man and God, between paper and the heart. Oh, a great difference, indeed! You have it, I say, this law of Christ, written in your hearts. I do not say [that you have] what is written in their books or the words which I speak to you here, but that by which you feel moved within.

Do you want to see if the inclination which is in your hearts comes from the law of Christ? Look at the fruit: *a fructibus eorum cognoscetis eos*[9] [Matt. 7:16]. If you want to identify an olive tree, you look at the fruit; if you want to identify an apple tree, you look at the fruit; if you want to identify a vine, you look at the fruit. Consider, then, if this law produces, in those who have

---

8. Ibid., quest. 93, art. 5.
9. "By their fruits you will know them."

it, the same fruit it produced at the time of the Apostles in the hearts of those who were converted and believed. They had this inclination toward living uprightly, doing good works, having a great love for Christ, loving martyrdom. So, this is the same law. You have seen and felt palpably that this is the work of Christ, wholly like His other works; I have shown you the similarities many times, and I could show you many more if I wanted to run through the Holy Scriptures.

Do you want to see one of them now? Look at those who believed in Christ: you will find that the scribes and the Pharisees, who were the learned and religious men at that time, did not believe in Him; rather, they contradicted Him and always have contradicted Him. But the people, the common folk, were the ones who believed in Him, in Christ. Thus, you know that it is written that the scribes and Pharisees said to their soldiers: *"num quid aliquis ex principibus credit in eum? [. . .] Turba haec quae non novit legem maledicti sunt"*[10] [Ioh. 7:48–49]. See, then, today the opposition of the priests to this work, while the populace and the common folk believe in it, and so it is similar to Christ's. *Furthermore,* tell me: did any leaders of the priests believe in Christ? You know well they did not. Thus, as our quotation says, they said: *"num quid aliquis ex principibus credit in eum?"* Consider if any prelates who are the leaders of the priests today believe in Him. But see if this work is similar to that. Go, see also that at that time they used to say of Christ: *quia "seducit turbas"*[11] [Ioh. 7:12]. That is, they said that He deceived the people. They say the same today of this work. *Moreover,* an edict was then issued that anyone who believed in Christ *extra Synagogam fieret*[12] [Ioh. 9:22], that is, they were to be excommunicated. Does it not seem to you that this is still done today against this work? *Moreover,* they said of Christ: *venient Romani et tollent locum nostrum*[13] [Ioh. 11:48]. That is, they feared that, for believing in Christ, the Romans would remove the rulership from their hands. Likewise today, our priests fear that for coming to hear the sermon they might lose their benefices. Does this not seem to you to be the same thing? *Furthermore,* when the scribes and Pharisees plotted to kill Christ, they did not want to enter Pilate's palace, because they were fearful, since it was Passover, of being contaminated, but they thought nothing of the death of Christ or of having Him crucified. Hear how subtle was the conscience of the Pharisees! Similarly today, they have scruples about excommunication, and, on the other hand, they keep a concubine and a boy. And

10. "Do any of the leaders believe in Him? . . . This multitude, which does not know the law, is accursed."
11. "That 'he seduced the crowd' "; *quia* is substituted for *sed*.
12. "Were to be put out of the synagogue."
13. "The Romans will come and take our place."

so you see that this work [of ours] is similar to that of Christ. If you have eyes, then, you must know that this is the work of Christ. *Furthermore,* if you are a philosopher and you want a reason, tell me: is not living uprightly what leads man to his purposed end? This doctrine leads man to live uprightly; *ergo,* it leads him to his end. What more manifest signs do you want?

Let us rejoice, then, all the good, for you know that this is the work of God, because you have the law of Christ written in your hearts, and, so, sing *alleluia, alleluia.* Let the first *alleluia* be for the joy you have here and now, so that you might remain ever joyful in these tribulations. The second will be for the joy we will have then, in the other life. Let this suffice as regards the title; now let us turn to the psalm.

In exitu Israel de Aegypto, domus Iacob de populo barbaro. The people of Israel, when they were in Egypt, lived among the Egyptians, such that they became half Egyptian in speech, in customs, and in almost everything, and yet God decided to free them. It so happened at that time that the lukewarm were mixed with the good, and the good could no longer be distinguished from the bad, and they were all becoming one big lump of dough, as it were. Is it not so? I remember that when I was in the world I had this thought, and I used to say, "What kind of life is this?" The ranks of the good could not be distinguished from those of the bad. I would wonder and say, "Are we Christians or pagans?" I saw many who had the names of Jove, Juno, and Venus in their mouths together with Christ's. I was stupefied. I would look at the prelates and not know how to tell whether they were lords or priests. For this reason, we were in the deepest darkness, and yet God has at this time sent light to the world and has taken us out of Egypt, that is, out of darkness, because "Egypt" is interpreted "darkness." Whence our psalm says: *In exitu Israel de Aegypto.* That is, we have come out from the darkness of Egypt. We have also come out of tribulation, for, as you know, you seemed to be in dire straits and unable to live any longer in that way. *Domus Iacob de populo barbaro:* you also have come forth from the hands of a barbaric people; you, I say, house of Jacob, which is interpreted "uprooter," that is, you who have uprooted vices and sins have come forth from the hands of a barbaric people. "Barbaric" is applied to a people without law. See, today the priests and religious are unbridled and without law. God has freed you from their hands; render thanks to God for this. Barbarians are said to be those who do not speak one of the three tongues, that is, Hebrew, Greek, and Latin, but in God's realm, a barbarian is one who does not have a Christian tongue, or one who has loosed it in murmuring and speaking ill. Barbarians are also said to be those with ugly faces, called barbaric visages. Look at those who believe and those who do not believe; you will be able to distinguish the barbarian faces from the angelic faces. So, you ought to thank God for separating you from all these barbarians. *Facta est Iudea sanctificatio eius:* "Judea has been made a sanctification." "Judea" means *confessio*. This means the confessions you have made, by which you have been sanctified in the Lord. *Israel potestas eius.* "Israel" means *videns Deum*,[14] that is, those who see God through faith and who have become good are made the power of the Lord. We have already been at war for seven years, and we have always conquered; whence has this power come? We have not had money or soldiers, but enemies nearly everywhere, and always we have won. This, then, has been Israel, that is, *videns Deum*, that is, the good, who see God; our arms have been prayers, faith and patience.

Mare vidit et fugit[15] [Ps. 113:3]. "The sea has seen and fled." The sea signifies "bitterness."[16] Bitter things and the temptations of the flesh have fled. This sea no longer disturbs you. Another sea is the devil, whom you have also conquered, and who no longer prevails upon you to commit sin, as he used to do. Another sea which has fled are the wicked, who have separated themselves from you, give you a wide berth, and no longer want you to remain among them. *Iordanis conversus est retrorsum*[17] [Ps. 113:3]. That is, "the Jordan has turned back." This means that you, who have heard that a judgment is coming upon Italy, have turned back and done penance. "Jordan" is interpreted "river of judgment," and, indeed, your judgment has turned back, but that of the wicked has not turned back. *Montes exultaverunt ut arietes*[18] [Ps. 113:4], that is, "the mountains (which signifies perfect men or preachers or prelates) have exulted like rams," that is, like guardians of the flock. The mountains are high places upon which the sun shines before it reaches other places. Have no doubt, my children, that the mountains were the first ones illuminated by the Sun of Justice, Christ Jesus, and so, they have exulted like rams, that is, like bellwethers and guides of the lambs. From the mountains the sun has then come upon the hills. *Et colles sicut agni ovium*[19] [Ps. 113:4]; you are the hills, who have rejoiced and have exulted like lambs; you remain joyful in tribulation, and you desire martyrdom, because the Sun of Justice has touched you. *Quid est tibi mare quod fugisti?*[20] [Ps. 113: 5] "But you, sea, what has happened to you that you have fled?" The sea, as I have said, is concupiscence, the devil, and the wicked. Come here, concupiscence, where have you fled? I speak to those who have become good, who used to be afire with concupiscence every hour of the day. Where have

---

14. "Seeing God."
15. "The sea saw and fled."
16. Savonarola puns here on *mare* ("the sea") and *le cose amare* ("bitterness").
17. "The Jordan was turned back."
18. "The mountains exulted like rams."
19. "And the hills like the lambs of sheep."
20. "Why is it, sea, that you have fled?"

you fled, devil, you who no longer overpower these good ones with temptation? Where have you hidden yourselves, you wicked ones? That is, where is the sword and your persecutions, which the good no longer fear? *Et tu, Iordanis, quia conversus es retrorsum?*[21] [Ps. 113:5] The Jordan stands for the good, who have turned away from sin back to penance. Come here, sinner, what is it that has made you turn back? What has been promised to you? Not gold, not silver, but rather, tribulations. *Et bene facere et mala pati;*[22] so, you have left your pleasures to come and suffer evil. It has been the grace of God, then, which has made you turn back. *Montes exultastis ut arietes et colles sicut agni ovium*[23] [Ps. 113:6]; "the mountains have exulted like rams and the hills like the lambs of the sheep." This means that the high mountains illuminated by God, as well as the humble hills and all the good, have made a great feast and have had and now have great joy, and they rejoice always and everywhere and sing, *ecce quam bonum et quam iocundum habitare fratres in unum*[24] [Ps. 132:1]. Indeed, you see that the good have rejoiced.

A facie Domini mota est terra[25] [Ps. 113:7]. That is, "by the face of the Lord the earth has been moved." O my Lord, what is Your face? Your face is Your Son; Christ is Your face. O holy face, O beautiful face, O sweet face, O face full of all graciousness! You, my Lord, with Your face have moved the whole earth. The earth of the good, I say, has been moved to goodness. The earth of the wicked has been moved to wickedness. *Hic positus est [. . .] in resurrectionem multorum [. . .] et insignum cui contradicetur*[26] [Luc. 2:34]. This Lord has been placed on this Cross for the salvation of the good and the ruin of the wicked. *A facie Dei Iacob*[27] [Ps. 113:7]. Jacob means "uprooter." The earth, then, will be moved by the face of Jacob. Have no doubt that we shall uproot sins in every way with the grace of the Lord, because He is the One Who converts every sinner. *Qui convertit petram in stagna aquarum*[28] [Ps. 113:8]. This is the Lord Who converts stone into pools of water. The stone is the hard heart. O my Lord, how many hearts of stone have You converted into pools of water? You have converted my heart into a pool of tears. *Et rupem in fontes aquarum*[29] [Ps. 113:8]. You have converted

21. "And you, Jordan, that you have turned back?"
22. "And to do good and suffer evil."
23. "[Why is it that] you, mountains, exulted like rams, and you, hills, like the lambs of the sheep?"
24. "See how good and how delightful it is for brothers to live together in unity."
25. "By the face of the Lord the earth has been moved."
26. "This [Child] has been put here . . . for the resurrection of many . . . and a sign which will be contradicted."
27. "By the face of the God of Jacob."
28. "Who has turned stone into pools of water."
29. "And cliffs into fountains of water."

high cliffs into fountains; the high cliff is the proud mind; You have converted it into a fountain of tears; You have subjugated it to humility. And
this has been through Your grace, not through the merit of men.

And so, Lord, let the praise be given to You, not to us. *Non nobis,
Domine, non nobis, sed nomini tuo da gloriam*[30] [Ps. 113:9/1]. "Give glory not
to us, Lord, but to Your name." May You be glorified, may You be blessed
a thousand times. *Super misericordia tua et veritate tua*[31] [Ps. 113:10/2]. May
You be praised, Lord, for Your mercy, because You have shown mercy to
the good and have given them Your light. May You also be praised for Your
truth, because You have always wanted and do want to attend to Your promises to them. Oh, Lord, come quickly to fulfill Your promises to Your elect,
ne quando dicant gentes: "ubi est Deus eorum?"[32] [Ps. 113:10/2] That is, "so that
the nations and the wicked might not say, 'Where is their God?'" And so
that they might not insult You, as they have done up to now. Lord, we pray
that You may be with us and that we may keep Your commandments. This
is Your law, which we want to have written in our hearts. This the lukewarm
do not have. But do you want to see whether it is true? Wait, and I will
show you what they are made of.

Whoever has this law is blessed; this is the law of laws. Hold fast to this
law so that God, having taken you out of Egypt, will help you and set you
straight. Go straight to God, and hold fast to this law and have no fear of
excommunication. "But," the lukewarm say, "we, too, have this law. We do
penance and many good works." You lukewarm, I remind you of one thing:
take care that you do not become martyrs for the devil; attend to what this
morning's epistle says: *si montes transferam, caritatem autem non habuero, nihil
sum*[33] [I Cor. 13:2]. I tell you, you lukewarm, that although you may be able
to perform good exterior works, if you do not have charity and this law of
Christ in your heart, you accomplish nothing, and you will end up in the
house of the devil. "But," you will say, "how do you know that I do not
have this law?" I will show you clearly that you do not have it.

Come along this way, you lukewarm, for I have taken you by the arm
this morning; stay a moment and listen to me, for I will show you clearly.
He will not want to listen, because he has no ears, as you will hear below.
Now, come close, you lukewarm; I know that you study philosophy, and
that you hold it dearer [to your heart] to be called a philosopher than a
Christian. When you go to him and tell him that he is a good philosopher,

---

30. "Not to us, Lord, not to us, but to Your name give glory."
31. "For the sake of Your mercy and Your truth."
32. "Lest the nations say, 'Where is their God?'"
33. "If I should move mountains, but do not have charity, I am nothing"; *si* substituted for *ut*.

he rejoices more and holds it dearer than if you were to tell him that he is a good Christian, and he waves his hand with that beautiful gesture and swells with pride. Now, since you hold it so dear to be called a philosopher, I want to demonstrate to you by means of your philosophy that you do not have the law of Christ in your heart. Aristotle says *in the second book of De coelo et mundo* — after proving that it is necessary for earth to exist, as well as its opposite, that is, the other elements [air, fire, water], because the universe is lacking in none of its species — he continues and says: *quod, posito uno contrariorum in rerum natura, ponitur et reliquum.*[34] That is, "if one contrary is posited, it *immediately* follows from this that the other must also exist." And so, if it is posited that earth is cold and dry, it shows that air is hot and humid by reason of contrariety. And if it is posited that fire is hot and dry, it follows from this that there must be a contrary entity which is cold and humid, and this is water. So, if you posit one contrary, it follows *immediately* from this that there must be an opposite. But if you were to say, "I see the fire here, and I see the water: how do I know that they are two contraries? How do I come to recognize this?" The method for recognizing them is this: put them together, one right next to the other, and you will immediately see a battle, one fighting against the other. But note that the substances of things are not contraries; water and fire, insofar as they are substances, are not contraries, but the forces within them are contraries. You see there a dog which appears to be a wolf; put it next to a wolf, and you will see that they are contraries and that they will bite each other. Likewise, if you see a wolf which appears to you to be a dog, and it lies still and sleeps, if you put a dog next to it, you will see that it is a wolf, and you will see them start a war of contraries and fight each other. This is due to the contrary forces within them. Consider also: you have poisonous food, but you do not know that there is a venomous power within it; eat it, and you will see that it is contrary to the life force which you have within you.

If, then, when one contrary is posited to be in the world, it follows that there is another contrary, and that one contrary is recognized in its battle against the other, since Christ and His law are in the world, there is also His contrary, which is the devil and his law. The law of Christ is His grace, and as soon as this law begins to operate in the world, up jumps its contrary, which is the devil. At the time of the Apostles, who carried out the law of Christ, His contrary immediately leapt into action, and the devil came into the world to make a great contradiction to Him. And then it became known that the scribes and the Pharisees were members of the devil and contraries to Christ, Who was not recognized at first. They did not have the grace of

34. "That if one contrary in the nature of things is posited, the other is also posited"; *De caelo*, bk. 2, chap. 2, 286a.

Christ, but its contrary. At the time of the martyrs, because they had this law of Christ in their hearts and taught it to others, His contrary, that is, the devil, came forth, and he stirred up the tyrants to wage war against Him. At the time of the heretics, they and their heresies were the contrary of this law, and the more the grace of Christ grew in the world and the more His law grew in the hearts of the faithful, the greater was the contradiction against Him, for when you set one contrary next to another, the second leaps up to attack it. So you will always see, wherever the grace of Christ is, that evil men contradict it.

If you, lukewarm ones, say then that you have the grace of Christ and His law, where is the contradiction made against you? You say that you give yourselves to prayer and to good works, and *yet* we see that the wicked, who ought to be your contraries and make war against you, tip their hats to you and accord you every honor. This means that the force which you have within you is not contrary to theirs, and so, you do not have the law and the grace of Christ as you say. Do you want to see that there is nothing of the grace of Christ within these lukewarm ones and evil priests? See how fearful they are to lose their benefices through the contradiction of the wicked. "Friar, there are also good religious who contradict you." I tell you that they are not good. Consider that they have friendship with and are at one with those who are manifestly evil, and they get along well with those who, as is evident from their works, do not have the grace of Christ. Therefore, you must be like them. For if [in your opinion] these are not evil prelates, you are in accord with them and have an understanding with those who pay children to throw stones and with those who are manifestly wicked. So, you are exactly the same sort as they and are not their contrary, because one contrary cannot be next to the other without a fight. You see, you lukewarm, how I have caught you this morning; you cannot escape. Tell me: what does it mean that you want to absolve the usurers and those who take ten benefices, and yet you do not want to absolve those who want to do good? Poor little women, because they come to the sermon in order to learn to live like a Christian, you do not want to absolve, yet you are ready to absolve the wicked. This, then, is perfectly clear: that you are as wicked as they. You help them, you favor them; therefore, they are not your contrary, because one contrary has no peace alongside the other. And so, since the wicked do not have the grace of Christ, you, being like them, do not have it either. You are earthly men, and your God is on earth, but our God is in Heaven: *Deus autem noster in coelo*[35] [Ps. 113:11/3]. Our Lord is He Who is in Heaven, and He has made the sun shine upon the mountains and the hills and has enlightened the good with His truth. And although you, evil

---

35. "But our God is in Heaven."

ones, contradict the good, our Lord, Who is in Heaven, will aid us in every way, and we shall overcome. We are your contrary, and we want to be so as long as you are earthly men. The Apostles overcame their contraries because God was with them, and since God is with us, we have no fear of your contradictions. Now you understand what the lukewarm are made of, and that they do not have the grace and the law of Christ within them. But stay a bit to understand even better about their condition.

"O friar, a great war will be waged against you." Was not a great war waged against our Lord until they finally crucified Him? I fear nothing; make war as much as you want; it is enough for me that the Lord is with me. But you do not believe that the Lord is with us; believe that I am not crazy, that I know where I am, and that I would know how to get out of here, if I wanted, by human means. I know well their cunning and their subtle humors, so that if I were to trample my conscience underfoot, I, too, would know how to be cunning and sell anyone at market. But because I know that the Lord is with me, I fear nothing, *quia Deus noster in coelo*. Our God is in Heaven and also with us, *et omnia quaecumque voluit, fecit*[36] [Ps. 113:11/3]. He does what He wants, and He can and will do what pleases Him; He wants this work to go forward and achieve its end, and He will make it happen. But these evil ones have idols for their gods. The idols are lukewarm preachers: *simulacra gentium argentum et aurum*[37] [Ps. 113:12/4]. They are idols, these lukewarm ones, who are engaged in no war at all. Tell me: have you ever heard of a war being waged against idols? Certainly not. They have been strongly preached against, yes. But against Christ and His Apostles and the martyrs the greatest war and persecution were waged continually. *Nevertheless*, their teaching still stands its ground, while the idols have vanished in smoke. Consider: it is seven years now that we have had so much conflict, so many preachers against us, and so many idols, and I have not preached against them, and *yet* we are still here, while they have vanished in smoke. These idols, then, are vain. *Simulacra gentium argentum et aurum:* they put their trust in gold and in silver. Gold signifies wisdom, silver, eloquence; that is, they put their trust in human wisdom and in knowing how to speak well, and they believe that with their ornamented speech they can shade the truth. *Opera manuum hominum*[38] [Ps. 113:12/4]. Because they, with their works, which are works of men, put their trust in human things, but our work belongs to Him Who is in Heaven, and in Him is all our refuge.

Os habent et non loquuntur[39] [Ps. 113:13/5]. These lukewarm ones have a

---

36. "And anything whatsoever that He wanted, He has done."
37. "The images of the nations [the Gentiles] are silver and gold."
38. "The works of men's hands."
39. "They have mouths, and they do not speak."

mouth and do not speak, but they howl and bark, murmur and speak ill, they flatter the great lords and do not tell them the truth. However, they do not know how to speak, and they talk [their way] through all the houses, coloring the facts in their favor and turning the little women around so that they do not attend the sermons. O lukewarm ones, this is not the way; if you want to win, and you believe that God is not with us but with you, say your prayers and live a good life, and God will enlighten you and will make you overcome and uncover the truth. But you do not know how to pray, as the psalm says here, and you do not know how to speak. Do you want to see that they do not know how to speak? How the little women confound them, and they do not know what to say, but they become enraged and begin to curse and speak evilly? At the very least, O lukewarm, since you are enjoined [to do so], at least open your eyes and see. *Oculos habent et non videbunt*[40] [Ps. 113:13/5]. "They have eyes, and they do not see." The eyes of their intellect have the spectacles and the veil of avarice, and they say, "I do not want to lose my benefices." I say nothing of the spectacles of lust. It is no wonder, then, if you do not see. At least, if you do not see, believe one who gives you good counsel, since you are so overwrought. But they don't want to believe, and they don't want to hear. *Aures habent et non audient*[41] [Ps. 113:14/6]. They have ears, and they do not want to hear the sermons, and they do not want to read them either, and they do not want those who are subject to them to read them or hear them. Come here, you lukewarm, for what reason are you so opposed? You speak against these sermons, and yet you do not hear them, and you do not read them, so you contradict what you do not know. "Oh, it has been reported to me what you say." Perhaps what has been reported to you is false. St. Jerome and St. Augustine and the other holy Doctors [of the Church] did not behave the way you do. They wanted to see all the books of the heretics, and then they contradicted them and knew what they contradicted. At least, O lukewarm, if you do not hear, at least you might sense the odor of this fame of living uprightly which, as you see, has spread all over. You do not smell this good odor: *nares habent et non odorabunt*[42] [Ps. 113:14/6]. "They have noses, but they do not smell," yet those who are far off smell this odor. I received letters only yesterday from one who lives in a city of Italy, who has seen two previous sermons and says that anyone who does not believe in this work is scarcely a Christian, and even from Germany we have letters from those who believe in this. You should at least smell this odor of good fame of the work of Christ spread all over. But for the evil, good things put them in a bad odor. *Aliis factus*

---

40. "They have eyes, and they will not see."
41. "They have ears, and they will not hear."
42. "They have noses, and they will not smell."

(as the Apostle says) *Christi bonus odor, sumus aliis vitae in vitam, aliis mortis in mortem*[43] [II Cor. 2:15–16]. The wicked hate living uprightly. Now then, if you do not smell this odor, at least do good. *Manus habent et non palpabunt*[44] [Ps. 113:15/7]. "They have hands, and they do not feel"; they do no good deeds, except for external works and ceremonies, which count for nothing since they are without rectitude of heart. To feel is when you touch the hand of your friend; you feel that warmth, you clasp his hand, and it gives you comfort. These people feel no warmth from good deeds because they are frigid, full of hatred, envy, and pride, full of all their vices. Do you also know, you lukewarm, why you have no gusto in your actions? Because your affections have become disgusting.[45] *Pedes habent et non ambulabunt*[46] [Ps. 113:15/7]; "they have feet, and they do not walk." The feet are the earthly affections. Your affections are turned entirely toward the earth. I have told you that you are idols; idols are fixed with nails to the earth; likewise, you are nailed and fixed to earthly things, and this is the cause why you are hindered from doing good.

Now then, lukewarm, at least call on God to free you from these hindrances—but they will not do it. *Non clamabunt in gutture suo*[47] [Ps. 113:15/7]. They have mouths, and they do not speak; they make no prayers to God. Even worse, being evil themselves, they also make evil anyone who consorts with them. *Similes illis fiant qui faciunt ea et omnes qui confidunt in eis*[48] [Ps. 113:16/8]. Hear what the Holy Spirit says: "They become like them, those who do what they do and who confide in them." So, do not encumber yourselves with them; do not go to confess to them, because you will become lukewarm like them. You who have a lukewarm priest at home, you will become lukewarm like him. *Cum sancto sanctus eris, cum perverso perverteris*[49] [II Reg. 22:26–27]; "If you keep company with a saint, you, too, will

43. "To some we have been made [if *factus* is read *facti*] the good odor of Christ; we are to some [the odor] of life unto life, to others, of death unto death"; significantly altered. The Vulgate has: *quia Christi bonus odor sumus Deo in his qui salvi fiunt et in his qui pereunt, aliis quidem odor mortis in mortem, aliis autem odor vitae in vitam* ("for we are the good odor of Christ to God among those who are saved and among those who perish; to some, indeed, the odor of death unto death, but to others the odor of life unto life").
44. "They have hands, and they will not feel."
45. A pun: *sapete . . . perchè voi non avete gusto . . . Perchè voi avete guasto . . . ;* literally, "you have let your affections run to ruin."
46. "They have feet, and they will not walk."
47. "They will not call out with their throats."
48. "Let those who make these things become like to them, and all who put their trust in them."
49. "With the holy, you will be holy; with the depraved, you will be depraved."

become a saint; if you keep company with the depraved, you, too, will be depraved." Look at those women who go to confession with the lukewarm: they do nothing but speak ill; they are full of hatred and envy, and they are lukewarm like them. Keep company, then, with the good, and put your trust in Christ, Who is with us. Let me take a pause, and we shall continue with the psalm.

Does it not seem to you that these things are true? It does to me. "O Father, we chanced to miss your sermon." Do you know why? Because only a few live according to Christ, fewer than you would think. And if many miss them [now], many more will be missing them [in the future]. Few of us are left from this sifting [Luc. 22:31], and I fear that yet another sifting will be needed. Our Lord, speaking certain words, once made [such] a sifting, so that few remained with Him. This happened when He said: *"Ego sum panis vivus qui de coelo descendi [. . .] Caro mea vere est cibus, sanguis meus vere est potus, etc."*[50] [Ioh. 6:51, 56] That is: "I am the living bread; My flesh is truly food, My blood is truly drink." I can tell you that few remained with Him after this sifting. All the disciples left, except for the Twelve, and all those who left—hear what they were saying: *"durus est hic sermo"*[51] [Ioh. 6: 61]; "this speech is hard: to say that we are to eat the flesh and drink the blood of a man"—and they left. The Savior turned to the Twelve and said: *"num quid et vos vultis abire?"*[52] [Ioh. 6:68] "Do you also want to leave?" And St. Peter replied: *"Domine, verba vitae aeternae habes"*[53] [Ioh. 6:69]. "Lord, You have the words of eternal life." *"Ad quem ibimus?"*[54] [Ioh. 6:69] "To whom do You want us to go? We want to stay with You." So you see that at times there are such rigorous siftings that few remain afterward. O my Lord, if it were to happen that only one person could go to Paradise, I want to strive to be that one. "O friar, if all the world were to contradict you, what would you do?" I shall remain steadfast, because I know it comes from God. I do not say that this has to happen, God forbid.

Now, you know I have shown you that these lukewarm know nothing, and I have told you how this saying is to be understood: *sententia pastoris sive iusta sive iniusta timenda est,*[55] which they quote so much, and if you

50. "I am the living bread come down from Heaven . . . My flesh is true food, My blood is true drink, etc."
51. "This saying is hard."
52. "Do you also want to leave?"
53. "Lord, You have the words of eternal life."
54. "To whom should we go?" Savonarola has Peter's statements reversed.
55. "The judgment of a pastor, whether just or unjust, is to be feared"; Gregory the Great, *Homilia XXVI in Evang.,* see *A Dialogue concerning Prophetic Truth,* bk. VII, page 125, note 33, above; and the Open *Letter against the Recently Imposed Sentence of Excommunication,* page 304, note 18, above.

gloss it in another way from what I have told you, how can you salvage that text of Pelagius [*sic;* Pope Gelasius I], which I have quoted to you, that is, that you are not obligated to observe an unjust excommunication? Are you so mad as to assert that, if a sentence is unjust, I have to observe it? If a thing is unjust, then it is contrary to justice. So, then, we have to observe what is contrary to justice. *Item,* if justice is Christ, then it is contrary to Christ. Must I, then, observe what is contrary to Christ? *Item,* if it is contrary to Christ, then it comes from His adversaries, and His adversaries are the devils and their members; shall I, then, observe the law of the devil and his members? You are mad if you believe that I have to observe a law made by devils. I have not sinned in this, in not observing the excommunication. The excommunicate is one who executes unjust excommunications, or one who causes them to be executed. I could present a hundred arguments to demonstrate to you that it does not have to be either observed or feared. "O Father, yet the canons say that, if the error [in it] should be hidden, even though the excommunication were unjust, it would have to be feared." Indeed, this is so. For example, if you were excommunicated for not giving a hundred ducats to a person to whom in truth you were not a debtor, but you were universally believed to be a debtor, then you would have to observe it, that is, not go to Mass, in order not to give scandal to your neighbor. But if everyone did not believe this, and you had publicly defended your case, then I say that you do not have to fear it, nor are you obligated to observe the excommunication, because the scandal has been removed; in that case, come to me, and I will give you Communion. But had you been excommunicated in such a way that, by observing the excommunication, you would act contrary to charity, then you would be obligated not to observe it. For instance, if you had been forbidden, under pain of automatic excommunication, to give food to someone in dire necessity, you would be obligated not to observe such a command. Do you think that the laws are made in order to do evil? If so, a wicked Pope could despoil the whole Church, if he wanted to, and his unjust decisions would be held valid. But come here, you priests who fear to take part with excommunicates: what about the decree of Pope Martin which states that taking part with an excommunicate, if he has not been publicly denounced by name, unless he has struck a clergyman in public, does not incur any censure?[56] "Oh, I do not know if that decree has been approved." Blessed Antoninus[57] says it is valid and that he

---

56. Bull of Martin V, *Ad evitanda animarum pericula,* in *Bibliotheca canonica, iuridica, moralis, theologica,* ed. F. L. Ferrari (Rome: Typografia Polyglotta, 1886), p. 469.
57. St. Antonio Pierozzi (1389–1459), Archbishop of Florence from 1446 to 1459. A Dominican and reformer like Savonarola, he attended the Council of Florence (1439).

has heard it held *to be worthy of faith* by men worthy of faith. Show me a man of equal authority who maintains the contrary.

These excommunications today are cheap commodities; for four lire anyone can have anyone he likes excommunicated. They are given to anybody who wants them, these excommunications. I tell the truth: I do not believe such excommunications carry any weight with God, because of the liberality and abundance with which they are handed out. The Church should not so quickly recur to excommunication on the slightest pretext. You can see for yourself how much these excommunications are worth. But you will remain obstinate, and I know you will not believe what I have told you. But if this had happened under the previous government, you would say that it had no validity and would welcome everyone as you did then. I have been well informed that in San Marco there was then a prior who meant to observe it. Now then, let us leave behind the excommunication; what are we to do now? Listen, for I shall tell you.

O you religious, O Rome, O Italy, I call on the whole world: come forward. What I tell you either is from God, or it is not. If it is from God, you cannot attack it, and if you do attack it, you will lose to your great harm. If it is not from God, it will soon fail by itself. Why so much contradiction, then? O Rome, *durum est tibi contra stimulum calcitrare*[58] [Act. 9:5, omitted in modern editions of the Vulgate; 26:14]. It will be a hard thing for you to kick against the goad. O Rome, I warn you, O naysayers and prelates of Rome, I warn you that if this is from God, *for the very reason that* it is from God, you must not spoil it, but it is this very thing which has made you tear down the wall. But it is not completely torn down yet. O wicked citizens, O you lukewarm, you will collapse under this weight. When you think you have stifled it, it will surge up again, livelier than ever, and the wall will fall down upon you. O Lord, I wish You would hasten. I can [do] no more.

And so that He may hasten all the more, I want you, dearly beloved, all to make orations on the day of Carnival, and all jointly to pray fervently to God and to say a Mass. I will take the Sacrament in hand, and I want everyone then to pray fervently, that if this matter is from me and I am deceiving you, Christ may send a fire from Heaven upon me to swallow me then and there into Hell, but if it is from God, that He may hasten quickly. And so that you may be very clear [on this point], have prayers said in all your monasteries, and tell even the lukewarm to come; tell them to pray on that morning that God may rescue you, and that if I am deceiving you, may a fire fall on this friar and kill me. Write it everywhere, dispatch messengers

58. "It is hard for you to kick against the goad."

to Rome and everywhere, and have prayers said on that day that, if this is not from God, evil may befall me, as I have said, but if it is from God, pray that the Lord may hasten and show a sign that this is His work. I do not mean right now, because it is not yet time. "O friar, you say you will hold the Sacrament in your hand, but you perhaps do not believe in the faith, and, therefore, it will be of no concern to you." You are right that I do not believe in it, because I already know it, I am certain of it, and I have touched it with my hand. So now, speak in this fashion to the lukewarm: that if they do not believe that I believe in the faith, let them pray to their God, that is, to Christ, Who they say is their God, let them pray, then, to that God that He might kill me on that day, if this work is not from God. "O friar, you put yourself in great danger." No, I do not put myself in danger. You will see how I will rejoice with my Lord. Believe that I am not crazy, and I know what I am doing, and I would not set myself up as a target if I did not know that God is with me. I shall be strong; have everyone pray fervently. I shall have that verse sung, *Excita, Domine, potentiam tuam et veni*[59] [Ps. 79: 3]. That is, "show Your power now, Lord, and come to free us." And let everyone sing that verse, and pray fervently to God to free you. On that day I will give Communion to my brethren and, since Fra Domenico has promised to give you Communion, also to the laity, but I give notice that no one come to Communion unless he feels purified.

Come all, then, and let us pray fervently to God that He may unravel this matter and unmistakably set you free, since reasoning is worth almost nothing against so much malice in the wicked. We shall be there, as I have told you, with the Sacrament in hand. Tell one of these lukewarm that he also, with the Sacrament in hand, in the presence of the people, should make this experiment and have everyone pray that, if the matter is false, God may kill him in the sight of the people. You will see if he will tremble all over. *Furthermore,* the procession of these children will march later in the day. But be sure, little children, that you are serious and modest and that the procession advances in an orderly way, and have everyone pray. *Moreover,* I remind you, children, that you no longer shout out, "Long live Christ," unless I ask you, because these things have to come from the Spirit, and they are not appropriate everywhere. Now then, we want to wage a great war against the devil at this time, and remove the fleshly delights of the devil, and introduce the spiritual delights of God. But the wicked will give themselves to worldly delights. Now on that day, let everyone pray that God may reveal if this is false and that, if it is His truth, *for the very reason that* it is, He may hasten

59. "Rouse up Your power, Lord, and come."

and come straightway to free us. "But you, friar, what will you do on that day?" *Domus Israel speravit in Domino: adiutor eorum et protector eorum est*[60] [Ps. 113:17/9]. The Lord aids those who hope in Him. I shall hope in my God, and He will be my protector. Have no doubt that God is with us. *Domus Aaron speravit in Domino: adiutor eorum et protector eorum est. Qui timent Dominum speraverunt in Domino: adiutor eorum et protector eorum est*[61] [Ps. 113:18–19/10–11]. Those who fear the Lord and hope in Him the Lord always aids.

Dominus memor fuit nostri et benedixit nobis. Benedixit domui Israel, benedixit domui Aaron[62] [Ps. 113:20/12]. "The Lord has remembered us and has blessed us. He has blessed the house of Israel," *that is,* those of the contemplative life, and those of the house of Aaron, that is, of the mixed life, and those of the active life when it says: *benedixit omnibus qui timent Dominum: pusillis cum maioribus*[63] [Ps. 113:21/13]. Fear nothing, for it is the Lord Who has given His blessing to both the great and the small. He has blessed you and has also blessed your children. *Adiiciat [sic] Dominus super vos, super vos et super filios vestros. Benedicti vos a Domino, qui fecit coelum et terram*[64] [Ps. 113:22–23/14–15]. May God add blessings on these blessings and a thousand more blessings on these blessings. The Lord, Who made heaven and earth, blesses you. May you be blessed a thousandfold. *Coelum coeli Domino terram autem dedit filiis hominum*[65] [Ps. 113:24/16]. Heaven is the soul of the just man, which is given to the Lord of Heaven. This [soul] has to be set above all the heavens. He has given the earth to the children of men, that is, earthly things to earthly men. *Non mortui laudabunt te, Domine, neque omnes qui descendunt in Infernum*[66] [Ps. 113:25/17]. Those who are dead in sin will not praise You, Lord, because they are already destined for Hell. *Sed nos qui vivimus benedicimus Domino ex hoc nunc et usque in saeculum*[67] [Ps. 113:26/18]. But we who live, that is, we who have spiritual life and the life of Your grace, will praise You eternally and shall never cease to give praise to Your Majesty,

60. "The house of Israel has hoped in the Lord; He is their aid and their protector."
61. "The house of Aaron has hoped in the Lord; He is their aid and their protector. Those who fear the Lord have hoped in the Lord; He is their aid and their protector."
62. "The Lord has been mindful of us and has blessed us. He has blessed the house of Israel; He has blessed the house of Aaron."
63. "He has blessed all those who fear the Lord, the lesser along with the greater."
64. "May the Lord increase His blessings upon you, upon you and upon your children. You have been blessed by the Lord Who made Heaven and earth."
65. "Heaven [belongs] to the Lord of Heaven, but He has given the earth to the children of men."
66. "The dead shall not praise You, Lord, nor all those who descend into Hell."
67. "But we who live bless the Lord on account of this, now and forever."

Who, not for our merits but because of His benevolence, has given us His grace and has redeemed us with the most precious blood of His Son. May You be praised, then, and blessed by us, Lord our God, and Your sweetest Son, Christ Jesus, our Redeemer, *cui est honor gloria et imperium per infinita saecula saeculorum. Amen.*[68]

68. "To Whom is honor, glory, and power forever and ever. Amen."

Luca Landucci, *A Florentine Diary*

27th February [Carnival]. There was made on the Piazza de' Signori a pile of vain things, nude statues and playingboards, heretical books, *Morganti*,[69] mirrors, and many other vain things, of great value, estimated at thousands of florins. The procession of boys was made as the year before; they collected in four quarters, with crosses and olive branches in their hands, each quarter arranged in order with tabernacles in front, and went in the afternoon to burn this pile. Although some lukewarm people gave trouble, throwing dead cats and other dirt upon it, the boys nevertheless set it on fire and burnt everything, for there was plenty of small brushwood. And it is to be observed that the pile was not made by children; there was a rectangular woodwork measuring more than 12 *braccia* [each about twenty-three inches] each way, which had taken the carpenters several days to make, with many workmen, so that it was necessary for many armed men to keep guard the night before, as certain lukewarm persons, specially certain young men called Compagnacci, wanted to destroy it. The *Frate* was held in such veneration by those who had faith in him, that this morning, although it was Carnival, Fra Girolamo said mass in San Marco, and gave the sacrament with his hands to all his friars, and afterward to several thousand men and women; and then he came on to a pulpit outside the door of the church with the Host, and showing it to the people, blessed them, with many prayers: *Fac salvum populum tuum Domine, etc.*[70] [Ps. 27:9?] There was a great crowd, who had come in the expectation of seeing signs; the lukewarm laughed and mocked, saying: "He is excommunicated, and he gives the Communion to others." And certainly it seemed a mistake to me, although I had faith in him; but I never wished to endanger myself by going to hear him since he was excommunicated.

---

69. On the *Morgante maggiore* of Luigi Pulci (1432–84), see page 254, note 12, above.
70. "Save Your people, O Lord." This combines the phrasing of Ps. 27:9 *(salvam fac plebem tuam)* with Ier. 31:7 *(salva Domine populum tuum)*.

Piero Parenti, *Storia fiorentina*[71]

IV.clxviii

When a new Signory was formed, whose members were not the friar's partisans, it seemed to them that they were in an evil case, since they figured they would have to take what they would have inflicted on others. . . .

And not being able to gain favor for themselves by other means, they [the Signory] agreed, in order to show consideration for the friar and the friar's party, that they might build on the Piazza della Signoria, as they had done the year before, a high structure in tiers in the form of Hell with many devils, and upon it would be many vanities for burning on the evening of Carnival, thereby providing a festival for the people, the purpose of which was religious and good and directed toward nothing else but the good.

Fra Girolamo for several days before had preached about this: how, on the morning of the day of Carnival, after saying a solemn Mass in San Marco, he wanted to give Communion to all his devotees and to pray to God that, if his teaching were false, God would make it evident by a miracle.[72] He wanted to demonstrate what he knew could not be otherwise, since, in the case that God should *not* perform a miracle, his pronouncement would be confirmed, for it would follow therefrom that his teaching was not false.

Yet he did not engage in controversies with the ignorant. He knew that his words would carry no weight with the foolish; it was only [cause for] a festival. So, having enjoined a fast on many people for the vigil of Carnival, on the appointed morning, after he had chanted a solemn Mass in San Marco, he gave Communion to about four hundred women and as many men. Then he came with the body of Christ in his hand to the door of the church, where there was a pulpit which he mounted and showed [the Sacrament] to the people and made his friars sing certain hymns, such as *Excita, Domine, potentiam tuam et veni*,[73] and without saying or doing anything else, he came down and returned into the church. A very large crowd had gathered on the piazza in front of the church, and many had gone there believing that Fra Girolamo would perform miracles, but they saw nothing. On ac-

71. This excerpt is from Joseph Schnitzer's edition, in his *Savonarola nach den Aufzeichnungen des Florentiners Piero Parenti*, vol. IV of *Quellen und Forschungen zur Geschichte Savonarolas* (Leipzig: Verlag von Duncker und Humblot, 1910).

72. See Exodus, Sermon III, page 332: "I will take the Sacrament in hand, and I want everyone then to pray fervently, that if this matter is from me and I am deceiving you, Christ may send a fire from Heaven upon me to swallow me then and there into Hell, but if it is from God, that He may hasten quickly."

73. "Rouse up Your power, O Lord, and come." An Italian rendering opens the second song included in this volume: *Excita Signor mio / La tua potentia e vieni.*

count of this, those who remained behind began to speak disparagingly [of him].

Nonetheless, he made them follow his orders. So, many children gathered at San Marco after dining, and, having divided them according to their quarters and with the ensigns of their quarters in front, he made them go in procession all around the city, with garlands on their heads and olive branches in hand. Certain citizens from among his partisans and many women trailed behind. At the bridge of Santa Trinità, where rock-throwing ordinarily occurred, the procession was impeded, but Messer Luca Corsini, a doctor [of law], was not ashamed to draw off his mantle and reply, with stone in hand, to any who impeded the procession, that for the faith he would put his life on the line. This was accounted the greatest foolishness, since such action was neither necessary nor suitable for him.

Later, the said procession was also impeded in the piazza by some unpleasant sorts who hurled dead cats and other filth at each other. As a result, before the procession had finished, the Signory, fearing some outrage because of the tumult raised in the piazza, ordered the fire to be started in the structure which had been erected, and, so, it was soon burned in despite [of Satan] much more hastily than it otherwise would have been. Not many stayed to throw the flaming brands, for the piazza had cleared in a moment when it appeared that some might be looking to pick a fight. And yet, in the end, for whatever reason, things remained calm.

Iacopo Nardi, *Istorie della città di Firenze*

I.xxx

But on the second day of March, the friar, while preaching in the cathedral, took leave of the people, saying that he was going to give way to the wrath of his adversaries, but he invited his audience to the Church of San Marco. There, continuing to preach on the explication of Exodus, he delivered sermons full of terror, more than ever severely chastising the clergy and all the other generations of men. Indeed, despite the respect due the excommunication, the crowd of auditors multiplied so much that, since this church lacked the capacity for such a multitude, it was necessary that he preach there to the men only, and it was ordered that Fra Domenico da Pescia preach to the women in the nuns' Church of San Niccolò on the via del Cocomero. Given the state of the times and of affairs, both the priests and the friars of the city, almost everyone in the parish—whether because of remorse and the prick of conscience, or because of envy and hatred, or because of fear and the danger of losing their benefices and other signs of respect—did not want to give absolution, or give Communion, or bury in consecrated ground the bodies of those who believed the prophecies of those friars or attended their sermons. In spite of such and so great a persecution and prohibition, it came about—I know not how—that the people, seized with a like conviction, not only went to hear the sermons, but more and more would go every day to the monastery of San Marco to join the religious life. So great were the division, the schism, the travail, and the confusion among every sort of people that in Rome and all over Italy they debated about almost nothing else, and in Florence, on Carnival day and the days preceding it, through the instigation and encouragement of the said Fra Girolamo and Fra Domenico, a great number of men, women, and young people went to confession and Communion, and in the said church he celebrated a devout and solemn sung Mass. When Mass was finished, the said friar came with the Sacrament in hand and mounted a pulpit erected for the occasion at the door of the church, and while the friars and the people, kneeling all around, sang many hymns and psalms, after he had silently said a few brief prayers, with the tabernacle of the Sacrament [i.e., monstrance] in his hand he blessed all the people who were in the piazza, admonishing and asking everyone to pray fervently, and he prayed to God that if he had not prophesied and said and done truly, without deception, all the important things which he had predicted and affirmed *by the word of the Lord,* that that God, Who among Christians is believed to be really and truly in that Sacrament, should expressly and clearly show a sign to that effect.

On the same day of Carnival, the people, divided according to the accustomed arrangement by quarters [of the city], carrying in procession a beautiful and most ornate tabernacle with the image of Jesus Christ represented as a child, went through all the city singing hymns and psalms and lauds in the vernacular. That same evening, having returned to the Piazza della Signoria, they burned many disgraceful, lascivious, and vain things, which had been begged for and collected by the children on the preceding day, in the same way as they had done the year before, and all [was done] with great delight and festivity by the children and by all those persons who accorded faith to the prophecies of the friar. In this way, those days which are customarily devoted to the pastimes and pleasures of the world seemed at that time all to have been consecrated to and celebrated for the honor and glory of Christ; however, on this occasion many insults and much villainy were said and done to these children in the procession, even to the point of tearing from their hands and breaking into pieces those little red crosses which they bore in their hands, and many other things besides, which manifestly resulted in contempt for our religion, whatever might have been the intention of that friar, and however much he might be excommunicate and a sinner and worthy of every shame and contumely.

Because of these things, a multitude of vices and the rage of his adversaries were seen and known to grow the more, the more goodness and piety grew in simple men, upright in heart. But in Rome especially an extraordinarily important scandal arose, there being no one there who could contain the Pope's fury, either with reasons or with pleas and prayers; wherefore, His Holiness wrote threateningly several more times that, since the censures of the Holy Church were held to be of no account, he would do all which he had at other times threatened to do, adding to them also arms and temporal force. For in truth, the Pope and all his court very much feared a universal schism and the division of Christendom, and for such disorder [to occur] it seemed that nothing else was lacking but some ecclesiastical leader of high repute and authority. For this reason, the Pope was encouraged and spurred on by the prelates and preachers in Rome to impose a remedy upon the affair. Among these was that Fra Mariano [da Genazzano][74] whom we have mentioned above, who had been banished from Florence with little honor on account of the things he had done against the city at the instance of Piero de' Medici. He was very fond of the Medici, since he had been particularly benefited and honored by Lorenzo, Piero's father, to such a degree that by his attentions he had restored almost the whole convent of San

---

74. An Augustinian and longtime foe of Savonarola, by this point Vicar General of his order.

Gallo. So the Pope wrote again, repeating the same threats and adding some much greater in a brief sent through a special emissary.

When this brief had finally been made public in Florence, and a division ensued between the Signory and the other chief magistrates, the city found itself in great travail, since many disputes and consultations took place concerning this issue. A great assembly of twenty-five citizens from every quarter [of the city] gathered, along with the senate of the Eighty and other magistrates accustomed to intervene in public consultations. In this assembly, after more than six hours of consultation and dispute, nothing was concluded, so balanced were these contrary opinions. But on the seventeenth of March, Giovanni Berlinghieri, a daring man, finding himself a Prior [of the Signory] and Piero Popoleschi Gonfalonier, they, along with their companions but against the wishes of the others, so managed it that it was expressly commanded, with many threats, that the friar stop preaching altogether. And so, the following day, he delivered a very grave sermon, once again protesting on God's behalf, and decrying the vices of the clergy, and threatening Rome and Florence in particular with various grave and imminent scourges, and saying that there was a need now more than ever to turn to Christ as universal source and cause, since no other remedy was to be found for the correction and reform of Holy Church, as has been said, more or less, above; putting an end to his sermon in this way, he took his leave. These words, and others similar to them, interpreted perhaps more maliciously than they should have been, were the principal and evil cause of every perturbation in Rome and Florence, for they could not reasonably be supported with patience. And so, in the election of the Signory at that time, his enemies were much favored, and for this reason Fra Domenico da Pescia began to preach.

I.xxxi

When he had preached for a few days, it happened that one Fra Francesco di Puglia, one of the Observant Friars of St. Francis, while preaching in the Church of Santa Croce, said one morning that he did not believe that these friars told the truth about this matter when they had maintained that they spoke through divine inspiration and *by the word of the Lord.* The same friar, adding that the excommunication imposed against Fra Girolamo was valid and reasonable, went on to say many other things like this to support his propositions, and he said that he was glad to ready himself right now to enter the fire, even though he thought he might die, if the said Fra Girolamo would also enter it with him and, should he save himself, manifestly show the truth of his prophecies by a supernatural sign. This agreed with what the same Fra Girolamo had stated publicly several times, that, should natural reasons not suffice to confirm the truth of what he had preached, he would not hesitate to prove them by supernatural signs. When Fra Domenico heard this proposal, he accepted the challenge and the conditions, and he said publicly that, in order to prove the truth of the conclusions preached by Fra Girolamo, he wanted to enter the fire himself, from which he believed he would escape miraculously, without a scratch, by the grace of God. I did not want to fail to make note of these conclusions in this place, for the memory of those who are to come. In brief, these were the conclusions:

> The Church of God is in need of reform and renovation.
> The Church of God will be scourged, and after the scourge, it will be reformed and renewed, and it will prosper.
> Infidels will be converted to Christ and to His faith.
> Florence will be scourged, and after the scourge, she will be renewed and will prosper. All these things will happen in our lifetime.
> That the excommunication made concerning our father, Fra Girolamo, had no force. Those not observing it would commit no sin.[75]

75. *Ecclesia Dei indiget reformatione, et renovatione.*
Ecclesia Dei flagellabitur, et post flagella reformabitur, et renovabitur, et prosperabitur. Infideles ad Christum, et fidem eius convertentur.
Florentia flagellabitur, et post flagella renovabitur, et prosperabitur. Haec omnia erunt diebus nostris.
Quod excomunicatio facta de patre nostro frate Hieronymo non tenet. Non servantes eam, non peccant.

Letter from Paolo de Somenzi, Orator, to Lodovico Sforza, Duke of Milan

My Most Illustrious, Excellent, and Distinguished Lord:

Today, that is, the day of Carnival, the friar has had a solemn procession made through the city, as it has been the custom to do in past years, in which the greater part of the populace has participated, but a great many went there not out of devotion, but rather just to watch. All the devotees of the friar held olive branches in their hands in order to be distinguished from the others. The people who participated in this procession were divided by quarters, as is the custom here; the boys of the most tender age went first, the others followed after, rank on rank, according to years, the last being those most mature in age, all in order. Last came the friars of San Marco, disciples of this Fra Girolamo. They conducted the procession through the middle of the city, passing the Piazza della Signoria, and then returned to San Marco, on the piazza before the door of the church; there they halted and all began to sing with one voice, *Ecce quam bonum et quam iocundum habitare fratres in unum*[76] [Ps. 132:1], all making a circle round this same piazza. And while they were singing, they sent twelve children dressed in white, with burning torches in hand, to set fire to the *capànna*[77] they had had erected in the middle of the Piazza della Signoria,[78] on which they had set a great quantity of lascivious belongings, such as mirrors, women's hats, cards, playingboards, dice, lutes, masks, pictures, perfumes in great quantity, and every sort of suchlike things, which were estimated at no small value. While the *capànna* was burning, and even before, guards from the Bargello [a palace housing the jail] appeared in arms because many times many young citizens who were adversaries of the friar and his followers have come along

76. "See how good and how delightful it is for brothers to live together in unity."
77. *Capànna.* Cf. *capannuccio*, page 217, note 17, above. Somenzi, a foreigner, does not use the local form.
78. Somenzi's account seems somewhat confused about the order and location of events, but because he was reporting "on the spot," Patrick Macey accords him greater credibility than the Pseudo-Burlamacchi version (below), composed decades after the fact (*Bonfire Songs: Savonarola's Musical Legacy* [Oxford: Clarendon Press, 1998]), p. 89, n. 69). Indeed, the latter glosses over the disruptions caused by the Compagnacci, witnessed also by Landucci and Parenti; however, a scenario in which the larger part of the procession fled the Piazza della Signoria, regrouped at San Marco, and then sent twelve children back no short distance into the fray to light the bonfire, as Macey interprets the sequence of events (pp. 88–89), is not convincing. Perhaps the procession's station in the Piazza della Signoria was briefer than in the previous year, but the participants most probably at least set the bonfire alight before moving on to San Marco.

who wanted to ruin the *capànna* and not allow them to celebrate their festival; for this reason, little was lacking to set off a tumult or great scandal. So, in order to avert it, the Signory had the piazza guard armed, and the matter was put down.

The enemies of the friar have taken heart because they are convinced they have the greater part of the Signory published yesterday on their side, that is, at least six of them, who make up two-thirds, because it seems when six are in agreement, they can carry every decision even if the other three were of a contrary opinion, although it is still not clearly known if there are five or six in accord against the friar, because they are not yet members of the Signory, since they become members on the first of next month. It has seemed [best] to me to give Your Excellency notice of all these things even though they are of small account; I have done all this so that you might understand minutely everything going on in this city. I commend myself humbly to Your Excellency, and I pray to God that He may preserve you for long and long in happiness.

Florence, 27 February 1498

With highest [regards], your humble servant,

Paolo Somenzi de Cremona

La vita del Beato Ieronimo Savonarola,
previously attributed to Fra Pacifico Burlamacchi

Chapter XLb
How he set fire to all the vanities

In the year of the Lord 1498, the children, carrying out their duties, began to purge the city anew and found more vain things and of a greater number and beauty, so that as a result, another edifice was built, larger than the previous one, of like model and form, on the top of which was an ancient serpent, and above it presided Lucifer with the seven deadly sins. On the day of Carnival, early in the morning, there was a solemn Communion of men, women, and children — several thousands of them — at the hands of the servant of God; afterward he climbed into the pulpit where he made that protestation . . .[79] as is written. And with great gladness the people went home.

After dinner they arranged a procession prepared by angelic hands. When the people had come to San Marco wearing their proper clothes, with red crosses in their hands, and the children with crowns of flowers on their heads, they went along two by two, according to the order of the quarters of the city, singing litanies and psalms and hymns and sometimes lauds newly composed for the occasion, and after them followed the ensigns of the quarters; that is, the quarter of Santo Spirito had the Virgin with the twelve apostles, upon whom the Holy Spirit descended, an admirably made sculpture, ornately painted, and set on a portable altar with two ornate poles running along each side, under which four youths dressed as angels set their shoulders and so bore it along, and they were all adorned in gold and silk. All these figures were placed in a marvelously constructed tabernacle, and upon them descended a dove representing the Holy Spirit, while the canopy

---

79. A blank space appears in the manuscript at the point where the Latin *Life* gives the words of Savonarola. See the conclusion to Exodus, Sermon III page 332, preached the preceding Sunday, above: "I will take the Sacrament in hand, and I want everyone then to pray fervently, that if this matter is from me and I am deceiving you, Christ may send a fire from Heaven upon me to swallow me then and there into Hell, but if it is from God, that He may hasten quickly. And so that you may be very very clear [on this point], have prayers said in all your monasteries, and tell even the lukewarm to come; tell them to pray on that morning that God may rescue you, and that if I am deceiving you, may a fire fall on this friar and kill me. Write it everywhere, dispatch messengers to Rome and everywhere, and have prayers said on that day that, if this is not from God, evil may befall me, as I have said, but if it is from God, pray that the Lord may hasten and show a sign that this is His work."

was raised high above the tabernacle, as we said earlier. There were children all dressed alike preceding this mystery, and they sang new lauds, and after [it] the cantors, the guardians with their soldiers, and almoners carried silver vessels to receive alms. After these followed another quarter in the same way with their ensign, St. John the Baptist, figured in a most beautiful tabernacle in high relief, borne in the same way by children and with a canopy, as I said before, according to the order of their quarter. Then followed the quarter of Santa Maria Novella with their emblem of the Virgin ascending into Heaven, also admirably sculpted, and carried in the same way by the children under its canopy. Last of all came the quarter of Santa Croce with its emblem, which was a golden cross rubricated with splendid gems and precious enamels, placed in an ornate tabernacle according to the manner and order of the previous ones, but you should know that in order to distinguish himself, the guardian had his red cross somewhat larger than the others. They were followed by a great multitude of men, and then the girls with the women, and, taking the road by the via Larga, they entered through the middle door of St. John the Baptist, patron saint of the city of Florence; then, exiting through a side door, they went to the corner of the Carnesecchi and turned round toward the river; after crossing the bridge of Santa Trinità, they turned to the suburb of Santo Iacopo, above the Arno, and came to the Ponte Vecchio, where, crossing the river once again, they came to the gate of Santa Maria. Turning on the via Vacchereccia, they finally reached the Piazza della Signoria, while all along the way every quarter with its cantors sang so sweetly and pleasantly that it seemed as if Paradise had opened.

When they arrived at the piazza, they found the great edifice better adorned than the previous one; there were some sculpted heads of antique women famous for their beauty, such as the beautiful Bencina, Lena Morella, the beautiful Bina, Maria de' Lenzi, sculpted in expensive marble by famous sculptors, not to mention the other Roman women, such as Lucretia, Faustina, and Cleopatra; there was a Petrarch adorned with illustrations in gold and silver which was worth fifty scudi. To guard this triumph there were soldiers posted at the piazza and servants of the Eight [of Watch and Ward; hence, the police], because, without these guards, many extremely beautiful figures of outstanding craftsmanship and high value would have been stolen. So when the procession reached the piazza, they went all around it; then the quarters positioned themselves according to the order observed in the previous procession and sang songs composed for the occasion of this feast, and after surrounding the edifice and triumph, they blessed it with holy water. The guardians with their lighted torches then came and set fire to it, while the musical instruments of the Signory were sounded along with the trumpets and bells of the palace to give glory, and all the people exulted and sang *Te Deum laudamus*. When this spectacle had been consumed by the fire in despite of Lucifer and his followers, the procession followed the via degli Adimari to the Cathedral of Santa Maria del Fiore, and here, praying and singing many lauds, they offered the whole city to God and commended it to the Queen of Florence, presenting to the officers of St. Martin gathered here on that account the coins, which grew and multiplied in greater and greater quantities every year.

Leaving the cathedral, they came along the via del Cocomero to the Piazza of San Marco. In the middle of this piazza they placed the image of Our Savior triumphant upon the holy Cross together with the four tabernacles and ensigns of the quarters; around these they performed three dances, all the friars in the forefront with great fervor. They removed their hoods as they issued from the convent, and each novice took as a companion one of the children dressed as angels, and [thus] they made the first round; then each of the young friars took one young layman and made the second round, singing; finally, the old friars and priests, setting aside all human wisdom, with olive garlands on their heads, each took an old citizen and made the third dance, enclosing the other two: the first circle was in the middle, the second came after the first, and the third last.[80] They were all exulting and jubilant, singing endless lauds to the image of the Crucifix, and they persevered in this devout fervor till the sun went down, and each went his own way. The servant of God felt such great fervor that he hid himself in a secret place to watch. He was jubilant for very lightness of spirit, and the following morning, while preaching, he greatly commended them, as is written in his sermon; he exhorted the whole city both to be cheered by this great consolation and to take great example [from it]—for all this God be blessed.

Nonetheless, these children suffered so many tribulations and persecutions for wanting to live uprightly and to do good works that many wondered why such warfare was waged against them by fathers and mothers, and child-followers of the lukewarm, and the wicked seemingly of every station; and yet, in spite of so much tribulation and opposition, they maintained such calm of spirit and peace, such great love and goodwill, such delightful obedience, so much patience and gladness in charity and joy that everyone was amazed. For, because of the divine grace overflowing from their bodies, their faces were bright and shining, so that to all those who contemplated them, they seemed angels, and the adversaries of truth sometimes became so enraged that, as if instigated by their leader and guide, Satan, they would begin to throw rocks at these people and to spit in the

80. Cf. the angels' round dance and the embracing men and angels in Botticelli's *Mystic Nativity*, painted in 1501. The Greek inscription at the top of this painting indicates the apocalyptic intentions of the artist, influenced by the death of Savonarola.

faces of the children and on the tabernacles, breaking the crosses, which they called mandrakes, and throwing them into the Arno, even going so far as to spit on the beautiful face of our Infant Savior [Donatello's statue], and they did things which [even] infidels would not have done, cursing the children and saying many nasty words to them.

Chapter XLI
How a young man who impeded the procession was punished

But hear the Lord's judgment. When the procession had already passed the Church of Santa Trinità and the Spini Palace, just at the point where there is a place which in the vernacular is called *la Pancaccia* [the Benches], where every day many noble and lazy youths hang around gossiping and wasting time, there were many Compagnacci, sons of the devil, who, carried away by the Furies, began to throw rocks at the back of the procession in order to confuse them. Suddenly the Spirit of the Lord came to the children of light and the friends of the truth and of the teaching of the servant of God, who, after removing their robes and making a shield of them, began to throw the rocks back, and so they began to prevail against their enemies, who turned tail and were put to flight. Do not suppose that these were [children] of the vulgar crowd; rather, they were [the offspring] of the leading men of the city who had been Gonfaloniers of Justice, Officers of the *Monte* [*comune;* the public debt], the Ten of the War Office, and counselors and ambassadors to various kings and princes and even to the Supreme Pontiff; and, nonetheless, laying aside all dignity and human wisdom, these children fought manfully against the enemies of Christ. But let us return to the great judgment of God, which was this: a noble youth of the Federighi family, passing by the procession on the bridge at Santa Trinità and passing the children with red crosses in their hands, hurled many insults and then snatched a cross from one of them, snapped it, and threw it in the river. In that very spot after not too many days, the Lord struck him down with the plague called *gavocciolo*.[81] There he was left in his sickness, abandoned by everyone and without the sacraments, and in that very place he died. This was revealed to the whole city and judged to be vengeance taken by God as a punishment.

---

81. Bubonic plague. Boccaccio uses the same term in *The Decameron*.

Last Moments

Savonarola's Execution: 22 May 1498

Luca Landucci, *A Florentine Diary*

22nd May. It was decided that he should be put to death, and that he should be burnt alive. In the evening a scaffold was made, which covered the whole *ringhiera* [a raised platform in front of the Palazzo Vecchio] of the Palagio de' Signori, and then a scaffolding which began at the *ringhiera* next to the "lion"[1] and reached into the middle of the Piazza, towards the Tetto de' Pisani; and here was erected a solid piece of wood many *braccia* [each about twenty-three inches] high, and round this a large circular platform. On the aforesaid piece of wood was placed a horizontal one in the shape of a cross; but people noticing it, said: "They are going to crucify him"; and when these murmurs where heard, orders were given to saw off part of the wood, so that it should not look like a cross.

22nd May (Wednesday morning). The sacrifice of the three *Frati* was made. They took them out of the Palagio and brought them on to the *ringhiera,* where were assembled the "Eight" and the *Collegi,*[2] the papal envoy, the [Vicar] General of the Dominicans, and many canons, priests, and monks of divers Orders, and the Bishop of the *Pagagliotti* [*sic;* Benedetto Paganotti, O.P., Bishop of Vasona][3] who was deputed to degrade the three *Frati;* and here on the *ringhiera* the said ceremony was to be performed. They were robed in all their vestments, which were taken off one by one, with the appropriate words of the degradation, it being constantly affirmed that Fra Girolamo was a heretic and schismatic, and on this account condemned to be burnt; then their faces and hands were shaved, as is customary in this ceremony.

When this was completed, they left the *Frati* in the hands of the "Eight," who immediately made the decision that they should be hung and burnt; and they were led straight on to the platform at the foot of the cross. The first to be executed was Fra Silvestro, who was hung to the post and one arm of the cross, and there not being much drop, he suffered for some time, repeating "Jesu" many times whilst he was hanging, for the rope did not

---

1. The *marzocco*, symbol of Florence.
2. The two "colleges"—the twelve Buonomini ("Good Men") and the sixteen Gon-faloniers of the Companies (or guilds)—had to approve any legislation proposed by the Signory in order for it to become law.
3. Given his Christian name, Benedetto ("well-said"), it is ironic that he misspoke during the ritual of degradation.

draw tight nor run well. The second was Fra Domenico of Pescia, who also kept saying "Jesu"; and the third was the *Frate* called a heretic, who did not speak aloud, but to himself, and so he was hung. This all happened without a word from one of them, which was considered extraordinary, especially by good and thoughtful people, who were much disappointed, as everyone had been expecting some signs, and desired the glory of God, the beginning of righteous life, the renovation of the Church, and the conversion of unbelievers; hence they were not without bitterness and not one of them made an excuse. Many, in fact, fell from their faith. When all three were hung, Fra Girolamo being in the middle, facing the Palagio, the scaffold was separated from the *ringhiera,* and a fire was made on the circular platform round the cross, upon which gunpowder was put and set alight, so that the said fire burst out with a noise of rockets and cracking. In a few hours they were burnt, their legs and arms gradually dropping off; part of their bodies remaining hanging to the chains, a quantity of stones were thrown to make them fall, as there was a fear of the people getting hold of them; and then the hangman and those whose business it was, hacked down the post and burnt it on the ground, bringing a lot of brushwood, and stirring the fire up over the dead bodies, so that the very least piece was consumed. Then they fetched carts, and accompanied by the mace-bearers, carried the last bit of dust to the Arno, by the Ponte Vecchio, in order that no remains should be found. Nevertheless, a few good men had so much faith that they gathered some of the floating ashes together, in fear and secrecy, because it was as much as one's life was worth to say a word, so anxious were the authorities to destroy every relic.

Simone Filipepi,[4] *Estratto della cronaca*

I copy here from a record that I made around 2 November 1499. Alessandro di Mariano Filipepi, my brother, one of the good painters who have lived in our city up to now, narrated in my presence at home by the fire, around the third hour of the night [between eight and nine P.M.], how he had been discussing the case of Fra Girolamo with Doffo Spini[5] one day in his workshop. Actually, Sandro asked him for the pure truth, because he knew that the said Doffo had been one of the interrogators in the affair, always present to examine Savonarola. So [Sandro] wanted [Doffo] to recount what sins they found in Fra Girolamo by which he merited to die such an ignominious death. And so, in his turn, Doffo responded, "Sandro, should I tell you the truth? We did not find any in him, neither mortal sins nor even venial ones." Sandro asked, "Why did you cause him to die so ignominiously?" He replied, "It was not I, but rather Benozzo Federighi. And if this prophet and his companions had not been put to death, but had been sent back to San Marco, the people would have destroyed us and cut us all to pieces. The affair had gone so far that we decided that if we were to escape, they must die." And then other words were exchanged between the two of them which there is no need to record.

4. (Ca. 1443–?), brother of Sandro Botticelli.
5. Leader of the Compagnacci, a member of the Eight irregularly appointed after the arrest of Savonarola (to weight this magistracy against him), and one of the "examiners" in his torture and trial.

Lorenzo Violi,[6] *Le Giornate*

This was Doffo Spini, who I have told you was the head of the Compagnacci, a daring and bold man, who had no qualms about telling the bad things
he had done; rather, he prided himself on them. I tell you, after the friar's
death, Doffo bragged many times and in many places of the methods and
tricks he used to get rid of that friar. And he proclaimed aloud this that I
will tell you now in a place where he said it many times and gave proof of
it.

Doffo often frequented the workshop of a painter called Sandro of Bot-
ticello, a man who was widely regarded in the city to be one of the best and
most excellent painters that ever were. There was always a crowd of loafers
in his workshop, such as the aforementioned Doffo. Many times when Doffo
was here and thinking about the death of the friar, he said that it was never
their [the Compagnacci's] intention to cast the friar of San Francesco into
the fire and that they assured him of this fact. Rather, it was enough for
them that he allow himself to be exploited so that by means of delay they
[the Compagnacci] might achieve their purpose to put an end to the activities of the friar [Savonarola] and drive him from Florence. Because Doffo
spoke about these things many times in Sandro's workshop, and since Simone, the brother of the painter, was also present, [the latter] made a record
of them in his chronicle, that is, in one of his books, where the aforementioned Simone described all the noteworthy things of these times. It appeared to him that this statement of Doffo ought to be noted so that the
secret truth of this matter would be discovered; therefore, he wrote in his
book bound in wooden planks a chronicle describing what things happened
in Italy in those times and how they were accomplished. I have seen this
book and read it.

---

6. A Florentine notary responsible for recording many of Savonarola's sermons *a
viva voce*. Though a dedicated, lifelong Piagnone, he became chancellor under the
restored Medici regime. His *Journals* are presented as a dialogue.

Postmortem

Marsilio Ficino,[1] *Apologia contra Savonarolam*

Apology of Marsilio Ficino on Behalf of the Many Florentines Deceived by the Antichrist, Girolamo of Ferrara, the Greatest of Hypocrites, to the College of Cardinals

I know, of course, Worshipful Cardinals, that many in the Sacred Council marvel that one hypocrite from Ferrara has deceived so many otherwise clever and erudite Florentine men for nearly a full five years. And with good reason they wonder exceedingly indeed when they consider that so many great persons have been duped by one particular man. But truly, no mortal man, but the most crafty demon, and not a single demon, but a demonic horde, has assaulted (alas!) miserable mortals through the most occult snares and duped them by means of astonishing machinations. No one really marvels anymore, but, rather, all grant without controversy that the first parents of the human race, fortified as if children of God with divine wisdom and virtue, established in Paradise, and instructed by angels, were nevertheless deceived by one certain diabolic spirit. Why, then, should it seem marvelous that the Florentines, exceedingly unfortunate especially at this time, have been clandestinely besieged and seduced by a strong horde of demons under an angelic mask? Do we not believe that the Antichrist will miraculously seduce many persons preeminent in both prudence and probity?[2]

Moreover, that Girolamo, prince of hypocrites, led by a spirit not so much human as diabolic, has seduced us, not merely setting traps for us but even sapping our vital energies, there are, in fact, many proofs: a certain utterly incomparable craftiness in this Antichrist persistently feigning virtues while in truth disguising vice, a vast passion, a savage audacity, an empty

---

1. Like Savonarola, Ficino (1433–1499) was the son of a court physician (to the Medici), himself trained as a physician, and was introduced to the philosophy of Aristotle through that training. Under Medici patronage he translated all the works of Plato into Latin and composed commentaries on many of them. He was ordained at the age of forty and eventually became a canon of the Cathedral. As a philosopher-theologian, he sought to reconcile Neoplatonism with Christianity, outlining a pagan revelation parallel to the Hebraic. Though not the head of a formal school, his circle of intellectual intimates is sometimes referred to as a Platonic Academy. His ideas on astrology and talismans, related to medical lore, were not generally accepted by colleagues such as Pico della Mirandola.
2. Triple alliteration: *vel prudentia probitateque prestantes*.

boasting, a Luciferean pride, a most impudent mendacity supported at every point with imprecations and oaths; the face, the voice, the speech frequently lightning fast while declaiming, carrying his listeners along not so much by voluntary persuasion as by violence. For often in the midst of disputation he would suddenly cry out, take fire, and thunder forth, being carried away exactly like those possessed by demons, or the Furies, as the poets are wont to describe it. Sometimes he would even fall into prophecy, mixed indeed with lies, so that while he might easily dupe or compel the populace by means of some of his predictions, such as they were, he might also, by means of his lies and evil works, be finally refuted.

Moreover, for what reasons the Astrologers, as well as the Platonists,[3] conjectured that Savonarola had been inspired by many and conflicting or unlucky influences of the stars, it is not expedient to dispute at present. But I might briefly say that from conflicting and unfortunate influences and confluences of the stars, just as from certain signs, the Astrologers conjectured, as did the Platonists, that Savonarola—or rather, as I should more correctly say, Sevonerola![4]—had become subject to various and wicked demons. But whether he was thus made subject by strange and marvelous means, or whether he rather subjected himself to evil spirits by his own pride and iniquity, it is certain that devils and similar influences, flowing together into his diabolic spirit as into their own workshop, at once breathed out a venom pestilential wherever exhaled; and not him only did they infect and destroy, but also those drawn near to him in whatever fashion and this very populace itself, committed to and too much believing in him. They say that a certain similar misfortune impending over the Ephesians was discovered and expelled by Apollonius of Tyana in the form of a certain squalid old man directed by evil demons.[5]

3. Ficino was a leading light of both groups and thus antagonistic to Savonarola, who makes clear his disapproval of astrological prognostications time and time again (see, e.g., the opening of the third sermon on Psalms above). See also Donald Weinstein's brief discussion of late Quattrocento Florentine astrology, in *Savonarola and Florence: Prophecy and Patriotism in the Renaissance* (Princeton: Princeton University Press, 1970) pp. 87–91.

4. Bernard McGinn, *Visions of the End: Apocalyptic Traditions in the Middle Ages* (New York: Columbia University Press, 1979), characterizes this as "Ficino's own word play—*saevus Nero* (savage Nero)" (p. 346, n. 22), referring to a figure in contemporary apocalyptic writings. See also Lorenzo Polizzotto, *The Elect Nation: The Savonarolan Movement in Florence, 1494–1545* (Oxford: Clarendon Press, 1994), p. 100.

5. Apollonius (first century A.D.), a wandering ascetic and wonder-working imitator of Pythagoras, was compared by some to Christ and after death became the focus of a pagan divinity cult. He is mentioned in Eusebius' *Gospel Preparation*, bk. IV, chap. 13. This bizarre episode is recounted in Philostratus' *Life of Apollonius*, bk.

I also long ago discovered the same thing in this Sevonerola, although in the beginning, after the Republic had undergone sudden change, while the French were agitating Florence with various terrors here and there, I myself also, together with the fearful populace, was terrified by I know not what demon and for a time deceived, but quickly I came to my senses and for three whole years now I have warned many known to me, frequently in private and often publicly, and not without great peril, so that they might flee far away from this poisonous monster, born to be a disaster for this people. I pass over the insurrections and lethal hostilities which have arisen there and the neglect of public affairs and the wasteful expense and most grievous damages which have made advances there.

This without doubt is the worst: that he has tainted so very many, partly by his pride and heretical pertinacity, partly, as I have said, he has demented and utterly stupefied them in the manner of that fish which they call the torpedo [the electric ray], a fruit undoubtedly worthy of such a diabolic seed. Moreover, that this can be done and is a common thing, we have that most weighty witness, Paul the Apostle, reproving the Galatians: "O stupid Galatians, who has so bewitched you not to believe the truth?"[6] [Gal. 3:1]. I also think that the addendum, "not to believe the truth," carries a good deal of hidden meaning. For those who have heedlessly consented to falsehood, bewitched by seducers, have not been deprived only once of the light of truth, but they also become more distrustful about receiving truth. Truly, everyone whosoever ought to be cautioned against "holy" preachers, when they hear them cursing and frenzied, so that they might have that Gospel passage ever before the eyes and ears of the mind: "Beware of false prophets who come to you in sheep's clothing but within they are rapacious wolves; by their fruits you shall know them" [Matt. 7:15–16]. Finally, Paul himself in the second letter to the Corinthians briefly encapsulates the whole matter thus: "Such pseudo-apostles are guileful laborers, transfiguring themselves into apostles of Christ, nor is this any wonder. For Satan himself transfigures himself into an angel of light. Therefore, it is no great thing if his ministers are transfigured as if into ministers of justice; their end shall be according to their works" [II Cor. 11:13–15].

And so, I conclude this brief apology thus: that clearly no one ought to

IV, chap. 10. The old man is stoned to a pulp by the crowd and shapeshifts into a slavering dog the size of a lion. Perhaps this is meant to stand as a counterweight to Christ's driving the demons from two possessed men into some nearby swine at Gadara (Matt. 8:28–34; Marc. 5:1–19; Luc. 8:26–39).

6. The Vulgate has *insensati* ("senseless") rather than *stupidi*. Also, the phrase *non credere veritati,* which so impresses Ficino, is attested in some manuscripts but is excised from the modern Stuttgart edition.

wonder at the Florentines. Not all, I say, for many had detected long ago the tyrannical malignity of Sevonerola and his quasi-satellites, but many, I say, have been seduced by his diabolic fraud; some even have been induced into this same malignity by a demon's instigation, especially since Florence had to contend not with one demon to be exact, but, as the Gospel also bears witness [Marc. 5:9], with a dire legion of demons attending Sevonerola. Indeed, from what a plague have divine clemency, the foresight of the Supreme Pontiff, and your diligence, inspired from heaven by the seraphic Francis [of Assisi],[7] happily just liberated us, with the College of Canons[8] of our Cathedral also assisting and a number of eminent citizens looking after affairs in the Republic, and Joanne [i.e., Giovanni] Canaccio[9] especially urging on this work. For we have taken up arms not against the gods, as they say that Aeneas and his comrades-in-arms fought unaware for the sake of Troy, so that afterward they rued it: "Ah, me! divine law does not require that one place one's trust in unfriendly gods,"[10] but against the inhabitants of the underworld and Tartarean monsters, as did Orpheus for the sake of Eurydice or Hercules for glory. Thus we have fought, with God's favor, to protect the liberty not only of Florence but also of the Roman Church, so that after battle, it may be sung of us: God has arisen and has dispersed His enemies in Antichrist, all who hate God have fled from before His face; as smoke dissipates, they have dissipated, as wax flows away from fire, so have these false and proud sinners run away to perdition from before the face of God [paraphrase of Ps. 67:1–2]. Because He, the All-Powerful, Who certainly resists the proud, but gives His grace to the humble, has shown strength with His arm; He has dispersed with Lucifer those proud in the thoughts of their hearts [paraphrase of Luc. 1:51–52].

Certainly, God often defers the punishment of other sins to the future judgment, but impious pride made oppressive with every pestilence He more often strikes also with present justice. What could be more manifest than this miracle? God, very indulgent till now, has borne with this blasphemer as long as he has deluded the people like a magician by means of the name and Cross of Christ. But truly when first he attempted publicly to desecrate the very body of Christ in the Eucharist through trial by fire, almighty God, shaking the heavens with sudden rain and thunder and lightning, exposed

7. The Franciscans were instrumental in Savonarola's downfall.
8. Of whom Ficino was one.
9. A leading citizen of Florence who advocated handing Savonarola over to the power of the Pope.
10. Vergil, *Aeneid* 2.402–403.

this arrogant and utterly barbaric impiety and instantly aroused His people to burn this man with the same fire. And so, after the special thanks owed first to God, we give great thanks to the Supreme Pontiff and to you, the Sacred College, and we humbly commend to you the people of Florence and the Cathedral College, most devoted to the Roman Church.

Francesco Guicciardini,[11] *The History of Florence*
From Chapter XVI

It will not be out of order to speak at some length of his [Savonarola's] qualities, for neither in our age nor in those of our fathers and forefathers was there ever seen a monk endowed with so many virtues, or one who enjoyed so much reputation and authority. Even his enemies admit that he was learned in many subjects, especially in philosophy, which he knew very well and used so skillfully for his purposes that one would have thought he had invented it. He was so well versed in sacred scripture that many people believe we would have to go back several centuries to find his equal. His judgment was very profound not only in matters of erudition, but in worldly affairs as well. In my opinion, his sermons demonstrate clearly that he knew very well the principles that govern this world. Endowed with these qualities, and with an eloquence that was neither artificial nor forced but natural and easy, his sermons were by far the greatest of his age. It was marvelous to see what audiences and what reputation he kept, for he preached for many years not only during Lent, but on many of the holidays as well. Moreover, he was in a city full of subtle and fastidious minds, where even excellent preachers came to be considered boring after one Lenten season, or at most two. These virtues were so clear and manifest in him that they are recognized not only by his supporters and followers, but by his enemies as well.

But questions and differences of opinion arise concerning the goodness of his life. It should be noted that if he had any vice at all, it was only simulation, caused by ambition and pride. Those who observed his life and habits for a long time found not the slightest trace of avarice, lust, or of any other form of cupidity or frailty. On the contrary, they found evidence of a most devout life, full of charity, full of prayers, full of observance not of the externals but of the very heart of the divine cult. Although his detractors searched industriously during the investigation, they could not find even the slightest moral defect in him. The work he did in promoting decent behavior was holy and marvelous; nor had there ever been as much goodness and religion in Florence as there was in his time. After his death they disappeared, showing that whatever virtue there was had been introduced and maintained by him. In his time, people no longer gambled in public and were even

---

11. Son of a Florentine aristocrat (1483–1540), he studied law and pursued a diplomatic career, as had his father. His *History of Florence* was written before his first embassy to Spain in 1512.

afraid to do it at home. The taverns that used to cater to wayward and vice-ridden youth were closed; sodomy was suppressed and decried. A great many women gave up their shameful and lascivious clothing. Nearly all boys were made to give up their many shameful practices, and brought back to a holy and decent way of life. Under his direction, Brother Domenico organized them into companies, and they went to church, wore their hair short, and would hurl stones and insults at lecherous men, gamblers, and women who wore lascivious clothing. At carnival, a day generally celebrated with a thousand iniquities, they first held a religious procession full of devotion; then they would go about collecting dice, cards, make-up, shameful books and pictures, and then would burn them all in the Piazza della Signoria. Older men turned toward religion, mass, vespers, and sermons, and went to confession and communion often. At carnival time a great number of people went to confession; alms and charity were distributed in abundance. Every day the friar urged men to abandon pomp and vanity, and to return to the simplicity of religion and the Christian life. To this end he proposed laws concerning the ornaments and clothing that women and children wore; but they were so severely attacked by his enemies that the Council only passed those concerning children—and even they were not observed. Through his preaching, men of all ages and stations joined his order, including many noble youths from the first families of the city, and many older men of reputation such as Pandolfo Ruccellai, a member of the Ten and ambassador to King Charles; messer Giorgio Antonio Vespucci and messer Malatesta [Sacramoro],[12] canons of Santa Reparata, good, serious, and learned men; maestro Pietro Paulo da Urbino, a physician of reputation and good life; Zanobi Acciaiuoli, who was very learned in Latin and Greek; and many others like them. In all of Italy there was not a convent like San Marco. He so enthusiastically directed the young men in their studies—not only of Latin and Greek but of Hebrew as well—that they promised to become ornaments to religion. And though he did all that for men's spiritual welfare, he did no less for the city and the public welfare.

When Piero had been expelled and the parliament called, the city was so badly shaken and the friends of the old regime were in such disfavor and

---

12. The "Judas of San Marco." He persuaded Savonarola against escape while San Marco was under attack and later clawed his way to the Vicar Generalship of the Order, in which role he worked zealously to suppress all remnants of devotion to his former superior's memory.

danger that even Francesco Valori[13] and Piero Capponi[14] could not protect them. That many of them would be done great harm seemed inevitable. If that had come about, it would have been a great blow to the city, for many of them were good, wise, and rich men of great houses and family connections. Dissension would surely have arisen among those who governed, as happened in the Twenty, and the divisions would have been deep because several men of nearly equal rank were seeking to achieve preeminence. New upheavals, more parliaments, further expulsions of citizens, and several revolutions would have been the result; and in the end, Piero would perhaps have returned, which would have meant disaster and ruin for the city.

It was Brother [Girolamo] alone who made it possible to avoid all this confusion and chaos. He introduced the Great Council, which put a bridle on all those eager to become masters of the city. He proposed the appeal to the Signoria, which acted as a safeguard for the preservation of the citizens. He brought about universal peace simply by impeding those who wanted to punish Medici supporters under color of re-establishing the ancient order.

Without doubt these efforts saved the city and, as he so truly said, worked to the advantage of both those who now governed and those who had governed. Because the results of his works were so good, and because several of his prophecies were fulfilled, many people continued to believe for a long time that he was truly sent by God and that he was a true prophet, despite the excommunication, the trial, and his death. For my part I am in doubt, and have no firm opinion on the matter. I shall reserve my judgment for a future time, if I live that long; for time clears up everything. But I do believe this: if he was good, we have seen a great prophet in our time; if he was bad, we have seen a great man. For, apart from his erudition, we must admit that if he was able to fool the public for so many years on so important a matter, without ever being caught in a lie, he must have had great judgment, talent, and power of invention.

13. Though of the Medicean party under Lorenzo, Valori grew disgusted with Piero because of his ineptitude. He became an ardent supporter of Savonarola and leader of the Piagnoni, serving in various offices of the Republic, including Gonfalonier of Justice. It was he who lowered the minimum age for participation in the Grand Council from thirty to twenty-four, opening the door to the Compagnacci. He also was chiefly responsible for denying the right of appeal to the Medicean conspirators of 1497, an incident which led many to criticize Savonarola for compromising his principles, since this right had been established at his urging. He and his wife were murdered during the riot which accompanied the attack on San Marco.

14. A leading Florentine citizen, one of the four ambassadors to King Charles along with Savonarola, he preferred an oligarchic form of government and became a fierce opponent of the friar. He was killed in battle at the siege of Soiana, near Pisa (1496).

Afterlife

After his arrest, Savonarola was imprisoned in the sardonically named *Alberghettino,* the "little hotel," a maximum-security cell at the top of the Palazzo Vecchio. His adherents, fearful that they, too, might incur the wrath of the populace, absented themselves from council meetings; as a result, the commission selected to interrogate the friar was composed entirely of Arrabbiati and Compagnacci (among them Doffo Spini; see Simone Filipepi's chronicle, above). Over the course of the following weeks (April 1498), he was subjected to repeated interrogations. His first, autograph "confession" convicted him of nothing, so his enemies resorted to torture, threats of torture, and trickery to gain a sufficiently damning document. The device used, the *strappado,* was a pulley and drop which would break or dislocate the victim's arms. Savonarola had never been robust, and his will broke under this abuse, along with his arms. When the pain became unbearable, the friar would confess that his prophecies were fabrication; when he had been allowed to collect himself, he would retract his confessions. Nonetheless, the notary employed to record the proceedings devised various means of inserting additional incriminating details after Savonarola had already signed.[1]

As his body recuperated, the pastor of souls could turn his attention once again to spiritual nouriture. First, his jailer, a man of hardened sensibilities, found himself inexplicably drawn to his suffering, saintly charge and received from him in recompense for his growing kindness a *Rule for Godly Living.* After this, Savonarola turned to his own spiritual consolation in meditations on Psalms 50 (the *Miserere*) and 30 (*"In te, Domine, speravi"*).[2] In the first, the speaker acknowledges his sinfulness but finds hope in the examples of the prodigal son's return and Peter's denial and repentance. Though he prays for rescue, he concludes with the resolve to face martyrdom. The aptness of this psalm is underscored several times over: "uncertain and hidden matters of Your wisdom You have shown to me" (Ps. 50:6), and "the bones which have been crushed will exult" (Ps. 50:8). As soon as this work was completed, it was smuggled out and hurriedly circulated.

The second psalm meditation plays out as a psychomachia between *Tristitia* (Sadness), armed with justice, and *Spes* (Hope), girt with mercy. The

---

1. For a full account of Savonarola's trials and the methods used to extract a usable confession from him, see Roberto Ridolfi, *Life of Girolamo Savonarola,* trans. Cecil Grayson (New York: Knopf, 1959), pp. 252–255.
2. Both texts have been ably translated by John Patrick Donnelly, S.J., in *Prison Meditations on Psalms 51 and 31* (Milwaukee: Marquette University Press, 1994). See his introduction for further analysis and a printing history.

speaker's soul becomes the battleground for these two opposing responses to his critical situation. No sooner had battle been joined, however, than all combatants were driven from the field: Savonarola had completed only two verses when his writing materials were confiscated, perhaps in response to the circulation of the *Miserere* text. Significantly, in this truncated form, *Spes* has the last word.

Matters moved swiftly once the papal commissioners arrived on 19 May. Savonarola was tortured once again in hopes of uncovering a conspiracy against the Pope. The prophet of Florence had threatened to call for a council to unseat the profligate who had usurped Peter's throne; how far had he gone in pursuing this? and, more importantly, with whom? But they discovered nothing of use to them, despite all their efforts. The judgment was swift and sure—though lacking in justice. Savonarola and his two companions were convicted of heresy and schism and handed over to the civil authorities for execution.

A large gallows and bonfire were hastily constructed on the Piazza della Signoria, the very place where the Savonarolan triumphs had so lately been celebrated. On the day following their sentencing, 23 May 1498, the three friars were led out and degraded from their clerical rank. The bishop assigned to perform this ritual, Benedetto Paganotti, had been a friar of San Marco and was even now no enemy of Savonarola. He was more likely dismayed by his responsibilities than overzealous in performing them, but he overstepped the bounds of his commission. As Ridolfi recounts it:

> As he accomplished his office, he said in his confusion: "I separate
> you from the Church militant and the Church triumphant." The
> Friar gently corrected him in his usual quiet voice: "Only from
> the Church militant; the other is not your affair." And the good
> Bishop corrected himself.[3]

The three friars were hanged one after another: Fra Silvestro, Fra Domenico, and last Fra Girolamo. A fire was lit beneath them, and the corpses and the gallows, too, burnt to ash. But even this pulverization was not sufficient for the authorities: lest any Piagnone make a relic of those ashes, every last speck was swept up and cast into the Arno.

Despite the zeal of both Church and State to eradicate all trace of their moral antagonist, the incendiary power of his words and example was not extinguished. His martyrdom and the refusal of ecclesiastical authorities to give heed to the crying need he had dinned into their ears lent support to the very cause they were attempting to crush and fanned the flames of their own near-destruction. Pope Paul IV sought to have all of Savonarola's works

---

3. Ridolfi, *Life,* p. 270.

listed on the Index of Prohibited Books (1558), but the censors found cause to suppress only the *Dialogue on Prophetic Truth* (above) and some dozen or so sermons. The publication of his many tracts and treatises went on apace, particularly in those countries eventually given over to Protestantism. Luther and other breakaway reformers co-opted Savonarola for their own purposes, hailing him as a champion of their cause. But he was not; he never questioned that there should *be* a Pope, only that the present occupant of that position was unworthy of his exalted role. He was not a herald of the Protestant revolt but of the Catholic reform, belated as it was. His truest descendants can be found among the most radically orthodox of saints, such as Filippo Neri (1515–1595), founder of the Oratorians, and the mystic Caterina de' Ricci (1522–1590).

Savonarola's reputation after death was as hotly disputed as it had been during his lifetime. In the religious arena, Marsilio Ficino, canon of Santa Maria del Fiore and a prince among humanists, who had at one time approved of his sermons, wrote a scathing but shamelessly self-serving diatribe against the "Antichrist," as he termed him, in his *Apologia* (above). Another cleric, that same Giorgio Benigno who had sprung to Savonarola's defense in the pamphlet wars of 1497, and now Bishop of Nazareth (an honorary title), took up the cudgels once again before the Fifth Lateran Council and exonerated the dead man from all charges of heresy (1516). Among historians and political theorists of the next generation, opinion also seesawed. Niccolò Machiavelli (1469–1527), last chancellor of the Republic and ever the pragmatist, condemned him for his failure to secure his power by force of arms.[4] A more balanced assessment can be found in Francesco Guicciardini's *History of Florence*, excerpted here; the historian postpones absolute judgment for a later and less biased age, but acknowledges the greatness of the man.

The battle between his devotees and detractors raged among the paint pots as well as inkhorns, if the arguments of present-day art historians are to be credited. Some see him in the central figure of Luca Signorelli's *Rule of Antichrist*, in the San Brixio Chapel of Orvieto Cathedral.[5] But he also takes his place among the saints, perhaps, in Raphael's *Disputation of the Holy Sacrament*, within the very walls of the Vatican, facing off against the entire

4. See *The Prince*, chap. 6; and *Discourses on Livy*, bk. III, chap. 30. In the *Discourses* see also bk. I, chaps. 11, 45, and 56. In the last, Savonarola is ironically categorized with fortunetellers.
5. See André Chastel, "L'Apocalypse de 1500: La fresque de l'antéchrist à la Chapelle de Saint Brice Orvieto," *Bibliothèque de l'Humanisme et Renaissance* 14 (1952): 122–140. Jonathan B. Riess challenges this identification in *The Renaissance Antichrist: Luca Signorelli's Orvieto Frescoes* (Princeton: Princeton University Press, 1995), pp. 136–138.

School of Athens for all eternity.[6] More to the point was his radical influence over the subject matter of Botticelli's later works, in particular his *Mystic Crucifixion* and *Mystic Nativity*.[7] Bartolommeo della Porta, painter of the most famous portrait of Savonarola, joined the Dominicans at San Marco after Savonarola's death, where he produced works distinguished by a stately equanimity. His *sacre conversazioni* paradoxically combine an intimacy between the viewer and the sacred personages represented with a monumentality of form. The echo of the preacher's voice reverberated in the psyche of Michelangelo to the end of his days, by his own account,[8] and although there may be no direct link with Savonarola's prophecies in his vast *Last Judgment,* there is certainly a consonance of spirit.[9]

That memorable voice has been carried down the ages in musical compositions, too, some reproducing his very words, others only harmonizing with his preferences for simplicity and clarity. The opening paragraph of his *Miserere* meditation, beginning *"Infelix ego"* (unhappy I), became the text for numerous motets, from Josquin des Prez's, commissioned by Savonarola's quondam patron, Duke Ercole d'Este of Ferrara, to Orlando di Lasso's, sponsored by Duke Albrecht of Bavaria. Inspired by processional hymns such as Benivieni's, given above, Palestrina wrote *laude* for the Roman Oratory of St. Filippo Neri, his confessor and a fervent devotee of Savonarola.[10]

This destroyer of vain fictions has put in an appearance in belles lettres, nonetheless, the magnum opus in this category being George Eliot's *Romola,* published in 1862. Though Savonarola is a central motivating force of the novel, he remains for the most part offstage. The minute particularity with which Eliot recreates the milieu of Savonarolan Florence, employing many of the sources excerpted here, is nothing short of genius, but the spiritual conflicts of her reluctantly and skeptically Piagnone-sympathizing heroine are steeped in a Victorian devotion to dutifulness as the supreme virtue. On the

6. In the Stanza della Segnatura. See Bruno Santi, *Raphael,* trans. Paul Blanchard (Florence: Scala Books, 1977), p. 28; and David Thompson, *Raphael: The Life and the Legacy* (London: BBC, 1983), p. 101. Thanks to Jane Kristof of Portland State University for these citations.

7. Creighton Gilbert discounts the Savonarolan imagery as possibly due to patronal influence. See his brief comment on the Filipepi excerpt included here, in his *Italian Art, 1400–1500* (Englewood Cliffs, N.J.: Prentice-Hall, 1980), pp. 218–219.

8. Related to his pupil and biographer Ascanio Condivi; *The Life of Michelangelo Buonarrotti,* trans. Herbert P. Horne (Boston: D. B. Updike, 1904).

9. Savonarola purportedly appears at Christ's right hand, among the elect in the extreme upper left of the fresco, immediately below the angels bearing symbols of the Passion.

10. See Patrick Macey, *Bonfire Songs: Savonarola's Musical Legacy* (Oxford: Clarendon Press, 1998), for a full account of Savonarola's musical influence.

opposite end of the spectrum, and dangerously flirting with the charge of vanity, is Max Beerbohm's " 'Savonarola' Brown," a decidedly irreverent confection. "The play's the thing," and Brown's unfinished drama plays fast and loose with many a major figure of the Italian Renaissance from beginning to end, the "plot" resembling a cutlet of "Monk" Lewis dressed with bits of Browning. Beerbohm draws a caricature contrived from all the worst and most ignorant stereotypes of religious and the Renaissance. Delight for the reader resides in recognizing the atrocities wreaked on fact.

For far too many English-speaking readers today, unfortunately, Savonarola (if they have heard of him at all) is just such a caricature, coinciding with the real historical personage in nothing but name. Even in Italy his reputation was obscured for a while by the indifference of the Enlightenment. The recovery of the three-dimensional, flesh-and-blood man began, fittingly, at San Marco in the mid-nineteenth century with a plan to republish his works, undertaken by the "New Piagnoni." But the tincture of republican radicalism still stained those pages, in the view of the Grand Duke, and the organizers of this project were sent into exile. Yet interest once aroused could not be suppressed; at the same time George Eliot was penning her fictional reconstruction of Savonarolan Florence, the first in a succession of scholarly biographies had recently been published.[11] Pasquale Villari synthesized a phenomenal range of original documents into his still essential *vita* (1859–1861),[12] and Joseph Schnitzer raised the bar half a century later (1924).[13] Roberto Ridolfi, scion of an ancient Piagnone heritage, capped the tricorona (1952).[14] The first (shorn of its appendices) and last of these have been translated into English;[15] not so the multiple volumes of the Edizione Nazionale of Savonarola's oeuvre. Though the current vitality of Savonarola studies is encouraging, much remains to be done, for it is only through exposure to his own words in the context of his own time that the fascination of the man who held sway over a city foremost in learning, culture, and commerce can begin to be understood.

Despite persecutions and a paucity of relics,[16] the cult of Savonarola has persisted through the centuries. Some Dominican convents devised lit-

---

11. Eliot argues against Villari's excusation of Savonarola's refusal to intervene in the Bigi appeal from the "six beans" (*Romola*, note to chap. LVIII).

12. *La storia di Girolamo Savonarola e de' suoi tempi*, 2 vols. (Florence: Le Monnier).

13. *Savonarola* (Munich: E. Reinhardt, 1924), trans. (into Italian) Ernesto Rutili, 2 vols. (Milan: Fratelli Treves, 1931).

14. *Vita di Girolamo Savonarola*, 2 vols. (Rome: Belardetti).

15. As Pasquale Villari, *Life and Times of Girolamo Savonarola*, trans. Linda Villari (New York: Scribner, 1888); and Roberto Ridolfi, *Life of Girolamo Savonarola*, trans. Cecil Grayson (New York: Knopf, 1959).

16. His cell at San Marco is maintained as it was.

urgies for his feast in direct and pointed opposition to the General of the Order. The cause for his canonization was raised early—during the papacy of his conciliar co-conspirator, Giuliano della Rovere (Pope Julius II)—and late—as recently as 1998, the quincentenary of his martyrdom.[17] But Mater Ecclesia has yet to come to terms with her prodigy of a son.

17. To put this ongoing campaign into perspective, consider that Joan of Arc (d. 1431), likewise burned at the stake for political reasons, was not canonized until 1920.

Index

Pages 136a and 136b are unfolioed pages that follow page 136.